MASIRAH

RAF Masirah 1976.
(Photograph: Sam Boyce)

Masirah

TALES FROM A DESERT ISLAND

Colin Richardson

First published in 2001

This edition published in 2003 on behalf of the author
by Scotforth Books,
Carnegie House,
Chatsworth Road,
Lancaster, LA1 4SL,
England
Tel: +44(0)1524 840111
Fax: +44(0)1524 840222
email: carnegie@provider.co.uk

Sales from the author
at Five Acres,
Fulbeck Lowfields,
Grantham,
Lincs, NG32 3JD,
England
p&p free.

British Library Cataloguing-in-Publication data
A catalogue record for this book is available from the British Library

ISBN 1-904244-30-0

Typeset in Adobe Garamond 11 on 13 by
Carnegie Publishing.
Printed and bound in the UK by
The Cromwell Press, Trowbridge, Wilts.

For my wife Ann.
With thanks for the bossing and badgering
and pushing me to finish.

Contents

Maps

Author's Note

THROUGHOUT THIS BOOK I have used the modern spelling of names transliterated from the Arabic, but omitting the apostrophe denoting the letter 'ain'. I have even done this when quoting some historical texts which use an earlier spelling. Without such consistency there can be confusion. For example, the settlement of Mersis was originally incorrectly transliterated as Umm Rasas (Mother of Rasas) which would have an identical spelling in Arabic. It was a natural mistake because the southern cape of Masirah is Ras abu Rasas (Cape Father of Rasas). The modern English spelling on maps is Umm Rusays, and although incorrect it has been used throughout the book. To add further to the confusion, the modern roadside signboard reads 'Marsis' instead of 'Mersis'.

Acknowledgements

I AM VERY GRATEFUL to the large number of people and organisations who have helped in the preparation of this book which could not have been written without their assistance. Amongst them are:

The Public Record Office. Documents AIR 27/1476 to 1480, 2729 & AIR 28/527, 1077, 1241, 1518 & 1615

The RAF Museum Hendon

The Air Historical Branch

The Naval Historical Branch

The Victoria and Albert Museum

The British Airways Archives

The British Embassy, Muscat

The Library of the RAF College, Cranwell

HQ P & TC, RAF Innsworth

The Netherlands Embassy, London

The Library of the Oriental and India Office. Files L/P&S/12 1951. R/15/6/86, 87, 88, 89, 206, 313 & 386.

The CRO, RAF Marham

The 244 Sqn and Kindred Spirits Association

Historians Ray Sturtivant, John Clementson, Christopher Morris, Charles Butt and John Peterson

Authors Bill Corser, Arthur Banks, Andrew Thomas and Fred Hitchcock

Local Masirah inhabitants Mohammed bin Khamis, Tahir Said al Qahtan and Adam Mohammed Abdi

Archaeologist Gerd Weisgerber

John Jackson of the Fisheries Civil Sector

Ron Paterson who provided the history of BERS

Bob Brand for Arabic language advice

Jack Sharing and Peggy Richardson for proofreading

I am also grateful to people for advice and personal reminiscences during the following periods:

Before the Second World War

Donald Cromar	Gavin Brown
Charles Whitelock	Jim Offer
Margaret Frame	

The Second World War

TOP CAMP	UMM RUSAYS
Eric Soar	Geoffrey Low
Jim Heslop	George Speer
Tommy Hazell	Arthur Davies
Mike Kerrigan	Ray Brazel
Keith Scott	George Chambers
Glen Anderson	Charles Meacock
Frank Moseley	Alan James
Mark Rowland	George Weir
Tom Booth	Jim Drew
Peter Mitchell	Pip Errington
Arthur Grimes	Terk Bayly
Johnny Walker	Dash Burridge
Clarence Pelham	Geoff Gibson
John Landrigan	
Don James	
Mike Allisstone	

1946–50

Les Bulmer	Tony Spooner
Bill Rogers	Jerry Lukes

1951–55

Bob Bolton	Jack Sharing

1956–60

Paul Hudson	Tam Syme
Gerry Baxter	John Rumens
Eddie Harding	John Graham
Terry Scott Collier	Peter Morris
John Campbell	Ray Raymond-Barker
Bob Roalfe	Tony Jeapes

1961–65

Jim Harrison	Jeff Mellor
John Fordham	Peter Wickenden
Richard Dive	

1966–70

George Willis	David Smith
Tony Pick	Mike Connett
David Barton	Frank Over
Mike Askins	

1971–77

Barry Hill	John Daniels
Peter Booker	Douglas Gow
Sam Boyce	Sir John Akehurst

1977–94

Frank Milligan	Ron Faulkner
Bruce Watts	Ken Lamprey
Paddy Mullen	Bill Liddle
John Merry	Andy Ley

Preface

IN HIS EXCELLENT BOOK *Flight from the Middle East,* Air Chief Marshal Sir David Lee GBE CB wrote the history of the RAF in the Arabian Peninsula and adjacent territories from 1945 until 1972. Of Riyan, Salalah and Masirah he wrote: 'The story of these tiny, isolated desert airfields is worthy of a separate book as they have played a significant part through the whole period of RAF activity in the Arabian Peninsula.'

This book recounts the story of one of these desert airfields – Masirah. Beginning in the mists of ancient history it tells as much as can be discovered about the island itself. The RAF began to take an interest in the island in 1929, and the Second World War brought a flurry of activity. Masirah played a part on a wider stage, so relevant events further afield are recounted here. The RAF tenure lasted until 1977 when the airfield was sold to the Sultan of Oman's Air Force, later renamed the Royal Air Force of Oman. The story continues for another twenty years, but on some aspects the author has, perforce, been somewhat circumspect, and there is regrettably no current map or photograph of sensitive areas.

Masirah is part of the Sultanate of Oman, a rocky offshore island in the Arabian Sea about 10 miles from the low-lying mainland coast. It is a little larger than the Isle of Wight or the Isle of Man, though narrow and approximately 40 miles long. There are sandy plains and dark hills rising to about 750 feet, these being of crumbling igneous rock which were once overlain by limestone. Indeed, in the north of the island some of the high ground still has a limestone cap. Rain is the exception rather than the rule, and in some years it does not rain at all. Winter storms are usually responsible for any rain, not the south-west monsoon of the summer months. The summer monsoon here is a cool wind from the south-west which persists for days on end. The rough sea is quite cold, and the murky air is salt laden from sea spray. Some sources refer to the north-east monsoon during the winter months, but it is not significant. The air is clear, the winds are light, and temperatures are similar to a fine summer day in Britain. Due to the lack of rain, vegetation is sparse and very hardy. On some still nights there is a heavy dew, and it is this which supplies most of the water for the plants.

Animal life is mostly small lizards, snakes, spiders and scorpions. There is

Masirah Wildlife: Gazelle
(Photograph: Peter Booker)

Masirah Wildlife: Donkey, neither donkey or gazelle are usually as tame as this
(Photograph: John Peterson)

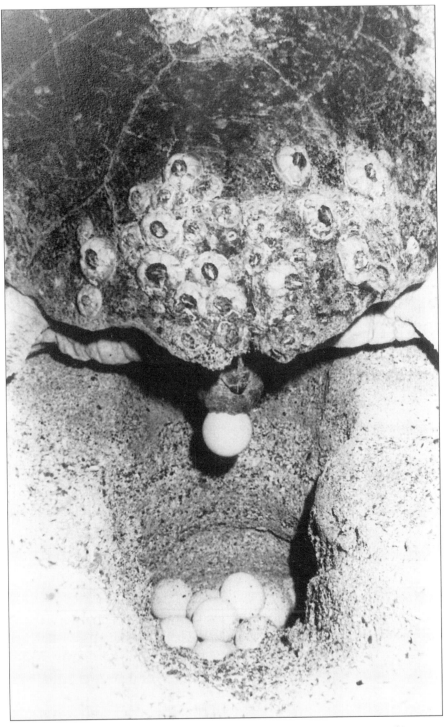

A Loggerhead turtle laying her eggs at night (Photograph: Tony Pick)

Tens of thousands of fossilised clams on the Jebal Humr
(Photograph: Ann Richardson)

.a small population of mountain gazelle, dainty and timid, which are obviously closely related to the Thomson's gazelle of Africa. One report states that these were introduced by the grandfather of Sheikh Khamis bin Hilal, the latter being the sheikh of the island throughout the RAF tenure. A tiny fox with huge ears has been seen, and there are some small cape hares. Feral cats abound, particularly on the air base. Near the south of the island large wild cats have been seen, much larger than any domestic cat. They are about the size of a small spaniel dog and have prominent vertical black stripes down their bodies and round their tails. Now that the local people possess Toyota Landcruisers and pickups, their domestic donkeys have been turned loose to fend for themselves as best they can. These donkeys have interbred with the grey donkeys which were not used as beasts of burden.

The vast majority of the local people live near the air base at the north end of the island. Their status symbol is the camel. The wealth from fishing has led to large numbers of camels roaming loose outside the airfield boundary fence. Herds of goats put further pressure on the environment. However, Mesquite (*Prosopis juliflora*) is now spreading outside the base where it was first introduced into the gardens by the RAF. It is a thorny leguminous tree, native in America from Mexico to Columbia. The upwind branches are stripped of their leaves during the south-west monsoon, but the tree survives and is distasteful to herbivores. It would flourish in the wadis of Masirah if permitted to do so.

If the land is barren, the sea is bountiful. There are rich fishing grounds which only now are beginning to be fully exploited. Masirah is a shell collector's paradise. On one stretch of coast, a little over a mile in length, can occasionally be found the shells of *Acteon eloiseae*, one of the world's rarest and most attractive sea shells. These shells are found nowhere else. Almost every known turtle nests on the ocean coast of Masirah, the northern coast being dominated by the loggerhead turtle. Over 35,000 nest here every year. It is an extremely large turtle and not edible, being an omnivore.

The bird life is varied and abundant, particularly during migratory seasons. The migration route is north India and Asia to Africa. During the migratory seasons Masirah is a birdwatcher's paradise.

Fifty years ago there were very few local people living on the island. They subsisted on the fish which they caught, and ate very little else. Brackish wells supplied just enough water to support the small population. They led a life of deprivation and squalor, their mean diet resulting in a poor physique and chronic ill-health. These days life is better.

This story of Masirah begins in the distant past before the discovery of oil in Oman, when the small local population were afflicted by disease and malnutrition.

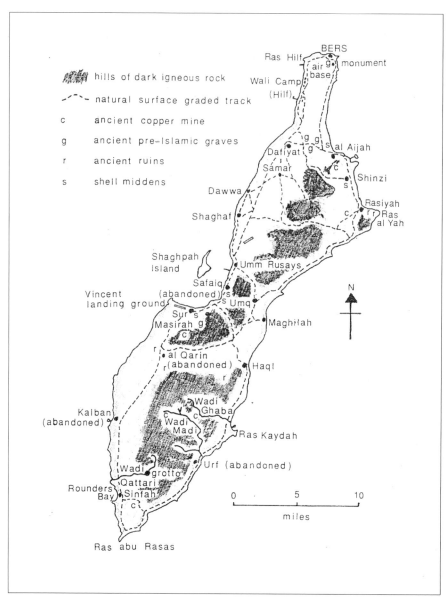

Map 1: Masirah Island

Map 2: Locations further afield which are mentioned in this book

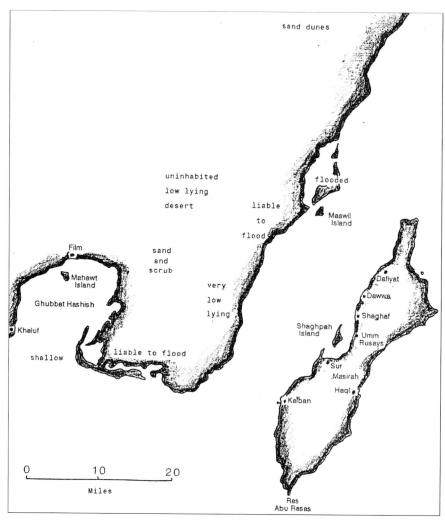

Map 3: Masirah area

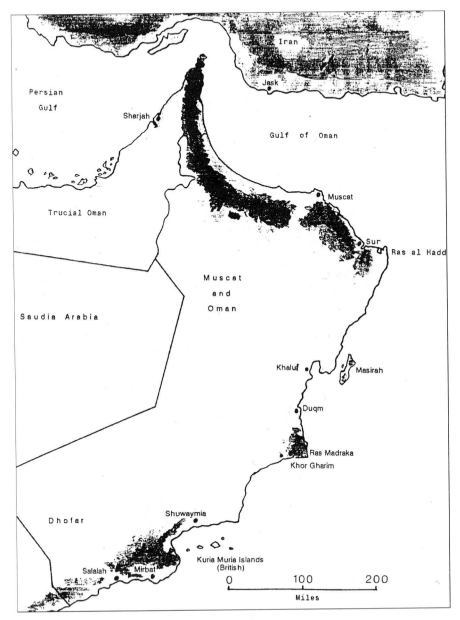

Map 4: Muscat and Oman, 1935

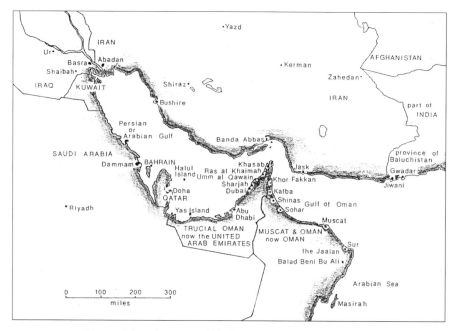

Map 5: The Persian Gulf before the Second World War

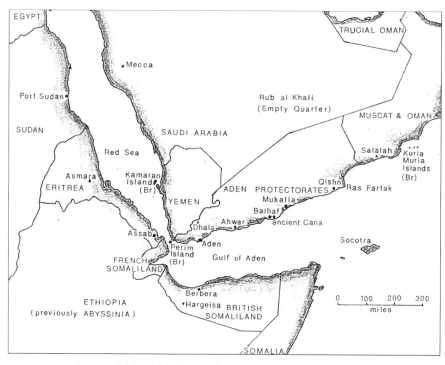

Map 6: The Gulf of Aden before the Second World War

CHAPTER I

Pre-History to the Twentieth Century

MASIRAH HAS BEEN INHABITED for many thousands of years. The evidence for this is vast shell middens, heaps of sea shells near the mouths of major wadis. A wadi is a dry watercourse which floods during the occasional storm. The island could not have supported a large population, so the vast accumulations of shells indicate a very long period of habitation. A visiting archaeologist, Gerd Weisgerber of the Deutsches Bergbau Museum, estimated 4,000 years. The shells themselves are mostly clams 30 to 40 mm across. Lying nearby are chips of flints for scraping out the contents, and fist-sized rocks for cracking open the shells. There are signs of very ancient stone shelters near al Qarin and below the hills to the west of Ras al Ya. 'Ras' means cape. This is the only part of the Masirah coastline which is protected from the tearing gales of the south-west monsoon of the summer months. Several hundred feet up above this cape are three ancient cairns and forty-two small stone shelters with flints and seashells scattered around This must have been a lookout post, not a settlement, because the nearest well is in the Wadi Rasiyah. Similarly there is another lookout post on the easternmost of the limestone-capped *jebals* (Arabic for hills or mountains). This is the Jebal Shabbah. There are only three places where it is possible to climb onto the plateau, and here there are chest-high defensive walls. Nearby are the foundations of two small buildings. In 1984 Gerd Weisgerber sifted the dust and found part of an ancient bracelet. He said it was certainly pre-Islamic and possibly neolithic. Also in the dust was an RAF fork dated 1952! On the tracks leading up to the top are potsherds of crude pottery.

The ancient inhabitants would have eaten fish as well as shellfish, but without fishing lines hooks or nets it would not have been easy. In the Kuria Muria Islands, 270 miles south-west down the mainland coast from Masirah, the primitive inhabitants were found to be fishing only with rectangular basket traps made of palm fronds.

In the north of the island there are ancient burial sites, now low mounds of stones, on low ridges, some with human bones which have surfaced. Some have been investigated but the graves were found to have been plundered long ago. There was still a little chlorite and pottery on the surface, and inside the mounds were agate beads, tiny fragments of copper, perforated shells, ceramic

Ancient shell middens on the channel coast between Umm Rusays and Sur Masirah
(Photograph: Richard Crowley)

beakers and carnelian beads. The skeletons were in a crouched position with their legs strongly tied. Men were facing south and women were facing west. Another pre-Islamic burial site 2½ km south-south-west of Sur Masirah is entirely different in character, the graves being mounds of large boulders which would need several men to lift. Some boulders are strewn around as if the graves had been purposefully destroyed, and again there are splinters of ancient bones on and near the surface.

According to old RAF histories of Masirah there were Persian inscriptions on gravestones near the abandoned settlement of Urf. There are none there now. Also, in 1957, there was an article about Masirah in the Geographical Journal written by Gerald de Gaury. He reported that there were weather-worn headstones of tombs with what appeared to be early Persian inscriptions. The location was in the Wadi Qattari near the 'sacrificial site' and 'grotto'. There are no such headstones there now, and the whole area is steeped in legend, folklore and superstition. Local legend had it that there is a big man named San at the south of the island. He is made of rock, and water from his mouth has miraculous healing properties. This would be the 'grotto' in the Wadi Qattari where there is a pool of mineralised water about 10 ft deep under an overhang. Downstream of the pool the wadi is dry and about 30 ft below the surrounding land. Above the north bank there are three graves which, certainly for at least thirty years, have been marked by flags and red bunting. These graves have no headstones and are of ancient divines of the Islamic era who died while returning from the pilgrimage to Mecca. The reputation of these saintly people is such that they are still revered, and people gather there to sacrifice goats and leave other food in bowls at the graves. There is a pole to which the goats are tethered for slaughter, and scattered around are goat skins, hooves, skulls and intestines, etc. This is not an Islamic practice, but it is still carried out frequently by those hoping to be blessed by good health or good fortune. Europeans survey the gruesome scene and shudder. To reinforce their unease they have invented the legend that the local people kill their deformed babies there. On the easternmost point of Shaghpah Island there is a similar grave marked by red bunting wound round a pole and the remains of goats scattered around on the ground.

There is another place where Europeans are seriously spooked. This is below the limestone cap of the Jebal Humr, below the cliff on its north-west side. Here there are a few palm trees and there is a freshwater spring when there has been recent rain. The islanders believe the place is haunted by a djinn. Offerings of food have been left there, and rope dolls and a hangman's noose have been seen. On one occasion a European happened to pass that way after a walk. The Royal Oman Police were waiting for him at the foot of the jebal and closely questioned him on what he had been doing.

Local people tell stories of how they have been pelted with small stones by an invisible poltergeist while sleeping overnight in a wadi. Another curious story is told by Bruce Watts, a level-headed British officer. He writes:

In April 1997 I was driving across the Salt Flats at Sur Masirah en route to the beach in search of the rare Eloise shell, a journey I had taken dozens of times since my return to Masirah in 1990. It was a warm, clear afternoon with excellent visibility.

As I approached the prominent rock I noticed in the distance what appeared to be a bright light. It must have been about a mile away in the direction that I was travelling. What was strange about this light was that it was brilliant white in colour. In fact it looked more like painted white rather than the whiteness associated with light.

As you can guess I was very intrigued by it and drove straight towards it. Except for the rock with the white cross painted on it there are no other obstructions on the flats themselves, so I was able to keep the light in view the whole time. Driving is easy on the flats and I soon began to approach its location.

Driving past the 'Rock' the light suddenly disappeared to be replaced by two figures walking westwards towards some low-lying hills. My first instinct was to assume that these men were fishermen from the nearby village. Some of them keep their fishing boats on the beach the other side of these hills. At this stage I must have been about half a mile from them.

3

The sacrificial site in the south of the island
(Photograph: Richard Crowley)

However, as I got nearer I was surprised to see the clothing of the man on the right. He appeared to be dressed in a very expensive/luxurious dishdash, the long shoulder to ankle garment worn by Omanis. It was light red and from a distance of about a quarter of a mile it seemed like it was made of a silk type material. It appeared very smooth and fine. Certainly not the type of attire you would expect to see a fisherman from Sur Masirah wearing! Then I noticed the other man.

He was all black from head to toe. Whereas with the first man I could easily differentiate the head from the rest of the body, with the second man I couldn't. There was an outline of a head attached to a body but I could not tell if he was wearing anything. It was as if he was a shadow but not of the other man. In addition he appeared to be walking slightly above the surface.

I increased my speed, but at a range of about three hundred yards they just disappeared. Although there was no way they could have reached the hills in front of them or the low 'cliffs' to their left, I drove around for a while trying to find them. There was no trace.

What was strange was that I did not find it an alarming experience but felt that I had intruded into something that did not concern me. Since then, I have been back on many occasions often on my own. I still find the beach at Sur Masirah one of my favourite places and have never felt before or since a sinister or frightening atmosphere. As for those 'men', I have not seen them since.

In this area, south of Jenkins Hill (Jebal Sur Masirah) there are some puzzling features. In a shallow saddle there is what could be an outcrop of large stones, except that the types of rock are mixed. It could be a large ancient tomb. A little further south there is a hill of dark rock on the western side of the road. It is covered in small stone enclosures two or three feet high. Some way to the west of this there are long lines of stones which have been laid on the ground and which meander aimlessly for some distance in random directions.

In his book *Die Alte Geographic Arabiens* A. Sprenzer offers two ancient names for Masirah: Orgyris and Orgen. This is where Nearchus, Alexander the Great's admiral, reported the tomb of King Erythras: 'A large one on a hill top with wild palms nearby'. Another account reports it as a tumulus. In about AD 60 the Romans produced a merchant's guide to the coastal route from Egypt to India and along the East African coast. It was written in Greek and called 'The Periplus of the Erythraean Sea'. It is not known if there is any link between King Erythras and the Erythraean Sea. Probably not. 'Eruthros' is an ancient Greek word meaning 'red', and led to the name Red Sea. The kings may have had red hair or a bloody reputation, or perhaps they dressed in red.

The author of the Periplus wrote:

> Sailing along this coast well out to sea for 2000 stadia from the Zenobian
> Islands [the Kuria Murias] there meets you an island called Sarapis, about
> 100 stadia from the mainland. It is about 200 stadia wide and 600 long,
> inhabited by three settlements of fish eaters, a villainous lot, who use the
> Arabian Language and wear only girdles around their waists made of palm
> fronds. The island produces a considerable amount of tortoiseshell of fine
> quality and small sail boats and cargo ships are sent there regularly from
> Cana.

'Stadia' is the plural of 'stadium', a distance of about 220 yards. The distance
from the Kuria Murias is approximately correct, but the size of Masirah was
estimated as about double its true length and width. Cana, where the Masirah
'tortoiseshell' (presumably turtleshell) was exported, was a city state about
three-quarters of the way to Aden, about 70 miles to the west of the present-day
port of Mukalla. Cana was the beginning of the overland 'Spice Road' to the
Mediterranean civilisations. It lasted for 1,300 years from 800 BC to the sixth
century AD. The route was nearly 1,500 miles in length and about 100 miles
inland from the Red Sea, the camel caravans carrying mainly frankincense
from the hinterland behind the present-day Salalah in Southern Oman. From
Africa and Socotra came other aromatics, cassia, tortoiseshell, cinnamon and
slaves. From India came pepper, spices, sandalwood, ebony, silk, ivory and
precious stones. It does seem curious that it was worthwhile taking Masirah
'tortoiseshell' to the Roman Empire. The author visited Cana in 1998 but there
was little to see compared to the magnificent ruins which mark the overland
route up to Petra. The camel caravans passed through a succession of city
states which were often at war with each other, but such wars were never
allowed to hinder the lucrative trade. The city states grew rich from their
protection rackets, but did protect the caravans from bandits. There could be
no such protection from pirates in the Red Sea where there could be strong
contrary winds.

From Cana the caravans passed through the now ruined cities of Shabwa,
Timna (which the author visited in 1958), and Marib with its huge dam.
This was the home of the Queen of Sheba. The route continued through
Sana, Mecca, Medina and the Wadi Rum to Petra which grew to be a city
of 30,000 people. Petra was the junction where routes branched off across the
Sinai to Gaza and Alexandria, north to Palmyra and Damascus, and east to
the Euphrates.

In the early 1980s two large Roman ship's amphorae were found on the
Qarin beach at Masirah. Large pottery water or wine containers, they were
about three feet long and one foot wide and in almost perfect condition.
They are now stored at the Department of Antiquities in the capital area of
Oman. Perhaps the ship was wrecked on one of the treacherous shoals in the

Masirah Channel en route to India. There was, apparently, a Roman agent living on the west coast of India.

It should be noted that during certain periods in ancient times it was possible to sail from the Mediterranean to the Red Sea. Ships could sail up a western arm of the Nile towards Cairo, and then down an eastern arm to where a canal had been excavated to the Bitter Lakes. In those days the Bitter Lakes were connected to the Gulf of Suez. Sometimes the canal was filled in for reasons of military defence.

Nothing else is known of Masirah until well into the Islamic era when the island was mentioned by Ibn Batuta, the North African traveller and chronicler. He is now studied at school in Oman and lesson 14 of the 7th class Arabic Literature is translated as follows:

> I left Tangier, my home town, on Thursday 2nd Rajab 725 [about AD 1324] heading for Mecca for the Haj and to visit the grave of the Prophet Mohammed (Peace be upon him). I was 22 years old ... I came to Oman by sea in a boat owned by a man from Masirah Island ... We arrived at Masirah, the home of the boat owner. It is a very big island and the inhabitants live on fish only. We did not land because the anchorage was far from the coast. We stayed on the boat one day while the boat owner went to his home. Then we sailed a day and a night.

A non-event, but it confirms the diet of the islanders and that domestic goats had not yet arrived. It also confirms the lack of local attractions.

Nearly halfway down the island, on the channel side, is an impoverished settlement of fishing folk living in hovels made of driftwood, corrugated aluminium panels, old 44-gallon fuel barrels, etc. This is Umm Rusays. Here there is a ruin known as 'the Portuguese Fort', but it seems unlikely that it was built by the Portuguese. A planisphere made for the King of Portugal in 1460 showed Masirah as having a castle of middle size. This was thirty years before the Portuguese arrived in the area. The fort is constructed of unfaced local stone, much of it fossilised coral, held securely in place by lime cement. Its size is not impressive and the standard of workmanship is less than might be expected of the Portuguese. There are two embrasures low down on the east wall with no signs of the bars which would have been necessary if (as has been reported) it had been used as a prison. The origin and purpose of the building remains obscure. Perhaps it was no more than a prestige residence at a place where visiting vessels would find relatively calm water during the strong winds of the summer monsoon.

Nearby, close to the roadside mosque, are the ruins of a large fortified house. There are photographs of it taken in the 1930s and 1940s before it had fallen into disrepair. There have long been rumours of a second fort on the island, with a number of alternative locations suggested, although there

The "Portuguese" Fort at Umm Rusays.
In 1967 the walls of the keep were still standing
(Photograph: Frank Over)

The "Portuguese" Fort at Umm Rusays.
By 1995 the inner walls of the keep had collapsed, and the outer wall has been
undermined by floodwater (Photograph: Richard Crowley)

8

is no sign of such a fort at any of these places. The large fortified house, which had castellations, is probably the origin of the rumour.

The Bait al Falaj fort in the capital area of Oman now contains the museum of the Sultan's Armed Forces. In it are reproductions of two old maps dated 1614 and 1749. They both show Masirah as two separate islands. To the south-east of Umm Rusays the island is quite low along the line of the present graded road across to Haql, with high ground on each side. Navigators on sailing ships must have assumed that a channel divided the island.

Ever since the Second World War there have been repeated references to Captain Kidd having buried his treasure on Masirah. No evidence for this is quoted; surely this story is fanciful? All such pirates operated off the Americas, didn't they? A little investigation shows that this speculation might just possibly be true. In 1695 in London he was granted a Royal Commission to apprehend pirates who molested the ships of the East India Company in the Red Sea and Indian Ocean. In February 1697 he arrived in the Comoro Islands off East Africa and turned pirate without conducting any legitimate business. He captured several small ships but his refusal to attack a large Dutch ship nearly caused a mutiny. In an angry exchange he mortally wounded his gunner, William Moore. His most valuable prize was the Armenian ship *Quedagh Merchant* which he kept, scuttling his own *Adventure Galley* which was old and unseaworthy. He sailed from the east coast of Africa to the west coast of India. There is no record of any visit to Masirah, but it is just possible. Later he sailed to the Americas and was apprehended by the Earl of Bellomont, Colonial Governor of New York. He was sent to England for trial and was found guilty of murdering his gunner William Moore, and was then hanged. He had buried treasure on Gardiners Island, off Long Island, and this was recovered.

Two or three hundred years ago the island's paramount sheikh determined to improve the culture of the islanders. Their adherence to Islamic practices and values left much to be desired. Clearly outside help was required. He turned to the Wadi Hadramaut which at that time was the most peaceful, prosperous and civilised part of the Arabian Peninsula. It is approximately halfway between Salalah and the entrance to the Red Sea, well inland of the port of Mukalla. Its inhabitants travelled widely, many working in the Far East. Its cities were, and are, gems of Arab architecture, and early European travellers were totally enchanted.

The missionaries from the Wadi Hadramaut came to Masirah and built a community at Safaiq which is between Umm Rusays and Sur Masirah. They were known to the islanders as the '*saddah*', a term of respect. The foundations of ruined houses can still be seen on both sides of the road. Around the ruins can be found broken pottery and china, some of which has been identified as Chinese. Their graves are in a walled cemetery to the west of the Jebal Safaiq, and are not in a good state of repair. The engravings on the headstones still

The large fortified house at Umm Rusays during the Second World War. It is now a pile of rubble (Photographs: George Chambers and Charles Meacock)

retain some of the original red colouring. These engravings give no dates, just quotes from the Holy Koran and the name of 'Mohammed bin Ali bin Haroon bin Ali bin Abdullah bin Soali bin Abdullah bin Haroon bin Abdullah'. Few Europeans can trace their ancestry for eight generations. Here lies a man of culture and distinction There are many more modern Moslem graves outside the walled cemetery. Nearby there are old walls on the summit of the Jebal Safaiq, and a short distance to the north are ancient pre-Islamic graves. On the beach is a shed and a large wooden trading vessel, known as al Khammam, which belonged to a previous sheikh. It is a bedan, extremely old and of a design which was superseded a long time ago.

The island's place of execution was a short distance to the south-east of the settlement of Sur Masirah. Its name is rooted in the Arabic word meaning punishment. Here can be seen the clearings and rocks where criminals were stoned to death.

Further south on the channel coast is the abandoned village of Kalban. It was a fishing village with a few date palms which still survive. Many years ago the paramount sheikh was invited to a formal feast at the village, and was offered fish instead of goat. This so offended his dignity that he banished the community from the island.

The first British survey of the South Arabian coast was carried out by HMS *Leven* in 1824. There was no landing on Masirah, but the Captain noted: 'Maseera, however, is remarkable for producing two harvests of dates in each year, but our Arabs did not praise their quality.' There are still two date harvests per year, and the Omanis still do not praise their quality. The Captain also noted that in the bay between 'Ras Hulf' and 'Ras Ya' they fished for whale: 'The tooth of the sperm species is in great request for sword handles, it being supposed to have a peculiar charm.'

The next survey was by the intrepid Captain Haines in the brig *Palinurus*, He was much respected in this part of the world. Sailing up from the south he turned north at Ras Madraka which at that time was called Ras Jezirah, and to Europeans it was known as Cape Isolette. It was the Indians who knew it as Madraka. Sailing north from there he surveyed the Ghubbat Hashish and then passed Masirah on the seaward side not wishing to risk his ship in the shoals and tidal rips of the Masirah Channel. He noted:

The island of Mosierah is of moderate height, its loftiest peak being about 600 feet high, as far as I could judge. Its outline is uneven, broken by numerous rocky points and sandy bays. Parts of it are cultivated, and its population (of the Jenaba tribe) tolerably numerous. When I was surveying at Ras Jezirah, Mosierah was governed by two sheikhs, apparently independent of each other, but nominally tributary to His Highness the Imam of Maskat. They have many boats, and I fear are much given to plunder when they meet any party weaker than themselves.

By the first part of the seventeenth century the Turks had become bored with Aden and simply walked out. In 1839 Captain Haines captured Aden from the local ruler and brought it under British rule. This proved to be a very astute move when the Suez Canal was opened thirty years later. But before then there was another survey, this time of the treacherous Masirah Channel by the survey brig *Palinurus,* in 1846. This had been Captain Haines's vessel but was now under the command of Captain Saunders. While the survey was in progress Assistant Surgeon Carter asked to go ashore to investigate the island. He had heard that in the distant past Persians had worked copper mines on Masirah. When the first boat came ashore the islanders were distinctly hostile. They threatened to murder the boat's crew who escaped with their lives and rowed back to the ship. Later the Sheikh of Sur Masirah successfully mediated a deal and Carter was able to begin his exploration. The islanders then became eager to help but knew virtually nothing of the old copper mines.

At that time of year (January and February) the weather was ideal and Carter was able to cover much of the island. He discovered the ancient copper mine near Sinfah at the extreme south of the island. It was the blue azurite which first caught his eye, and then he found the smelting places, slag heaps and the remains of small stone shelters. Later he found the copper deposits in the Wadi Rasiyah and a few miles to the north in the Wadi Ghard. When the islanders realised what he was looking for they told him of an old mine at al Qarin, where pottery smelting jars have recently been found. However, by that time the ship had finished her survey and was about to move on. Carter submitted his report and specimens to the Bombay Branch of the Royal Asiatic Society. Evidently the Society was not much impressed. Carter had not found the three richest mines. Firstly there is one at the top of the Wadi Madi where later geologists found an underground shaft, and secondly one to the south of the Wadi Ghaba where there are twenty-three stone dwellings and about nine waste dumps. The slag from smelting is a reddish colour, some with a black lining where the slag has vitrified in the fire. There are the remains of pottery vessels in which the ore was smelted, and rock oyster shells have survived the centuries to give a clue to part of the miners' diet. The third old copper mine is in the Wadi Muhasi which is 6 km down the track from Sur Masirah. At the best none of these mines was more than a cottage industry. It is not known when the mines were worked, but the one at Sinfah is certainly far older than the others. In the Wadi Jizzi in Northern Oman the old copper mines were worked from about 2500 BC until a couple of hundred years ago. The Persians (if that is who they were) must have been desperate for copper to go to so much trouble for so little reward. Even the supply of charcoal must have been a major undertaking.

In 1877 there was a rumour that eighty Abyssinians had been brought by sea from Mukalla to Masirah where most of them had been sold. The British

Political Agent in Muscat, Mr P.J.C. Robertson was instructed to sail to Masirah to investigate the rumour. His report is as follows:

I left Muscat for Masirah in HMS *Arab* on 24th December accompanied by Musellim bin Bedui of the Beni Ruahah on behalf of H.H. Sayid Turki. On arriving at the village of Umm Rusays I landed with Captain Dicken and found that the poverty of the place and its inhabitants had not been exaggerated at Muscat. The village consists of about 60 huts built of date branches, but several of them were deserted. The people live entirely by fishing, having neither cattle nor cultivation. There is a small clump of date trees at the upper end of the bay, but it belongs to the sheikh of the Jenaba who lives on the mainland and rarely visits the island. With this exception the island is entirely barren as I saw from the top of a hill which stands behind the village.

The villagers spread a mat for us and I told them why we had come. They said that the bughlah had anchored at the entrance of the bay but had landed no slaves on the island although slaves might have been sent in her boats to the mainland opposite. They swore that their collective wealth was insufficient to purchase a single Abyssinian. I questioned them at some length to ascertain if their boats had assisted in conveying the slaves to places on the coast but it did not appear they had done so.

Judging from the destitute appearance of the people, it seemed to me that the smallest pecuniary penalty would prove irrecoverable and neither the strength of the case against them, nor my instructions, appeared to justify the infliction of punishment by destroying boats or huts. I warned the islanders that if slaves were again landed in the neighbourhood and they failed to give notice of it, they should be held responsible and punished for the old and new offence at the same time. They appeared to be impressed and I trust you will consider that what I did was advisable in the circumstances.

In 1869 the Suez Canal had been opened and the sea passage from Britain to India became much quicker and easier. Aden became prosperous, and from there to Karachi many ships hugged the coast. This may not have been wise in the foul weather of the south-west monsoon during the summer months. On 29 July 1904 the SS *Baron Innerdale* set out from Karachi with a cargo of grain and timber. She was of 3,340 tons and was bound for Liverpool but on 2 August she ran aground in squally weather on Hallaniyah, the largest of the Kuria Muria Islands. The Kuria Murias were British crown territory having been given to Queen Victoria as a present by the Sultan of Muscat in 1854. They were given back to Oman in 1967. Incidently Kuria and Muria were two Portuguese sisters. The islands are now officially named the Juzor al Halaaniyaat. Anyway in 1904 ships had no radio, so the crew of the *Baron Innerdale* would have had to wait until a passing vessel came to the rescue. After only three days the British skipper and twenty-three members of the mainly Greek crew left on two of the ship's lifeboats. It is not clear why the captain decided to leave the ship so early. Perhaps he intended to use the current and wind to sail along the coast to Muscat with the prospect of being rescued on the shipping route. The smaller lifeboat contained only six crew who were never seen again. The larger lifeboat contained seventeen crew including the skipper and a boy passenger.

Some days after the departure of the Captain, the SS *Prome* sighted the *Baron Innerdale* and took off some of the remaining eight men. The *Prome* sailed to Aden where the matter was reported. The *Baron Innerdale* was refloated and sailed to Perim Island for temporary repairs. Perim Island was primarily a coaling station, British colonial territory at the mouth of the Red Sea west of Aden. Aden was also a British colony, administered by the India Office. The hinterland from the Red Sea to the Oman border was British protected territory.

From Perim Island the *Baron Innerdale* sailed to Bombay, arriving on Christmas Day and going into dry-dock. Repairs cost £500. On 27 October 1914, on passage from Calcutta to Port Said with a cargo of salt, she collided with the steamer *African Monach* in the Red Sea and sank.

Meanwhile, after the *Prome* had reported the grounding to Aden, the steamer *Dalhousie* sailed from Aden to search for the lifeboats, When she arrived off Masirah she learned of the fate of the Captain and crew. All had been massacred when they landed on the island. One account states that the boy was spared and taken aboard the *Dalhousie*.

It is not known whether the lifeboat was driven ashore by monsoon winds or whether the Captain had decided to land. After 270 nautical miles in an open boat in rough weather a landing would have been an appealing prospect. After landing the crew were met by a local sheikh. At first the reception committee was friendly, but then there was some incident. Perhaps curiosity led the locals to investigate the contents of the lifeboat, and the crew thought it was being looted. Perhaps it was. In any case one of the crew drew a pistol and fired, presumably to warn the locals to keep their distance. This was misinterpreted, and in the resultant mêlée the crew were slaughtered. Their bodies were buried in the sand close to where they landed on the north-east corner of the island.

News of this caused some consternation to the Sultan at Muscat. His neighbours in the Gulf were the British protected states of Trucial Oman (now the UAE), and his neighbour on the south coast was the Sultanate of Qishn and Socotra. This was part of the Eastern Aden Protectorate. Across the sea to the east the British Raj in India was the jewel in the crown. The previous year Lord Curzon, the greatest of all the Viceroys of India, had toured the Gulf and Arabian Sea in the *Hardinge*, a ship of the Royal Indian Marines. He was accompanied by the East India Squadron of the Royal Navy. In Muscat harbour there was a solemn durbar on the brightly illuminated *Argonaid*. Here the Viceroy presented Sultan Faisal with the Grand Cross of the Order of the Indian Empire.

The slaughter of the crew of a British ship was not an incident which could be ignored.

HMS *Merlin* was despatched from Karachi to Muscat where she picked up H.H. Sultan Faisal and Major W.G. Grey who was the British Political Agent. They sailed to Masirah to join HMS *Lapwing* which had sailed there directly from Karachi. No evidence of a massacre could be found so HMS *Merlin* returned her passengers to Muscat.

Letters continued to arrive at Muscat from the interior giving details of the crime. So a couple of weeks later the Sultan and his son Taimur sailed again to Masirah in the *Nour-el-Bahr*, the Sultan's steamer. At the village of Hilf at the northern end of the island there was a house-to-house search which revealed a seaman's jacket riddled with bullet holes and stained with blood. The search party started making arrests on the spot, and one discovery led to another. After twelve days the Sultan returned to Muscat with nine of the actual murderers and twenty-one of the chief residents of the island including the Sheikh. There were actually nineteen murderers but nine had escaped to the mainland and another was hiding somewhere on the island.

On the voyage to Muscat one of the prisoners jumped overboard and was drowned.

At Muscat the prisoners were put on trial. Those who had covered up the crime were imprisoned in Fort Jalali for a while and the Sheikh was permanently banished from the island. The village of Hilf was burnt and all the weapons found there were confiscated. The murderers were returned to the island for execution. They were shot at the site of the massacre and their bodies buried nearby in a communal grave without religious ceremony. In Taimur's words: 'I built one small commemorative mound of stones.'

The ten murderers who escaped arrest were never found.

It was an RAF legend that the islanders were forbidden to have permanent housing as a perpetual punishment for the massacre. This does not appear to be true because the locals knew nothing about it and old photographs do show permanent buildings at some settlements.

In 1943 a group of RAF airmen built a monument on behalf of the Captain's widow. It is close to the point where the massacre took place. Unfortunately the mason who cut the lettering misspelt the ship's name as 'Baron Inverdale' and this was perpetuated when the monument was refurbished by British contractors in the 1980s. The wording on the monument reads: 'IN MEMORY OF THOSE OF THE BARON INVERDALE WHO WERE MASSACRED AT THIS POINT IN THE YEAR 1904'.

The original monument built in 1943 carried a standard Christian cross but the refurbished one built in the 1980s carried (and still carries) a cross of the

The monument in 1994
(Photograph: Ann Richardson)

Celtic form. The reason for the change is not known but may merely have been to add structural strength.

CHAPTER II

A Stepping Stone on the Air Route from Iraq to Aden

I N THE 1920s the RAF established an air route to British India along the northern coast of the Arabian Gulf which was then known as the Persian Gulf. In those days the airfield staging posts were known as 'landing grounds', one of them being situated at Bushire. This was a port in the northern Gulf on the Iranian side. It was here that His Britannic Majesty's Political Resident in the Persian Gulf held sway. Around the area he had a number of Political Agents and Consuls. One of them was at Muscat where the ruler was His Highness the Sultan of Muscat and Oman. This country is now known as Oman and has long had a close and friendly relationship with Britain. It was never a British Protected State like the states of Trucial Oman (now the United Arab Emirates), its neighbours along the Gulf coast.

The Royal Air Force Air Headquarters at Baghdad (AHQ Iraq) had an area of responsibility which extended south to include the Sultanate of Muscat and Oman. The southern province of Muscat and Oman was Dhofar, its principal town being Salalah. The RAF Air Headquarters in Aden had an area of responsibility as far as the Dhofar border.

There were RAF bases in Iraq and Aden, but between the two there were no landing grounds until the late 1920s. In 1926 AHQ Iraq was beginning to have doubts about the air route to India north of the Persian Gulf. The British Government had an uneasy relationship with the Shah of Iran, and the landing ground at Bushire was far from ideal. It was soft and frequently flooded. In December 1926 the intelligence staff at AHQ Iraq began tentative investigations, and wrote the following letter to the Political Agent in Muscat:

> There is a proposal under consideration, if it should be politically and topographically possible, to establish a subsidiary air route to India via the Arabian coast and Muscat, and thence across the sea to British Baluchistan. This would provide an alternative route for reinforcement by air in the event of political factors rendering use of the Persian coast route impracticable.
>
> Before the matter is taken up officially by the Air Officer Commanding, it would save much time if you could kindly send us preliminary notes

unofficially by the first available mail on the following points:

Topographical possibility of establishing landing grounds and refuelling stations at Kuwait, Khaburah and Muscat, with intermediate landing and refuelling grounds in the vicinity of the Musallamiyah Islands and Mirfah.

A few weeks later this was followed by another letter from the AHQ intelligence staff to the PA in Muscat which read, in part, 'Do you know anything of the coast round from Muscat to Aden, and are there any other political officers to whom we could apply besides Aden to whom we are already writing?'

1929

In April 1929 the Residency in Aden wrote the following letter to the Political Agent in Muscat:

The Air Officer Commanding in Aden has been informed by the Air Ministry that every opportunity should be taken to extend reconnaissance and to establish landing grounds along the southern coast of Arabia to the maximum distance from Aden as is consistent with safety, the object being to keep moving further and further east.

The Air Ministry point out that there must be no suggestion of bringing in the civil authorities to set up an administration in outlying districts, nor are any treaty arrangements with tribal chiefs envisaged.

The influence of the Aden Residency extends as far eastwards as the territory of the Sultan of Qishn and Socotra who is in treaty relations with His Majesty's Government, and it is hoped in the near future to establish a landing ground in the vicinity of Qishn. A reconnaissance party is now at Mukalla and a chain of landing grounds will shortly be completed along the coast at Aden, Ahwar, Balhaf, Mukalla (Shuhair) and (probably) Qishn.

I am requested by the Resident to ask your advice as to the possibility of extending reconnaissance along the Dhofar and Oman coast as far as Muscat with a view to linking Muscat with Aden for the purpose of communication by air.

The Sultan at Muscat was also keen to establish an air route between his capital and Salalah, the principal town in his southern province. In November 1929 he granted permission for a landing ground at Sohar and another at Bait al Falaj near Muscat. Thus all the interested parties were in favour of the South Arabian air route, but there were practical difficulties. North-east of Dhofar the desert was reported to be infested with roaming bands of lawless bedu, principally Jenaba who owed no loyalty to their Sultan. The Amirs of the Jaalan could perhaps exercise some small influence over the bedu through their puppet Jenaba Sheikh of Masirah, but unfortunately parts of the Jaalan had slipped from the Sultan's control. At this time there was some hint of oil deposits near Duqm in Jenaba territory north of Ras Madraka. The Sheikh of Masirah was obviously to be a key figure in negotiations concerning the air route and the oil.

At this time (early 1929) No. 203 Squadron with its Southampton flying-boats moved its base to the turbid Euphrates river at Basra in southern Iraq. Away from base they were not reliant on landing grounds, any long stretch of sheltered water was acceptable. Often a Royal Navy sloop was required for refuelling or protection. The title 'sloop' is an old and honoured term from the days of sailing ships. In the Victorian era it became associated with small long-range vessels driven by steam with auxiliary sails. Sloops were used extensively on distant stations to supplement the small cruisers which operated there. The smaller sloops enjoyed the evocative term 'gunboat' and provided an economic way of imposing the rule of law in the days of the Pax Britannica. After the First World War the sloop enjoyed a revival. There were different classes, but all were small, very stable, and able to undertake almost any task.

There was a plan to send flying-boats from Basra to Aden in October 1930. As a preliminary, two Southamptons flew as far as Ras al Hadd in May 1929 but the next step down the coast was open to doubt. The AOC at Baghdad wrote to the Political Resident at Bushire: 'With regard to the flight to Aden next October it is most important that we settle on where we should refuel. From the map I suggest Mahawt or Masirah Island, but I have little or no information about them or whether the island is even inhabited.' The PA at Muscat provided the information a month later. Quoting his report:

Masirah Island. The east coast would be exposed to the north east monsoon and would be unsuitable. The Channel towards the mainland would be most satisfactory on weather grounds for seaplanes, but it is full of shallow two fathom patches at the north entrance, and is not anywhere buoyed so that a sloop may conceivably be chary about navigating it. On the south west side of the island, with approach from the south, conditions would appear to be most favourable. Alternatively Mahawt (more correctly Ghubbat Hashish) is a better sheltered harbour and is navigable for a sloop.

At neither Masirah or Ghubbat Hashish could safety of seaplane crews be guaranteed with certainly unless a sloop stood by: the inhabitants have an unsavoury record.

On other grounds both places would appear to be feasible, but it would be unwise to fly low over land at either. The Sheikh of Masirah is the Sheikh of the mainland too, and divides his time equally between Umm Rusays in Masirah and Khaluf in the Ghubbat Hashish where I stayed with him.

1930

In 1930 the RAF landing ground at Bait a Falaj outside Muscat was cleared by Lieutenant Dove RE.

The Aden Command also showed considerable zeal in pushing further and further east, as required by the Air Ministry in London. Disregarding the boundary of the Aden Protectorate, Flt Lt Rickards sailed from Aden to Ras al Hadd in a dhow and laid out a landing ground there. Then Sqn Ldr Betts and Lt Col Lake sailed from Aden to Masirah in HMS *Lawrence*. On the way the ship called in at Balhaf, Qishn, Salalah and Mirbat. The purpose of the visit to Masirah was to investigate the island as a stepping stone on the South Arabian air route, but this was not divulged to the inhabitants. The report reads as follows:

> We reached Masirah at 7 am on the 2nd May and dropped anchor off the northern point. At about 8.30 we put off in the motor boat for Dawwa about 5 miles south on the landward side. We only found a few fishermen there who gave us a cordial welcome. There was no one of any authority on the island and I was informed that the Sheikh (Said bin Sultan bin Khamis) was on the mainland at Ammar, and that he visited the island now and then. They also acknowledge the authority of Ali bin Abdullah, Amir of Jaalan.
>
> It was the opinion of the representative of the Sultan of Muscat at Mirbat that there would be no objection to making a landing ground on the island on the part of the Sheikh provided he had orders from the Sultan. I am of the opinion that a landing ground could be constructed at any time especially if the constructing party brought with them a few luxuries for the inhabitants in the shape of coffee, sugar and rice.
>
> Dawwa consists of 40 or 50 huts constructed of palm branches and a mud-built building which serves as a mosque. Fishing is the chief industry of the inhabitants who are poor. They export shark fins and import dates and rice.
>
> We only passed two villages on our way to Dawwa, one called Hilf near the northern end with a hill of the same name, and the other Dafiyat about half way between Hilf and Dawwa. On our return to the ship Commander Garatin sent off a bag of flour, a bag of rice, and about 15 tins of ship's biscuits for the inhabitants.
>
> The highest point of the island is reported as 743 feet, and the Gazetteer of Arabia estimates the population to be about 600. The inhabitants belong chiefly to the Jenaba tribe, are very poor and subsist chiefly on fish, which abound in the sea there. The exports are tortoiseshell, shark's fins and dried fish; most of the trade seems to take place with Muscat.
>
> In view of the reported unfriendly attitude of the inhabitants a heavily armed party was sent in the ship's motor boat.

During the discussion which followed our arrival and reception at Dawwa, the villagers stated that they had heard of the visits of aeroplanes to Dhofar and did not seem to be in any way hostile to the idea of such a visit to Masirah. Any difficulty in making a landing ground on the island will not be due to the attitude of the inhabitants who stated that the Sheikh would be equally well disposed. Time did not permit a visit to any of the other villages, in particular Umm Rusays where, judging from the chart, there would seem to be a suitable seaplane anchorage.

The plain near Dawwa is composed of hard sand and shells, with numerous tufts of dried grass; the ground rising gently from the sea to the hills. A landing could be effected on narrow patches of clear ground running inland at right angles to the coast. This, however, is at right angles to the prevailing winds. A really suitable landing area near Dawwa would require much preparation as the ground is cut up by narrow shallow water channels. It is possible, however, that the plain nearer the middle of the island, where the hills are not so high, might prove more suitable, as the water channels might not be so pronounced, or be entirely absent.

Off Umm Rusays village there is a long narrow inlet, 3½ miles long with a width of 400 to 800 yards and depths of 1 to 3 fathoms (6 to 18 feet). It is protected from the Masirah Channel by an island 2¼ miles long, running north-north-east to south-south-west. The inhabitants of Dawwa stated that this was a very good dhow anchorage during the south-west monsoon and was extensively used at that time. But it was not so much used during the north-east monsoon as it is exposed to the winds which occasionally blow very strongly from the north-east. In view of this the site would not appear to be suitable as a seaplane anchorage (other than an emergency one) as all the other anchorages on the coast are more suitable during the north east monsoon.

A copy of this report was sent to Bushire where it was read by Colonel Biscoe, the Political Resident. Evidently it angered him, judging by the missives he fired off in the general direction of Aden. He was disturbed that the landing party was armed, something expressly forbidden in his area of responsibility. Letters of apology explained that it seemed a sensible precaution in view of the islanders' reputation, and that the armed party did not come ashore from the motor boat.

1931

The proposed Basra to Aden flight did not take place in 1930 because of the failure of the dhow carrying the fuel. Instead it was decided to visit Masirah to gain the confidence and co-operation of the islanders so that a landing ground could be established there. Much would depend on the attitude of the Sheikh and the islanders, and an alternative location in the Mahawt Inlet could also be reconnoitred. This is a wide shallow bay on the mainland, due west of the south point of Masirah. The following letter was written by Colonel Biscoe at Bushire to the PA at Muscat:

Dear Fowle

Your letter of 11th March – Masirah Island.
The matter has since been fixed up by telegram and I hope you will have a successful trip. I may be entirely wrong, but my own impression is that the warlike propensities of the inhabitants of that coast have been considerably exaggerated. It suited Thomas's book to describe them as ferocious warriors, but I personally shall be very surprised if when you go there they do not turn out to be a lot of poverty stricken fisher folk ekeing out a miserable existence by catching sharks. The tribes in the interior of course are somewhat different: and the above remarks refer to the people along the coast.

Colonel Biscoe was absolutely correct.

In March 1931 two Southampton flying-boats of 203 Squadron, under Squadron Leader Bentley, arrived at Muscat harbour, followed the next day by the sloop HMS *Penzance*. She was under the command of Commander Startin. A conference was called by Major T.C. Fowle CBE, the Political Agent at Muscat, who then embarked on the sloop for the journey to Umm Rusays on the channel coast of Masirah.

On his return from Masirah the PA submitted a long report to Colonel Biscoe. He related how he had sailed from Muscat on the sloop, calling in at Sur to pick up three influential Omanis who might be able to assist with the negotiations at Umm Rusays. These three Omanis were put ashore at Umm Rusays on the evening that the sloop arrived, and spent the night there. The purpose of the visit was explained to the islanders.

The PA went ashore the following morning and discovered how the island was governed. It was apparently divided into many strips of land, each owned by its headman. Some of the islanders were of the Hikman tribe, but most were Jenaba, the same as the three influential Omanis picked up at Sur. While the PA was ashore more headmen (*muqaddimeen*) were arriving but none seemed to acknowledge the sovereignty of the Sultan.

There was also a sheikh of Masirah. He was Jenaba and always of the Majali family which had originally come from the Hadramaut. The newly elected sheikh was Khamis bin Hilal who was away fishing. He owned no land on the island but the assembled headmen acknowledged him as 'first among equals'. He was destined to be sheikh for the next forty-seven years, until 1978 which was after the RAF had left the island.

Later in the morning one of the Southampton flying-boats arrived from

Muscat. After refuelling from the sloop it departed for an aerial reconnaissance of the Mahawt Inlet which might also be suitable for flying-boats. By the time it returned the PA was back on the sloop. After lunch he went back ashore with Commander Startin, Squadron Leader Bentley, Flying Officer Drew and a couple of interpreters. The RAF officers inspected a possible landing ground for wheeled aircraft and then all sat down in the shade while coffee and dates were served. Although the Omanis from Sur had explained it already, the PA repeated the requirements which were for a refuelling barge, moorings for flying boats, and a landing ground. The headmen replied that this would require the agreement of all the sheikhs of the Jenaba, not just Khamis bin Hilal (who had still not arrived). Since there were Jenaba sheikhs over a wide area of the mainland, the headmen's terms were a non-offensive way of refusing permission. The PA said how much he regretted their decision because it would deprive them of the financial benefits that an agreement would bring to them. He left a bag of rice as 'ground bait' and returned to the ship with the others.

The PA went ashore again next morning to see if the headmen had changed their minds. They had not. He invited them to the ship for any medical treatment that they might need, but they all declined. The PA returned to the sloop in time to join another aerial reconnaissance of the Mahawt Inlet, and later that day returned to Muscat on the Southampton.

The PA, Major Fowle, was quite optimistic in his report. He noted that the islanders were friendly and that an agreement was only a matter of time after a few more visits. These could be by flying-boat without the protection of an accompanying sloop. The new Rangoon flying-boats of 203 Squadron would be able to return to Muscat without refuelling.

At exactly the same time as the above there was a probing expedition of land planes from Aden. Four Fairey IIIFs of 8 Squadron staged through the landing ground at Mukalla and continued to Salalah where Flt Lt Rickards had previously positioned 2,500 gallons of petrol. Another similar flight was planned for October, immediately after the south-west monsoon, but it had to be cancelled due to another failure of the fuel dhow. It was not until September 1931 that 8 Squadron returned to Dhofar and established the landing ground at Mirbat, another 50 miles up the coast from Salalah. As a landing ground it was far superior to Salalah itself, but the local inhabitants from the hinterland were a law unto themselves. There were persistent difficulties and the following report forty-five years later shows that matters had not improved:

On 3rd July 1976 the scheduled Skyvan to Mirbat landed on time there and disgorged its passengers in an orderly fashion. The Army staff sergeant (i/c crowd control) informed the loadmaster, who informed the pilot that there were fifteen adult passengers and seven children for Salalah and this was accepted. The passengers began to embark, women and children first, but it soon became apparent that there were many more passengers than stated, even allowing for the fact that some of the more developed children wore beards. The staff sergeant, wishing to remove those who had not booked, started with a tall gentleman in one of the rear seats, a Jebali, who said it was absolutely imperative that he get to Salalah. An argument then seemed to develop between the staff sergeant and the Jebali, at one point of which the staff sergeant leaned across this passenger and touched him, one assumes to emphasise a point. The next instant the staff sergeant appeared upside down with his feet waving in the air and shortly after a bout of fisticuffs started, in which all the male passengers immediately joined. After several minutes it was apparent that the action was likely to last for some time so the pilot informed Operations Salalah that the engines were being closed down because of the fight in the rear of the aeroplane.

After completing the 'close down' checks the pilot descended from the front of the aeroplane, and with great coolness and deliberation, as befits an ex-member of Bomber Command, went and sat on a nearby burmail.

After a while a group of struggling figures appeared from the back of the Skyvan (amongst which was the tall Jebali) and at this point the pilot went to the rear of the aeroplane to determine what was happening inside. The scene inside was a little more orderly so the pilot told the loadmaster and staff sergeant that no more than the original load would be acceptable, with no one sitting on the floor and no children with beards.

At this point the pilot happened to look behind him and saw the tall Jebali had broken away from the group of struggling figures and was making back towards the Skyvan in some haste, clutching his FN rifle by the barrel. The pilot then executed some rather fancy footwork which took him to one side and the Jebali once again entered the Skyvan, laying about him with considerable energy. Other figures followed the Jebali into the Skyvan and the pilot returned to his burmail.

Some time later the group of struggling figures once again emerged from the aeroplane onto the sand. At this point frantic signals from the loadmaster indicated to the pilot that now would be a suitable time to start the engines and leave; so the latter, with as much speed as was commensurate with dignity, entered the aeroplane, started one engine and taxied to the far end of the strip. There the second engine was started and the aircraft returned to base without further incident.

In spite of its excellent runway Mirbat always had one serious drawback!

Returning to 1931, a second visit to Masirah was planned, this time by the new Rangoon flying-boats of 203 Squadron. The flight was to be under the command of Group Captain Welsh who was the station commander at Basra and therefore responsible for 203 Squadron. No final decision had been made on the location of the refuelling station; it could have been off Masirah or off the mainland in the Mahawt Inlet. This time no sloop was to accompany the flying-boats. The following telegram was sent from AHQ to Bushire and Muscat:

> Request concurrence for cruise of two Rangoons as follows. Leaving Basra 13/5. Bahrain, Yas Island, Ras al Khaimah, Muscat, Masirah Island and return to Basra. Object of flight: development of friendly relations with inhabitants of Masirah and photographic reconnaissance. Request PA Muscat be permitted to accompany flight if he can be spared from his duties for maximum of two days. Propose giving minor presents to headmen on this occasion.

Unfortunately Major Fowle had gone to Karachi for medical treatment so the PA at Bahrain took his place, boarding the Rangoon at Bahrain. On his return he submitted the following report to Colonel Biscoe at Bushire:

> We arrived at Muscat at about 5.30 pm on 19th May. The next day we waited for the second Rangoon to catch up and attempted to leave for Masirah on the following day. But we were forced back by excessive oil temperatures, the day being unfortunately very hot. We left two days later after adjustments to the plane, arriving at Masirah some four hours later. At first sight the island appeared deserted and even after anchoring scarcely a soul could be seen. Group Captain Welsh and I went off in the rubber dinghy and Squadron Leader Bentley followed in another with a bag of rice, or 'ground bait', as my colleague at Muscat euphemistically terms it. I could see one or two men hiding behind houses, and it was not until we were leaving the beach that a body of some 20 men sallied out to meet us. We went into their majlis and sat down and discovered that the so called Sheikh Khamis bin Hilal was on the mainland. The emptyness of the place was explained by many of the inhabitants having gone to the mainland to help in the date harvest.
>
> I could not discover any of the persons mentioned in Fowle's report, and the islanders did not volunteer any information. They were evidently as shy as hawks though one or two were nearly persuaded to come over to the flying-boats. The way they all took cover at the distant sight of the aircraft showed that they still consider them as fraught with unknown dangers and it will be some time before they become accustomed to them. It must be remembered that few of these people have ever seen a European before, let alone their mechanical horrors.
>
> ... The island evidently has as many owners as a suburban allotment, and having lived in glorious isolation since the dawn of history, its inhabitants see little advantage and many drawbacks in providing a link in a present day air route.
>
> Masirah is Muscat state territory and there appears little to be gained by waiting until these savages are willing to execute an agreement. If a dhow laden with petrol were preceded by a flying-boat I doubt very much that any attempt would be made upon it. Later a barge might be substituted and

203 Squadron Short Singapore piloted by Clayton Boyce at Khor Jarama en route to Masirah on 4 April 1939 (Photograph: Sam Boyce)

once the islanders had become accustomed to aircraft an agreement regarding an aerodrome should be easy to arrange if it is still considered advisable to get them to make one.

There were approximately two more visits to Masirah during 1931. One was a single Rangoon flown by Flt Lt Ragg (later Air Vice-Marshal). Quoting from his letter: 'We went ashore at Umm Rusays in a rubber dinghy under cover of our machine guns while the Sheikh and his braves came down to the beach to meet us; and the old men, women and children retired behind the village among the hillocks. But eventually we made friends – with the help of a few bags of rice.'

In 1929 the Sultan, Taimur bin Faisal, abdicated and two years later his son, Said bin Taimur, was appointed as the new Sultan. Later in 1931 the new Sultan sent an emissary to Masirah to speak to Sheikh Khamis about an agreement with the RAF. He found the Sheikh who showed himself to be a master of obfuscation and procrastination. An agreement was as far off as ever.

1932

Khor Jarama is a most remarkable harbour. It is about 3 miles west of Ras al Hadd in the direction of Sur and Muscat. The entrance to the khor is a narrow fjord winding its way between cliffs, and then opening out into a large lagoon about 1½ miles wide and 3 miles long. Due to a lack of fresh water it is virtually uninhabited. In rough weather it provides sheltered water. It was therefore ideal as a refuelling stop for RAF flying-boats in the 1930s but a petrol store was an obvious requirement. Instead of a blockhouse full of four-gallon tins, there were to be two cylindrical 4,000-gallon petrol tanks. They were to be buried in trenches 11ft deep and entombed in concrete. In addition there were to be two 250-gallon oil tanks entombed in trenches 6ft deep. The Sultan granted permission for this and the installation was carried out by the Works Department of AHQ. For increased security the tanks were not laid on the shore but on a rocky island just inside the twisting entrance.

Khor Jarama proved a useful advanced base when trouble was brewing early in 1932. Exactly what happened is not recorded but it appears likely that the Sultan's customs officials were roughed up and ejected at gunpoint from the customs post at Ayja which is across the bay at Sur. Sheikh Ali bin Abdullah al Hamuda was the ringleader. The following operation order was issued on 24 February by AHQ Iraq:

Sur Operations. 1932

1. Authority has been received from the British Government for the Combined Operations by the Royal Navy and the Royal Air Force to be carried out at Ayja if rendered necessary by the attitude of the Beni Bu Ali tribesmen.

2. The political aim of the Combined Operations is to prevent further interference with the administration of the Muscat State at Ayja.

3. Three sloops of the Royal Navy will arrive at Muscat on 2nd March.

4. The Hon'ble the Political Resident in the Persian Gulf will arrive at Muscat on 2nd March.

5. The Senior Naval Officer, Persian Gulf will arrive at Muscat on 2nd or 3rd March.

Aim

6. The aim of No. 203 (Flying-Boat) Squadron will be to destroy the fort at Balad Beni Bu Ali.

Execution

7. The three Rangoons are to arrive at Muscat not later than 2nd March.

8. At the same time as the Naval forces arrive off Sur, or at a time to be decided by the Political Resident, the Rangoon flying-boats are to carry out a demonstration over Balad Beni Bu Ali and drop proclamations warning Sheikh Ali of the Beni Bu Ali that his fort will be bombed if he

resists the Muscat Government at Ayja or interferes with the Customs Post at that place.

9. If the Beni Bu Ali tribesmen molest the Customs Post, which it is intended to establish at Ayja, the fort of Sheikh Ali at Balad Beni Bu Ali is to be bombed by the Rangoons beginning at the time that the sloops bombard the fort at Ayja.

10. If it is found that Beni Bu Ali tribesmen are at Ayja when the Naval forces arrive off that place, and that they have to be ejected by force, the Air Officer Commanding has asked the Hon'ble the Political Resident in the Persian Gulf to agree that the bombing of the inland fort at Balad Beni Bu Ali by the Rangoons shall begin at the time that the fort at Ayja is destroyed by shell fire from the sloops. The reply from the Political Resident has not yet been received at Air Headquarters.

11. Warning proclamations are to be dropped on the village and fort during the day previous to the commencement of the bombing. When the bombing has once started no further warning proclamations prior to each attack will be necessary.

12. Authority to begin bombing is to be obtained from the Hon'ble the Political Resident.

13. Bombs are to be dropped from a height of not less than four thousand feet above the fort and above any country in the immediate vicinity from which fire might be directed against the aircraft.

14. In the first place bombs of 250 lbs. are to be used. After the buildings have been well shaken by the 250 lb. bombs, 112 lb. bombs should be tried. It is feared, however, that they may prove of little use for destructive effect. It is not proposed to send additional 250 lb. bombs to Muscat for the first phase of the bombing.

15. Bombing is to be intermittent and the following programme is given as a general guide for the first seven days:
    (a) First and second days. Intensive bombing.
    (b) Third day. No bombing.
    (c) Fourth day. One heavy attack during the afternoon.
    (d) Fifth day. Intensive bombing.
    (e) Sixth day. No bombing.
    (f) Seventh day. Intensive bombing.

16. Bombing is to be continued until the Officer Commanding No. 203 Squadron decides that in view of the aim defined in para. 6 of these orders, sufficient damage has been done, unless in the meantime the political aim of the combined operation (vide para. 2) has been attained.

17. Aircraft may operate from the advanced base at Khor Jarama during daylight

hours, but are not to stop there at night. The proposals for the security of this base, put forward in Section VIII of the Report by Group Captain W. L. Welsh under reference No. 203S/103/3/Air of 14th February, 1932 are approved.

Officer Commanding No. 203 (Flying-Boat) Squadron is responsible to the Air Officer Commanding for the safety of the advanced base and is to satisfy himself that the posts are sited in the best possible positions and are suitably constructed to resist any attempt to rush them.

Administrative Arrangements

18. Officer Commanding No. 203 Squadron is to arrange for the supply of petrol and bombs for Khor Jarama from Muscat.

Intercommunication

19. Signal arrangements will be the same as for a normal cruise.
Acknowledge by signal.

On 4 March the Sultan's warning proclamations were dropped to the people of Ayja. The English translation is at follows:

I am informing Sheikh Ali of your rebellious action and telling him that unless you accept the customs post the fort at Ayja will be destroyed by warships and the fort at Balad Beni Bu Ali will be destroyed by aeroplanes. I enclose for your information a copy of my letter to him.

To Sheikh Ali bin Abdullah al Hamuda. Today the Muscat State sent some customs officers to Ayja to establish a post there in accordance with former custom. Your tribesmen at Ayja threatened the customs guards with rifles and refused to allow them to remain there. I am therefore writing to give you notice that unless you send instructions to your people not to resist the establishment of a customs post your fort at Ayja will be destroyed by ships and your fort at Balad Beni Bu Ali will be bombed by aeroplanes. Your people at Ayja should come on board the ship and inform me by noon on Monday at the latest that they are willing to accept the customs post.

signed Said bin Taimur.

Sheikh Ali replied saying that he would not come on board the ship, but suggested a meeting at Ayja or Sur. He demanded rent and an allowance to be paid in addition to dates and rice. He also demanded the return of a dhow which had been impounded and taken to Muscat. He got short shrift from the Sultan who wrote:

As you have not complied with my orders by noon today, I write to inform you that your fort at Ayja will be bombarded and your fort in the Jaalan bombed by aeroplanes. In order to enable your tribesmen to escape from the danger, this will not be done until Wednesday morning. I enclose for your information a notice addressed by the Senior Naval Officer to the people of Ayja, and also a notice which you should send to the people of the Jaalan.

Warning

The people of Ayja are warned that about four hours after sunrise on Wednesday 9th March the fort at Ayja will be bombarded. 15 minutes before opening fire each ship will fire two rounds of blank ammunition. Anyone remaining in the town of Ayja after that time will do so at the peril of his life. No one should return to Ayja until a letter is received telling them it is safe to do so.

The Political Resident, who was on board HMS *Shoreham*, also wrote to Sheikh Ali:

O Sheikh, I advise you to make your peace with His Highness while there is yet time. The demands of the Muscat State are just and the High Government will enforce them.

Sheikh Ali capitulated but still refused to come aboard the Sultan's ship. No doubt he feared abduction and imprisonment. The customs post was re-established but because Sheikh Ali would not come to the ship he did not receive his allowance and rent or any dates and rice. Major Fowle had now been promoted to Lieutenant Colonel. On hearing of the promotion the Sultan wrote the following letter to him:

I take this opportunity to express from the bottom of my heart my thanks and gratitude to our friend the High British Government for the valuable assistance rendered in securing the demands of our government, which we highly appreciate. I request you kindly to convey my cordial thanks to H.B.M.'s Government.

I also offer my best thanks to the Hon'ble the Political Resident, Lieut-Colonel H. V. Biscoe, and to yourself for the trouble taken in the Sur question and the zeal shown with regard to our rights: that is the establishment of the customs post at Ayja similar to the former one, and the submission of the Sheikh of the Beni Bu Ali to our Government after he had been rebellious. We will never forget your help and always recognise your true friendship. I trust that you will convey my friendly sentiments to the Hon'ble the Political Resident.

In conclusion I trust that the perfect friendship existing between us may endure.

Please submit the text of our letter to the High Government for which I thank you.

Your sincere friend,
Said bin Taimur.

With Said bin Taimur's rule firmly re-established over this part of the Sultanate the Jenaba became much more co-operative over the landing rights at Masirah. Incidently, in 1930 Sheikh Hasan of Musandam province entertained thoughts of independence and ignored an ultimatum. When the sloop HMS *Lupin* shelled his house he capitulated.

Further attempts were made to obtain an agreement at Masirah. During March Gp Capt Welsh flew a Rangoon down to Muscat where he picked up Colonel Fowle. Together they flew to Umm Rusays and as usual were accorded a very friendly reception. But as usual the Sheikh was absent, so no meaningful discussion could take place. In his report to Bushire, Colonel Fowle wrote: 'their Sheikh was absent. He always is: he may have been really absent or he may have been hiding behind the nearest sand-hill.'

Two months later there was another attempt to contact Sheikh Khamis at Masirah. In his report to Bushire Colonel Fowle wrote:

On 22nd and 23rd May two flying-boats under command of Gp Capt Welsh arrived at Muscat. Also on the 23rd HMS *Triad* arrived with the Senior Naval Officer on board. The object was to establish a refuelling base at Masirah for RAF air-craft. All that was required for the moment was a rough stone building which could be constructed by the islanders themselves providing they were supplied with beams and matting. These were put on board *Triad*...

Triad left Muscat on 24th and I left by air with Gp Capt Welsh on the morning of 25th. Stopping at Khor Jarama on the way we reached Umm Rusays that afternoon some time ahead of *Triad*. Three of the islanders came to meet the flying-boat, the first occasion on which the first move has come from the Island. They had a letter from the elusive Khamis whom we had been pressing for more than a year. He said that he had gone to Sur.

The report continues, saying that the building materials were landed from *Triad* and that the islanders were told that a flying-boat or sloop would arrive and show them how to build the petrol store. Some cash was handed over together with rice, flour and sugar. Colonel Fowle boarded *Triad* for the return journey, stopping at Sur. Sheikh Khamis was here and came on board where the situation was explained to him. Colonel Fowle wrote of him: 'He is a pleasant enough individual of about 35 and professed himself completely obedient to the Sultan's orders.'

Colonel Fowles's report also contains the following observations:

On previous visits to the island, where the Bani Bu Ali – who were still more or less recalcitrant – have influence, our policy was to keep the State in the background. On this occasion, however, owing to the recent success gained at Sur by the submission of Sheikh Ali bin Abdullah to the demands of the state, the time seemed to have come to work through the State ...

... There is no doubt that our success at Sur had a beneficial effect on the attitude of the islanders. Sheikh Khamis was in Sur after the capitulation of Sheikh Ali, and on his return to Masirah must have passed on his impressions to the rest of the island. You will remember that – in advocating operations at Sur – you mentioned this point, the effect on Masirah, in your telegram No. T 77 of 30th November 1931 to the Government of India.

Early in 1932 some doubt was thrown on the necessity of a refuelling station at Masirah. AHQ wrote to the Resident at Bushire:

The discovery of the khor at Ras Madraka may affect the importance of Masirah (Umm Rusays) as a flying-boat refuelling point. Reconnaissance from the air last December shows that Khor Madraka has a sufficient expanse of water, but further reconnaissance by 203 Squadron on the ground is necessary. If this khor proves suitable it would be preferable to Masirah as a refuelling point, being nearer Aden and at a convenient distance (260 miles) from Khor Jarama.

The khor (creek) was not actually at Ras Madraka, but at Khor Gharim which is 19 miles further west. Before the summer months the Sultan escaped the heat of Muscat by sailing to Salalah which is cooled by the south-west monsoon. He allowed Flt Lt Ragg and Flt Lt Finch of 203 Squadron to join him on his dhow which stopped at Khor Gharim for an inspection. They found that the khor was not long enough for a heavily loaded flying-boat, so interest in Masirah was rekindled.

Incidently, it was not only the Sultan who fled from the oven-like heat of the Muscat summer. The Political Agent also absented himself from mid-May to mid-September, carrying on his duties as best he could from Quetta or Simla in the hills of northern India. In the early 1800s four successive PAs at Muscat had died due to the Muscat climate. Air conditioning did not arrive until the late 1940s.

In November 1932 an agreement was finally reached at Masirah. By this time there was a new PA at Muscat, Major Bremner. Colonel Fowle had established a close personal relationship with the new Sultan, his letters to him beginning 'My Dear Friend' and ending 'I am Your Highness's sincere friend'. The Sultan's replies also started 'My Dear Friend' and ended 'Your sincere friend'.

Sultan Said bin Taimur had been educated in India and wrote English in a neat hand. He was softly spoken and had considerable personal charm. However, he was obsessed by the debts which he had inherited from his father, and in later life gained a reputation for parsimony. He became a benign autocrat, a sultan of the old school.

Colonel Fowle was a serving officer in the Indian Civil Service. On leaving Muscat he was posted to Bushire where he became the Political Resident, replacing Colonel Biscoe. A few years later the correspondence shows him as none other than Sir Trenchard Fowle KCIE.

Major Bremner wrote to Colonel Fowle explaining how the agreement had been achieved. The letter was dated 28 November 1932 and reads:

Sir,

I have the honour to submit herewith a report in D.O. form by Captain R.G.E.W. Alban on the establishment of the Masirah Island oil depot.

A copy of the actual agreement has not been submitted by Captain Alban but the same will be obtained and forwarded to you in due course.

Captain Alban's report modestly makes no allusion to his own skilful handling of the negotiations, the successful result of which is entirely attributable, as I am informed by Flight Lieutenant Ragg, RAF, to his tact, patience, and determination. I regard the accomplishment of his mission as a most creditable performance.

I have the honour to be,

Sir,

Your most obedient Servant,

C.E.U. Bremner, Major

The attached report by Captain Alban reads:

Dear Major,

In accordance with the instructions of the Political Resident and yourself and with the approval of H.H. the Sultan, I accompanied Flight Lieutenant Ragg in a flying-boat to Masirah on 14th November 1932.

On arrival at Umm Rusays it was found that Sheikh Khamis bin Hilal, Sheikh of Masirah, was away at the fishing grounds. The settlement of Umm Rusays is a small collection of huts and three or four stone buildings where most of the fish caught in those parts is dumped for drying and export. Chartering a dhow which happened to be lying at anchor there, we despatched it in search of the Sheikh.

In the meantime we occupied ourselves in examining any building likely to prove suitable as a petrol store. With the assistance of Captain Mackay RE such a building was found. It belonged to one Salim bin Said who was willing to let it subject to the approval of the Sheikh.

Later the boatman who had been despatched in search of Sheikh Khamis returned saying that there was no trace of the Sheikh, and that he was thought to have gone to the mainland. As there was no object in staying any longer at

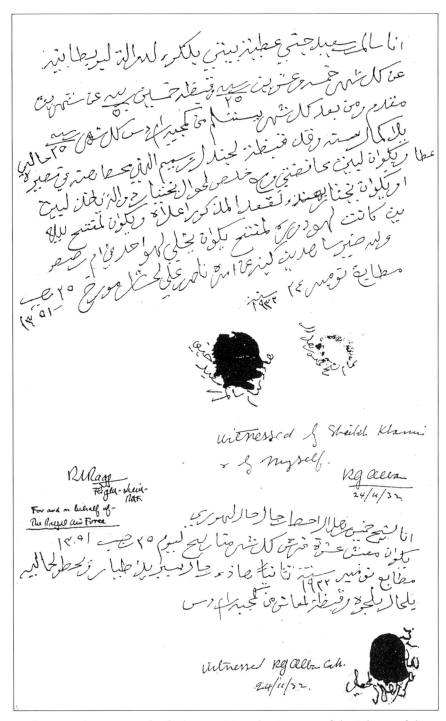

The original agreement for facilities at Masirah. Courtesy of the Library of the Oriental and India Office – File R/15/6/89

Umm Rusays, we decided to return to Muscat visiting Sur en route on the chance of finding Sheikh Khamis there. Owing to the roughness of the sea, however, we were compelled to pass it by and return direct to Muscat which we reached on Wednesday the 16th.

On Wednesday the 23rd we again left Muscat hoping to be able to land at Sur and locate Sheikh Khamis. On arrival at Sur it was ascertained that Sheikh Khamis had left Sur a few days before and would, without much doubt, be now on the island of Masirah.

Next day we proceeded to Umm Rusays. We took with us Sheikh Nasir bin Ali who is the paramount sheikh in Sur and of the Jenaba tribe, the same tribe as the people of Masirah. On arrival at Umm Rusays we despatched a man to fetch Sheikh Khamis from a village at the other end of the island.

Next morning, Sheikh Khamis having in the meantime arrived, we broached the subject in view. There ensued a great deal of beating about the bush, Sheikh Khamis being a typical bedu. The Sheikh was evidently torn between his desire to provide a building (and take the rent himself) and his fear of assuming a responsibility which might give his enemies a chance of bringing him into bad repute by, for example, setting fire to the dump.

In the meantime the owner of the selected building, thinking himself to be the only pebble on the beach, was engaged in raising the rent, the sum demanded having already reached the figure of rupees 50 per month. We sent him about his business with the intimation that we had no further use for his house.

We settled down to see if some arrangement could be made with the Sheikh. He agreed to build a store himself at any spot selected by the RAF and let it to them for a rental of rupees 30 per month. But he also insisted upon having four guards to look after it at a salary of 15 Maria Theresa dollars per month each. This would have brought the total of rent and salaries up to nearly rupees 80 per month.

At this point it was found that Salim bin Said, the owner of the house, was bewailing his fate outside. He was accordingly called in and offered rupees 25 per month for his house with two months advance cash down. Sheikh Nasir bin Ali wrote out a form of agreement which Salim signed without any more ado. Flight Lieutenant Ragg signed on behalf of the RAF and the document was witnessed by Sheikh Khamis, Sheikh of Masirah, and myself. Salim bin Said agreed to look after his house and the petrol himself. Sheikh Khamis further agreed to engage a boatman/caretaker who would be given a houri by the RAF at a salary of 10 Maria Theresa dollars per month.

Although the rented house is some distance from the sea, this arrangement is probably the best as the whole village, and their relatives in other villages around, will be interested in the safety of the store. This would not be the case had the Sheikh himself taken on the contract. The price also, of rupees 33 per month inclusive of watch and ward, is very moderate compared to the other proposition. The boatman/caretaker will be provided by the Sheikh and his houri will be supplied by the RAF. He will visit flying-boats immediately on arrival, take their orders, and arrange as far as possible for labour for loading petrol.

Rupees 200 was paid to Sheikh Khamis as a personal present from the Honourable the Political Resident and another rupees 40 was paid at the rate of rupees 10 each to four minor sheikhs and influential men in the village. Thirty Maria Theresa dollars was given to Sheikh Nasir bin Ali of Sur in consideration of the trouble incurred by him, expenses of food etc. In addition to this some head dresses, coffee and sugar were distributed. An order for the monthly payment of rent for the godown, i.e. rupees 25, and of 10 Maria Theresa dollars for the boatman/caretaker was given to Messrs Khimji Ramdas of Sur.

I have to thank Flight Lieutenant Ragg for his hospitality and kindness under somewhat exacting conditions.

Yours sincerely,

R.G.E.W. Alban, Captain

When writing the laudatory covering letter to this report, the new PA at Muscat did not mention that the building materials for a petrol store had already been delivered to Umm Rusays. Furthermore he failed to recognise two flaws in the agreement. Firstly, at such an extended distance, it would be difficult for Khimji Ramdas at Sur to make the regular monthly payments. Secondly, there was no mention in the agreement of any payment of porterage charges for carrying the petrol tins from the store to the beach. This would cause difficulties the following year when the agreement was put to the test by a visiting flying-boat. The visiting aircrew were all from 203 Sqn and should have given more consideration to a landing ground at Umm Rusays. It would have to be close to the petrol store, but the local terrain was really not suitable. It would appear that nobody wanted to draw attention to this unpalatable fact.

The mention of the Indian rupee and Maria Theresa dollar requires an explanation. In the coastal area of Muscat and Oman where trade was largely in the hands of Indians, known as banians, the currency in use was the Indian rupee. In the interior of Oman it was the Maria Theresa dollar.

Maria Theresa became Queen of Hungary and Archduchess of Austria in 1740. Her thalers or dollars were particularly fine coins weighing 28.35 grams with an 83.5 per cent silver content. Austrian ships from Trieste introduced them to Alexandria on the Mediterranean coast of Egypt. The coins became trusted for their silver content and their use spread throughout Egypt to the Sudan, Ethiopia, Somaliland and throughout North Africa. To the east the coins gained currency in the Levant and throughout the Arabian Peninsula. Many states established local currencies for nationalistic reasons but the Maria Theresa dollar was more acceptable for many years and served alongside them as an unofficial local currency which had the advantage of being acceptable in neighbouring states.

Queen Maria Theresa died in 1780, but due to popular demand the mint at Vienna continued to produce them for export. Those minted after that year all carry the date 1780.

In 1935, under pressure from Hitler and Mussolini, Austria signed a treaty whereby the mint at Rome was authorised to produce them. The British had wide interests throughout the area, and in view of the fact that Vienna's monopoly had been broken, decided to produce them at the Royal Mint. Between 1936 and 1940 the Royal Mint produced 15 million of them, many of them earmarked for use in Ethiopia once the Italians had been ejected and the Emperor restored. Following the entry of Italy into the War it became difficult to transport the newly minted coins from Britain. The dies were therefore flown to Bombay where another 19 million coins were struck. After the War the dies were returned to London. Manufacture continued in Rome until the expiry of the treaty in 1960. The Royal Mint in London ceased manufacture in 1962. The coins are still being produced in Vienna, but being bulky are not so much in demand as the better-trusted paper currency of the local governments. Indeed, the production is now so small that the coins have acquired a rarity value.

1933

Flt Lt Ragg was the Captain of the first flying-boat to visit Masirah after the agreement. His letters and the aircraft's log tell the following story:

11 Feb 33 – Rangoon S 1433 left Ras Al Khaimah at 0250 GMT (0650 local time) and arrived at Muscat at 0615 (time of flight 3 hours 25 minutes) alighting off Mutrah to swell, and taxied to mooring.

12 Feb 33. A heavy swell prevented any flying.

16 Feb 33 – left Muscat at 0555 and proceeded via Sur (where message from the Political Agent at Muscat was dropped) to Masirah Island alighting off Umm Rusays. Salim the caretaker did not row out, so I went ashore with Fg Off Sorel and Fg Off Crosbie. The Sheikh was not present but I saw Salim and through him tried to obtain coolie labour as agreed. I wanted 70 tins of petrol and 3 drums of oil on the beach – a distance of 360 yards. The only inhabitants present wanted 1 Maria Theresa dollar per 8 tins, whereas the payment should be 1 anna per 2 tins [one rupee was 16 annas]. Petrol and oil was therefore transported by the officers and crew of the S 1433 from the petrol store to the beach from whence the boatman/caretaker employed by Salim was persuaded to convey it to S 1433. Salim himself is nearly blind.

The petrol and oil had been carefully stored in the storehouse but several tins of petrol had leaked.

The conveying of 70 tins of petrol and 3 drums of oil from the storehouse to the flying-boat and fuelling took 3½ hours, no assistance being obtained from the natives who became almost truculent until the Sheikh himself arrived about 1½ hours after fuelling had started. Although the Sheikh was friendly he did not order the services of the natives. In the absence of an interpreter it was a little difficult to discuss the situation, but it was understood that the Sheikh was perplexed as to the method of payment for the labour. It was impressed upon him however that at noon the following day 70 tins of petrol were required on the beach with the 'houri' ready to take it off to the flying-boat as soon as she had anchored.

Fg Off Crosbie walked over the suggested landing ground and reported that in his opinion it was suitable for Wapitis, but care should be exercised and the northern end should be used as far as possible owing to the bare sandstone surface of the southern end.

17 Feb 33 – S 1433 left Umm Rusays at 0230 and flew direct to Ras Madraka.

After seeing Flt Lt Ragg's report, the PA at Muscat (Major Bremner) wrote to the Officer Commanding 203 Squadron (Group Captain Welsh):

It must be borne in mind that the sparsely distributed population of the island come somewhat under the category of 'wild men' being quite unsophisticated and unaccustomed to any sort of business methods or 'necessity to hurry'.

Practically speaking the advent of the flying-boat has heralded their first contact, for the purpose of direct dealings, with white men or civilisation.

The PA went on to suggest that visiting crews should pay the porterage on the spot. This was agreed by Group Captain Welsh. There were a number of letters about payment including the following from Major Bremner to Group Captain Welsh:

In the agreement with Sheikh Khamis drawn up on 24 Nov 32 the terms of porterage however are not mentioned. Presumably they were settled verbally between the parties, but unfortunately no note to that effect has been entered by Capt Alban who is at present on leave. I should be grateful if you can enlighten me on this point at your earliest convenience.

In his reply Group Captain Welsh said that the portage was included in the monthly payment of 10 Maria Theresa dollars to the boatman/caretaker, but that he would now agree to 1 anna per two tins as was normal in the Persian Gulf. The Sheikh appeared to claim excessive back payment until it was realised that it included the original porterage from the beach to the storehouse when the petrol first arrived.

There was a further visit by a Rangoon later in the year. The Captain's report cast doubt on the landing ground and suggested that it should be relocated to Shaghpah Island. He was also not impressed by the state of the RAF houri. Major Bremner again wrote to Group Captain Welsh:

It is apparent from the experience of the only two occasions that flying-boats have alighted at Masirah Island to refuel that the existing arrangements are not only exceedingly unsatisfactory but are almost irremediable ... I have now obtained the Sultan's permission for use of Shaghpah Island for aeroplanes in lieu of the existing landing ground.

At the very end of the year Gp Capt Saul, the new Commanding Officer of 203 Squadron and RAF Basra, wrote to AHQ Iraq:

On 16 Dec 33 I landed at Masirah Island to inspect the fuelling arrangements

A houri on the beach at Umm Rusays
(Photograph: Ann Richardson)

A Masirah fishing boat with the nets on board and towing a houri
(Photograph: Gerry Baxter)

there, and have to report as follows:

I landed at 1114 hours GMT in a south east wind of approximately 28 knots, and a rough sea, and was forced to anchor a mile off shore from Umm Rusays where the present petrol store is positioned, owing to various shoals and banks not indicated on the present chart.

After waiting half an hour no native craft appeared, and Fg Off Coates was sent ashore in the rubber dingy to investigate.

He found the native boat, the property of the RAF, in a dilapidated condition and unfit for further service, as it had apparently been left in the open on the beach unattended for some considerable time.

The petrol store was found to be in a satisfactory condition, but it was only after a period of approximately one hour that sufficient local labour could be found to transport the petrol tins to the foreshore. Additional delay was incurred in acquiring a boat to take the petrol out to the flying-boat, and eventually a small native houri was requisitioned for this purpose.

This craft could only carry a limited amount of petrol, and it was necessary for it to make three trips from the shore to the flying-boat, a somewhat perilous proceeding owing to the state of the water and the strong tide running at the time.

Refuelling to the extent of 200 gallons was completed in approximately 4½ hours, the last trip by the houri being carried out in darkness.

The question of the native boat, the property of the RAF, and the scarcity of available labour, is being taken up with Sheikh Khamis by the Political Agent at Muscat and a further communication on these matters will be addressed to you in due course.

If the intention is to use the uninhabited island of Shaghpah as a landing ground in the future, the delay in the provision of fuel for aircraft is likely to be very considerable as no means of communication with Umm Rusays exists, other than by attracting the attention of stray native boats which may by chance be in the vicinity.

In the event of a decision to use Shaghpah Island as a landing ground, it would, I feel, be a more convenient arrangement for land aircraft and flying-boats to have a new petrol store built on Shaghpah Island in such a position as to be convenient for the use of both types of aircraft. This would in the long run prove an economy owing to the amount of rent paid for the use of the present petrol store.

There is a considerable extent of tidal foreshore around Shaghpah Island which is not accurately detailed by available charts, and I am therefore not prepared to state, without further investigation, the best site for the suggested new petrol store.

The Political Agent states that in the event of a decision to build a petrol store on Shaghpah Island, the permission of the Sultan will have to be obtained, but that there is likely to be no difficulty in acquiring sanction.

A photograph showing Shaghpah Island and part of Masirah Island is attached for easy reference.

The Fg Off Coates who was put ashore by Gp Capt Saul was 'Jasper' Coates who will feature again in this story of Masirah. He spent most of his life in this part of the world, retiring in the rank of Group Captain as the Senior RAF Officer Persian Gulf. After retirement in 1957 he became a major in the Army of the Sultan of Muscat and Oman and played a prominent part in the Jebal Akhdar War. Later he founded the Sultan's Navy. In November 1976 he wrote a long letter to the last station commander of RAF Masirah. Part of this letter concerns the problem of payment to the islanders for porterage later in the 1930s.

I solved the problem of payment for coolie labour in refuelling at Masirah which Tony Ragg had so much trouble over on his early visit. Money was of little or no use in Masirah at that time as they had little chance of spending it. Having the advantage of two way communication (I was an Arabic interpreter) I paid them in empty flimsies, the old four gallon petrol tins for which they had myriad uses. Both Stores Officers and Auditors insisted that these should eventually be returned to base for sale! I dodged the issue by officially writing off the tins used for paying the coolies as 'U/S due to holes caused by rusting in the damp and heat of the monsoon'. It was never queried.

After leaving Masirah, the flying-boat, which had the Political Agent on board, continued its voyage down the coast to Salalah. The purpose of this was to allow the PA to talk to the Sultan there about the establishment of a landing ground between Masirah and Mirbat. The Sultan agreed to this subject to some precautionary stipulations. For instance he said that his uncle, Sayid Shahab, and nine selected sheikhs and other individuals from Sur and Masirah should be aboard the sloop and should be put ashore without any British presence in the first instance. Only when they had given the 'all clear' could British officers go ashore to investigate any of the eight sites which had been earmarked during earlier aerial reconnaissance. He said that there should be two expeditions, firstly the preliminary reconnaissance of the likely sites, and later a 'marking out' expedition when the best site had been chosen.

By 1933 the Imperial Airways route from Britain to India had moved to the southern coast of the Persian Gulf. From Basra the staging posts were Bahrain, Sharjah, Gwadar, and finally Karachi. The magnificent Handley Page 42 airliners flew this route. Civil aviation interests and the RAF were keen to complete the route from Aden to Iraq or India. There is no sheltered water between Masirah and Aden, a distance of nearly 1,000 miles. The Rangoons of 203 Squadron could usually fly this route outside the period of the south-west monsoon, refuelling in the open sea. But a regular year-round schedule was out of the question. The 1,000-mile non-stop flight was impossible.

The first flight between Iraq and Aden was carried out just after the south-west monsoon in 1933. Two Rangoons of 203 Squadron left Basra on 30 October and arrived in Aden on 4 November. After visiting ports on the African coast they left Aden on 12 November and arrived back at Basra on 17 November. Group Captain R.E. Saul DFC was the commander of the cruise with Air Commodore A.D. Cunningham as a passenger in his aircraft. The pilot of the other Rangoon was Flight Lieutenant L.K. Barnes with Flying Officer Jasper Coates as his second pilot. The aircraft did not visit Masirah, flying non-stop between Khor Jarama and Mirbat on both the outward and return flights. The cruise was entirely without incident, although the refuelling at Khor Jarama was not as easy as expected. It had been hoped that the petrol from the buried fuel tanks would syphon down to the flying boats after the flexible hose had been primed, but this did not happen.

1934

In 1934 there was a more thorough survey of Masirah Island. The largest settlement on the island was Dafiyat where about forty families lived. Haql, where the Sheikh later lived, was reported as a small fishing hamlet. There is no mention of any other settlements on the east coast of the island. On the channel coast there is no mention of Sur Masirah although it was certainly inhabited then. Dawwa had a large flat white mosque built of stone, about thirty dwellings and a few palms. There were also a few palm huts at Shaghaf. At Umm Rusays there was a large stone house, the property of the late Sheikh Mansur bin Nasir al Majali. There was also a large flat stone mosque and a dozen palm-leaf huts. Sheikh Khamis bin Hilal lived here (when he was not away!). The RAF petrol hut here had two rooms and was built of coral limestone.

The survey from Masirah to Mirbat was conducted from the sloop HMS *Bideford*. She sailed up the Masirah Channel and arrived off Umm Rusays during the afternoon of 9 February 1934. The crew of the sloop then replenished the petrol in the storehouse. Major Bremner, the Political Agent from Muscat, and Sayid Shahab (the Sultan's uncle) went ashore to collect Sheikh Khamis who was required on board for the survey. Once again he was away fishing. The accompanying Rangoon flying-boat was not there either, its departure from Basra having been delayed by bad weather. The Rangoon was to bring the AOC, Air Vice-Marshal Burnett, to Umm Rusays to board the sloop for the survey, and to take him for an interview with the Sultan who was still at Salalah.

The following morning there was dense fog. The Rangoon arrived at 9.45 in the morning with insufficient fuel to return to Khor Jarama. Fortunately there was a small and temporary break in the fog over the sea, 8 miles north of Umm Rusays and to the west of Dafiyat. The pilot, Flying Officer Littlejohn of the Royal Australian Air Force, took advantage of this fleeting opportunity and skilfully alighted on the mirror-calm sea. When the aircraft had nearly stopped it grounded on a coral reef on a falling tide. There was no serious damage, but the keel was scored and there were a few small leaks where rivets had been torn. There was plenty of time to repair the leaks. The sloop's motorboat was sent out to find the flying-boat but the fog was so dense that the search was abandoned. It was not until 2.30 p.m. that the motorboat located the Rangoon and brought the AOC, his ADC and Jasper Coates back to the sloop. During the intervening period the ship's whaler had rowed ashore with a working party to carry the petrol from the hut to the beach. The Rangoon refloated shortly before dusk and flew to Umm Rusays to refuel. This had to be completed in the dark.

The following day there was again thick fog which delayed the departure of the sloop until 1.30 p.m. This was lucky because during the morning Sheikh Khamis was located and brought on board with four of his followers.

The sloop and the accompanying Rangoon carried out the reconnaissance down the mainland coast to Mirbat. Of the eight possible sites for a landing ground the best was at Khor Gharim which is about 19 miles west of Ras

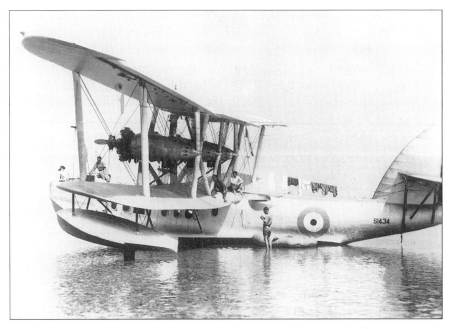

10 February 1934. Short Rangoon S1434 of 203 Sqn aground off Masirah
(Photograph: Jasper Coates courtesy of the RAF Museum)

Madraka. During the cruise from Basra to Aden the previous year the Rangoons
had photographed this site. The AOC reported that HMS *Bideford* could
anchor here about a mile from the shore. It was difficult to land on the steep
sandy beach owing to surf even in the prevailing calm weather. About 100
yards inland an oblong lake (Khor Gharim) ran approximately north to south
(perpendicular to the coast), but curved to the west further inland. The lake
was some two miles long and 150 to 200 yards wide, but due to the curve
only a marginal 1,400 yards was available for flying-boats. At high tide the
lake was about six feet deep, reportedly falling only one foot at low tide. On
the north-east shore of the lake there was a flat plateau of hard limestone with
loose stones and small ridges about one to two inches high. With little difficulty
the plateau could be cleared and made available for aircraft with wheel brakes
and tailwheels. The small ridges would break tail skids. An area 700 to 800
yards wide could be used. Fresh water was reported at the north-east end of
a small wadi leading into the lake. In the event of a southerly gale flying-boats
could shelter in the lee of a small island just off Ras Madraka.

The sloop sailed as far as Salalah where the AOC was landed for his interview
with the Sultan. After this he reboarded the sloop for the first part of his
return journey. The Rangoon picked him up off Ras Madraka where the sea
was relatively calm, and returned him as far as Basra.

A couple of months later Jasper Coates was again in the area in a Rangoon
flown by Flt Lt Waring. The main purpose of this cruise was to supervise the

refilling of the bulk fuel store at Khor Jarama, and 12,000 gallons in 4-gallon 'flimsies' were transferred from the fuel dhow – evidently additional fuel tanks had been installed. At the same time Jasper walked over to Ras al Hadd to check the landing ground there. The Rangoon then continued to Umm Rusays where Jasper surveyed the landing ground with a view to small improvements and more permanent markings in concrete. The Captain's report on Masirah included the following:

> The Rangoon alighted opposite Umm Rusays at 1500 hours and anchored in 1½ fathoms about 400 yards from the shore and four of us went ashore in the dinghy. There was no sign of anybody about except a few women among the houses in the village who took no notice of us. We walked up to the petrol store and after shouting at the top of our voices about half a dozen old men and some small boys emerged from the mosque nearby. A blind man named Salim produced the key and we took out the 30 tins of petrol we required. We then tried to induce the men to carry the petrol to the beach; at first they declined to help at all but after much haggling they set to work with a will. One of them, younger than the rest, owned a houri which was tied up near the beach and we soon had our 30 tins of petrol on board and taxied out into deeper water as the tide was falling.

There is no mention of payment for porterage of the petrol tins to the beach. Jasper Coates was aboard the Rangoon and payment was probably in empty petrol tins.

By the end of May the PA at Muscat was wondering whether to obtain the Sultan's permission for a landing ground and petrol store at Shaghpah Island. A 300-yard square had been cleared and the corners marked in concrete. The PA queried the lack of any further news and received the following reply from Air Headquarters:

> It is quite true that we were considering building a new store at Shaghpah Island, but we have now decided to retain Umm Rusays landing ground in preference to establishing a new one at Shaghpah Island and therefore we do not now require a new store.
>
> The present store at Umm Rusays seems quite satisfactory although, as you have pointed out in previous correspondence, there is usually some difficulty in obtaining labour or getting the houri out to the flying-boats. From our letter of 19 May you will see that we are proposing to renew the original agreement for facilities at Masirah.

Major Bremner's departure for the hill station in northern India appears to have been delayed in 1934. On 18 June he wrote to Air Headquarters:

> I note that you do not now want to construct a petrol store on Shaghpah Island and I am accordingly renewing the Umm Rusays storehouse contract.

While I am on the subject may I offer it as a suggestion that tins stored there or at any other bad climatic spot may be dipped in varnish or some such thing to make them more damp or rust proof? I personally tidied up your store and re-arranged the existing store of petrol in February last to make room for the consignment we imported in HMS *Bideford*. Any amount of the old stored petrol had just leaked away due to rust, whilst there were many half empty tins which gushed like watering cans on picking them up.

Please don't think I'm butting in on what isn't my concern but it struck me that it might be helpful to you to know this in the interest of economy and otherwise.

There is no recorded reply to this suggestion; the correspondence in the files later in 1934 being chiefly concerned with establishing the landing ground at Khor Gharim between Masirah and Mirbat. It was necessary for the short-range land planes of those days and could serve as an emergency landing ground for longer range aircraft. It was to be the scene of a tragedy a few years later.

1935

Correspondence shows that there was difficulty in laying out the landing ground at Khor Gharim. The surface was far from ideal and Colonel Biscoe's prophetic words written in 1931 come to mind. Concerning the Masirah islanders he wrote: 'but I personally shall be very surprised if when you go there they do not turn out to be a lot of poverty stricken fisher folk ekeing out a miserable existence by catching sharks. The tribes in the interior of course are somewhat different.' Khor Gharim was uninhabited and there were no poverty stricken fisher folk. But in the hinterland there were lawless bedu who owed no loyalty to their Sultan and adopted an uncompromising attitude towards interlopers. These bedu arrived on the scene when a working party had been put ashore from the sloop. Worse, the Asian foreman had mistakenly taken the working party too far inland. There was a confrontation which could have ended violently but Major Bremner's diplomacy averted a disaster. News of this reached London where the Air Ministry sent the following message to the India Office: 'Selection and preparation of Khor Gharim Landing Ground. The Council wish to express their most grateful appreciation of Major Bremner's extremely skilful handling of the situation at Khor Gharim.'

Before the hot weather of 1935 there was more correspondence about Masirah. The Officer Commanding 203 Squadron wrote to Major Bremner at Muscat:

The present petrol store at Masirah Island is unsatisfactory as regards condition, size and site.

Authority has been given for the construction of a new store at a site as marked on the attached plan.

This site would be more convenient for the refuelling of flying-boats as well as land aircraft.

In order to avoid any ill feeling it is proposed to pay a ground rental of rupees 300 per annum for the proposed new site. This is similar to what is now paid for the present store and will, therefore, not involve any financial loss to the Sheikh. I would be glad if you will inform me at an early date if there are any difficulties to the above proposal.

Major Bremner wrote back to 203 Squadron saying that the Sultan considered rupees 300 per annum was excessive. The Sultan would agree a small monthly sum to a *chowkidar* (guard) at the rate of about rupees 80 to 90 per annum. In addition there should be rupees 50 or 60 plus some coffee to Sheikh Khamis and others who had helped in protecting the building during construction. It was also suggested that the new store should be large enough to accommodate a houri which should always be left half full of water.

There the matter rested until after the heat of midsummer. Up until then the establishment of landing grounds and the provisioning of them had been the responsibility of the local Political Agent, the Royal Navy and the flying-boats of 203 Squadron. Jasper Coates had special responsibilities for landing grounds and was detached from AHQ Iraq to 203 Squadron for this purpose. Although the landing grounds had been constructed with Wapiti aircraft in mind, there is no evidence to show that Wapitis had ever ventured as far as Aden. There were only two Wapiti squadrons in the Iraq Command, 84 at Shaibah, a few miles west of Basra, and 55 Squadron at Hinaidi near Baghdad. 84 Squadron re-equipped with Vincent aircraft in January 1935, and 55 Squadron nearly two years later.

After the hot weather of 1935 203 Squadron was busy re-equipping with the new Singapore flying-boats and was unable to accept the commitment to the landing grounds. This commitment was passed to 84 Squadron with its new Vincents. There were some landing areas which were for flying-boats. These were at Dubai, Ras al Khaimah and Umm al Qawain on the Persian Gulf coast, and another at Khor Fakkan on the Gulf of Oman. All of them are now in the United Arab Emirates, then known as Trucial Oman.

There was another alighting area at Khor Quwai in the lee of 'Goat Island' at the very north of the Musandam Peninsula which is the northernmost point of Oman. The Royal Navy had built recreation facilities on 'Goat Island'. A little further south in the Musandam Peninsula is the Elphinstone Inlet which is a fjord to the east of Khasab. Round a bend in this twisting fjord ruins can still be seen on Telegraph Island. These ruins are the remains of a telegraph station which was for communication between London and British India. The telegraph station was in use only between 1864 and 1869 and was merely a ruin when it was visited by Lord Curzon in 1903. When it was in use the operators were reputedly there for a year. When relieved by a new crew, the old crew were found to be completely 'round the bend', which is the origin of this expression.

On 25 September 1935 a formation of three Vickers Vincents of 84 Squadron left Shaibah to check the southern landing grounds. Flt Lt Teddy Nuttall was the leader with two other crew members in the aircraft. The other two Vincents were flown by Flying Officers Craig and Stubbs, both South Africans, each with their own crew which included a spare pilot, Sgt Donald Cromar. Flt Lt Nuttall retired as a Group Captain and will be remembered by generations of post-war Cranwell flight cadets as the College Mess Secretary. He was extremely tall and was reputed to hold the Cranwell high jump record well into the post-war era.

The formation refuelled at Bahrain and continued on to Sharjah for a total of over seven hours in the air. Aircraft travelled slowly in those days. The members of the formation spent the night in the Imperial Airways fort at Sharjah, and continued on next morning to check the petrol stored at the landing ground at Ras al Hadd on the very easternmost tip of Arabia. En route to Ras al Hadd Flt Lt Nuttall dropped the keys of the petrol store to the sloop HMS *Shoreham* at Khor Jarama. After checking Ras al Hadd the formation flew back to Muscat, landing near the fort at Bait al Falaj and spending the night at the British Political Agency (later the British Embassy) on the waterfront at Muscat.

The following day, 27 September 1935, the three Vincents flew round the coast and landed at Umm Rusays. This was the furthest that they were required to go. Khor Gharim was not yet ready for them.

All three Vincents landed safely at Umm Rusays and checked most of the 5,776 gallons of petrol in the storehouse. Flt Lt Nuttall commented 'some sweat' in his pilot's flying log book which is now kept in the library at the RAF College Cranwell.

Flt Lt Nuttall viewed the Umm Rusays landing ground with deep misgiving, and decided that an alternative site should be found. The comment in his pilot's log book is 'very bad L/G. Condemned it.' All three Vincents were able to take off and had a quick look at the Shaghpah Island landing ground before returning to Muscat. Here Flt Lt Nuttall signalled to AHQ giving his opinion of the Umm Rusays landing ground. AHQ promptly signalled back:

From AHQ to PA Muscat for Flt Lt Nuttall, repeat to 84 Squadron. Agree not necessary revisit Masirah to check remainder of petrol but most important to find alternative landing ground to which fuel can be taken if you consider Umm Rusays unfit for Hardy and Valentia. In the latter case make any arrangements you can through PA Muscat for 4000 gallons petrol 200 oil to be transferred to Shaghpah or any other suitable site as soon as possible. Report by signal defects Umm Rusays landing ground whether above aircraft could land there if necessary and any action taken.

The Hawker Hardy was a single-engined biplane, a two-seat general-purpose aircraft developed from the Hart. The Vickers Valentia had two of almost everything. It had biplane wings and tailplane, two wheels on each of its two undercarriage legs, two engines and two crew. It could carry 22 troops and had a huge bulbous, blunt nose. It was developed from the Victoria. In fact most of them started life as Victorias, the aircraft which was used for the evacuation from Kabul in 1928 and 1929.

Unfortunately the above signal arrived too late, and the next morning the three Vincents began their return journey to Shaibah. Their first landing was at Sharjah where there was a signal recalling them to Muscat. They returned to Muscat where they spent the night. On this day AHQ sent another signal as follows:

> From AHQ to 84 Sqn, repeat to PA Muscat. Immediate for Sqn Ldr Fogarty. If Nuttall unable to make satisfactory arrangements for refuelling in Masirah are you ready to proceed there yourself immediately to do so? If you confirm Umm Rusays definitely unsafe for Hardy and Valentia and can find no other suitable site on Masirah or mainland, fuel must be transferred to Shaghpah Island as quickly as possible. This matter is urgent and you may fly on 29/9. Forward your recommendations for siting of intended new fuel store at Masirah bearing in mind requirements of flying-boats.

Squadron Leader Fogarty, the Officer Commanding 84 Squadron, immediately replied as follows:

> From 84 Sqn to AHQ, repeat to PA Muscat and Basra for Coates. In view of probability of having to move landing ground from Masirah Island to Shaghpah Island or to mainland and that petrol store will if possible have to meet flying-boat requirements request that Flt Lt Coates accompanies me. Propose leave for Muscat am 29/9 unless favourable report received from Nuttall.

Again on the same day AHQ sent the following brief reply:

> From AHQ to 84 Sqn repeat to PA Muscat and Basra for Coates. Flt Lt Coates is to accompany Sqn Ldr Fogarty.

Again on 28 September there was yet another signal, this time from Flt Lt Nuttall after he had returned to Muscat:

> From Vincents Nuttall to AHQ repeat to 84 Sqn, copy PA Muscat. Returned to Muscat but too late to carry out recce for landing ground today. Flt Lt MacDonald 84 Sqn landed on Shaghpah Island in July. Suggest his views be obtained with regard to using this as alternative landing ground if considered suitable. PA Muscat could arrange dhows to transfer 4000 gallons petrol 200 gallons oil from Umm Rusays as soon as possible and will arrange

for temporary shelter to be built. Unconfirmed rumour that Shaghpah Island sometimes covered by sea. Will proceed Masirah 29/9 with PA Muscat to reconnoitre for new landing ground and will also land Shaghpah Island. If no suitable landing ground can be found on Masirah or Shaghpah Island is there any objection to using mainland near Ras Sheiballa? Umm Rusays totally unsuitable for Hardy and Valentia and hazardous for Vincent due to very small size and apparent prevailing wind being across aerodrome which is only 100 yards wide with approach from ENE over high soft sandhills and WSW over sea and small five foot cliff. Ground outside boundaries and part of landing ground soft.

There was a final signal of 28 September:

From AHQ to Vincents Nuttall repeat 84 Sqn. MacDonald reported Shaghpah Island good, only defect being inaccessibility. Have no definite information about flooding. If you find no alternative fit for immediate use, arrange transfer fuel Shaghpah Island as quickly as possible using local craft if available to save time. Understand cannot establish landing ground on mainland for political reasons, perhaps PA can confirm. In order that permanent arrangements may be made, obtain all possible information about alternative sites, flooding of Shaghpah Island and its accessibility for refuelling flying-boats. Also take up question of safe custody of fuel there. Fuel store will be built shortly when most satisfactory site decided.

The following morning Flt Lt Nuttall decided to take only one other Vincent to Masirah, the one flown by Fg Off Craig. The comment in his pilot's log book is: 'Craig only. To select new LG landed at Shaghpah but condemned it due to bird colony. Collected two young gulls for pets.' To gauge the size of the problem, an ornithological expedition in November 1979 estimated that there were 15,000 birds on Shaghpah Island. Soon both Vincents were in the air again to look for a more suitable site. This did not take long. After fifteen minutes in the air both aircraft landed on the long smooth surface to the west of the settlement of Sur Masirah. The available runway length was over 1,000 yards. It was ideal except for a single vehicle-sized rock halfway along, but there was sufficient width to easily avoid it. The comment in Flt Lt Nuttall's log book is: 'Landed on site for new LG. Very suitable. On seashore just south of Shaghpah Island went paddling & a shark took a squint at me!' The purpose of his paddling was to assess the depth to see how close flying-boats could approach to the shoreline. Both Vincents then took off and landed at Umm Rusays. The comment in Flt Lt Nuttall's log book is: 'Landed, also Craig, to find out if Sheikh would transfer petrol to new LG. Sheikh away and Arabs v. unintelligent. No advance.' No doubt the problem was caused by the lack of an interpreter rather than the lack of intelligence. Both aircraft took off and returned to Muscat, but instead of the usual coast-crawl they took the direct route over the Wahiba Sands and through the mountains. The scenery drew appreciative comment in Flt Lt Nuttall's log book. It had been a good day. On arrival back at Muscat he sent the following signal:

From Vincents Nuttall to AHQ repeat 84 Sqn, SNOPG, copy PA Muscat. Landed on Shaghpah Island. Almost complete island can be used as LG. Surface is softish but wheel tracks bed down hard. Consider it is as accessible as Umm Rusays for flying-boats and is immune from flooding. Chief objection for use as permanent LG is that island is a bird colony and as such is dangerous for landing and take-off. Found alternative LG on Masirah situated due south Shaghpah Island on south shore of Shaghpah Bay. LG of immense size with good approaches from all directions. Flying-boats could approach to within 120 yards approximately of shore allowing 4 foot draught. Surface the same as Shaghpah Island and no risk of flooding. Sheikh of Masirah absent so unable to ascertain move of petrol store at either Shaghpah Island or new LG. Ascertained that local Arabs would transport 4000 gallons petrol 200 gallons oil to new LG for rupees 160. Other petrol store at Umm Rusays checked and found to contain 164 gallons petrol 130 gallons oil and 175 empty tins. Total stocks now at Umm Rusays 7640 gallons petrol 330 gallons oil.

The following day, 30 September, another four Vincents arrived at Muscat. They were led by the Squadron Commander, Sqn Ldr 'Joe' Fogarty who was on his third tour of duty on 84 Squadron. A group photograph of 84 Squadron shows Sqn Ldr Fogarty seated in the centre of a surprisingly large number of personnel. He looks supremely confident and superior. He is cross-legged and wearing riding breeches, a riding crop in his lap, and the solar topee (made of cork) had an RAF puggaree wound round it. He eventually retired as Air Chief Marshal Sir Francis Fogarty.

Sergeant Pilot Donald Cromar cannot remember ever speaking to his Squadron Commander who always communicated through his flight commanders. Relationships were very formal in those days and only surnames were used. Donald Cromar can remember only one Christian name, that of his close friend Sergeant Pilot George Higgs. A later 84 Squadron Vincent pilot was Sgt Charles Whitelock who writes:

I can confirm Cromar's comments on relations between officers and other ranks, very formal at all times and with very little contact off-duty. The age of the Christian name had not yet dawned; nicknames and abbreviated surnames yes, but rarely first names. My best friend in 84, a contemporary, Sgt Pilot Nobbs, was always 'Nobby'. I have no idea what his first name was. In those days – pre 1939 – officers and other ranks (the very term OR defines the gulf between us) came from very different backgrounds. We all knew what was expected of us and, by and large, generally supplied it. A

84 Squadron Vincents at Muscat (Bait al Falaj landing ground) en route to the new Sur Masirah landing ground, 1 October 1935 (Photograph: Donald Cromar)

very minor and usually light-hearted whinge by Sgt Pilots was that after landing the officer pilots disappeared on various social activities. The Sgt Pilots, after flying all day, stayed with the ground crew and refuelled and put the aircraft to bed before relaxing. It was a bit different, of course, on unmanned landing grounds, but I must admit that I never saw an officer pilot refuelling on the top mainplane in temperatures of 120°. It was a different world, and I would be the last to complain about it.

When Sqn Ldr Fogarty arrived at Muscat he sent the following signal:

From Vincents Fogarty to AHQ repeat 84 Sqn, copy PA Muscat. Will proceed Masirah 1/10 to confirm contents of Vincents Nuttall NR3 29/9. Will arrange for fuel and oil to be moved from Masirah store to new site and will make temporary markings on LG.

On 1 October three Vincents left Muscat for Masirah, the Squadron Commander with Jasper Coates, OC 'B' Flight and Flt Lt Nuttall. Their first landing was at Umm Rusays for the Squadron Commander to assess it and to put out the petrol to be taken to the new landing ground. Leaving behind a Persian interpreter they then had to take off across the runway in a strong westerly wind. The runway was only about 100 yards wide, ending in little cliffs down to the sea. All three aircraft just managed to take off before reaching the sea. They had to run up to full throttle against the brakes, hoping that they would release evenly and fully. Wheel brakes were not reliable in those days. Then they flew to the new Sur Masirah landing ground for the Squadron

Flt Lt Teddy Nuttall (left) and Sgt George Higgs (centre), 84 Squadron, Shaibah –
Christmas 1935 (Photograph: Donald Cromar)

Commander's assessment. Sqn Ldr Fogarty concurred with Flt Lt Nuttall's
judgement, condemning the Umm Rusays landing ground and confirming the
new one at Sur Masirah. The three Vincents then flew back to Muscat against
a stiff headwind. The next day the Squadron Commander sent the following
signal:

> From Vincents Fogarty to AHQ repeat 84 Sqn copy to PA Muscat. Further
> my NR 9 1/10. Unable make satisfactory arrangements at Masirah for move
> of fuel to new site. PA has very kindly arranged to despatch motor dhow
> on 4/10 to transfer fuel and erect temporary shelter at new LG. Estimates
> seven days to complete work. Approx cost rupees 250 to 300. Proposed
> itinerary for return. 3/10 Muscat Sharjah via Sohar Shinas Ras al Khaimah.
> 4/10 Sharjah Doha Bahrain. 5/10 Bahrain Shaibah.

Actually the Vincents did not begin their return journey the next day. They
had to return to Masirah to pick up the Persian interpreter they had left at
Umm Rusays the previous day. Flt Lt Nuttall's log book shows that he flew

to the new landing ground with two other Vincents flown by Sgt George Higgs and Sgt Donald Cromar. Flt Lt Jasper Coates was in Nuttall's aircraft and Fg Off Stubbs was with Sgt Higgs. At the new landing ground everyone was put to work marking out the runway with the bags of lime they had brought with them. The standard runway markers were at least four right-angled corner marks and a large white circle. At the new Sur Masirah landing ground the large circle had an 'A' in the middle. At some stage the vehicle-sized rock had a white cross painted on it which has lasted to this day.

During the day Flt Lt Nuttall flew to Umm Rusays to pick up the Persian. Presumably he had been left there to inform the Sheikh and local inhabitants of all the recent developments which would affect them financially. At the end of the day the Vincents returned to Muscat. After spending the night there all seven Vincents began their long return journey to Shaibah.

A week later the Sultan wrote to Sheikh Khamis, the English translation being as follows:

> I have already written you a letter in connection with keeping the petrol at Sur Masirah. I have no objection if the officials of my friend the British Government want to erect a building out of wood or stone at that place. If it is possible for you to keep somebody to look after the building on its completion please do so. A monthly salary will be paid to that man by them.

Later in October Jasper Coates hired a dhow in Muscat to take the building materials and masons to Sur Masirah to build the petrol store. He did not travel on the dhow himself. When the dhow was close to Masirah it was boarded and pirated by Masirah fishermen. On board was the excellent Works and Bricks supervisor, a Pathan Muslim by the name of Mohammed Khan. He had a good command of Arabic and remonstrated with the boarding party. He told them that 'Abu Shuwarib' (Jasper's nickname) would make life extremely difficult for Sheikh Khamis until the appropriate punishment for piracy had been carried out. He reminded them of the punishment for piracy and told them that the Sultan would be kept informed of developments. The boarding party then reconsidered their actions, returned all the goods and money, and left with their tails between their legs. In their anxiety they actually returned more money than they had taken. On arrival at Masirah the crew transferred the fuel and oil from Umm Rusays to the new Sur Masirah landing ground.

A month later a single Vincent of 84 Squadron staged through Sur Masirah and ventured one step further to the Khor Gharim landing ground. It was the first time an aircraft had landed on it. There was no fuel there. The aircraft was on the ground for forty-five minutes while the crew inspected the landing ground. The pilot kept the engine running during this forty-five minutes in case hostile tribesmen arrived.

At the end of December 1935 Lieutenant Hasler of the Royal Engineers was at the Sur Masirah landing ground with a working party building the new petrol store there. In a letter written on 4 November 1976 Jasper Coates says that he was present when the petrol store was built. The following signal from them on 30 December 1935 showed that trouble was brewing.

> From Masirah to AHQ repeat Muscat. A man from mainland Sur named Ali bin Mosalim bin Tabah is here claiming that site of aerodrome is on land belonging to his tribe. He objects to our work and does not admit authority of Sheikh Khamis over this piece of land. Today Ali prevented coolies cutting stone at point of rifle. Local men are for us and prepared to protect but seem unable to get rid of Ali. Khamis fears him. Work 31/12 uncertain. Signal instructions.

Fortunately there was a flight of Vincents at Muscat at the time. AHQ reacted immediately, sending the following signal:

> From AHQ to PA Muscat repeat Vincents Allsop, 84 Sqn, Masirah for Hasler. Suggest Vincents proceed Masirah 31/12 taking you if necessary. Work to proceed. Ali bin Mosalim being told claim will be dealt with by Sultan. If you agree arrange with Allsop and inform me.

The reply was:

> PA Muscat to AHQ. In my opinion trouble is carefully arranged scheme staged by Sheikh Khamis himself to further his own ends but it is advisable for me to proceed Masirah personally to see into matter. Am arranging with Allsop to leave tomorrow morning. Meanwhile I suggest it preferable Hasler not to continue work pending our arrival.

The PA at Muscat (now Major Watts) sent a note across to Flt Lt Allsop:

> I have a letter from the Sultan's representative in Muscat for Sheikh Khamis of Masirah and one letter for Ali bin Mosalim of Sur regarding the dispute over the new petrol store at Masirah. Before your departure for the aerodrome tomorrow morning please call at the Agency Office for the above mentioned letters which I would request you to be good enough to take to the individuals concerned. At the same time I shall inform you whether I intend to accompany your flight to Masirah or not.

Unfortunately the above note is the last enclosure in the file, and subsequent files lack detail. However, the petrol store was completed at Sur Masirah, and the landing ground there continued in use for some years.

1936

The 70 Squadron records show that in January 1936 a single Valentia transport aircraft was sent from Iraq to Masirah to pick up personnel and radio equipment. Presumably the Sur Masirah petrol store had been completed by then and the Valentia was sent to pick up Hasler and his party together with their equipment.

The 55 Squadron records were kept extremely badly with no entries for months on end. January 1936 is a blank in the 55 Squadron records. However, the records of 8 Squadron at Aden show that some of its Fairey IIIFs flew to Mirbat to meet a detachment of 55 Squadron Wapitis. The range of the Wapiti was 360 miles, so they must have refuelled at the new petrol store at Sur Masirah. There was no petrol at Khor Gharim which in any case was unsuitable for aircraft with tail skids like the Wapiti. The distance from Sur Masirah to Mirbat was within the range of a Wapiti, but not against any appreciable headwind. The 8 Squadron records do not say that the 55 Squadron Wapitis continued to Aden. Their return to Sur Masirah against the north-east monsoon must have been a hazardous undertaking.

At the beginning of 1936 the 84 Squadron Vincents were regularly venturing as far as the unpopular Khor Gharim landing ground. In January Flt Lt Evans-Evans, one of the flight commanders, was fired at by fishing boats. This hostile act was totally unexpected. Two months later another Vincent landed at Khor Gharim, the pilot reporting that the surface was extremely poor and that he was lucky not to damage the aircraft. He also reported some signs of sabotage by tribesmen. Some concrete markers had been broken. Investigation

55 Squadron Wapitis at Bait al Falaj in January 1936, en route to Mirbat
(Photograph: Jeff Mellor)

by the PA at Muscat subsequently revealed that the damage had been caused by one particular tribesman, and did not represent widespread discontent.

A year after his first visit Flt Lt Nuttall returned to Masirah. On the way south he spent the first night at Bahrain, and the following day carried out an inspection of the landing ground and petrol store at Doha in the sheikhdom of Qatar. From there he flew to the fort at Sharjah for his second night stop. The following day he checked the landing ground and petrol at Abu Dhabi, and again returned to Sharjah for the night. The next day he flew to Muscat, taking a photograph of Shinas en route. After a night at the British Political Agency he flew to the new landing ground at Sur Masirah for an inspection of its condition and the condition of the petrol store building which had recently been completed. It was constructed of local stone and above the door 'RAF 1936' was inscribed in concrete. Forty years later this building was still standing, but the cyclone and torrential rain of 13 June 1977 began its slow destruction. In 1996 it was no more than knee-high rubble, but the concrete block inscribed 'RAF 1936' had been saved and let into the stonework of the pool bar at the Sergeants' Mess at RAFO Masirah.

After the inspection at Sur Masirah Flt Lt Nuttall flew to Shaghpah Island and collected two more gulls as pets for personnel at Shaibah. This may seem rather strange but in 1995 was explained by Donald Cromar (Sgt Cromar, see above) in the following words: 'I can understand his need for gulls as pets. Shaibah was universally regarded as the worst of overseas postings and tempers ran high during the summer months. Mental stress was fairly common especially among non-drinkers. Each year we were sent to Summer Camp in Kurdistan.'

After taking off from Shaghpah Island with his gulls Flt Lt Nuttall never

The petrol store at the Sur Masirah landing ground in 1967, now knee-high rubble
(Photograph: Frank Over)

The date block over the door is now preserved in the Sergeants' Mess pool bar
(Photograph: 1994, Ann Richardson)

returned to Masirah. He carried out a landing ground inspection and petrol
check at Ras al Hadd and returned to Muscat. The following day he flew to
Sharjah 'through a gorge in the mountains' and again spent a night in the
Imperial Airways fort. The next day he flew all the way back to Shaibah,
refuelling at Bahrain, and battling against headwinds. It took 7 hours and 50
minutes flying from Sharjah to Shaibah. In 1937 Flt Lt Nuttall returned to
the United Kingdom after two tours on 84 Squadron at Shaibah totalling 4½
years. But before his return he took part in the Squadron's 'grand tour' from
Shaibah to Singapore and back, a stately progress across the Empire.

In many ways the Vickers Vincent was a remarkable aircraft. It came into
squadron service in 1934 and eventually equipped eleven squadrons, all of them
based in the Middle East. It was certainly an ungainly design with few
refinements and little streamlining. In the air it was not very stable so on long
flights it was tiring to fly. But it was very reliable and enormously tough while
operating in conditions of extreme heat and dust. It could operate off short
and primitive landing grounds which would tax the suspension of a motor
vehicle.

The Vincent was a single-engined biplane with three seats. In addition there
was a prone bomb-aiming position below the pilot's seat. With an auxiliary
fuel tank between the undercarriage legs it had a range of 1,250 miles,
approximately 10 hours of flying at its cruising speed of 120 m.p.h. The main
tanks in the top wings were 14ft above the ground. Each main tank had a

capacity of 75 gallons. To raise the 4-gallon petrol tins to the main fuel tanks required a chain of three men. One man on the ground pierced the petrol tins with a long spike and passed them to the man on the lower wing. He passed them up to the man sitting on the top wing who used a large funnel lined with a chamois leather to trap any water in the petrol before it went into the tank. A splash of petrol onto bare legs was agonising in those temperatures. The man in the middle had the worst job, often getting a spill down his neck.

The most popular pilots were those who used the auxiliary belly tank, down to the last drop if necessary. Filling it was easy, and the aircraft could be positioned so that refuelling could be done in the shade of the wings. Providing the aircraft was flying reasonably high there was no risk in using the belly tank until it was empty. When the engine stopped the other crew members were instantly roused, the sudden silence claiming their full attention. But the pilot merely had to change over to the top tanks to get the engine running again. In flight, at the cruising air speed, a little propeller-driven pump raised the petrol from the auxiliary tank to the engine. At low speed or on the ground the little propeller would not 'windmill' fast enough to pump up the petrol.

The radial engine was the 650hp Bristol Pegasus which, when worn, used a gallon of oil every hour. The oil tank held 14 gallons, but the oil overheated when the oil level fell. It was oil rather than petrol which limited the range of the Vincent. The armament was a fixed Vickers gun firing through the propeller, and one Lewis gun on a Scarf ring over the back cockpit. Up to 1,000lb of bombs could be carried, and there was a reconnaissance camera. Messages could be picked up from the ground by a hook on the end of a long pole. The front of the pole was hinged on the right-hand mainwheel spat, and the crewman could lower and raise the hook. The message container was attached to a loop of string which was held aloft between two poles.

All the crew members were in tandem open cockpits. The pilot's seat was substantial and comfortable, but close behind him the centre cockpit seat was only a plain board suspended by steel cables at each corner. Below it was a sliding hatch to the bomb aimer's position in the tunnel. Unfortunately the sliding hatch would never stay shut, being quickly forced open by the slip-stream. This added to the general level of ventilation which was never less than generous. The wireless operator had a swivel seat in the rear cockpit, and the fuselage sides only came up to slightly above his elbows. This led to a general sense of insecurity in turbulent conditions. A canvas safety belt could be clipped into his parachute harness to stop him falling out. The Vildebeest was the torpedo-bomber version of the Vincent. 42 Squadron's first fatality of the Second World War was when an unfortunate crew member fell out of the back cockpit of a Vildebeest in flight. The radio in the rear cockpit of the Vincent was for sending signals only. For communication from one aircraft to another the pilots used hand signals. This was known as 'zogging'. It was based on the Morse code, a long slow downwards movement of the forearm being a 'dash', and a short quick one being a 'dot'. Flying the aircraft with the other arm out in the slipstream was difficult. Zogging usually ended in a fit of giggles.

Vincent pilot Charles Whitelock comments favourably on the reliability of the engine. He writes:

> In two years on 84 Sqn I recall only one engine failure on the squadron. Three of us were returning from a trip out west of Shaibah when the leader glided down and landed with a dead engine. The other two of us got down too. An inlet valve had broken up on one cylinder, almost shaking the engine out of its mountings. We took-off again and went back to base, arriving after dark. The next day a new cylinder and piston were flown out and fitted on the spot and all was well.
>
> Sunburn was a problem for the pilots who were sitting ahead of the top mainplane and close to the engine. After a Gulf trip one's cheeks and a strip of forehead between goggles and helmet were almost black. I carried a pot of Vaseline to grease my face occasionally. The Pegasus was a great oil-slinger, fortunately, so having forgotten the Vaseline one could always wipe oil from the windscreen and smear that on one's face.
>
> Peeing was another problem for the pilot on long trips. There was a pee tube but I never knew anyone who managed to use it through the complications of clothing, parachute harness and seat harness. After five or six hours in the air there was a pressing and urgent requirement on landing, and for some reason the tailwheel seemed the natural target. An order appeared in the Pilots' Order Book to the effect that the wheel bearings were becoming seriously corroded, and would we please do it elsewhere.

The engine starting procedure provided an amusing spectacle for the interested observer. The centre crew member walked up the right lower wing to as far forward as possible. From there he could just reach the catch on a drop-down hatch 8ft off the ground just ahead of the pilot. Executing a sideways splits the crewman put his right foot on the protruding hatch door. He could then reach the starting handle crank which was clipped to the inside of the hatch. Unclipping it with his right hand he could fit it into the ratchet of the inertia starter gear. Winding the handle, slowly at first, he increased the revs of a highly geared flywheel. When the whine of the flywheel had increased to the required pitch the crewman shouted 'contact' to the pilot and with his left hand operated the dog-clutch lever to engage the flywheel to the engine. The contortions of the pilot could not be seen from the ground. He had one hand on the throttle and another turning the starting magneto. Yet another hand was needed to operate the priming pump, and another to pull the stick back. When the flywheel was engaged to the engine there would sometimes be no more than a few coughs and puffs of smoke, but luckily

Starting the Vincent engine
(Photograph: 8 Squadron Archives)

the engine started readily on most occasions. This was the part of the procedure which provided the most entertainment for the observer. The crewman desperately needed something to hold on to. A few feet in front was the huge propeller throwing back a gale while the pilot blipped the throttle to clear the sparking plugs. The unshielded exhaust pipe was rapidly heating up and very close. Stepping back onto the wing the crewman had to clip the starting handle into the hatch. Next he had to shut the hatch and screw home the quick release studs without burning himself on the exhaust pipe. From there on it was only a matter of weaving rearwards through the flying wires and entering the middle cockpit head first. In temperatures of over 40°C it was not a popular task.

The distance between Khor Gharim and Mirbat was the longest on the South Arabian route. It was thought prudent to establish a new landing ground between the two which could be used in an emergency. Better still, it might allow short-range aircraft to overfly Khor Gharim which was not a popular spot. The establishment of this new landing ground was the quickest and easiest on the whole South Arabian route. A site was identified a couple of miles east of the fishing village of Shuwaymia, and about a mile inland from the coast. This is on the mainland north of the Kuria Muria islands. A runway was cleared and the first visit by aircraft was at the end of November 1936.

The terrain was good and the local people were friendly and co-operative. Then at the beginning of December a flight of five 55 Squadron Vincents landed there accompanied by a 70 Squadron Valentia transport aircraft. 55 and 70 Squadron were based at Hinaidi in Iraq. En route they had landed at Khor Gharim but met only a working party which had been landed from a sloop. The improvement to the surface of the Khor Gharim landing ground was much appreciated. The flight continued to Aden and British Somaliland, the first land planes to fly from Iraq to Aden.

1937

On 16 June the American aviation pioneer Amelia Earhart overflew Masirah on her attempt to fly round the world. She had started from Florida in her Lockheed Electra with her navigator Fred Noonan. They flew down the coast of South America to its easternmost point at Natal in Brazil. In those days there was no airfield on Ascension Island so they flew the Atlantic non-stop, 1,900 miles to Senegal. They then flew across Africa to Assab at the bottom of the Red Sea. The next leg was the longest of the entire circumnavigation, from Assab to the Drigh Road airfield in Karachi in what was later to be Pakistan. It appears that she was under the impression that the whole Arabian Peninsula was Saudi Arabia. The book *Winged Legend* states that at first she was refused permission to fly over the Peninsula, but overflight was later permitted by the King who still refused permission to land. The King could not have given permission to land because none of the south Arabian coastline belonged to him. She flew over Aden to establish her position and continued up the coast, apparently ignorant of the RAF landing grounds which she could have used in an emergency. She and her navigator died when they failed to find Howland Island in the Pacific.

On 26 October 1937 three 84 Squadron Vincents set out from Shaibah to check the southern landing grounds as far as Salalah. The formation was led by Pilot Officer Robert McClatchey, a Canadian, and in the rear cockpit was AC Leslie O'Leary, the signaller. The passenger in the centre cockpit was Wing Commander Aubrey Rickards OBE AFC, of AHQ Iraq, who was based at Bahrain.

Aubrey Rickards had been a pilot in the First World War but was shot down and taken prisoner in 1917. After the War he served mostly in Egypt, Palestine and Aden. Then, after an Arabic course at the School of Oriental Studies, he returned to Aden as an intelligence officer in 1928. He distinguished himself leading tribal levies at the Battle of Dhala in 1929. He journeyed amongst the tribes, carried out aerial mapping of the area, and established most of the thirty-five landing grounds in the Aden Protectorates and further up the coast in Oman. It was Aubrey Rickards who established the landing ground at Ras al Hadd in 1930. The RAF was responsible for the ground defence of Aden from 1928 to 1957, and of all those involved Rickards has been described as probably the greatest of them all. From 1933 to the end of 1935 he moved from Aden to Iraq to command 55 Squadron at Hinaidi. After a year back in the UK he returned to the Middle East to take up his new appointment at Bahrain for 'air liaison duties'. It was this that led to the fateful flight to the southern landing grounds.

The other two aircraft in the formation were flown by Sergeant Pilot Frame and Sergeant Pilot Whitelock. All three aircraft had a crew of three and were fitted with the auxiliary fuel tank underneath the fuselage which extended the aircraft's range to 1,250 miles, oil permitting. This would enable them to fly non-stop from Masirah to Aden. But this was not their task.

On the first day the three Vincents landed at Bahrain and Abu Dhabi, and spent that night in the Imperial Airways fort at Sharjah. The following day they landed at Shinas and flew on to Bait al Falaj, spending two nights at the W/T station at Muscat. This was run by a sergeant with three airmen and was next to the British Political Agency. On the 29th they flew on to Ras al Hadd and from there to the landing ground at Sur Masirah for another night stop and refuel. Charles Whitelock writes:

We slept on the ground under mosquito nets slung from the mainplanes. We left Masirah at about 0700 hours on 30th for Khor Gharim where the only feature was four white concrete corner markers, very hard to find when largely obscured by dust and sand. McClatchey went in to land first, touched his wheels and apparently saw that he was somewhat across wind – I saw that from the dust that he threw up – and opened up to go round again. He climbed probably to about 500 ft and started a turn to port, then suddenly flipped over in the start of a spin and went straight in on the edge of the lake there. I was at about 1000 ft away to starboard of him and saw the whole thing.

Sergeant Owen Frame's report includes the following:

At the time of the crash I was at 6000 ft taking vertical photographs of the landing ground. After completing this duty I looked around for the other two machines and saw one flying a bit behind and above the other. The leader flew over the landing ground and then made off in a south westerly direction and I assumed that we were to set course for our next landing ground and that a landing at Khor Gharim was not being attempted due to the rough state of the ground. Before leaving Shaibah we were told only to land at Khor Gharim if the surface was suitable. As I altered course to follow the other two machines I kept a lookout beneath me in case they went back to the landing ground to attempt a landing after all. The next thing I saw was one machine just settling in a cloud of dust on the very edge of the khor.

En Route to Khor Gharim 1937.
The Vincents at the Bait al Falaj landing ground near Muscat
(Photograph: Charles Whitelock)

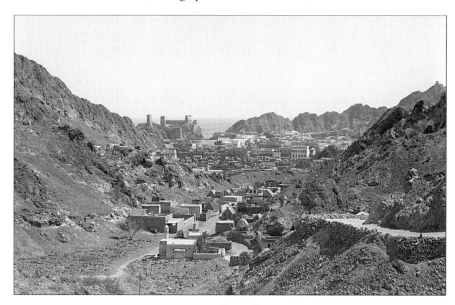

En Route to Khor Gharim 1937.
Muscat seen from the approach road
(Photograph: Charles Whitelock)

The other machine was circling round and I could not tell whether it was the leader or not. As senior pilot in the formation as far as experience went, I flew straight back to the landing ground, checked the wind for drift (as I had no smoke bombs) and went in to land. The surface was very rough at my selected spot and I landed cross wind but safely. Once on the ground I ordered a smoke candle to be burned to recall the remaining machine. This turned out to be K6345 piloted by Sergeant Whitelock.

After detailing AC1 Harris to stand guard over the two aircraft, armed with Sergeant Whitelock's revolver, the remaining five of us set out on foot for the scene of the crash. We took with us first aid kits, two spades, an axe and a tool roll. The going was hard and a detour round the khor had to be made before we arrived at K6346 about one hour later. Sharpe, Funnell and myself were first on the scene and found the occupants still in the aircraft, harnessed, and parachutes not used. I climbed into the wreckage, made a rapid inspection, and found all three to be dead. The impact appeared so severe that I assumed that all three had been killed instantaneously. Later, on removing the bodies, this fact was fairly obvious. When I climbed out of the wreckage after my first examination Sergeant Whitelock and Corporal Bougourd came up and I communicated the knowledge of the deaths to them. These two had been carrying the heavier stuff and when they realised that the need for any great hurry was over, Corporal Bougourd very wisely sat down to rest. As there was nothing that we could now do for the crew of K6346, we all followed suit. I believe that this action helped to keep the airmen in the party calm.

After two or three minutes rest we removed the body of O'Leary, the wireless operator. The injuries to his head were very severe and when he was handed down, from necessity head first, I was covered in grey matter. We placed the body under a ledge in the lava-like rock and I covered the face with a strip of fabric from a mainplane. It was impossible to remove the body of Wing Commander Rickards or the pilot, Pilot Officer McClatchey. The only wireless set was in the crashed aircraft and had been smashed beyond hope of repair so that communication by that was out of the question. I now decided that Sergeant Whitelock should fly back to Muscat, if possible that day, to report the accident. I told him to land at Ras al Hadd if a daylight landing at Muscat was at all doubtful. I ordered all kit to be removed from Sergeant Whitelock's machine for lightness, and detailed only LAC Funnell to fly as passenger for the same reason. I sent Corporal Bougourd back to the landing ground with them to inspect the aircraft for airworthiness.

When they left, Sharpe and I set about cutting away the port mainplane. Having cut these away with the aid of a hacksaw, a hammer and a cold chisel, we found that it was still impossible to remove the two remaining bodies. The kit and luggage had shot forward on impact and the occupant of the middle cockpit was trapped. Sharpe now climbed into the fuselage and started unloading kit, but as soon as he removed a bedroll from the tunnel the

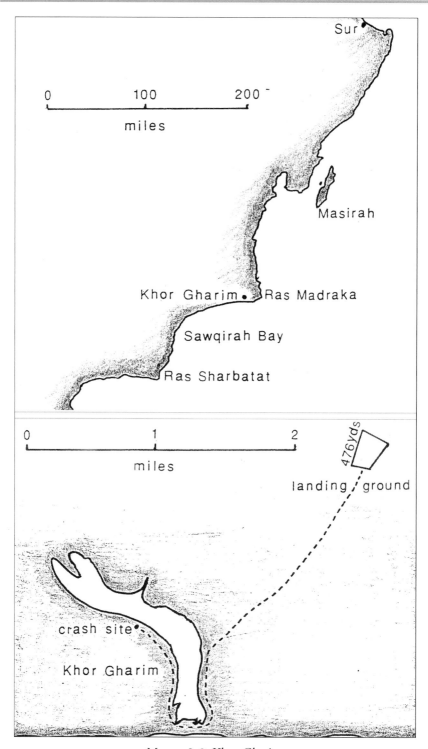

Maps 7 & 8: Khor Gharim

fuselage started to collapse. Seeing the danger of Sharpe becoming injured I told him to abandon that work and to come out. We then started cutting away the side of the fuselage by the middle cockpit.

Again the fuselage creaked and slipped a bit more and I was afraid of a longeron snapping completely and injuring either myself or Sharpe. By way of a rest I removed the sidcot flying suit from the body of the radio operator and took all personal articles from his pockets and substituted a towel for the fabric on his face. All our water was gone and we were both fatigued and thirsty. The water in the khor was very rank and salty but I bathed my arms therein and Sharpe did the same. This had a refreshing effect and we were able to carry on with our salvage operations until Harris came on the scene from the landing ground bringing water and some old tea in flasks. He had been sent by Corporal Bougourd who remained to guard the aircraft.

Corporal Bougourd had sent word by Harris that he thought it would be easier for all concerned if the remaining aircraft was taxied as close as possible to the scene of the crash. There was a lot of carrying to be done and the walk was long and over difficult ground so I saw that he was right. This meant that I now had to leave Sharpe in charge at the crash, and I left for the landing ground carrying as much of the salvaged gear as I could. Before I left I cautioned Sharpe to proceed with the greatest of care with salvage work but not to attempt to cut any more of the fuselage away until Corporal Bougourd arrived.

While Sharpe and Harris were alone at the crash about 50 natives arrived on the scene. They made it impossible to work on the aircraft and guard the salvaged gear at the same time. However, they did see ammunition being removed from the crashed aircraft and to them it was like gold. At one time some natives did get hold of some, and when Sharpe attempted to take it back from them he was nearly knifed for his trouble. An enormous amount of pilfering went on and a lot of gear was lost. At the time I did not know this was happening but when I later checked the ammunition I found that it was all there and congratulated Sharpe and Harris on their good work. All the guns were saved and I believe all the personal effects.

After leaving Sharpe and Harris at the crash I met Corporal Bougourd at the landing ground. We loaded all the kit into and onto K4117 and I taxied the machine as near as possible to the crash. Due to the very rough nature of the ground and the surrounding hillocks this was only to the edge of the landing ground. I then sent Corporal Bougourd back to the crash with a Field Service Pocket Book. I had told him about the state of the fuselage, and I wanted him there mainly on account of his greater technical knowledge and his superior strength. I also wanted him to send Harris or Sharpe back to the aircraft to guard it so that I could get back to the crash, but as this meant a wait of over two hours in changing over I decided to stay with my aircraft. I had previously inspected the ground around the crash and found it unsuitable for digging. I had therefore selected a ledge and told Corporal

Bougourd to place the bodies under this if they succeeded in removing them. I very much doubted that the bodies would be removed that day so I expected to be present to carry out the burial service myself next day.

After Corporal Bougourd left I set up camp and half an hour before sunset I made tea. One hour after sunset Corporal Bougourd and Harris arrived back at the landing ground, guided by Very lights and flashes from my torch. Each carried a very large bundle of salvaged gear. They were both fairly well worn out, as were we all, having worked all day with no food since breakfast at or before dawn at Masirah. I warmed up the tea and we soaked ration biscuits in it and made a hasty meal. Corporal Bougourd told me that the bodies of Pilot Officer McClatchey and Wing Commander Rickards had been removed and all three were now buried. He had observed the short service from the Field Service Pocket Book I had given him. Sharpe had been left behind to guard the guns and ammunition salvaged from the wreck. He had volunteered to do this.

Having refreshed ourselves Corporal Bougourd and I set off in the dark to carry back some more salvaged gear. There were no stars so we got lost and did not find the khor until one and a half hours later. We found the lake eventually by making our way towards where I could hear birds crying. I had previously noticed lots of birds on the water and hoped that what I could hear were the same birds. Luckily they were. On arrival at the lake

En Route to Khor Gharim
Left to Right: Funnel, Bougourd, Sharpe, Harris, O'Leary
(Photograph: Charles Whitelock)

I stood on high ground and flashed my torch all around. I got an answering flash from Sharpe on the other side. He struck several matches at once to make a small flare. This showed us our position and we set off around the side of the lake over extremely difficult ground When we eventually arrived at the crash we were so worn out that I decided to carry the heavy gear, such as bed rolls etc., only a short distance and then hide them by burying them in the sand at a convenient spot, and retrieve them in the morning.

We planned to take only the guns and ammunition back to the landing ground that night.

At this moment two camel drivers and two camels arrived on the scene. I suspected them of coming only for loot. They were very villainous looking so I decided that we had better show them that we were not afraid of them by making friends. I greeted them in the usual manner and asked them if they would carry away the remaining gear. At first they refused and I began to worry as to how I was going to get the heavy stuff to a suitable hiding place without their knowledge. I offered payment for their services and they still refused. But when I showed them the money they agreed, so we set about loading the two camels. This was a most difficult job because we needed the torches to load the camels, and this upset the camels to a very great extent. Then we ran out of cord and I had to cut the shrouds from an unserviceable parachute to get enough to tie the gear on with. The ammunition was safely hidden in a bag and I do not think that they knew it was there, but the guns they had seen so I decided that we would carry them ourselves. After describing our destination we set off, the camel drivers leading. Even now I was not very sure of these natives and I was constantly on the lookout for any signs of treachery. My revolver was loaded and hidden in my pocket. Throughout our stay at Khor Gharim my policy was not to show firearms at any time except in emergency. After a great number of halts to readjust the camels' loads we arrived back at my aircraft some time after midnight. The camels were snorting and making a lot of very frightening noises, and I thought that as we neared the machine Harris might become alarmed and start loosing off a few rounds at us. So I went ahead of the main party to warn him of our approach. But I was too late and Harris, partly to scare what he thought were intruders and partly to see who they were, fired off a Very light. This so much upset the camels and the drivers that I had visions of chasing off over the desert trying to catch all our gear again. However, the drivers soon settled down again and got the camels to the aircraft without further mishap. After the salvaged gear had been unloaded and placed near the aircraft I paid the natives six rupees each and they seemed much relieved. As a more personal mark of gratitude I offered them bread and water which they accepted and we all sat down in a circle and ate a few biscuits while the natives refreshed themselves. I made very certain that as far as possible we observed the rules of native hospitality because in view of the hostile nature of the

The crashed Vincent at Khor Gharim
(Photograph: Charles Whitelock)

tribes thereabouts we would stand a far greater chance of survival if we could manage to get friendly with some of them. Seeing our obviously friendly intentions, the two drivers had removed their camels to a reasonable distance to the lee of our camp, for which act we were very grateful! When they left we had a meal of tinned meat and vegetable that Harris had prepared in our absence. Harris had appointed himself cook which duty he carried out exceedingly well all the time we were there – not that there was very much to cook! After eating the stew we agreed to do about an hour's guard duty each while the others slept. There were only about 3½ hours of darkness left, so one hour each was quite enough. I had previously decided not to leave a guard on the crashed aircraft as this would mean splitting up our party of four which, in the event of any hostilities, would probably prove fatal to all of us. All the loose salvageable gear was now away from the crashed aircraft, so I felt quite justified in my action although contrary to regulations.

At daybreak on 31st October I took stock of our food and water and upon rationing it out found that we could live for eight days if Sergeant Whitelock failed to reach Muscat. If at the end of eight days no relief was forthcoming I would burn or bury the surplus kit and fly the complete party back to Muscat. I told the rest of my party of my plans and they seemed quite satisfied. They took my lead for granted and everything that I said went without query.

A propeller blade marked the site of the temporary burial
(Photograph: Charles Whitelock)

After collecting a lot of dry camel thorn we built a fire and Harris set
about making a breakfast of sorts. After breakfast Corporal Bougourd and
Sharpe set off for the lake to collect water for washing the cooking and
eating utensils. Harris and I remained to set the camp in some sort of
order and to collect some more of the scanty camel thorn for fuel. This
had the effect of partially clearing the landing ground which was in a very
bad state.

At about this time three natives arrived armed with rifles stamped 'VR
ENFIELD'. I went out alone and apparently unarmed to greet them. They
asked for bread and water which I gave them, and they told me that they
had seen us come down the day before and had set out to see us. They
had seen three machines fly over and then one machine fly back, and
thought perhaps something was wrong. They appeared to be friendly but
were very inquisitive. About an hour later they left and Corporal Bougourd
and Sharpe returned with water from the lake. This water was very salty
and quite a lot of salt remained on the dishes and mugs after they had
been boiled in it. We had no cloth to wipe the things with. This salt,
coming into contact with our lips, made them dry up and they subsequently cracked and became very painful. In a few days these cracks

opened to fair sized cuts and to use one's mouth was agony at times. This discovery led us to wash that portion of the mug that touched our lips with tea before we started to drink.

Personal washing and bathing was out of the question. The sea was shark infested and the shore was very abrupt and with no sheltering sandbar to act as a shark stop. The lake was made by seepage from the sea. It was below sea level and was stagnant even though it was so salty. It had a very bad smell and contained innumerable small red wriggling worms. I told the party that they were not to enter either the sea or the khor, and our fresh water was to be used for nothing except drinking. We cleaned our teeth in the remains of our tea.

Several parties of natives came to us during the day. They were exceedingly inquisitive and all asked for ammunition. They showed us money (mainly Maria Theresa dollars) and were willing to pay almost any price. It was very difficult and required very great tact to prevent them from clambering over the machine and the salvaged gear which was now stacked beside it. To start ordering them about would most likely have meant trouble so I told the three others to be as careful as they could be. As it happened they knew very little Arabic and the onus of dealing with the natives fell mainly to me. The presence of these natives made it inadvisable at this time to visit the crashed aircraft or to leave my aircraft. They knew the ammunition was there having seen it removed from the crashed aircraft the previous day. They were intent on having it. The cartridges will not fit the majority of their guns and rifles, but they use the cordite and cap and the metal of the bullet to manufacture crude ammunition of their own. They were originally issued with guns and rifles of various makes and calibres by the Sultan of Muscat, in whose territory they live, but with only a limited supply of ammunition. To deal with this problem they saved all their old cartridges and made more ammunition from time to time from whatever material they could get.

About midday we had some tiffin during which meal I said that I would go out to the crash to see that all was well there. Corporal Bougourd was to stay behind with the other two to deal with any more natives that turned up. Most of the crowd had gone away and the remainder had withdrawn to some distance and were just watching us. Before I set off, however, Sergeant Whitelock arrived back from Muscat in K6345. Needless to say we were very much relieved. We were now stronger by two, we had an extra aircraft to use in case of emergency, and a little more water. He had brought back 10 gallons of fresh water, some fresh limes, bananas and a flask of naval lime juice and six bottles of beer that the airmen of Muscat wireless station had sent us. He gave me copies of all signals relative to the accident and told me of the hospitality extended to himself and Funnell while at Muscat. I was exceedingly pleased and relieved to see Whitelock again. Not only had we got news through to Shaibah and AHQ, but Whitelock and Funnel were safe. I had been a bit worried about them because Whitelock was not very experienced in Vincent aircraft at that time, and had not been down the Persian Gulf before. The charts supplied for that district are not very reliable from the point of view of air navigation. I congratulated him on his navigation and thanked him for his co-operation.

Sixty years later Charles Whitelock wrote to the author:

I left Khor Gharim at about midday and got to Muscat some 3½ hours later. In my haste I took a more or less direct line across country, which I soon realised was most unwise. A forced landing inland in a single aircraft is an experience we would be lucky to survive. However, we did arrive safely and after sending a signal to AHQ and Shaibah I called on the British Political Agent at Muscat. I do not recall him having much to say about it; my chief memory is of the stacks of empty gin bottles along the veranda – legacy of Empire I suppose. I refuelled next morning and flew back to Khor Gharim with tins of water and food. Shaibah had signalled that two Valentias of 70 Squadron would come down to Khor Gharim.

Two of the signals were as follows:

From AHQ To Muscat repeat to 84 Sqn. Following for Sgt Whitelock. You are to proceed back to Khor Gharim with food and water am 31 Oct and remain until arrival of Valentias.

From AHQ to 70 Sqn SHQ Dhibban repeat 84 Sqn and PA Muscat. Detail two Valentias to proceed Khor Gharim to collect three bodies killed in crash. Aircraft to proceed Shaibah tonight. At Dhibban emplane F/Lt Whitehead and one medical orderly. F/Lt Whitehead responsible for deciding if bodies are in fit state to be taken back to Muscat for burial or if they should be buried locally. At Shaibah emplane W/Cdr Savile and three coffins. Aircraft to leave Shaibah in time to arrive Muscat before dark 31 Oct but if arrival at Muscat in daylight is in doubt night stop to be made at Sharjah. On arrival at Muscat itinerary of aircraft to conform to W/Cdr Savile's require-ments. W/Cdr Savile is president of court of inquiry. Pilots of Valentias are detailed as members. Collect key of Masirah petrol store from 55 Sqn.

To continue with Sergeant Owen ('Oscar') Frame's report:

Whitelock and I now set out together to the crashed aircraft to inspect the temporary grave. This was quite intact and bore no signs of having been tampered with by natives or animals. Natives had stripped most of the fabric from the machine and most of the rubber from one tyre was missing. Five natives were among the wreckage and I made a great show of dismay at what had happened. I told them that the machine was the property of our king and did not belong to me at all. They seemed to have a certain amount of respect for stuff that belongs to the government and I thought it was worth trying this angle. I also told them that in a day or two some big officer sahibs were coming here and when they saw what had been done they would be very angry with me. They seemed somewhat sympathetic and I begged them not to touch anything else until the officers had been, and then they could have the lot for themselves. This seemed to please them quite a lot and they even set about collecting the bits and pieces that were scattered about and placed them with the rest of the wreckage. When next I went to the scene nothing further was missing.

Sergeant Whitelock took photos with his private camera for official use, and after cautioning the natives we returned to the landing ground. The rest of the day was taken up with keeping the natives under control. They were a very great trial to us as we had to be alert the whole time and could never relax. They were not openly hostile but were exceedingly quick tempered. It was almost a danger to give an empty tin to one and nothing to another, and when we did we had to keep our wits about us to pacify them. The natives who came from afar always needed water. I pleaded a grave shortage but they knew it was there and it was policy to give them some. Having broadcast our shortage of water and food it would have been very bad policy to eat with them in the vicinity. We had to wait until there were no natives around every time so that we could have our meals. As they were with us, like the flies, during all daylight hours it meant that we had to get up just on dawn to have our breakfast and then wait until after dark to have our dinner. Tiffin had to go by the board. Even as darkness fell there was very often still a crowd around us, and it was only with the greatest verbal difficulty that we persuaded them to go away. That night I doubled the guard and we each did about 3 hours in pairs. We had buried the beer to keep it cool and during the night we split a bottle between us. I had told the natives that a very big aeroplane would be coming on the next day with a lot more white people, and they seemed very impressed.

On the morning of 1st November Whitelock, Funnell and I went out to the crash again to see if we could salvage any more parts. There were still a few things left on the fuselage such as a generator and the tailwheel, and we were going to see if there was anything else worth salvaging. On arrival we found everything intact and no natives about. Having arranged a system of signalling in case of trouble at either end, I left Whitelock and Funnell and returned to the landing ground to mark out a decent runway for the Valentia. On the way back I noticed several fresh tracks left by some fairly large animal but did not see anything of it.

When I arrived at the landing ground there were several natives around the aircraft but I could see no sign of my party. I feared for their safety and was temporarily at a loss to know what to do. I was unarmed at this time, having left my revolver with Whitelock who had left his with the party at the landing ground. However I went forward prepared to put as best a face on things as I could, but inwardly scared to death. My fears were groundless however, as they were only sheltering under mosquito nets from the hordes of flies that were prevalent during all hours of daylight. Nevertheless it gave my already jagged nerves such a bad jolt that I was never without my revolver again. I also ordered that no one was to go anywhere outside our range unarmed. Shortly after I arrived back at the landing ground more natives came up armed as usual with guns, rifles and knives, all of very widely varying design. Really they were quite picturesque but we failed to notice that at the time! They were most persistent in their quest for ammunition and after I had admonished two particularly nasty types they left in opposite directions to one another and in a short time a great crowd returned with one of them. The other one had not yet returned. It looked very much as if we were going to have some trouble and I fired off a Very light ordering the return of Whitelock and Funnell. The situation was becoming pretty critical. I still endeavoured to make friends with all of them but it was becoming increasingly difficult. It was obvious that the non-arrival of the big aircraft made them disbelieve my story and made them think that we were only playing for time. They obviously meant to get the ammunition and I began to fear an attack. Then the other man returned with his crowd. The natives were still just pottering about, worrying us for food, water and ammunition when Whitelock and Funnell came back about an hour and a half later. The natives didn't seem to understand where Whitelock and Funnell could have come from, and most of them left. In the heat of the afternoon only two natives remained with us, but by standing on the centre section of the top mainplane of my machine I could still see the others in amongst the dunes. Later in the afternoon a very old man approached and upon sighting us he did his prayers and then came up to us. I went out to greet him. His eyes were in a very bad state and he complained of pains in the head. I brought him up to the aircraft and gave him some aspirins, two cascaras and a roll of bandage and told him what to do. This seemed to satisfy him no end and he again did his prayers. This incident greatly relieved me as it was the best act of friendship that I had been able to perform and, I thought, if I cure this old man's headache he would spread it abroad and I might get the reputation of being a bit of a healer which would greatly ease the situation. I told Bougourd of my views and he agreed with me. Being an old man he said that they would probably listen to him and he might be able to keep the peace for us. Later, however, there was some trouble over an empty tin that I had given to the old man. One of the two natives who had stayed with us during the afternoon tried to wrest the tin from the old man. We parted them with some difficulty and the old man kept his tin. It was obvious from this that they had no respect at all for age.

Sergeant Whitelock and I now went over the landing ground again and I showed him where I thought the Valentia ought to land. As we were expecting the Valentia that day we thoroughly inspected the landing ground and selected suitable runways free from rough ground. When we returned to the aircraft I succeeded in making the remaining natives go away. After they left Harris started to prepare the second meal of the day but half an hour before sunset two more natives came and demanded water. One looked very capable of causing trouble and after telling him we were exceedingly short of water I gave him a very small quantity. They said they were tired and wanted to camp with us. This was quite out of the question as to have any natives in our midst if trouble broke out would have proved fatal. Again I succeeded in sending them away. In the short twilight we saw the distant forms of natives moving about. While we had our meal it was decided to have three on guard at a time. Corporal Bougourd inspected all our Lewis guns and rifles and these were loaded. The Lewis guns of K4117 and K6345 were left on the mountings ready for use, and the salvaged Lewis gun was placed ready for use on the ground. Each man now had a firearm of some description.

Several lights were seen twinkling round about showing the presence of natives. This was very disconcerting as everyone's nerves were on edge. However, Corporal Bougourd succeed in restoring our confidence in ourselves. Three of us went to sleep while the remaining three mounted guard. We changed the guard during the night and although many lights were seen no disturbance occurred.

While breakfasting under our mosquito nets shortly after daybreak one Valentia arrived bringing Wing Commander Savile, the PA Muscat and Squadron Leader Stevens who was our squadron commander. The two natives who were on their way to us were questioned by the PA and when they left no more came near us.

The stay at Khor Gharim had been a very great nervous strain for everyone concerned but I have great pleasure in informing you that one and all worked really hard and put up a magnificent show of courage, patience and endurance.

Sergeant Frame's pilot's log book shows that he continued to fly until 16 November. After this entry he wrote: 'Complete nervous breakdown. Hospitalised and so missed special rôle in 2nd Singapore reinforcement flight by 84 Sqn.' It was not until the following May that he began flying again. This was still on 84 Squadron Vincents. In June 1938 the following signal was sent from AHQ to 84 Squadron: 'The AOC sends his congratulations to 562112 Sgt Frame WRO and 360000 A/Sgt Bougourd WT on being awarded the BEM.'

In his letter to the author sixty years later, Charles Whitelock writes:

There were three coffins on the Valentia but due to the state of the bodies it was decided to leave them where they were to dry out before removing them for a proper funeral. All the aircraft left Khor Gharim on 3rd November, arriving back at Shaibah on the 5th after nights at Muscat and Sharjah. Sergeant Frame and Corporal Bougourd did a marvellous job.

I still have an open mind on the cause of the crash. It was an awful shambles in the cockpit area and I do not know if the wreckage was sufficiently investigated to check the position of the gravity tank and belly tank cocks. Belly tank fuel was pumped up to the engine by a windmill-driven pump and one always changed over to gravity tanks in the top mainplane for landing, but I would be surprised if failure to change over would cut the fuel supply at landing approach speed, and, as the windmill was in the slipstream of the propeller, it could be expected to keep pumping when opening up to go round again. In the absence of evidence that the top tanks were not turned on I think it just as likely that he spun in doing a tight turn to get back for another go. If he had lost power so low down he would surely have realised that he had no chance of getting back to the landing ground and that his only option was to land ahead which might not have been too difficult as I recall the ground there. It was certainly a very quick flip over into a spin, perhaps halfway through a turn, and fairly straight down.

'A' Flight did another Gulf trip in 1939 not long before I came back to the UK. The landings included Doha in Qatar, Kalba on the Gulf of Oman coast of Trucial Oman (now the UAE) and Shinas a few miles south in Muscat and Oman. Another place we landed was Sohar which was another few miles further south on the Gulf of Oman. South of Masirah we landed at Shuwaymia, Mirbat and Salalah. On one occasion at Masirah the usual fluttering bag of rags came over the horizon and squatted some distance from us. He pulled his rags up over his head; we heard a metallic clanking sound, followed by puffs of smoke. Then he emerged smoking a primitive pipe which he had apparently lit from a spark struck from a flint and a bit of old iron.

On the 60th anniversary of the fatal accident at Khor Gharim the following appeared in the *Daily Telegraph*. It was placed by Charles Whitelock.

In memoriam
'THEIR NAME LIVETH FOR EVERMORE'
IN MEMORY OF – W.Cdr. AUBREY RICKARDS, O.B.E., A.F.C.,
P/O ROBERT McCLATCHEY and A.C.1. LESLIE O'LEARY, killed
in the crash of Vincent K 6343, 84 (B) Sqn. R.A.F.,
at Khor Gharim, Southern Arabia on October 30,
1937, and buried there that day. The grave is
unmarked.

1938

In the early 1990s a photocopy of most of an old letter was found in a 'put away' file at SOAF Masirah. The file dated back to the early days of the SOAF tenure, and the letter was written by the late Jasper Coates. It was dated 4 November 1976, a few months before the RAF left Masirah. It contained the following information:

> After two years as a flight commander on 201 flying-boat Squadron at Calshot, I returned to the Gulf in April 1938 as Air Liaison Officer Bahrain to take over from the late Wg Cmdr Tex Rickards, killed in a flying accident at Sawqirah Bay a few months previously [Khor Gharim is located in the wide Sawqirah Bay]. He, and later I, were the first RAF to live in Bahrain, and it was whilst I was there that I acquired for the RAF the land and marked out the landing ground and boundaries of what later became RAF Muharraq [now Bahrain International Airport, the home base of Gulf Air].
>
> July. It could have been a little later, but one did not keep a record of passenger flying in those far off days, I flew to Masirah from Bahrain in a Vincent of 84 Sqn piloted by Flt Lt Peter Holder, later to be C in C Coastal Command, accompanied by a second Vincent with a fitter and rigger. We had the W/T operator and I navigated. Our task was to see if the bodies of Wg Cmdr Rickards and the pilot and W/T op of the Vincent which had crashed in trying to land at Sawqirah Bay landing ground were fit to be exhumed and flown to Habbaniya for burial in the RAF cemetery.
>
> We nearly followed them because when Peter was turning over from the 'belly tank' to the main, shortly before Sawqirah, a manoeuvre which necessitated reaching low down forward of the stick, he must have inadvertently knocked off the main ignition switches with the cuff of his old type flying gauntlet. I, dozing on the centre seat, leapt up at the cessation of all engine noise and looking over Peter's shoulder noticed that the main ignition switches were off. I shouted to him and he said he thought he must have turned them off as normal forced landing procedure. Nevertheless he tried them and the engine started up again and we were saved what might have been a very tricky forced landing in some pretty rough country.
>
> After inspecting the bodies, which were mummified by the dry heat, we took off again and landed at Sur Masirah where we spent the night. I have a couple of old photographs in my album of the two aircraft, with our camp beds below the wings, and another of Peter and the other crew eating bully and drinking tea in the shade of the petrol store.
>
> On my return to Bahrain I duly reported the results of our exhumation to AHQ, but the war put a stop to any further thoughts of removing the bodies, and as far as I know they are still there, buried on a slight mound

close to the remains of their aircraft. No other aircraft have ever landed at Sawqirah since Peter, myself and the second Vincent did.

The year 1938 was not a good one for the flying-boats of 203 Squadron. In February one of them drifted onto a submerged rock at Mirbat, but it was later successfully salvaged and repaired. Less than two months later another Singapore hit a rock as it was taxiing at Umm Rusays. The pilot was able to beach the aircraft before it sank, and again it was successfully repaired on-site and returned to the Squadron. Then at the end of July another flying boat was damaged, this time at Khor Jarama. There was no wind and the water was a glassy calm. The pilot was unable to judge his height when landing and the aircraft hit the water with a high rate of descent. A wing tip float was torn off and the lower wing hit the sea. A repair party was sent from Basra and the aircraft was returned to the Squadron. Many of these Singapores ended their days as decoys, moored out in Aden harbour at the beginning of the Second World War.

In April 1938 the fuel store at Shuwaymia was built and this marked the completion of the South Arabian air route for short-range aircraft. Even long-range aircraft might require an emergency landing ground. In 1974 the author landed five times at Shuwaymia in a Beaver carrying medical teams and the Civil Liaison Officer Dhofar. The fuel store was still there. Much of the runway had been washed away by flash floods but sufficient remained for an over-load take-off with some villagers and their goats as well as the medical team. At the time the author was puzzled by the Shuwaymia landing ground not knowing who had built it, when, and for what purpose.

In the summer of 1938 55 Squadron undertook a grand tour of the Middle East and Africa. The Squadron was based at Habbaniya near Baghdad, and equipped with the ubiquitous Vincent. Obviously the planning officers did not know about the south-west monsoon which affects Masirah and Salalah during the summer months. The grand tour started down the Gulf and continued down the South Arabian coast to Aden. All twelve aircraft were readied and fitted with long-range tanks.

In early August the Squadron took off and headed south over the Euphrates valley. This part of the Fertile Crescent seemed particularly arid after the irrigated gardens of RAF Habbaniya. After 2½ hours the head of the Gulf slowly approached. The blue of the Gulf on the left was a welcome change, but on the right was the featureless khaki of Kuwait. The tiny sheikhdom was still dependent on fishing and pearl diving, and it would be another decade before its huge wealth of oil began to be fully exploited. In 1938 it was nothing more than a poor British protectorate. They flew onwards for another two hours of deafening boredom until the island of Bahrain manifested itself out of the heat haze. The RAF airfield was on Muharraq Island to the north of the main island of Bahrain. The two islands were joined by a causeway in 1940.

The landing ground was easy to identify, and the squadron descended from the cool upper air. Slowly they circled the landing ground and landed one by one for their first night stop of the grand tour. Bahrain had been exploiting its small oil reserves for some years, and the modest wealth which this produced had not ruined the authentic Arab flavour of the place. Surprisingly, there were fresh water springs which watered date groves and other crops. For the British it was the most settled and civilised of the Gulf states. For the aircrew this would have been the most favoured place to have an unserviceable aircraft, yet all twelve started up and took-off the following morning.

The route was across the base of the flat Qatar peninsula and a coast crawl to Sharjah. This Gulf coast is low lying, threaded with convoluted creeks, and with shoals and sandbars so extensive that it is difficult to distinguish the land from the sea. The Vincents crawled over the barren scene at a snail's pace, the crews peering through the haze at the passing geography lesson. It took 2½ hours to reach the desolate poverty of Sharjah where the Squadron refuelled. After take-off the Squadron gathered itself together over Sharjah and set off east over the low dunes and scrub towards Muscat.

Soon the craggy spine of Oman passed beneath, and then the blue water of the Gulf of Oman appeared ahead. Turning slightly right the Squadron converged on the coast. Onwards past the landing grounds at Kalba, Shinas and Sohar. No creeks or shoals, the monotonous coast was utterly featureless and curved gently to the left. The coastal plain was cultivated here and there, and with the cultivation were built-up areas with ancient forts. At last the coast turned rocky, and the Squadron began the long descent to the Bait al Falaj landing ground. As the aircraft lost height the appalling smell of drying fish reached up to give warning of what was to come. The landing ground was in mountainous terrain with the runway between two ridges, and near the end of the runway an impressive fort sat four-square. The heat was unbearable. All landed safely and when the aircraft were picketed and refuelled the crews departed.

Somehow everybody was accommodated inside the British Political Agency in the tiny walled city of Muscat. The accommodation was in 'The Rest House' which was formerly the American Consulate, established in 1880 and closed in 1917. The building had not been occupied for many years when, in 1929, it was leased to the RAF which needed a permanent wireless post in Muscat. It was used mostly by 203 Squadron, the flying-boat squadron at Basra.

At Muscat there was a curfew at night, and the city gates were closed at sunset. The Squadron spent the following day in Muscat, deeply disturbed by the squalor and poverty. Eye disease and blindness was endemic, and next door to the Political Agency was the grim facade of Jalali jail. It had a heavy wooden door with a three-inch gap at the bottom, and through this gap came the hands of the wretched prisoners pleading for scraps. Everywhere there were

Muscat Harbour where the 203 Squadron flying-boats moored for the night. Lower left is the prison of Fort Jalali, and next to it on the waterfront is the British Political Agency, later the Embassy (Photograph: Tommy Hazell)

flies. Nobody was sorry to make a very early start on the following morning and hurry away from this nightmare place.

Again the reliable and robust Vincents had no technical problems and all twelve aircraft departed south. They flew high in clear skies between the deep blue sea and the daunting limestone mountains cut with awesome ravines. Ras al Hadd was ignored, the Squadron continuing the extra hundred miles to Masirah. The mountains gave way to desert, its features barely visible through the heat haze which surrounded the aircraft. Everything became grey and the sun's disc enfeebled. The aircraft huddled together in the encircling gloom and gradually lost height to keep the surface in view. Soon the sea and coast was blanketed below by the white top of cloud or fog. Out to sea it extended to the horizon, but parts of the featureless desert were visible. This was no help with map reading. Then, in the distance, hilltops protruded through the cotton wool, and this could only be the island of Masirah. Was it fog or low cloud? Sqn Ldr Stowell took his life in his hands and descended into the cotton wool. He knew that his altimeter was not telling him his correct height because he could only guess the atmospheric pressure.

If it was fog he would descend into the ground or sea. If it was low cloud he could fly into the hills. The minutes ticked past. Anxiety increased in the crews of the circling Vincents. Eventually, after fifteen minutes, Sqn Ldr

Stowell's Vincent burst out of the cotton wool. He rocked his wings and his squadron fell into line astern and followed him down through the clammy and embracing blanket. They emerged from the bottom at about 500 feet over Masirah and followed the boss to the Sur Masirah landing ground where all twelve Vincents landed successfully. They clustered round the petrol store building and then began the long task of refuelling out of the 4-gallon tins. The aircraft were inspected and picketed for the night. Then it was time to prepare the meal of Maconochies beef stew in a huge cook pot. An Omani and his son watched from behind a rise in the ground. In the Arab culture they would have been invited in to share the feast, and this would have been an honour and a pleasure for the hosts. All they got were the empty meat tins and petrol tins, but these would have been prized containers.

That night the aircrew slept under the wings of their aircraft, too tired to worry about centipedes and scorpions. It was difficult to sleep due to the increasing humidity as the night air cooled. Aircraft and sleepers became drenched in dew as the temperature dropped. There was the distant sound of waves breaking on the shore, but also a closer clicking noise. This was the ungainly hermit crabs, armoured gentlemen in second-hand sea shells which had come to investigate the remains of the meal. Larger and somewhat more ominous was the small army of curious ghost crabs which also arrived to investigate the meal. It was not a good night's sleep for those of a nervous disposition.

In many ways 55 Squadron were lucky to encounter the low cloud at Masirah.

August 1938. A 55 Squadron Vincent at Sur Masirah with Jenkins Hill in the background (Photograph: Jasper Coates, courtesy of the RAF Museum)

A more usual hazard during the summer months is a gale force wind from the south-west, laden with dust and salt whipped up from the sea. At this landing ground the monsoon wind direction is almost straight across the runway. The Vincents could not have landed in a crosswind of this strength, and would have been forced to land across the runway. There was sufficient length available to do this, but there would have been broken ground and a low cliff at the upwind edge of the landing ground. The turbulence would have been daunting, and these lightly loaded aircraft would have been almost impossible to control during the landing. When the wind speed reaches 25 knots there is rising sand which reduces the visibility to a few hundred yards. The wind often reaches a strength which would have destroyed the Vincents on the ground unless they remained securely picketed, perhaps for some days.

However, the following morning was calm and grey and wet with dew. Toilets and breakfast were hurried, and the weary aircrew soon struggled to start their sodden engines. All were successful and soon the Vincents were climbing through the gloom to the south-west. Overflying Khor Gharim and Shuwaymia it was 300 miles to Mirbat, a landing ground of generous proportions about 50 miles short of Salalah. The weather remained hazy but the Squadron was lucky to have no low cloud over the destination. For most of the summer this stretch of coast is covered in very low cloud and drizzle, and just to the north-east of Mirbat there is a 6,000-foot high escarpment. The top of the cloud sheet is usually about 4,000 feet. In the normal weather conditions to be expected at that time of year it would not be possible to land. With no navigation aids any attempt would be suicide.

The Squadron landed at Mirbat in time for a Maconochies lunch. The aircraft were refuelled from the petrol store with the help of some sturdy negroes who were working for smaller but highly vocal Arabs. This was slavery, although a more politically correct euphemism may have been used to describe the relationship. Mirbat was not a good place to spend the night. Armed mountain tribesmen could arrive, unsmiling in their demands and accustomed to being obeyed. So the Squadron flew low level fifty more miles to Salalah, landing beside a V-shaped inlet from the sea. Salalah was the provincial capital, a more settled and peaceful environment for the Squadron's night stop. While the evening meal was being prepared a dozen Arabs appeared, squatted on their haunches and subjected the crews to unblinking scrutiny. Each wore a *kunja* (dagger) on his belly, and their garb and kohl eye shadow presented a somewhat threatening appearance. Not a word was said, and not a morsel of food was offered. As they drifted off into the night no doubt the tribesmen talked about the strange lack of hospitality of the *Nazranis* (Christians). 'What a backward and uncultured bunch they are!' must have been their comment.

With the first grey streaks of dawn it was apparent that the low cloud had returned. The Salalah plain was ringed by mountains so the take-off had to be towards the sea for a straight climb into the gloom. After a few minutes eleven Vincents successfully burst out into brilliant sunshine, joined in loose formation and headed south-west for Mukalla. The twelfth Vincent was the first unserviceability, but the crew had all they needed for rectification. It had been arranged that they would follow as soon as possible.

After an hour or so the low cloud became patchy and eventually disappeared altogether. With the coast in full view map reading to Mukalla was easy. On landing the Squadron was greeted by the son of the Sheikh who had had a university education in England. He spoke impeccable English and had laid on a mutton stew lunch for everybody. Some of the more suspicious aircrew probed the stew for the sheep's eye, but thankfully without success. It was a good meal and it was good to be back in British Protected Territory. The town of Mukalla was a jewel of traditional Arab architecture tucked into a bay below the barren hills. It was the chief town of the Eastern Aden Protectorate which was a haven of peace compared to the more turbulent Western Aden Protectorate in the hinterland behind the colony of Aden.

The missing Vincent did not arrive that day. But the following morning, as anxiety increased, a small dot appeared above the coast to the north-east. It was the twelfth Vincent.

From Mukalla it was only a short 2½ hour flight to RAF Khormaksar at Aden, home of 8 Squadron which was also equipped with Vincents. Two of the 55 Squadron Vincents were unable to join the others for the flight to Aden. The following day there had been no signal from them so two 8 Squadron aircraft went to see what had happened. They were recalled when the two missing Vincents finally arrived. There are conflicting reports about what had caused the delay.

It was oppressively hot and humid at Aden, but the facilities were much appreciated by the crews of 55 Squadron. Until arriving at Aden they had only the water they carried with them, so had drunk sparingly and washed only the parts which showed. It was heaven to get clean again and wear freshly laundered clothes. The fleshpots of Aden beckoned and not all the crews behaved wisely. After a few days nine 55 Squadron aircraft joined twelve aircraft of 8 Squadron for a show of strength over the recalcitrant Mansuri territory. After a week 55 Squadron departed for Port Sudan, then south to Kenya, and finally north again to Egypt, Transjordan, and home to Habbaniya.

By 1938 it had become obvious that the Sur Masirah landing ground was not ideal. Although the maximum length of 1,000 yards was generous for the aircraft of those days, it lay across the direction of the monsoon wind. Furthermore, the landing ground flooded at exceptionally high spring tides. On a geological timescale, the whole island of Masirah is rising very rapidly and this flooding is rare these days. An alternative landing ground elsewhere on the island seemed a wise precaution, and this was established in 1938 on a plateau 50ft above sea level at the northern tip of the island, which is the site of the present airfield. No petrol was stored there due to its distance from the sea.

Late in 1938 a Royal Navy survey vessel, HMS *Challenger*, conducted depth soundings and carried out a triangulation survey of Masirah Island. On top of one jebal there is a blue disc cemented into the rock. It is inscribed: 'HYDROGRAPHIC DEPARTMENT ADMIRALTY LONDON SWI TRIANGULATION STATION HMS CHALLENGER DEC 13 38'. Almost all the trig points on the island have now been smashed or removed, so the author demolished the cairn which had been built over this disc, and is not divulging its location.

1939

The survey by HMS *Challenger* continued during January and February 1939. The ship's surgeon spent two weeks ashore and submitted the following report:

26th January 1939. I landed at 1200 with Leading Telegraphist Damon, A.B. Coates, and Hassan, the native interpreter. Camp was pitched 50 yards beyond the high water mark at a spot about five miles north of Mersis (Umm-Rasas on the Chart) and about two miles south of Dawwa (Daua or Datti on Chart). 500 yards to the south were two wells (Ras Shaghaf Wells), one of them silted up with sand, and a hut used as a rest house and called Makan-el-Raha. The three ridge-pole tents were erected in the shape of a 'T' so that an extra fly supported by their poles could form a roomy sun-shade. Stores were kept in the Arctic tent. As the camp was being erected a native arrived by canoe from Dawwa and offered fresh water. In the afternoon a shark merchant from Dawwa called, name Abdulla bin Thabet. He asked if we knew Major Watts (Political Agent), but was otherwise uncommunicative. In the evening a fisher boy passing by was induced to come to the camp. He was frightened to say much about the Sheikh but obviously hated him, saying that his mother and father were killed about seven years previously by order of the Sheikh. 24 hour tide readings were commenced. Several figures were seen in the distance on the plain, but they did not approach the camp.

27th January. About 0200 a dhow was seen close inshore approaching the camp, but made off when the Aldis lamp was directed on it. In the forenoon, accompanied by Hassan, I went to Dawwa, about 40 minutes walk. As we approached we could see women and children running away, and hear shouts of 'Farangie cagie' ('Europeans coming'). We managed to collect a few natives, and through the interpreter I told them that I had come to treat the sick and wished to see the head man. Some said he was in another village, others that he was out in a dhow. After answering many questions, it was conceded that he really was in the village, and he was sent for. The natives were timid at first, the women hiding in their houses, but not in the least unfriendly. None of them bore arms, wearing their daggers only on special occasions, and there were no soldiers present with rifles. When the head man arrived, he was immediately friendly and hospitable, offering us tea and coffee. He was obviously much respected, everyone keeping silent when he spoke and doing as he ordered them. His name is Aba Salim bin Ahmed, but everyone, even the Sheikh, refers to him as 'Aba' Salim – 'Father Salim' – as a mark of respect. He mentioned that the villagers were frightened by the surveying flags which had been erected on the island, and was very grateful when I explained that they meant no harm. He did not even attempt to conceal his contempt of the Sheikh, saying, when his name was mentioned, 'Spit on his face'. Nevertheless, much as he disliked the person, he maintained his loyalty to the Sheikh as Sheikh. It was stated that the Sheikh was in Oman, but that he visited Masirah for a few days each month. (It came to light later that the Sheikh was actually in Dafiyat, the village to the north of Dawwa, where he had also been staying when the Political Agent had previously attempted to get in touch with him and was told he was at Sur.) Aba Salim promised to convey my message to the Sheikh, and to try to induce him to come to the camp. Later in the day several people voluntarily came to the camp for medical attention.

28th January. At 1000, while attending to two female patients at the rest house 500 yards from the camp, a native messenger came running in a state of great excitement and announced that the Sheikh had arrived at the camp. When I got to the camp, I found the two ratings rather dismayed, as 100 yards from the camp stood the Sheikh surrounded by 30 soldiers armed with rifles, cartridge belts, and daggers. However, when I went forward and greeted him in Arabic, he was perfectly friendly but obviously ill at ease and nervous. Through Hassan I explained the purpose of the camp and he said how grateful he was for the medical attention given to his subjects. His name is Sheikh Khamis bin Hilal – 'Thursday son of the Moon' – a wary, beady-eyed individual of about 35. After he had been entertained to coffee he became more confident and I suggested that he should meet the Captain of 'Challenger'. At first he refused. Then, after many promises, oaths on the Koran, etc. that he would not be poisoned, killed or kidnapped, he promised to meet the Captain at the camp on Thursday the 2nd February, Thursday being his lucky day. He also promised to go on board the ship and to bring no soldiers. He gave permission to remain in the Island, to shoot gazelle, put up marks, etc. Aba Salim was present, but remained in the background, getting quite embarrassed if any special favour was shown him in the presence of the Sheikh. He said the Sheikh would not have come to the camp had the ship not been beyond the horizon. Eleven fresh medical cases were attended to, many also returning for daily treatment. Four natives arrived from Mersis by dhow after dark to hear our 'talking box' – gramophone – which was always a source of great amusement. They said they had been slaves in Jezirat Daiyinah under one called Hamwod bin Hamed, but had fled to Masirah because of his cruelty, six months previously, and were now soldiers of the Sheikh.

Sheikh Khamis bin Hilal in 1965. He was Sheikh of Masirah from before the first arrival of the RAF in 1931 until after the RAF withdrew in 1977 (Photograph: Peter Wickenden)

31st January. Today the natives celebrated the Mohammedan feast of 'Bekra-idd', and few came to the camp. In the afternoon I went to Dawwa to study the celebrations and was made most welcome. All the inhabitants were dressed in clean clothes, and many had the palms of their hands dyed with henna.

2nd February. In the early morning a dhow from Mahawt anchored near the camp with four invalids seeking medical attention. This was proof of the comparative rapidity with which news travels to the mainland, as we had only been in camp six days and these people stated that they had heard three days previously that there was a good Hakeem now in Masirah. One of these patients was Saued bin Saeed, son of Saeed al Sultan of Mahawt, and cousin of the Sheikh. The Sheikh had promised to meet the Captain of 'Challenger' at 1000 today, without a bodyguard, and to go on board to be entertained. The Captain, First Lieutenant, and Paymaster-Commander landed at the camp about 0900. At 1000 natives started arriving at the camp from other villages, and the sound of drums could be heard from Dawwa. At 1045 we were rather surprised to see a large banner approaching across the plain surrounded by 70–80 natives, singing and dancing to the sound of drums. The procession stopped 500 yards from the camp, and as no further move was made towards the camp, Hassan and I went to meet it. The Sheikh was sitting in a circle with about a dozen soldiers and merchants. He greeted us nervously, and it was obvious he was not looking forward to the promised meeting. After about 30 minutes delay, the procession came to the camp, where all was confusion, people singing and dancing, and many whispering advice to the Sheikh. One merchant in particular, Mohammed bin Khamis, who could read and write, and had been to India, was overheard advising the Sheikh to order us to remove the surveying marks and clear out of the island immediately. He was one of my patients, and I later refused to give him further treatment. The Sheikh was perfectly friendly and reasonable in the privacy of a tent with the Captain, but refused to go on board, apologising profusely and saying that if he went without his (over 80) followers they might shoot him when he returned. He became quite confident with the Captain, and explained that he had torn up a letter from the Sultan of Muscat some time previously (a testimonial carried by geologists who landed on the island by 'plane), because they had offended the villagers by paying too much attention to their womenfolk. The majority of the Sheikh's followers on this occasion were his soldiers.

3rd February. Awakened by singing from a dhow near camp at 0130. 6 fresh medical cases. Visited Dawwa in the afternoon to see patients and while photographing on the shore was approached by a soldier who became very menacing, loading his rifle, and accusing us of being spies. He was placated by announcing that we would report his behaviour to the Sheikh. Was entertained by the Sheikh in his house in Dawwa. He later came to the camp on a white donkey with 8 soldiers. He was shown the chart, and was very helpful checking, correcting, and making additions to the names. He showed an excellent knowledge of the local reefs and islets. He was also given medical attention for a certain complaint; was much more communicative and confident now, saying that he would like to visit the camp daily.

4 February. Sheikh's brother and some soldiers visited camp in morning. Later the Sheikh arrived and was full of confidence and very friendly indeed. He expressed his gratefulness to the 'Hakeem' and asked whatever was in his power to do, he would do it for him. He mentioned a monetary present of 500 'riyals' (Maria Theresa dollars) which was declined with thanks. He stated he would remain in the island until the camp broke up, to protect us from his 'wild ungrateful' subjects, and asked that the ship might leave as soon as possible as he wished to return to the mainland. It was apparent that his anxiety for our safety was only an excuse to prevent us becoming more friendly with the real Masirah islanders, as they had from the start been friendly and hospitable. Only the Sheikh's soldiers and friends from the mainland showed any sign of enmity or ungratefulness. The Sheikh's brother took the interpreter aside and told him to ask the Captain for a monetary present ('backsheesh') for him, but to say nothing about it to the Hakeem or Sheikh.

6th February. Sheikh spent two hours in camp, becoming almost embarrassingly friendly and intimate. The Sheikh's cousin and son of the Sultan of Mahawt, who had been receiving injection treatment, became so offensive that I refused to treat him more, but after the Sheikh had asked to continue treatment for his sake, as he wished to remain friendly with the Sultan, I did so.

7 February. This being the last day, there was a constant stream of natives at the camp, many merely to say 'goodbye', others to get medicine to continue treatment, and a few to scrounge whatever they could. The Sheikh called and presented me with a fine silver mounted dagger and sheath. He bought it for 35 riyals from a soldier after much haggling, mentioning that his own was not a sufficiently good one. He said how sorry he was he had not had a real feast in our honour, but we would understand that he could not supply a table, forks and knives etc., and we might not have enjoyed it.

8th February. Camp broken up A.M. The Sheikh spent the whole morning at camp until we left, and was a pathetic figure as he stood alone on the beach with tears in his eyes waving farewell.

Part II. Summary.
Medical

In all, 64 patients received medical attention, 16 of them not natives of Masirah, but travelling merchants or Bedouins from the mainland, some of whom came specially to consult me. Many attended daily for treatment; 15 minor operations were done under general or local anaesthesia – opening of abscesses, operations for piles, enucleation of superficial tumours, extraction of teeth, etc.

Typhoid and dysentery are endemic. Malaria is only found in natives who have lived on the mainland. Eye diseases are very common. Smallpox epidemics occur about once a year, and two months previously 15 children died of it in Dawwa alone. Phthisis is common. Several cases of venereal disease were met with, including gonorrhoea, congenital syphilis, secondary and tertiary syphilis. 4 cases of cancer in a late stage were seen. Owing to religious reasons, female patients could only be examined under difficulties, and were always seriously ill. One woman in Dawwa had a large ulcer of the ankle down to the bone, and gangrene of the toes. Her husband made the wound with his dagger ten months previously because she was eloping with another man; he also shot the man, but was in turn shot himself by order of the head man. Amputation was refused by the relatives despite the efforts of Aba Salim and the Sheikh, who fully realised the good it would do.

Much valuable experience was therefore gained. The majority of the medicines used were medical samples in my possession and the cost in medical stores was negligible.

No medical attention of any kind is available in the district.

Political

The largest village is Dawwa (Daua or Datti on Chart). It consists of 45 dwellings made of dried palm sticks and wood, a white washed stone building near the shore which is used as a mosque, and two stone built store houses for dates and dried fish. There are between 450 and 500 inhabitants, but the population varies according to the number away fishing or trading. There are five wells in Dawwa, giving the purest and most plentiful supply of water in the island – the water is clear and sweet. Aba Salim bin Ahmed is the head man, owning 7 dhows, 3 camels and the stores. He was the most intelligent and helpful person met with, and is liked and respected throughout the island, and as far as Ras al Hadd on the mainland. He has been to Mecca. He would be Sheikh if the present line was broken, and would undoubtedly be most popular. His son, Hamood bin Salim was a soldier in the 1st Yemen Infantry 1919–1922, and can read and write a little; is now a soldier with the Sheikh. Dafiyat, 2½ miles to the north of Dawwa, is not marked on the chart. The Sheikh spends most of his time here when he visits the island for a few days each month. Hilf, to the north of Dafiyat, is another village not marked on the chart.

In order, to the south of Dawwa, the villages are named Mersis (Umm-Rasas on chart), Sur Masirah, Safaiq, Kalban. Except Dawwa, the population of each village is between 50 and 100, and there are a few scattered dwellings; so that the total population of the island cannot exceed 1000.

The head man of Mersis, Saleh bin Saeed, is a complete nincompoop, and it is suspected that the head men of the other small villages are in a similar category.

Sheikh Khamis bin Hilal, aged about 35, is hereditary Sheikh of Masirah, his family line unbroken for many generations. He is illiterate, but can speak Suris and Muscatese dialects. He is cunning. He lives mostly on the mainland, where he stated he was also Sheikh, and has property in Sur. He is intensely disliked and despised by everyone, even his own soldiers. The following reasons were given for this dislike: He is cruel; he maltreats his five wives; he keeps boys and indulges in homosexual practices (this can be confirmed, as one of these transvestist boys was pointed out while being entertained by him); he is not a good Moslem; he has a monopoly of the local shark trade, and gives unfair prices that the natives are bound to accept. He is a weak character, and he is far too prone to accept advice from anyone. His brother has a charming personality, but is a rascal.

The Sheikh has about 100 soldiers in all, whom he pays 5 riyals (Maria Theresa dollars) a month each, and some grain. They are generally a hetero-geneous crowd of ruffians, although there are some decent islanders among them. Many of them, questioned as to their antecedents, became embarrassed, and refused to say. Some are runaway slaves, some fugitives from justice, and there are several Ethiopians who left Abyssinia three years ago.

The Sheikh himself has a very low opinion of his subjects, and said quite frankly that cruelty was the only discipline they could understand. He owes loyalty to the Sultan of Muscat whom, he says, visits the island about once a year. He obviously pays more allegiance to the Imam of Oman, whom he considers superior to the Sultan. He says the Sultan comes under the British Government.

Trade is done with Bombay, Karachi, Sur, Muscat, Mukalla, Aden, and all along the Arabian coast. The chief export is dried shark. It was stated dates are brought from Zanzibar and sold in Muscat, which appears like taking coal to Newcastle.

The natives can be classified as the real islanders; friendly and hospitable, mostly fishermen; and the traders, merchants, soldiers and Bedouins from the mainland arrogant, uncouth, ungrateful, wild, and difficult to get on with.

The Sheikh himself was always friendly enough and easily managed in the absence of his advisers. His confidence was completely gained, and he promised to be helpful to any of H.M. Ships whenever he had the opportunity.

Geology

There are signs of old copper ore workings in the southern part of the island.

No ores are worked now. The island is of volcanic origin. Several coloured ore outcrops were found.

Natural History

Gazelle are numerous. Hyena footprints were numerous, but none were seen. Camels are bred and roam the plains in twos and threes. Small harmless lizards are numerous. Two dangerous species of snake were described by the natives, said to be common when it rains. One is called 'Abu seha', locally, and the other 'abu raqat', described as the 'bad one', and having wings – apparently a cobra. Snake bite is not rare. The common fly is a nuisance. No mosquitoes were seen. No other noxious arthropods.

On 3 May a Vincent of 84 Squadron crashed on take-off from the Sur Masirah landing ground. The pilot, Pilot Officer D.H. Walsh, and his crew were uninjured but the aircraft was destroyed. No further details are available but it must have been one of the last Vincents to visit the Sur Masirah landing ground because the Squadron was at that time re-equipping with the Bristol Blenheim Mk1. The first of them arrived on the Squadron on 17 February and by 3 June the Squadron had been completely re-equipped.

Also in 1939 the Sultan married his only wife who was a lady from Dhofar. She bore him a single son, Qaboos, who was to become the next Sultan.

CHAPTER III

The Second World War

O N 30 NOVEMBER 1939 the British Consul (as he was now more appropriately known) at Muscat wrote the following secret letter to the Sultan:

Your Highness,

I have been directed to inform Your Highness that His Majesty's Government
in consultation with the Government of India have considered Your Highness's
statement of conditions on which you are prepared to afford them necessary
facilities in your territories and territorial waters during the present war. At this
stage when it is not possible to foresee how the course of the war will develop
His Majesty's Government are unable to give any precise definition of the further
facilities if any which they might require but it is possible that in addition to
the continuance of the facilities already granted to the Royal Navy and the Royal
Air Force it might be necessary for them to ask for other facilities of a similar
nature. In that event they would inform Your Highness as long as possible in
advance of what is required in order that with your goodwill and co-operation
the necessary arrangements may be made.

2. They wish in the first place to re-affirm their readiness to protect Your
   Highness's territories including Gwadar from any external aggression resulting from the war, while in the event of internal disturbances they are
   prepared to give Your Highness such assistance as may be possible.

3. In reply to your specific requests they desire to state that in return for Your
   Highness's co-operation:

   (a) They agree that Your Highness should be a party to any peace
   treaty to the extent that it may involve Muscat territory or Muscat
   interests.
   (b) They understand that unless specific permission is given by Your
   Highness any facilities that might be desired during the war (i.e.
   apart from those which Your Highness had already granted in peace
   time) will terminate on the conclusion of peace.
   (c) They undertake to consult Your Highness on all political matters
   relating to your territory and to obtain your permission before
   entering into direct communication with tribal leaders of Oman.

(d) Special consideration will whenever possible be given to the needs of your State in connection with the export to Muscat from India of staple foodstuffs such as wheat, flour, rice and sugar.

(e) To enable Your Highness to undertake essential security measures they will grant you for the duration of the war and for a reasonable period after the cessation of hostilities of a monthly allowance of rupees twenty thousand (to date from September 3rd; two monthly payments being made in advance) together with an immediate grant of rupees fifty thousand for the repair and construction of fortifications, and an advance of rupees fifty thousand in respect of the Zanzibar Subsidy. It is understood that receipt of these payments does not impose any obligation on Your Highness to provide at your own expense guards for the protection of facilities granted to the Royal Navy and the Royal Air Force.

(f) Finally as soon as supplies can be made available they are prepared to provide Your Highness free with war stores as specified below which include stores already offered to you:

(1) Four light lorries.

(2) 300 rifles and 300 bayonets.

(3) 350 thousand rounds ammunition.

(4) Two 2.75 inch guns and carriages with 225 shell H.E. and 125 shrapnel with 200 reduced charge cartridges and friction tubes.

(5) Two semaphores and one Vickers gun and one Lewis Gun.

(6) 250 rounds for 3-pounder guns.

(7) First aid equipment (including dressings and drugs).

(8) An annual allowance of 10,000 rounds ammunition for training purposes.

Your Highness will appreciate that in the existing circumstances some delay in supply is unavoidable but His Majesty's Government and the Government of India will do their best to minimise delay so far as they can.

4. I have been further instructed to require Your Highness to state clearly the scope of the security measures to be undertaken and to inform Your Highness that continued payment of the war subsidy will be conditional on their prosecution.

5. I shall be grateful if Your Highness will let me have your reply in writing confirming your acceptance as soon as possible.

Your Highness's
sincere friend,

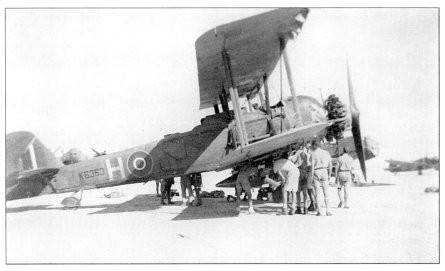

244 Squadron Aircraft.
The rugged and stately Vincent at Shaibah (Photograph: Frank Sheppard)

1940 and 1941

At the beginning of the Second World War Masirah was a backwater. Neither side had much interest in the Arabian Sea, and the first action in the area was in East Africa where the Italians were being evicted from Somaliland, Eritrea and Ethiopia in early 1941. The Aden base was crucial to this but the action was all in Africa and the Red Sea. At the same time, in April 1941, a serious incident occurred in Iraq when Rashid Ali established a pro-Axis government in Baghdad.

The previous year another Vincent squadron had been formed at Habbaniya (see Map 20). For some reason it was not given a squadron number but was known as 'S' Squadron. It was used for policing patrols and communications work around the Persian Gulf and Iraq. We will follow its fortunes because it was the only RAF squadron ever to be based at Masirah. On 18 September 1940 the Squadron moved from Habbaniya to Shaibah to take over from 84 Squadron which had re-equipped with Blenheims and was about to move to Heliopolis in Egypt. On 15 November 1940 'S' Squadron was redesignated as 244 Squadron. There were detachments further north in Iraq at Habbaniya and Mosul for reconnaissance as well as general communications. This relaxed existence was suddenly shattered by the Rashid Ali revolt. Rashid Ali, who was working with the Germans, became Prime Minister. The pro-British Regent, Emir Abdul-Ilah, fled from Baghdad.

A British battalion was brought in to Shaibah by air on 17 April 1941. It immediately moved to Basra to cover the seaborne arrival of a brigade group from India the following day. 244 Squadron at Shaibah helped secure the area against hostile Iraqi forces, but further north at Habbaniya the outlook was bleak. On 29 April a battalion flew into Habbaniya from India, increasing the number of fighting men to 2,200. Unfortunately there were also 9,000 civilians on the base which was not an operational airfield. It was a flying training school, and to reinforce the training aircraft a few Gloster Gladiators flew in from Egypt. This increased the number of aircraft at Habbaniya to eighty-two. The airfield had 7 miles of insecure perimeter fence, and by 2 May there were 9,000 Iraqi troops with artillery on the plateau overlooking the airfield. 244 Squadron flew key personnel into Habbaniya but most of its work was attacking Iraqi army units which had not withdrawn from Basra. While attacking the railway between Shaibah Junction and Ur one of the Vincents was brought down by small arms fire. Seeing this PO Wooley landed alongside and picked up the stranded crew, taking off as Iraqi troops approached. That day two other Vincents were damaged by ground fire, and another was shot down and the crew killed. Help arrived the following day with the arrival of Fairey Swordfishes of 814 Squadron of the Fleet Air Arm.

At Habbaniya hostilities began in the small hours of 2 May when Wellingtons detached to Shaibah bombed the Iraqi positions on the plateau. Out of the ten Wellingtons nine were seriously damaged with some aircrew killed. There were further determined attacks by Habbaniya-based aircraft as well as the Wellingtons from Shaibah. The Iraqis naturally replied by shelling the airfield, killing or wounding forty men and destroying twenty-two aircraft. There was no Iraqi ground assault on the airfield. Indeed, the Iraqi gunners wilted under the attacks by British aircraft. Soon the RAF was able to turn its attention to the Iraqi Air Force bases, and by the end of the campaign all of the sixty Iraqi Air Force aircraft had been destroyed. After four days of attack by the RAF, the Iraqis had had enough. On the night of 5 May they withdrew from the plateau and moved back in the general direction of Baghdad, about 55 miles to the east. They were followed up on the ground, and a reinforcing column was caught on the road and destroyed by forty aircraft from Habbaniya. More RAF fighter aircraft arrived from Egypt, and the British women and children were evacuated to Basra. On 30 May 1941 British Troops from Habbaniya reached Baghdad. They were few in number, but enough to achieve their objective. Rashid Ali fled to Iran, and a new regime was established under the Regent.

Although the British were reacting to the Rashid Ali revolt, there was a far more serious threat. The Axis powers realised that the Rashid Ali Revolt presented a golden opportunity to occupy Iraq. The Germans were keen to capture the oilfields and sever the British corridor to India. In mid-May there were German Heinkel 111 bombers and Messerschmitt 110 fighters at Mosul and Italian Fiat CR42 fighters at Kirkuk. Although these Axis aircraft did attack Habbaniya, it was all too late. The aircrew had nothing except what they stood up in. The RAF attacked their airfields and prevented any resupply by rail from Syria where there was a Vichy French government following the fall of France. The significance of the Rashid Ali revolt to Masirah will become apparent later. When hostilities finally ceased the Habbaniya training aircraft and aircrew had suffered catastrophic losses but had aquitted themselves extremely well.

Three months later, in August 1941, British and Soviet troops occupied Iran. Again, 244 Squadron played its part in this operation, its only loss being a Vincent shot down by an over-eager Hurricane pilot of 261 Squadron. In Tehran the pro-Axis Shah was evicted and spent the rest of his days in comfortable retirement in South Africa. His 22-year-old son was placed on the Peacock Throne. This secured the Iranian oil fields and provided a land link to the Soviet Union. By the end of the War five million tons of supplies had been sent to the Soviet Union up the Gulf and across Iran, a longer but safer route compared to the Arctic convoys to Archangel.

The Germans had begun to take an interest in the Indian Ocean and Arabian Sea as early as 1940. At first a few disguised merchant raiders were sent round the Cape of Good Hope. They looked like innocent merchant ships, but were armed with guns and torpedoes. Additions to the hull and extra funnels could be erected or removed overnight. Eventually there was a total of nine of them in the area, the numbers gradually building up between 1940 and 1943. They were victualled by a small number of supply ships. Altogether they sank a total of 128 Allied ships.

On 7 December 1941 the Japanese attacked Pearl Harbour, bringing the United States into the Second World War.

1942

In 1942 U-boats began to replace the merchant raiders. First the *Eisbär* (Icebear) group of four U-boats and then the *Paukenschlag* (Drum-Roll) group of five U-boats rounded the Cape with their supply ships. During 1942 the U-boats and surface raiders sank 205 Allied ships. In addition to the war supplies to the Soviet Union, the British war effort relied on oil from the northern Persian Gulf. War supplies were also shipped to India for the war in the Far East against the Japanese. This brought five Japanese submarines into the area, together with their two supply ships.

After the island of Madagascar had been taken from the Vichy French, there was a most audacious attack by the Japanese on the northern port of Diego Suarez. On 29 May 1942 a small spotter plane with floats circled the harbour, having been launched from a large Japanese submarine. The British noticed it but never suspected that it could possibly be hostile. The following evening the tanker *British Loyalty* and the battleship *Ramillies* were torpedoed in the harbour by a midget submarine. It had been brought to the area by another large Japanese submarine. The midget submarine did not escape. It was scuttled by its crew of two officers who swam ashore and made their way 12 miles north to their pick-up point. For two days they were pursued by a 15-man British patrol. The Japanese killed one of them and wounded another four before themselves being hunted down and killed. Clearly the British had to strengthen their anti-submarine operations.

The dwindling number of Vincents on 244 Squadron started shipping patrols on the approaches to Basra. In January and February a total of five aircraft were destroyed but not by enemy action. To widen the area covered by its patrols, in January 1942 the Squadron established a detachment of thirty men with eight Vincents further down the Gulf at Sharjah. An Airspeed Oxford then arrived at Sharjah. The purpose of this training aircraft was to convert the pilots to twin-engine aircraft. The first of these were three well-worn Blenheim IVs which arrived in April. The Blenheims were more effective in the anti-submarine role, and the number of Vincents continued to decline.

The Sharjah detachment continued for three months until May when the entire Squadron moved there from Shaibah. Pre-war Shaibah had the reputation of being the worst posting in the RAF, but 244 thought it preferable to Sharjah which won hands down for pure awfulness. The Squadron's patrols met no success at all, and not a single submarine was sighted until 2 October 1942 when Sergeant Chapple's crew found and bombed a U-boat. They missed. The very last operational Vincent sortie was on 28 November 1942, although this aircraft remained as a squadron hack for another couple of months.

To counter the submarine threat in the Arabian Sea, in July 1942 aircraft once again began to visit Masirah. Initially it was 203 Squadron's old flying-boat anchorage at Umm Rusays which was brought back into use for refuelling the Catalinas of 209 Squadron, which was based at Mombasa on the East African coast. Except for the derelict petrol store building no facilities had been built at Umm Rusays, and the petrol was stored in the open behind the beach. 209 Squadron simply used Umm Rusays to extend the range of its Catalinas in the hunt for submarines.

The flying-boats in this part of the World were American Consolidated Catalinas. The RAF did not have enough Sunderlands, and the Saunders-Roe Lerwick was not a success. Only twenty-one were built. The initial RAF evaluation of the Catalina in 1939 was not encouraging. It was found to be slow, underpowered, and did not meet the specification. It was suspected that it would not last long under combat conditions. However, at that time there was no alternative, so the RAF ordered an initial batch of forty and were very well satisfied. It was an inspired design. The wing-tip floats retracted to form the wing tips. The parasol wing gave the aircraft great stability in the air and allowed the two engines to be mounted close together. This very much reduced the pilot's difficulties in the event of an engine failure. However, the Pratt & Whitney engines were exceptionally reliable.

The pylon joining the wing to the fuselage was not wasted space, as the flight engineer's position was inside. Further aft on the fuselage there were very large perspex 'blisters' on each side. These afforded an excellent view outside and were the rear gunners' positions. Further aft still there was a position for a prone gunner facing backwards and firing through a hatch in the floor. There was yet another gun position in the nose ahead of the pilot. The most important crew member was considered to be the rigger/front gunner. He did not do much rigging or gunning but hooked up to the mooring cable when mooring to a buoy, which was quite important, and he was the cook, which was very important.

There were more Catalinas built than any other flying-boat in the history of aviation. They were also produced in large numbers in the Soviet Union. The Americans call their aircraft types by a sequence of letters or letters and numbers. For instance, the Catalina was the 'PBY'. The name 'Catalina' was invented by the British, who prefer names, and this name was later adopted by the US Navy. Santa Catalina is an island off Los Angeles. Due to its airborne endurance of twenty hours (twenty-four with extra fuel tanks) the Catalina had a crew of nine to man seven positions. Up to 4,000 lb of bombs or depth charges could be carried.

In December 1942 and January 1943 the Catalinas of the Canadian 413 Squadron started visiting Umm Rusays. Their main base was in Ceylon (now Sri Lanka) but they dispersed widely escorting convoys and hunting submarines and their depot ships. They used Kamaran Island which is in the Red Sea close to the Yemen coast, and Perim Island at the very south end of the Red Sea. Aden provided facilities unobtainable at other ports of call. South of Aden, on the Somaliland coast, Berbera was another refuelling base. Up the Arabian coast the Catalinas stopped at Mukalla, Raysut (a few miles west of Salalah), Mirbat, Masirah, Khor Jarama, Muscat, Dubai, and Bahrain where routine engine maintenance was carried out. Here they were entertained by British oil company employees who were completely isolated from the outside world. On the north side of the Gulf there were refuelling stations at Bandar Abbas, Jiwani and Gwadar which at that time was a possession of Muscat and Oman.

At Umm Rusays there were now mooring buoys in the bay and a couple of tents on shore for the labourers who looked after the fuel and oil which was stored in tins on the beach. There was a large rowing boat which was used for bringing the tins to the beach from the dhow when it was delivered, and for taking it from the beach to the Catalinas for refuelling. The shore party were a mile or so south of the village of Umm Rusays, where the present-day mole extends out into deep water. Some crew members slept aboard the Catalinas, officially to guard the aircraft, but unofficially to avoid spending the night on the 'depot ship'. This was His Majesty's Indian Navy Ship *Doorani* which was an ancient cockroach-infested dhow moored in the bay. The Indian crew cooked the meals, and the sleeping accommodation was below deck. The 413 Squadron Catalinas usually spent only one night at Umm Rusays before moving on.

The Rashid Ali revolt had given the British pause for thought. The air route to India and the Far East was across territory which was politically unreliable. Of more importance, the Desert War along the coast of North Africa was a series of huge advances and retreats until the final victory in September 1943. While the Mediterranean coast of Africa was occupied by enemy forces it was often impossible for British aircraft to fly the 2,000 miles from Gibraltar to Egypt. Most supplies for the North African Campaign and the Far East went by sea around the Cape of Good Hope, but there was also an air route for reinforcement aircraft. They arrived by sea at Takoradi in the Gold Coast (now Ghana) where up to 120 aircraft per month could be reassembled. From there they flew to Lagos, and then north-east up Nigeria to Ikeja, Kano and Maiduguri. The next staging post was at Fort Lamy which was just inside French Equatorial Africa (now Chad). This had been secured by Free French Forces. There was next a long leg overflying French Equatorial Africa and landing at Geneina which was just inside the Sudan. From there it was east to El Fasher and on to Wadi Halfa via Wadi Seidna. It was then plain sailing up the Nile to Cairo. Central Africa was poorly mapped and most of the staging posts were small, primitive and difficult to find. The majority of the reinforcement aircraft were destined for Egypt at this time, but those continuing to the Far East took the route across Palestine, Transjordan, Iraq and down the Gulf to Karachi.

As an alternative there was the 'Hadramaut Route' which was Cairo – Luxor – Port Sudan – Asmara – Aden – Riyan – Salalah – Masirah – Jiwani – Karachi. Short-range aircraft refuelled at intermediate landing grounds such as Kamaran Island, Shuwaymia and Ras al Hadd. The infrastructure was completed in the second half of 1942. The landing ground at Mirbat was abandoned in favour of an airfield inland of the town of Salalah, and enough accommodation was built for both the RAF and the personnel of the British Overseas Airways Corporation (BOAC), previously named Imperial Airways. There was also enough accommodation for the passengers and crew of transit aircraft who spent the night at Salalah. The Sultan of Muscat and Oman was pleased to have a permanently manned airfield near his palace at the capital of his southern province. At Masirah the Sur Masirah landing ground had not been used for some time. It was abandoned in favour of the site at the north of the island which had been marked out as an emergency landing ground in 1938.

BOAC was involved at Salalah with the provision of runways, hangars, quarters for passengers and staff, radio communications, food and water, etc. The inaugural service on the BOAC Hadramaut Route from Cairo to Karachi was started by Capt. W.R. Dunderdale in May 1942. Lockheed Lodestars

A Cairo-based Lockheed Lodestar of BOAC
(Photograph: Tony Spooner)

were used almost exclusively, and initially the schedule was only once per month. This was enough to keep the service ticking over until such time as the northern route might be denied by the enemy. Throughout its period of operation the service was never more than weekly. The passengers were VIP civilians on important government work. Early on BOAC examined the possibility of using 'C' class flying-boats, but this was quickly dismissed due to the lack of sheltered water between Aden harbour and Umm Rusays. Such a sector length (nearly 1,000 miles) would have dictated a heavy fuel load and therefore a much reduced payload. The 'C' class flying-boats were so called because each one was individually named with an initial 'C' such as Canopus and Cassiopeia. They were large four-engined aircraft from which the military Sunderland was derived.

Early in 1942 the Masirah runway was improved by the trader and contractor Khimji Ramdas. There were about 300 Baluch labourers under a single Englishman. His identity is uncertain, but he was later known as 'the Captain'. No buildings were erected except for the Captain's hut on the east side of the runway. The Captain's sole task was to lengthen and smooth the surface of the single north-south runway aligned 19/01. It was lengthened to 1,000 yards and improved by a roller crushing gypsum onto the surface. The roller was 7ft wide and 5ft high and was manually pulled by teams of Baluch. The labourers' tents, food and other equipment were brought by Khimji Ramdas by dhow. The coolie camp was halfway between the airfield and Ras Hilf, approximately where the RAF later built its bomb dump. There was a limited resupply by the BOAC schedule from Aden.

In May and June the state of the Masirah airfield was checked out by Vincents of 244 Squadron who spent the night there as guests of the Captain. They refuelled from a petrol store which had been established there. On at least one occasion a Vincent continued as far as Salalah but did not land at Khor Gharim, Shuwaymia or Mirbat. These Vincents also landed at Ras al Hadd and Bait al Falaj where the runways were also being improved. The natural surface at the Ras al Hadd airfield was soft so tarmac several inches thick was laid over the surface. This tarmac remains to the present day although somewhat ragged. The Masirah working party did not leave until about November.

In July 1942 the permanent RAF occupation of Masirah started when twelve personnel were drafted in from No. 73 Operational Training Unit in Aden. Sgt Matthews was in charge of the party which was named No. 33 Staging Post. After four months a pilot officer arrived to become the CO. His revolver enhanced the fire power of the unit. Until then the wireless operator's Lee Enfield rifle was the only protection against a landing party from an enemy submarine. At first their rations arrived on the BOAC Lodestar but later chartered dhows brought most of life's necessities including 4-gallon tins of water. Well water from Hilf was used for washing and could be used for making tea after the scum had been skimmed off. The personnel lived in tents which were located to the east of the runway. For illumination after dark they had hurricane lamps. Their diet was repetitive. Breakfast was porridge, red with weevils, followed by tinned Australian streaky bacon with perhaps a fried egg or tomato. Lunch ('Tiffin') was biscuits with bully beef or tinned Indian cheese. The evening meal was the best with the popular Maconochies tinned beef stew with ships' biscuits which could be soaked in the gravy. Initially, and during the south-west monsoon, they were able to supplement their diet with turtles' eggs. There were no vegetables.

Dhows brought petrol and oil for the transit aircraft. These were unloaded off the north beach onto a small barge towed by a seaplane tender which actually belonged to Umm Rusays. The RAF lads waded out to the barge to bring everything ashore. There was no native labour to help them. The 4-gallon tins were carried to the camp. The tins of petrol and water were identical, but the petrol tins floated in sea water. In December some of the petrol arrived in 33-gallon drums, and these also floated. The lads had to roll them up the 50 feet to the airfield. There were no vehicles of any type on the island. The first aircraft to stage through were Bisleys, coming through in groups of six. Each required 100 petrol tins to fly on to Karachi. Beauforts and Beaufighters followed later, and American DC-3 Dakotas and DC-4 Skymasters which required 800 gallons each. By this time a semi-rotary handpump had arrived and could be used for refuelling from the petrol drums.

In their few off-duty hours the RAF lads had few recreational facilities. Reading material was limited to one *Hotspur* comic and two copies of *Readers' Digest*. There was a pack of cards, a game of Ludo (for high stakes) and a gramophone with a broken spring. There was one record, 'Shine on Harvest Moon' with 'I paid for the Lie I Told' on the flip side. The gramophone turntable was driven by a propeller in the wind. One of the RAF lads had brought a chameleon from Aden. It was hobbled to prevent escape and the huge number of flies provided an ample source of food. These swarms of intrusive flies were the primary characteristic of Masirah. Their main interests seemed to be in people's eyes, noses and mouths, and these appeared to be a

The Bisley in characteristic pose at Sharjah
(Photograph: via Arthur Banks)

compelling obsession which they would pursue regardless of their own personal safety. To compensate for their hard living the RAF lads were awarded an allowance of 10 rupees per month. Toothpaste, razors etc. were issued free, and there was a weekly allowance of fifty free cigarettes. Of the original twelve RAF personnel the last to return to Aden was Eric Soar who was at Masirah for nine months. When he arrived at Aden he was told to report to the small American hospital at Sheikh Othman where the medical officer was appalled by his physical condition. His legs were covered in sores and it took some time to restore him to health. At Masirah the staging post was left with only nine personnel.

In September 244 Squadron began to extend its range by detaching some of its aircraft and crews to Masirah. The south-west monsoon had almost finished, and the change in the weather was very welcome after a most uncomfortable summer at Sharjah. It was at this time that the Blenheim Mk Vs, known as Bisleys, began to replace the Blenheim Mk IVs. This change was not welcome. These Bisleys were truly dreadful aircraft. They had been kept for some time in storage and others had been used operationally by other squadrons in North Africa. The rot had set in. The undercarriage legs were one of the main problems, and the engines were unreliable. These engines, Bristol Mercury Mk XXs, were 'lifed' at only 240 hours but there was no guarantee that they would last this long. The aircraft were overweight and underpowered so the failure of one of the engines was a serious emergency. Later the performance was improved by removing the weight of the armour plating and limiting the armament to four 100-lb depth charges. Nevertheless, the loss rate was so high that a total of fifty Bisleys were issued to the Squadron in sixteen months. It should be noted that the range of the Vincent exceeded that of the Bisley, its war load was greater (two 450-lb depth charges) and its engine was reliable.

In November a Bisley force-landed near Shaibah with engine failure. Temporary repairs were carried out, and the aircraft took-off for Habbaniya in the late afternoon of 26th November. As darkness fell the aircraft flew into a dust storm with heavy rain. The starboard engine caught fire with flames licking back over the petrol tanks in the wing. The intercom between the crew members was not working and nor was the radio receiver. Distress messages were transmitted to Habbaniya without any confirmation that they had been received. With the engine still on fire the pilot flew on, passing over the lights of several villages. Then the pilot saw two parallel lines of lights which he took to be a runway. He made an approach but realised at the last moment that it was a bridge over a river, either the Tigris or Euphrates, but being lost he did not know which. With the engine blazing the aircraft climbed to about 5000 ft for the crew to bale out before the wing structure failed. A scribbled note telling him to bale out was handed to the signaller, Jack Earnshaw, who put on his parachute and attempted to use the escape hatch on the floor. The hatch was too small and he got stuck half way out. Eventually he wriggled out and was relieved but surprised when the parachute opened. He was not so pleased when he landed in a village cesspit although it did have the advantage of breaking his fall. He was uncertain about the reception he would receive in the village following the Rashid Ali revolt of the previous year. Making good his escape he waded through irrigation ditches, climbed over walls, and walked for about an hour before seeing a light on higher ground. It was a power station. He knocked and went in. The Iraqi engineer was startled by this evil smelling apparition which appeared before him, and telephoned the police.

The police arrived in a horse drawn Landau and took him, accompanied by a large number of clammering villagers, to the local British authority. This was none other than Wing Commander Jasper Coates, who features earlier in this book. Earnshaw knocked gingerly on the door and began to explain that he was in a thoroughly unsavoury condition. Jasper cut him short with 'I don't care a fart. Just come in'. There followed a detailed interrogation followed by a shower (an Iraqi pouring buckets of cold water over him) and a change of clothes. Jasper was extremely tall and they must have been his clothes because the jacket came down to Earnshaw's knees and the trousers came up to his armpits, with Persian slippers for his feet. He was given a meal and a bed for the night. After breakfast next morning they visited the crash site and the cesspit where his parachute had been found, but Jasper took the opportunity of visiting all the police stations on the way. 'Come on Earnshaw, let's have a look at these scruffy buggers'. Earnshaw tagged along, mortified by what a prat he looked in his ill-fitting clothes. Then he travelled by road to Habbaniya where the Court of Inquiry wondered why an unqualified Leading Aircraftsman was acting as aircrew.

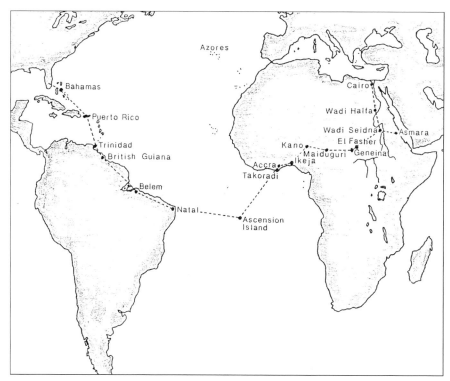

Map 9: The US Army Transport Command Route to India

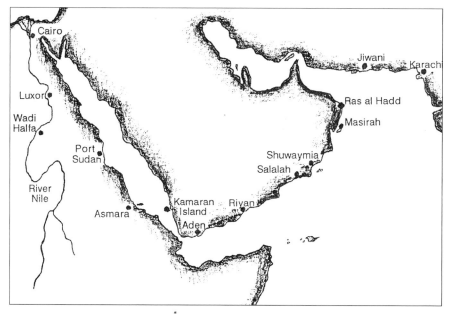

Map 10: The South Arabian Route with emergency landing grounds

1943

In January 1943 244 Squadron lost three of its Bisleys, written off due to engine and undercarriage failures. This was the month that the Blenheim Mk IVs were withdrawn and the last of the faithful old Vincents was scrapped.

At Masirah a new source of drinking water was exploited. The well water at Dawwa was pure, but it was 10 miles from the camp and no transport was available. So it was carried to the camp by the women of Dawwa. Such a menial task was below the dignity of the men. The women appeared to welcome this opportunity to escape from their cloistered existence. As the number of RAF personnel increased the need for water overtaxed the supply from Dawwa and the 4-gallon tins arriving by dhow. So a water barge was towed in and replenished every two or three weeks by shallow draft ships from the Euphrates river near Basra. Even at the beginning of the journey the water was far from pure and contained all manner of unwelcome creatures. It had to be vigorously boiled, and each man's daily ration remained one service water bottle.

Back in late 1942 American transport aircraft had begun to stage through Masirah. This resulted in additional work for the tiny RAF staging post. Starting in August 1942 the Americans began to build their own staging post which was completed by the end of the year. In February 1943 the Americans moved in and their staging post became fully operational. For the first month or so there was resentment and suspicion between the British and Americans who placed armed guards round their facilities. Thus the RAF were denied access to what they regarded as part of their own airfield. Then relationships thawed, to be replaced by firm and lasting friendships. The airfield became a link in the chain of US Army Transport Command staging posts to India, Burma and China. Most of the aircraft were C-47s (DC-3 Dakotas) and C-46s (Curtiss Commandos), but B-17s (Flying Fortresses) and B-24s (Liberators) also passed through frequently. Their route from the USA was via the Bahamas, Puerto Rico, Trinidad, British Guiana (now Guyana) and down the Brazilian coast to the easternmost point of South America. From here they crossed the Atlantic to Ascension Island where the Wideawake airfield had been built in July 1942. From there the route was to Accra in the Gold Coast (now Ghana). From Accra they joined the British ferry route across Central Africa. Reinforcement aircraft for the Soviet Union continued north to Egypt, then east to Iran. Aircraft flying to the Far East left the British ferry route in the Sudan, staging through Khartoum and Asmara to Aden. They then took the South Arabian route to Karachi and the Far East.

After the Allied victory in North Africa in September 1943 another USAAF route was across the Atlantic via the Portuguese Azores and across North Africa to Cairo.

At Masirah the Americans lived comfortably in Quonset huts. Their mess hut was air-conditioned. Fresh fruit, meat and vegetables arrived weekly, and enough films for a different 'movie' every day. The RAF lads were allowed to watch the films, bringing their empty 4-gallon tins to sit on. Variety shows passed through with famous American actors, singers and comedians; and on their way through there was a performance for the GI Joes and the RAF.

A water desalination plant was built at Ras Hilf on the north-west corner of the island. Later they built another on the slightly higher ground behind the camp. The sea water for this was piped all the way from the east coast. The helically wound pipe and the sea-water well behind the beach can still be seen. The Americans also built a concrete hardstanding for their aircraft. It measured 80 yards by 35 yards. Beneath it were buried fuel tanks for hydrant refuelling of their aircraft. A senior American officer passing through enquired about the native labour camp at the foot of the dark hills. He was told that this was the Royal Air Force camp.

The RAF buildings were constructed by the lads themselves. Their tents flapped a lot during the tearing gales of the south-west monsoon, and were rotted by the salt-laden rising sand. On concrete floors the lads built huts out of 4-gallon petrol tins filled with sand and lightly cemented together. Roofs were improvised, and doors and windows were just holes. These self-help buildings were a source of pride, the mess buildings being quite large. Later the lads built two churches. The Roman Catholic church of St Patrick and St Theresa of Lisieux took three months to build. It took 1,500 petrol tins and the altar was made from an aircraft fuel tank. For many years Masirah was known as 'Petrol Tin Island' due to these buildings.

In January 1943 the 244 Squadron detachment at Masirah was upgraded to an Advanced Flight. The Flight Commander became the Commanding Officer

A hut being constructed of sand-filled 4-gallon petrol cans
(Photograph: Keith Scott)

of Masirah, and a proper Operations Room (or, more accurately, an Operations Tent) was established for the Squadron and for the 413 Squadron Catalinas at Umm Rusays. It was at this time (January and February) that 244 Squadron began detachments at Ras al Hadd and Jask which is on the Iranian coast north of Muscat. Before the War Jask had been a staging post for KLM airliners on the route to the Dutch East Indies. 244 Squadron lost another two Bisleys through accidents in February, but one of the Ras al Hadd detachment aircraft managed to damage a Japanese submarine.

It was also at this time that an amazing machine appeared at the Masirah airfield. It looked like a steam traction engine but without any of the driving parts. The firebox was a hydroburner fed with drips of oil and water, and this iron-wheeled monster was towed around the domestic sites. It was the Steam Cleaner. Personnel put all their soiled clothes into a drum to which the steam pipe was connected. After the required length of time the steam pipe was disconnected and the clothes tipped out. Then personnel had to undress and put the rest of their clothes into the drum. After the second steam cleaning the belching juggernaut was towed away to the next site. Evidently this monster was indestructible. In 1995 it was lying on its side behind the bulk fuel tanks at Ras Hilf.

Due to the impending monsoon it was important to lay down stocks of supplies to last through the summer months. Petrol, oil, water and food were the most important bulk items. At first local dhows were used to ferry supplies ashore from the ships, but too much was stolen. It was a serious problem. So the RAF brought in a couple of flat-bottomed boats for the ship-to-shore ferrying duties. They were Eurekas, small American infantry landing craft which were very dependable.

In the November of the previous year a detachment of RAF Levies had been brought in from Iraq for local defence. The intended role of the Levies was to protect the base from attack from the sea. The Diego Suarez incident had been a warning. A landing party from a submarine or merchant raider could wreak havoc on an unarmed station. The Levies were unable to safeguard the huge quantity of stores which were being stolen by the local inhabitants. The RAF could ill afford to have the predatory islanders living nearby at Hilf. Their ringleader was Sheikh Said bin Sultan al Majala. He was expelled from the island by the Sultan. In April the Consul at Muscat arranged to burn down three native villages between Hilf and Umm Rusays. The record does not name the villages but undoubtedly Hilf was one of them because the record states that 'the burning of shacks near Ras Hilf had the salutary effect of reducing the number of flies'. Compensation was paid to the villagers. They moved to the mainland but their absence did not deprive the RAF of a workforce because they were reluctant and unenthusiastic workers. Instead the workforce was shipped in from Northern Oman. Apparently many of them were Baluch, and some of them were criminals. There were about

The Second World War steam-cleaning monster, derelict here in 1951
(Photograph: Bob Bolton)

120 of them initially, each batch staying for six to nine months. They worked in gangs of eight or nine at the disposition of the Clerk of Works. Two deep wells were dug but the water was brackish and undrinkable, although it was used for washing. The steam cleaning monster could be used to distil sea water, but it used a gallon of fuel to produce a gallon of distilled water. Pure distilled water is not good for the gut. For drinking water the RAF station was reliant mostly on the generosity of visiting ships. A flat-bottomed Eureka would tow the water barge to the ship and hold it in place while it was being filled. All drinking water was boiled and the ration was still one bottle per day per serviceman.

In April 1943 a small jetty was built just to the east of Ras Hilf, on the north beach. The station became 'RAF Masirah', and by June the strength was 22 officers and 337 other ranks. This did not include the Americans, or the Omani labour force, but did include the Baluch company of RAF Levies which numbered 120 men. The RAF CO was Squadron Leader Mackenzie who was later replaced by Squadron Leader Gus Walker, later Air Chief Marshal Sir Augustus Walker.

Details are sketchy, but it appears that the second runway was laid down at about this time. It was in a more east-west direction, being aligned 25/07. It was in use as a sand runway for the remainder of the RAF occupation, and is now a concrete runway of a generous length. In 1943 it was 1,720 yards long, and runway 19/01 had been lengthened to 1,620 yards.

In February 1943 a detachment of 212 Squadron Catalinas arrived from Korangi Creek near Karachi. They replaced the visiting Catalinas of the Canadian 413 Squadron. At first 212 Squadron sent a single aircraft to Umm Rusays, joined later by another and finally a third to bring the detachment up to full strength. By this time the dhow, HMIS *Doorani*, had become infested by rats as well as cockroaches, so the aircrew preferred to sleep on deck. Each Catalina and crew stayed about three weeks, so there was one new aircraft arriving weekly with fresh and tinned food. The tinned food seemed to consist mostly of bully beef, akin to corned beef which has never been a popular buy with Second World War veterans. Often the Indian crew would supplement the rations by fishing, and less often (by popular request) by catching turtles. The Squadron also kept a detachment at Jiwani, which is on the coast to the west of Karachi close to the Iranian border. It had sheltered water near the airfield.

The aircraft were maintained by the aircrew but the dictum was 'if it ain't broke, don't mend it'. Fortunately the aircraft were incredibly reliable in spite of the lack of maintenance, but every now and then a 'sick' aircraft had to be returned to Korangi Creek, and any sick aircrew returned in it. Water for the detachment was from the water barge at Ras Hilf, and brought down by dhow. There was just enough for drinking, but not for washing. Everybody washed in the sea using salt water soap which produced a reluctant scum. In those days before stainless steel blades, salt water reduced the life of a razor blade to a single shave. Some did not shave, and the dress code was very relaxed. When not airborne the standard dress was sandals, shorts and bush hats. The lack of rank insignia did not seem to matter very much when often the aircraft Captain was a sergeant and his co-pilot was an officer. Clothes were also

Umm Rusays 1943. His Majesty's Indian Naval Ship *Doorani* which served as living accommodation (Photograph: Masirah Scrapbook at RAF Marham)

1943. 4-gallon petrol tins being moved from the beach at Umm Rusays to the rowing boat for refuelling a 212 Sqn Catalina (Photograph: George Speer)

washed in sea water which was not entirely satisfactory because after drying they were impregnated with dried salt which was not good for the skin. As at the airfield further north (known as the 'Top Camp') the urinals were 'desert lilies'. These were 4-gallon petrol tins stuck into the sand and filled with sand. On top was another petrol tin jammed in at an angle, its bottom perforated and its top removed. The 'crappers' were excavations lined with 4-gallon tins and not noted for their privacy.

Later there was no need for a petrol store on the beach. The petrol tins were brought down by dhow from the Top Camp. The Indian Navy crew rowed the boat full of tins from the dhow to the aircraft. A row of Indians swung the tins up to the crewman who was sitting on the wing. He sat astride the refuelling funnel and poured the petrol into the tanks. There was a chamois leather in the funnel to filter out impurities and soak up any water in the petrol, which also slowed down the refuelling; 1,600 gallons of fuel was 400 petrol tins, the empties being returned ashore supposedly for eventual re-use. Refuelling was a long, hard, hot, slow process. One crew tried to speed it up by not using the chamois leather, but on the subsequent flight both engines stopped. They were both successfully restarted, but after this the chamois leather was always used.

Flying-boat bases should have, at the minimum, a flying control, a crash tender, and dinghies with engines. Umm Rusays had none of these, and there

The loaded rowing boat
(Photograph: Masirah Scrapbook at RAF Marham)

were no spare parts and no flare path available for night flying. With an airborne endurance of at least twenty hours, and operating at extreme range, the ability to take-off or land at night was highly desirable. Without a flare path the Catalinas were limited to flights of no more than about the twelve hours of daylight. One crew badly misjudged its return and arrived back at Masirah after dark. There was nowhere else to land but there was enough light to drop a stick of three flame flares across the bay. The aircraft landed alongside these, but there was little chance of finding its mooring buoy in the dark, and a greater chance of taxiing into one of the other Catalinas. After groping around in the dark, the aircraft ran aground on a sandbank. The skipper tried to gun it off at full power, but succeeded only in driving it further up the sandbank. The crew jumped into the water and tried to push the aircraft back, but this also failed. Had they succeeded there is no knowing where the aircraft would have drifted. The skipper, Sgt Jock Mathews, rightly decided to sit tight until daylight and a rising tide. Actually, he had no choice. When first light came they discovered that they were not alone on the sandbank. Also stranded was what they took to be a giant stingray. This was peered at from a safe distance, but it was probably only a harmless manta ray.

There was not much to do during any free time. Only the brave went swimming, those of a more cautious nature being mindful of stone fish, sea snakes, sharks and evidently giant stingrays. They imagined nameless horrors with claws or sharp teeth. At low tide all sorts of unappetising things could be seen on the sea bottom – red or green squashy sea cucumbers and large

Above and Below: Refuelling a 212 Squadron Catalina at Umm Rusays, 1943
(Photographs: George Speer)

worms standing vertically out of their holes and swaying around like the gorgon's hair. There were floating lumps of mottled grey gristle. Nobody knew what they were. Ashore it was possible to walk up and down the beach, but the boat was not always available. Again, those of a more nervous disposition were on the lookout for snakes, scorpions and camel spiders. The local fishermen also enjoyed an unsavoury reputation, but this was undeserved.

Contact with the rest of the human race was no more than tenuous. There was a radio watch at certain hours to receive instructions, and mission reports were dropped on the airfield at the north of the island. The paper was stuffed

Above and Below: 212 Squadron Catalinas at Umm Rusays, 1943
(Photographs: Masirah Scrapbook at RAF Marham)

into an empty food tin and thrown out of the blister as close as possible to the Operations Tent. This entailed some spectacular low flying. The crews became very proficient, and one crew claimed its tin bounced into the tent and ended up on the ops officer's desk. The tent must have flapped about a bit; it required a steady nerve to be a Masirah ops officer. Later a field telephone line was laid between the two bases, but of course the inevitable happened – the islanders found the telephone wire ideal for fishing. On one occasion an enterprising islander tried to sell a large roll of telephone line to the RAF.

On 10 May a visiting 240 Squadron Catalina was damaged during a difficult take-off in rough weather. A wing-tip float was torn off when it smashed into a wave. The aircraft would probably have been lost if that wing-tip had dipped into the sea. With considerable skill the skipper managed to keep the wings level while turning the aircraft towards Umm Rusays and driving it up onto the beach. A repair team was brought in from RAF Drigh Road at Karachi and most of the crew returned to their base in Madras.

At Umm Rusays on 8 June Catalina FP 175 of 212 Squadron was detailed for an anti-submarine patrol. Some activity had been reported about 150 miles south-east of Masirah. At a little after midday the crew spotted a lifeboat containing sixteen people. By 8 June there is no doubt that the south-west monsoon had started, but nevertheless the Captain of the aircraft, Sgt John Gallagher, radioed Korangi Creek for permission to land in the open sea. Korangi Creek unwisely acquiesced to this request. Before landing the crew attempted to jettison the aircraft's six depth charges. Three of the five which fell off exploded in the sea, which they should not have done as they should have been safe. In spite of trying everything the sixth depth charge refused to fall off the aircraft. The Captain imprudently decided to risk the landing anyway. The sea was rougher than it appeared, and on the roundout to land the aircraft's nose was smashed in by a large wave. The aircraft began to sink. The crew took to the dinghies and paddled away as quickly as possible, conscious that there was a 50:50 chance that the hung-up depth charge would explode when it reached the prescribed depth. They were lucky. It did not. After about an hour they reached the ship's lifeboat and linked up with it. Its occupants were Americans from the ship *Montana* which had been torpedoed three days earlier. Now, instead of sixteen survivors there were twenty-five. The next day a US Army Air Corps DC-3 flew over and saw the Very light which was fired from the lifeboat. At dusk a Catalina of 191 Squadron, also based at Korangi Creek, arrived and dropped some supplies and a map which gave their position as only 50 miles from Masirah. The ship's navigator and the Catalina's navigator conferred and set course for the island.

Early the following morning the ship's lifeboat hoisted its sail. No aircraft were seen all day, but land was sighted in the distance that afternoon. At sunset when they were nearing the coast a 212 Squadron Catalina arrived and stayed in the area until all were safely ashore. It dropped some more supplies and a message that they would have to wait until the next day to be picked up. Their landfall appears to have been only about three miles from the south point of Masirah on the ocean side. This is the south end of a long sandy beach which is a favourite habitat for ghost crabs. These are light yellow, of insubstantial physique, and live in burrows above the high-tide mark. At dusk they appear en masse as a seething carpet, particularly if any unusual activity might suggest the arrival of food.

That night the ghost crabs conducted their usual reign of terror, playing 'grandmother's footsteps' with the exhausted survivors. The game is to stalk close enough to try an investigative nip. The irate response sends them scuttling back to their burrows. When all is quiet again they re-emerge and begin another cautious advance. The survivors had little sleep that night. When dawn broke Masirah had never looked so good. All were alive and safe. The sailors had been in their lifeboat for five days. Howard Price, one of the Catalina crew, had been on his first operational sortie. He had 29 flying hours and 56 hours in a rubber dinghy.

The trucks arrived from the Top Camp at about 11 a.m. The Catalina crew were dropped off at Umm Rusays where they were examined by an RAF doctor from the airfield. He treated them for sunburn and minor cuts and bruises. The next day they were flown back to Korangi Creek and given two weeks survivors' leave. The sailors were taken back to the Top Camp and flown to Karachi in an American transport aircraft. It was at this time that the RAF lads built the memorial to the SS *Baron Innerdale*. No doubt they told the American sailors what happened the last time a lifeboat made a landfall at Masirah.

There was another lifeboat full of survivors from the *Montana* which was found by a 244 Squadron Bisley and escorted to Ras Hilf by one of the Eureka craft.

While all this was happening, on 9 June, a Bisley force-landed on a sandbar between Umm Rusays and Shaghpah Island. It was visible until the cyclone of 13 June 1977 but its engines were removed by an RAF expedition in 1974. One of the engines can still be seen a few miles south of the airfield, just outside the boundary fence of the BERS HF site.

Later in June 1943 another 244 Squadron Bisley crashlanded on the sand close to the monument to the north-east of the airfield. The observer, Flight Sergeant Symons, was killed but the pilot and navigator survived. The wreck of the aircraft was a landmark for some years after the end of the War. The worst Bisley accident was in August 1943. The aircraft was taking off on runway 07 when one of its engines failed. It crashed in the rocky overshoot area and its depth charges exploded. All were killed, Sergeant Nash (the pilot) and his crew, Sergeants Keir and Sublet.

Another two Bisleys were destroyed when an 8 Squadron Wellington from Aden landed at Masirah without wheelbrakes. At the end of the landing run it left the runway and ran into the two Bisleys. All three aircraft were damaged beyond repair. An American B-17 Flying Fortress was lost when it came down in the Masirah Channel to the west of the airfield. It was reputed to contain a fortune in Chinese bank notes.

In June 1943 another group of German U-boats, the Monsoon Group, left for the Indian Ocean There were eleven operational U-boats plus two which were 'milch cows'. Seven of them were sunk en route in the Atlantic in the first month, mostly by American escort aircraft carriers and land-based aircraft at Ascension Island. At the same time another four supply ships for the U-boats

A 244 Squadron Bisley in shallow water opposite Umm Rasays
(Photograph: Jim Drew via Arthur Banks)

were sent to the Indian Ocean. They contained fuel, ammunition, torpedoes, food and water, etc. If a rendezvous was not possible for any reason the U-boats had to go to Penang Island for replenishment. This was an Imperial Japanese Naval Base on the west coast of Malaya. After months in a U-boat, rest and recreation in Malaya must have been paradise. But the Japanese were unsmiling, unwelcoming and very formal. The Germans thoroughly disliked them. Much later in the war U-boats returning from the Far East carried war supplies as ballast in the keel. They were vital to Germany's war effort and included tin, wolfram, manganese, raw iodine and latex rubber.

Also in June there was a most audacious rendezvous between the supply ship *Charlotte Schliemann* and no fewer than six U-boats in the Indian Ocean. There was a luncheon aboard the *Charlotte Schliemann* for the six U-boat captains, all of them holders of the Knight's Cross. One of them had sunk forty-seven allied ships. The U-boat crews were able to have showers, beer, and stretch their legs on deck.

Muscat harbour is enclosed by a crab's claw of hills on both sides, but on the eastern side there is a narrow and shallow gap. On 28 June the Norwegian ammunition ship *SS Dahpu* was at anchor in Muscat harbour, and the Captain was taking leave of the British Consul when he heard a huge explosion. Looking round he saw his ship blow up. Bits of the ship rained down on the town, and the anchor chain can still be seen wrapped round a rock on the eastern side of the inlet. A Japanese midget submarine had fired a torpedo through the gap. For many years the ship's bell hung in the Embassy courtyard.

At this time, before the Allied victory in North Africa, the Suez Canal was not in use. Allied shipping had to round the Cape of Good Hope. The U-boats and Japanese submarines were thinly spread around the Indian Ocean, and the Catalina squadrons were also thinly spread around the periphery in a giant semi-circle from South Africa, East Africa, Arabia, India and Ceylon (now Sri Lanka).

Also in June the 212 Squadron detachment was withdrawn due to the south-west monsoon. The small working party from Drigh Road was left behind to repair the damaged Catalina of 240 Squadron, together with three of the crew. By this time there was a seaplane tender and a building made of concrete blocks. The Indian Navy dhow *Doorani* had departed a few weeks earlier. It was a lonely and uncomfortable summer for them at Umm Rusays. They had a native cook and a light truck to bring their supplies from the Top Camp. The Catalina did not finally leave until the end of September, 4½ months after it lost its wing-tip float. The repair team were glad to leave Masirah, and the three crew members were very happy to return to their base at Redhills Lake in Madras in South India.

Another Catalina squadron which had detachments at Masirah was 321 Squadron. Originally it was a squadron of the Royal Netherlands Navy in the Dutch East Indies. During the Japanese advance the aircraft were hidden in mountain lakes in the interior of the island of Java. Their orders were to evacuate senior colonial and military staff. Four of the Catalinas flew non-stop to Ceylon, one of them force-landing in a lagoon. Nine of them flew to Australia where four of them were destroyed by Japanese Zero fighters at Broome. The five which survived flew an amazing 3,000 miles non-stop to Ceylon. Here they were all reformed into No. 321 (Dutch) Squadron of the RAF, but allowed to retain Dutch national markings. All aircrew and ground-crew were Dutch including some KLM engineers who managed to join the Squadron. Eventually it became a very large squadron with twenty aircraft, almost all of them being the amphibious version. At the beginning of 1943 part of the Squadron was detached to three ports in South Africa because of the increasing U-boat menace there. In September 1943 the Mediterranean and the Suez Canal were once again available to Allied shipping, so the U-boats moved north into the Arabian Sea. The 321 Squadron detachment followed them north, basing itself at the desolate island of Socotra.

In September the following signal arrived at the Top Camp: 'Arrange to accept max number of amphibious Catalinas to be based Masirah. If necessary withdraw Bisleys to Ras al Hadd or Jask.' This caused some consternation but in the event only one amphibious Catalina arrived during September. Another arrived in mid-October. The Bisleys stayed at the Top Camp. At Umm Rusays two 259 Squadron Catalinas arrived from Dar-es-Salaam in East Africa and so did a non-amphibious Catalina of the Dutch Squadron.

During the summer monsoon the mooring buoys had deteriorated and the seaplane tender had broken free from its moorings. It had drifted off to the mainland coast where it was found and stripped by local fishermen. Another seaplane tender, 447, was sent from Basra to undertake the repairs to the buoys. It reached Ras al Hadd on 13 September. The south-west monsoon still persisted and four times the tender set out for Masirah and four times it had to turn back. It finally reached Umm Rusays on 6 October battered and leaking badly. By this time a rickety jetty had been built and there were a few more concrete block buildings including a large mess and cookhouse. The coolie labour force slept in the smaller buildings but the Europeans preferred to sleep in tents. Apart from the Catalina crews there was a section of RAF Regiment for protection and also the crew of the seaplane tender. Towards the end of October another seaplane tender, No. 211, arrived as deck cargo together with a powered dinghy and a lifeboat. The following month a bomb scow arrived together with a fourth Catalina, this time from 209 Squadron.

There were now too many people at Umm Rusays: 20 officers, 51 senior NCOs and 70 other ranks, while up at the Top Camp there were 51 officers, 116 senior NCOs and 476 other ranks. In addition there were 120 soldiers of the RAF Levies. The number of coolies had increased from 120 to 450. The big influx occurred after the end of the monsoon.

A more substantial jetty made of wood was constructed to the south of Ras Hilf, a little further south than subsequent jetties. It was decided that a narrow gauge railway would be a convenient method of bringing supplies and fuel from the jetty to the airfield. On 27 October two Decauville locomotives arrived from the USA together with twelve wagons and 7 miles of 2-ft gauge railway track. Initially the construction of the railway was under the direction of a Polish prince by the name of Lieutenant Poniatowski who had previously constructed railways in South America. The prince left Masirah after only a few months and was replaced by Captain Glendinning from one of the Indian railways. The ship bringing the railway also contained five lorries, 200 live sheep, 200 tons of cement, stores, fodder, rations and fresh water in a barge which it had towed from Basra. This barge stayed at Masirah because the original one had deteriorated during the monsoon.

There were small wooden barges for unloading ships, but they leaked because they had not been properly tarred. So the new water barge had to be used for bringing supplies from ship to shore.

Dhows bringing the coolie labour had called in at Sur where there was a smallpox epidemic, and twelve of the coolies caught smallpox although none of them died. Eighty of them had already had smallpox and these were put to work nursing the sick and laying the railway track. Aden was unable to supply enough serum for everybody, but the shortfall was made good by the Americans. The Medical Officer quarantined the coolies who had not had smallpox and had their clothes burnt. For the rest of their time at Masirah they wore sackcloth.

There were five flying-boats at Umm Rusays after the monsoon. At the Top

Camp there were three Dutch amphibians and a fourth by December in addition to the 244 Squadron detachment. The Americans used 66,730 gallons of petrol during September alone. Consumption exceeded resupply. The problem was compounded by theft and leaking 4-gallon tins. This caused a deficiency of 252,000 gallons of 100-octane and 98,000 of 90-octane aviation gasoline. At Jask and Ras al Hadd there was plenty of petrol and tons of oil. As a short-term measure 856 tons of petrol were moved by dhow to Masirah from Ras al Hadd, and 280 tons of petrol and 54 tons of oil from East Africa. At the end of October the island's petrol stock was down to one week's usage, 110,000 gallons having been used that month.

Enter the good ship *Tinombo* – without it Masirah would not have been able to operate. She had arrived out of the blue from the Dutch East Indies, and the large bearded Dutchman who commanded her merely said that he wanted to get closer to the War. She brought aviation fuel in 4-gallon tins, about 40 per cent of them leaking to some extent. These were stacked on railway sleepers which were laid on top of depth charges. A more lethal cargo is difficult to imagine. Later, when the loss from 4-gallon tins was recognised as unacceptable, the fuel arrived in 33-gallon drums, which did not leak. If the sea was calm these could be thrown off the *Tinombo*. They floated and could be pulled ashore by a rope between two Eurekas. Later the fuel drum size was increased to the normal 44 gallons, the ubiquitous 'burmail' which is still in common use today. The Arabs think that the word 'burmail' is an English word and the British think that it is an Arabic word. It probably derives from the name 'Burma Oil' written on the drums in those days.

The lighter items and personnel were brought to the island by the RAF Habbaniya Communications Flight. The aircraft used were Hudsons, Wellingtons, the archaic Bristol Bombay, and on one occasion the Americans were amazed to witness the arrival of a Vickers Valentia. This ancient biplane was almost hovering as it made its approach to land against a 40-knot headwind during the south-west monsoon.

Although newcomers arrived regularly it became apparent that no personnel were leaving at the end of their authorised time, which caused increasing discontent towards the end of 1943, although the word 'mutiny' was never used.

In addition to the one bottle of fresh water per person per day there was also a ration of a bottle of beer per week. Cordial too was available in the mess to help with the fluid intake. Food was monotonous. Mostly it was tins of Maconochies beef stew and vegetable (M & V). In addition there was soya link sausage, powdered egg, bully beef, ship's biscuits and bread. Local fish was popular but there were not enough local fishermen to satisfy the demand. The Armament Officer helped by fishing with 1¼-lb depth-charge primers thrown out of a ship's lifeboat. RAF auditors queried why the consumption of primers exceeded the consumption of depth charges, but the armoury's goat was able to dispose of such unwanted paperwork.

At one time there were several ships' lifeboats available. One of them was from the *Montana* and others came from a liberty ship which had been torpedoed 30 miles south of the island. There had been no radio distress call so the arrival of the lifeboats at the Top Camp was a surprise. The ship was later spotted from the air, listing slightly and drifting in a busy shipping lane. Apparently it had a refrigerator full of frozen duck which was there for the taking, but there were no high-speed launches which could be used to reach the ship before the ducks thawed out. The Navy sank the wreck a week later. The Medical Officer took one of the lifeboats out for a trip. He ran out of fuel and drifted over to the mainland. To teach him a lesson the CO left him there overnight. He was rescued the following day but his lifeboat had been seriously holed and was abandoned on the mainland coast.

Occasionally lobster-sized crayfish were produced by local fisherman once they had realised that, for some perverse reason, the *Nazranis* (Christians) regarded them as a delicacy. Seagulls' eggs were sometimes found, and during the summer months a prodigious quantity of turtles' eggs could be found under the sands of the beach on the ocean coast. These were laid by large loggerhead turtles which would come ashore at night, excavate a deep hole with their rear flippers, and lay about 100 eggs each. The islanders ate them, and the RAF tried them too. The eggs were the size of large table tennis balls, but the white shells were soft and leathery. No matter how long or hard they were cooked the whites never set but remained a clear viscous fluid. The yokes tasted like a chicken's egg but were a little coarser in texture. There was no taste or smell of fishiness so the CO thought it a good idea to try it out in the Airmen's Mess as an alternative. The whites were separated from the yokes which were mixed with a little powdered milk and chopped onions. This was scrambled and proved very popular until the airmen were told what they had eaten. The islanders also ate the loggerhead turtles when they came ashore to lay eggs, turning them onto their backs and cutting their throats in the Islamic fashion. There were one or two occasions when the RAF thought that they would try this ready source of meat, but it was disgusting, and so was turtle soup. The reason was that loggerhead turtles are omnivores and not edible. The only edible turtle is the vegetarian green turtle.

The Catalinas and Bisleys were used for anti-submarine patrols, and for convoy escort which was the most productive use of the aircraft. Ships were not sunk when escorted by aircraft. Searching for a submarine was like looking for a needle in a haystack. But on 17 October 1943 244 Squadron was lucky. Sergeant Pilot L. Chapman was flying a Bisley from the main squadron base at Sharjah. He was letting down through a thin layer of cloud over the Gulf of Oman near Shinas when he spotted a submarine on the surface 4 miles ahead. It was the U-533 which was one of the two larger Type IXD2 U-boats of the Monsoon Group. The aircraft was ideally placed for a diving head-on attack, and Sgt Chapman carried this out perfectly. The

U-boat quickly submerged but there was still a short length of its stern above the water as the Bisley approached. All four depth charges were dropped, bow to stern, and two were seen to fall in the swirl. After about five minutes an oil patch appeared on the surface followed by air bubbles and a few white objects. The pilot also thought that he saw a survivor but this could not be reported at the time due to the aircraft's radio failure. There was only one survivor. He and one other crew member were in the conning tower when the U-boat dived. The survivor was a young, tall, blond seaman by the name of Günther Schmidt. He was picked up by the Royal Navy and landed at Sharjah where he was handsomely entertained by the Squadron. Squadron morale soared and the official record states:

> The known presence of the enemy – more indeed, the actual presence in the camp of a real German prisoner – has been a spur to the efforts of air and ground crews enabling us to realise that we really are taking part in the same war as others.

No doubt the German felt ambivalent about the celebrations he had joined, with his fifty-two comrades dead. One account states that the German swam 28 miles to reach the coast. This is almost unbelievable, but perhaps he did and was later picked up from the beach by the Royal Navy. On subsequent interrogation Schmidt said that they had been depth-charged for a whole night by a destroyer during the outward passage. The U-boat had been seriously damaged and it had been a harrowing experience for the crew. He said that many members of the crew had no U-boat training before joining U-533. He also said that landing parties were able to come ashore on the Arabian coast and were even able to make local purchases there.

A few days after the sinking of U-533, on 26 October, Flight Sergeants Frank Moseley (pilot) and Mark Rowland (navigator) with Warrant Officer 'Palmi' Palmerson (wireless operator) left Masirah at dawn in Bisley BB 154. Their task was to give protection to a convoy 70 miles south-east of Ras al Hadd. The convoy included a precious ship load of water for Masirah. They were flying at only 1,000 ft when the oil pressure of the left engine began to drop. Frank Moseley's diary, written at the time, reads as follows:

> Start climbing pronto. Palmi sends a WJR3. After climbing from 1000 to 3000 feet the port engine gives a series of sickening bangs which shake the whole kite. Being dead scared of a fire breaking out I throttle back and switch off the engine in a hurry – none too soon either for with a dull thud, and Mark looking very worried, the engine seizes up altogether. Palmi sends a WJR1. I drop the depth charges and attempt to jettison the outer tanks. However, there must be something wrong with the system because the fuel gauge still reads 'tanks full'.

I open up the starboard engine as much as I possibly dare (to +4 boost and 2350 rpm) but still unable to maintain height – coming down at 200 feet per minute. Palmi piles on the WJRs. For a time it seems as though we will have to ditch and hope for air-sea rescue from Masirah (100 miles away).

Lower and lower we get but thankfully reach the coast after what seemed like years with 2300 feet still on the altimeter. I turn right for Ras al Hadd. The starboard engine is heating up terribly with all the gauges easily surpassing their maximum permissable readings (oil temperature over 100°C). Mark is all for attempting to lob down in the desert and hoping to walk the 30 odd miles to Ras al Hadd. The mountain arabs are reputed to be none too friendly though. Then comes a last effort to cross the low range of rocks to Ras al Hadd. Up to +5 and 2400 rpm with the engine nearly vibrating out of its sockets. Still dropping like a stone.

Within sight of the short runway at about 600 feet. Short runway, downwind, no flaps (hydraulics U/S with the port engine). I see now that I should have done a belly landing. However Mark jettisons the escape hatch and I try to be clever, firing the wheels down with the cartridge. Result – fairly good approach – touching down about halfway along the runway – wizard smooth wheeler – Palmi thought we had made it, and undid his straps. As we run along the runway I realise we can never stop, and we don't stop for a few seconds either.

Then the kite leaves the end of the runway and leaps with one bound into the sea. There was no time to think about anything at all. My next impression was of being surrounded by water and unable to move an inch. I remember quite clearly struggling for a while and then thinking quite casually and without worrying much, that this was a hell of a way to pass out. Then it suddenly dawned on me that I had not undone my safety harness. The next thing I know I was bobbing up to the surface and viewing the scene.

The kite had hit the sea and the undercarriage legs submerged in the waves. The kite had nosed under, completed a half somersault and stopped upside down in the sea. It lay now completely submerged except for the tail and part of the wing with a few air bubbles gurgling from the cockpit. Suddenly Palmi emerges from the other side and a little later Mark pops up. He was semi concussed and had not realised that the escape hatch was underneath him until he fell through it.

Luckily we had scarcely a scratch between us. As we started swimming for the shore the first thing we saw was Sam Vesey, wearing nothing but a pipe, followed by about 20 others coming to the rescue.

Strange to say the C.O. congratulated me for getting the kite back to land. There had been supreme panic at Masirah with WJRs pouring into Signals for an hour. Palmi did well getting them through.

The crew remained at Ras al Hadd for about four days before returning to Masirah. The wrecked aircraft was dragged ashore by ropes and the big end

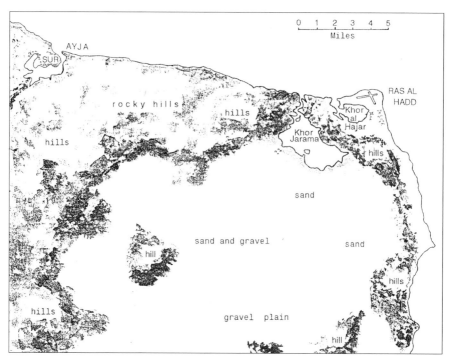

Map II: The Eastern Tip of Arabia

on the left engine was found to be seized up. The aircraft remained there for over 30 years.

Frank Moseley's diary is more like an illustrated album with photographs and maps. One map shows three blue circles which he is unable to explain. They circle Khor Gharim, Shuwaymia and Mirbat which had evidently been retained as emergency landing grounds. There is some evidence to suggest that the blockhouse at Shuwaymia contained a stock of 4-gallon tins of petrol.

Another extract from nineteen-year-old Frank Moseley's diary sheds further light on the activities of the Squadron at this time. Twelve of the aircrew, including Mark Rowland and the Canadian Palmi Palmerson, were taken from Sharjah to Bandar Abbas on the Iranian coast to the north of the Straits of Hormuz. The diary relates:

> The garry from camp took us to Sharjah village, down to the creek past beached dhows and filthy hovels where we absorbed a greater variety of odours than I knew existed. We piled into an arab punt which took us across the narrow waters of the shallow creek. On the far side we jumped out and walked past more hovels on the sand bar down to the sea where an arab boat was waiting. A couple of Arabs rowed us out to the *Tosiri*, an 800 ton Dutch East Indies coaster which was to be our transport. Funny way these Arabs row, sometimes backwards and sometimes sitting on the side of the

boat, all the time keeping up a mournful chant, or else talking to each other at a tremendous rate.

The purpose of the trip was to attend a convoy briefing at Bandar Abbas, and also to eat as much as possible in the time available. Sharjah nosh was awful. It took 17 hours sailing to reach the convoy mustering point in the Clarence Strait, and we didn't arrive until the morning of the following day. It was rather warm here, Bandar Abbas being cut off from winds by great mountains. Visibility was good and the islands of Qishm and Hormuz were quite distinct, whilst the small Persian port of Bandar Abbas appeared due north. It looked much like Sharjah from this distance. Only a few miles inland the desert became vertical, soaring to the rocky summit of Kuh Ginau (7,700 feet), appearing from where we were to rise from nothing in a terrific elliptical sweep. Other giant peaks reared to right and left to 8,000 and 6,000 feet respectively, whilst the 10,100-foot summit of Furgan was visible behind, and all a perfection of desolation.

We pulled alongside the *Alonia* where the conference was held, with the masters of all the freighters and tankers in the convoy attending the briefing. The *Alonia* was the naval base ship (14,000 tons) and contained all the stores etc. It was revealed that three Japanese submarines were known to be operating quite close to our area. Then we went back to the *Tosiri* again to partake of another great meal. We really did stoke up, all this good food just for the eating.

We left Bandar Abbas and passed between the rocky barren islands of Qishm and Larak on our way to Khor Quwai where we were to drop some passengers at the naval shore station on Goat Island. This is south of the Straits of Hormuz on the northernmost point of the peninsula on the arab side. At about 5 pm we arrived, passing between the rock bound island and the rock bound mainland, which formed the harbour. After dropping off the passengers we passed on down the channel which became narrower. The cliffs on either side also became higher and more precipitous, the mountains of the northern Hajar rising beyond. It was dark and almost full moon when we passed out of the channel and headed towards Sheikh Masud, the cliffs under a ghostly illumination flanking either side of the exit, and the cape and mountains forming a gloomy skyline. Arabian Nights!!!! The following morning we were back at Sharjah having again eaten well and not looking forward to the food to come. No fault of the cookhouse, just supplies. We left the *Tosiri* on the RAF launch. The crew of the *Tosiri* were British and Dutch officers and Javanese hands, waiters, etc. Benny, our friend the chef, has his home in Batavia and is pretty good on the guitar.

We had to cross the creek again on an arab punt, and found that since we left a goat had died. It was beginning to get rather high. Its owners, having turfed it out of the parlour, seemed to be leaving it at that. Still, the dead goat smell blended perfectly with the numerous other distinctive odours.

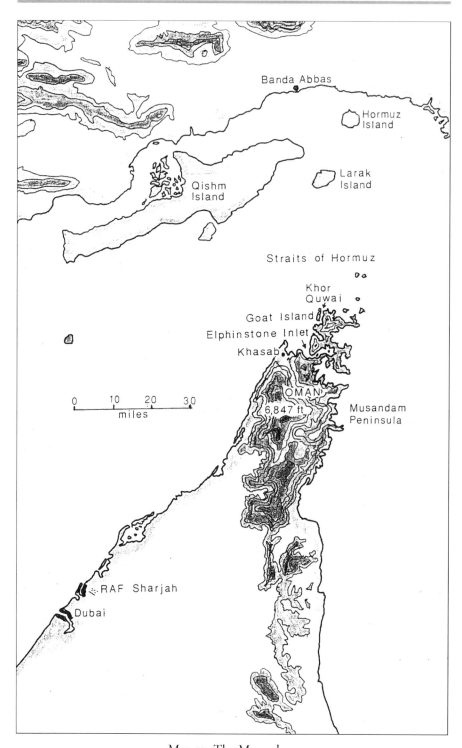

Map 12: The Musandam

Back at Masirah the stock of petrol gradually increased, and by November was up to two weeks' usage. This was still a wafer-thin margin. The sheer number of empty petrol tins and drums was also causing logistical problems. A ship full of them was torpedoed and could not be sunk. It drifted through busy shipping lanes until some enterprising skipper took it in tow to claim salvage at Aden. At the Top Camp the railway sidings were not only for dispersing the stock of fuel, but also for huge dumps of 'empties'. The locals used some of the 33-gallon drums as building material. At Umm Rusays the empty 4-gallon tins were no longer returned to the Top Camp, but after refuelling they were punctured and thrown off the Catalinas one by one. In single file they floated off, taking up the mean direction of the tidal stream and the wind before disappearing below the waves.

At Umm Rusays the living conditions were even more primitive than the Top Camp. Drinking water from the barge at the Top Camp was also rationed to a bottle per day. There were unsuccessful attempts at well digging, so acceptably fresh water was taken from the wells at Dawwa and Sur Masirah. An improvised shower was rigged from an empty fuel tin with small holes pierced in the base. Sometimes clothes were washed in petrol, using the fuel left in the old rusty tins which had leaked some of their contents. The dhow from the Top Camp was now bringing 33-gallon drums instead of 4-gallon tins. The converted bomb scow used for refuelling could carry only seven drums at a time and required three trips compared to the single trip normally required using 4-gallon tins. At low tide it was not possible to refuel because the water was so shallow. December 1943 was a very slack month for operational flying, which was fortunate in view of the shortage of petrol. There was only the occasional short trip 'to keep the barnacles off the bottom'.

The field kitchen at Umm Rusays was primitive. For cooking there was a sloping channel down which ran a drip feed of oil. This was ignited by the cautious addition of a little petrol. A drip of water on to the oil fire made it flare up. For sport there was one football and two complete sets of hockey sticks and balls. Later 'softball' became popular. This was a game like rounders or baseball. Living conditions deteriorated on 15 December when storm clouds gathered and a third of an inch of rain fell. The roofs leaked, and so did the tents. The track to the Top Camp became dangerously boggy in parts, and the sides of the shallow wadis became little cliffs. Even before the rain the official record at the Top Camp noted: 'The condition of both runways leaves much to be desired.' After the rain the airfield became unusable for a week or so, and the petrol-tin buildings were only a little more rain-proof than the buildings at Umm Rusays. A huge number of petrol tins had rusted and 91,000 gallons was written off.

Dropping things into the sea is one of the hazards of working on flying-boats, and plug spanners littered the sea bed at Umm Rusays. Eventually there was only one left on the island, the property of the United States Air Transport

Umm Rusays – a game of softball in the evening
(Photograph: George Chambers)

Command. In December it fell into the sea from one of the 265 Squadron Catalinas – December 1943 was not a good month.

Then very early on Christmas Eve the Operations Tent at the Top Camp received a radio message from a ship named the *River Raisin*. She was north-east of Masirah in the Gulf of Oman and being pursued by a submarine. A Dutch amphibian of 321 Squadron and a 265 Squadron Catalina took off to fly to the given position. Neither aircraft could find either the ship or the submarine. Then the pilot of a US Air Transport Command aircraft picked up an SOS from a ship 200 miles south-west of Masirah in the direction of Salalah. Another Dutch amphibian left to investigate this, but again nothing was found. On Christmas Day another Catalina of 265 Squadron took off at 02.20. It was flown by Flying Officer Robin who had sunk U-197 south of Madagascar the previous August. Two hours later another Catalina took off from Umm Rusays, this time a 209 Squadron aircraft. At some stage the Top Camp received a message that the *River Raisin* had been sunk, but the search had to continue for survivors. The telephone line to Umm Rusays had deteriorated and communication was very difficult. The original pair from 265 and 321 Squadrons joined the search. These were seventeen-hour flights, and all fruitless. Christmas festivities were seriously interrupted. The mess at Umm Rusays had been tastefully decorated with stars cut from petrol tins, improvised paper chains and palm leaves from the only palm tree within sight. Due to the flying task only one officer was available for serving the men's Christmas Dinner, so the senior NCOs helped out. The last Catalina did not land at Umm Rusays until 20.30 on Christmas Day. It was arranged that the officers should go to the Top Camp for their Christmas festivities on the evening of Boxing Day, dining with the other RAF, Dutch and American officers.

The *River Raisin*'s first signal never reached Masirah. At 10.30 a.m. on Christmas Eve she reported that she had twice sighted the submarine which had so far fired one torpedo which had narrowly missed. She was continuing on course but using evasive steering. It was subsequently revealed that the *River Raisin* was not sunk and survived the War. This was indeed fortunate for the crew because the submarine was the Japanese I-26. Japanese submarines always machine-gunned survivors, and none were left alive. The Germans did not do this, and sometimes gave assistance to survivors.

There was yet another drama on that busy Christmas Day. An American merchantman was torpedoed close to Masirah and the crew took to the lifeboat. Fortunately the sea was calm so seaplane tender 447 was sent to pick up the survivors. The lifeboat was led back to Umm Rusays where it remained for some months and was used for ferrying Catalina crews to and from the shore.

1944

Apart from the *River Raisin* incident the closing months of 1943 had not provided much business for the Catalina detachments at Umm Rusays. Elsewhere a large operation was planned, so most of the Catalinas departed. Some remained due to the very poor serviceability of the Bisleys at the Top Camp, and because the Dutch detachment had decreased to only two amphibians.

Back in England the 'Ultra' team at Bletchley Park had cracked the code of the German 'Enigma' machines, and it was vital that the Germans did not realise that their classified signals were compromised. For this reason German classified information was used only sparingly for the most important operations. One of these was the destruction of the notorious German supply ship, the *Charlotte Schliemann*, during a rendezvous with U-boats. Seven naval vessels and a dozen Catalinas from East Africa were earmarked for this large operation, which was not straightforward. There were alternative dates and positions, and a cyclone caused extra difficulties. The *Charlotte Schliemann* was eventually located by a 259 Squadron Catalina in the southern Indian Ocean, and then sunk by the destroyer HMS *Relentless* in the early hours of 12 February. A short time later the German supply ship *Brake* was also sunk. The loss of these two ships was a body blow to the German U-boat offensive in the area.

Also in February 1944 it appeared likely that Sergeant Weale at Masirah had contracted smallpox, so it was important to remove him from Masirah as soon as possible and take him to the hospital at Aden. Frank Moseley was detailed to take him in Bisley BA 408, together with Palmi and Dicky Larcombe who was another pilot on 244 Squadron. Mark Rowland was away at a commissioning board at Habbaniya, and Dicky Larcombe was to fly a Fairchild Argus back from Aden for use by the Squadron. The Argus was a small high-wing communications aircraft with three seats which was supplied from the USA under the Lend-Lease agreement.

On the first day the Bisley had to return to Masirah with generator failure. Quoting from Frank Moseley's diary:

The second day we started again, past Cape Madraka and the deep bays thereabouts, past the Kuria Muria islands, rocky barren and lifeless, past Mirbat and to Salalah where we landed and refuelled. Salalah airfield is two or three miles inland between the coastal village and the mountains which are about 3000 feet high. At the airfield there is a small RAF camp which seems quite pleasant with few flies. When we took-off again the starboard engine cut several times in rapid succession accompanied by terrific bangs. This somewhat worried us so we landed again. The fitters cleaned up a few things and said 'Right, that'll be OK'. Just about then, before we could decide whether we were still worried, a fusillade of gunfire came from the direction of the arab village. This sounded interesting and we learnt later that it had been quite exciting. We were told that the Sultan of Muscat and Oman had been inspecting his guard at his palace there when suddenly some of them upped their rifles and had a go at him. The guard captain threw himself in front of the Sultan and was killed. But the Sultan survived. What happened after that I know not.

After that we forgot about the ropy kite and took-off for Aden. We went across the sea to the rocky promontory of Ras Fartak and then followed the coast to the landing ground at Riyan where the mountains are just a few miles inland. From Riyan, a few miles from Mukalla, we set course inland, climbing to 7000 feet to get over the mountains. We were now in the Hadramaut. Extremely craggy mountains with giant cliffs were occasionally visible through a layer of stratocu. Eventually, 3 hours and 45 minutes after leaving Salalah we landed at Khormaksar at Aden.

As soon as we landed a garry rushed out and guided us away to the far side of the aerodrome. When we got out with Sgt Weale everyone retreated before us. Smallpox is very catching and they said we would have to be quarantined. When the MO examined Sgt Weale he decided that it was not smallpox after all. So we were allowed to go to the mess and find ourselves a billet. But Sgt Weale was still taken into hospital.

The kite was due for an inspection before its next flight, and they found that it was dropping to bits. So we had to stop at Aden until it was put together again. We didn't mind; the food was quite good. The carburetter air intake on the port engine was loose, all its fastenings broken and the air

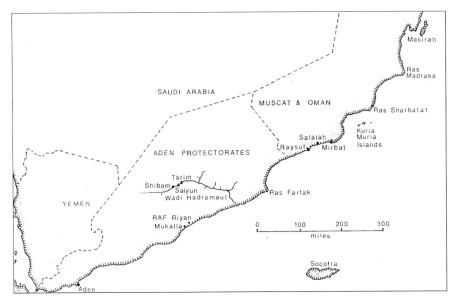

Map 13: The South Arabian Coast in the Second World War

filter stays were all that stopped it from dropping out of the engine. The nuts and bolts were missing off the exhausts on the starboard engine, and there was something else wrong with it too. The priming pump on the port engine was U/S, and there was a hole in one of the wings. It took two or three days to put all that right.

Some of that time I flew around with Dicky, testing the Argus. We had a look at the nearby landing grounds at Sheikh Othman, Little Aden and Hiswa. One afternoon we went into town. A taxi took us to Crater which lies through a rock tunnel. There is a great mass of rock which rises to 1500 ft above the sea. We had a look at the cisterns, ancient man-made hollows 3000 years old I believe which were for holding rain water. They were nearly empty but their rock sides soared upwards for several hundred feet and looked like excellent climbing material. The rock extends upwards to the mountain summit, but it was a bit too warm to do much climbing then. There is a museum at the entrance to the cisterns. Then we went to Steamer Point to do some shopping. The bazaars are nearly all in The Crescent and are run by Indians. Silk to send home was quite cheap, and so were shirts. We ate very well at the Services Club before going back to the camp for another pretty good dinner in the mess.

The following day was similar with an attempt to do some climbing. The day after that Dicky started off back to Masirah in the Argus. He had to land to refuel at the small landing grounds that we saw from the Bisley. He did his own refuelling from petrol cans carried in the back of the kite. Quite an exiting trip. On 20th the Bisley was proclaimed serviceable and

Palmi and I returned to Masirah by the same route. On arrival I was told that Mark and Neil Wren had been commissioned, but were still at Sharjah. I did a sortie with Fg Off Davis as navigator, but had to return with the starboard engine cutting. Guess which aircraft? No prizes. It was of course BA 408. Still no one could find out what was wrong and a few days later Sam Vesey had the same problem.

Down at Umm Rusays eight Sunderland flying-boats passed through in transit from Dar-es-Salaam (East Africa) to Koggala (south Ceylon). This was No. 230 Squadron. One crew member recalls the ditched Bisley in the shallows; he also remembers that they were ferried to and from the aircraft in a ship's lifeboat. The seaplane tenders are not mentioned. The ship's lifeboat was presumably from the American merchantman which was sunk on Christmas Day 1943.

Umm Rusays, however, acquired a new role in 1944. It became the base for Florida-built high-speed rescue launches known as 'Miamis'. They were supplied to the RAF under the Lend-Lease agreement with the United States, and arrived at Basra as deck cargo on freighters. They were 63ft long with a crew of ten and powered by two unreliable Hall-Scott Defender petrol engines of 650 horsepower each which gave them a top speed of 33 knots.

After acceptance trials at Basra two of them sailed to Masirah and a third to Ras al Hadd. They were all No. 214 Air Sea Rescue Unit, although they were later joined by some launches of No. 215 ASR Unit. At Masirah the launches were initially moored off Ras Hilf but it was obvious that they could not remain there during the south-west monsoon. At the end of February one of the launches surveyed a sheltered site in the lee of Ras al Yah, and in April a dhow was hired to establish a mooring there. However, at the beginning of the south-west monsoon the ocean swell proved unacceptable and the high-speed launches moved to Umm Rusays. Here they joined the Marine Craft Unit, an entirely separate organisation which was established there for the flying-boats.

But before the monsoon the Miami at Ras al Hadd was kept busy as a taxi service to Muscat. It was usually moored to the jetty in the Khor al Hajar next to the airfield, and it was there at about 4 p.m. on 23 March when the crew heard the throb of engines. Above the sandbar at the entrance to the khor a yellow flag was seen approaching. A few minutes later the crew heard shouting and saw that the flag was flying above one of two ship's lifeboats. The Miami towed them into the khor. In the lifeboats there were thirty-three survivors from a torpedoed Norwegian tanker which had been en route to Abadan. After the U-boat had fired three torpedoes into the tanker the crew took to the lifeboats. A few hours later an Omani fishing boat arrived and the owner offered to lead the survivors to the 'Inglaise'. En route to Ras al Hadd one of the survivors died, but his comrades could not bring themselves to tip him overboard into the shark-infested sea. The dead man was still sitting upright when the lifeboat reached Ras al Hadd. There had been no previous death on the station, and no one knew what to do. An RAF driver had been a member of the Salvation Army and had a prayer book. He conducted a simple funeral service when the body was buried in a shallow grave in a square marked out under the windsock.

Signals passed between Ras al Hadd, Masirah and Aden. At Masirah there was a Wellington which had recently arrived to re-equip 244 Squadron. It was airborne at 4.40 a.m. the following morning, and landed at Ras al Hadd in the first grey streaks of dawn. Here there were three survivors with serious burns. The tail of the aircraft was jacked up so that their stretchers could be put into the aircraft through the belly hatch. This was the gentlest way of loading them into the aircraft. The Wellington was airborne again at 7.10 a.m. bound for the British Military Hospital at Karachi. Sadly one of the three survivors died a short time later.

After a week a Royal Navy sloop arrived at Ras al Hadd to pick up the rest of the survivors. By this time they had seriously depleted the Ras al Hadd food stocks. The Miami ferried the survivors three miles out to the sloop, which kept moving in case an enemy submarine was in the area. At the same time one of the Masirah-based Miamis sailed to Ras al Hadd to collect and tow back one of the lifeboats. But there was bad weather at Ras al Hadd so the Miami had to shelter in Khor Jarama for a few days before returning to Masirah with the lifeboat in tow.

Meanwhile, the Omani fisherman did not move out from Ras al Hadd. He wanted his reward, and he did not want to be paid in rupees. Finally the Senior Naval Officer at Aden authorised a payment of 50 Maria Theresa dollars.

By this time a fourth Miami had arrived and it was decided to spread them more widely in the area. One was sent to Muscat to take up station there and another was sent to Salalah where it moored close to the shore at Raysut. Later it was replaced by a fifth Miami, No. 2541 which sailed up from Aden.

The early months of 1944 also saw significant changes at the Top Camp. Operational Control of Masirah had passed from AHQ Iraq and Persia to HQ British Forces Aden in December 1943, and in January 1944 Administrative Control also passed to Aden. Masirah remained in the Aden Command until the British withdrawal from Aden in 1967. In early 1944 a new steel jetty was erected to augment the older wooden one. A crane on catapillar tracks also speeded up the unloading from the Eurekas and dhows which were again being hired. Both the unloading and the railway were now the responsibility of the Royal Engineers. Three more locomotives arrived, making a total of five. There were also additional flatcars, more track, and of course more petrol dumps. There were now about 700 coolie labourers, and in addition 200 artisans, masons, carpenters and mechanics were employed by AMWD (Air Ministry Works Department). For ground defence against hostile landing parties there were two companies of RAF Levies together with their battalion HQ. A concrete reservoir was constructed very close to the sea at Ras Hilf, and later a second one alongside it. A subsidiary reservoir was built on the station on higher ground behind the camp. All together the total capacity was 440,000 gallons which should have been sufficient to cover the monsoon period. As previously, the water was brought from Basra and still contained a number of undesirable creatures. The reservoirs were covered by tarpaulin to try to stop any more falling in. The station had now become so large that the arrival of NAAFI had become inevitable.

The U-boat menace had appeared to ease at the end of 1943, and the destruction of the *Charlotte Schliemann* and the *Brake* should have resulted in a further decrease in U-boat activity. This did not appear to be the case, particularly in the choke of the Gulf of Aden leading into the Red Sea. At Aden itself 8 Squadron had converted to the maritime version of the Wellington bomber. In early 1944 it was joined by 621 Squadron, also equipped with Wellingtons, which had been formed in East Africa and had been moving steadily north up the African coast. In January five ships were sunk by submarines in spite of 524 anti-submarine sorties being flown. There had been sixteen sightings of submarines, but none were sunk. Enemy submarines were not, however, limited to the Gulf of Aden. The files of the Consul at Muscat show that Omani dhows too were being sunk by enemy action.

In February and March 244 Squadron also began to convert to the white maritime version of the Wellington, the Wellington XIII, and at the same time moved its base from Sharjah to Masirah. But what could be done with all the obsolete and worn-out Bisleys? The easiest solution would be to leave them to rot at Sharjah, but they did represent useful scrap which could be recycled. Some of the Bisley aircrew were tasked to fly them up the Gulf, across Iraq, Transjordan and Palestine to the Mediterranean. It was a slow and halting move as the aircraft fell by the wayside with faults which were difficult to rectify. At the end of the journey the RAF bases were reluctant to accept the aircraft, and told the crews to move them somewhere else. Eventually they ended up at Heliopolis in Egypt.

The main move of personnel and stores from Sharjah to Masirah was on the SS *Baroda* in March. Masirah may have been primitive but the move was a welcome change for the Squadron. Particularly during the summer months, Masirah's cool south-west wind was infinitely preferable to the stagnant oven-like heat of the Gulf. 244 Squadron was the only RAF squadron ever to be based at Masirah. In March the number of Dutch amphibians increased from two to four, and with the arrival of 244 Squadron the base was over-crowded. Two of 244's Wellingtons were detached to Aden where most of the action was taking place.

One of the 244 Squadron Wellingtons was on convoy escort in the Gulf of Aden in April. Perhaps it was a sudden engine seizure, but whatever the reason some of the right-hand engine mounts broke and the engine fell forwards. The aircraft was flying at about 800 feet and the pilot was unable to stop it descending into the sea. Four of the six crew escaped, swimming under burning petrol, and boarding the inflatable dinghy. They were picked up by one of the ships and put ashore at a port in the Red Sea. The second pilot died from his injuries but the others eventually returned to the Squadron.

At the beginning of May one of the 244 Squadron Wellingtons should have been in on the kill of U-582 which had withstood a prolonged air attack in the Gulf of Aden, when forty-seven depth charges had been dropped from the Aden-based Wellingtons, and 7,000 rounds of ammunition had been fired at her. Before the 244 Squadron Wellington could administer the coup de grâce the Captain beached her on the coast of British Somaliland and destroyed her with scuttling charges. The Captain had previously machine-gunned the survivors of a ship which he had sunk in the Atlantic. For this atrocity Captain Eck was tried after the War and executed by firing squad. He was the only U-boat captain to suffer this fate.

During all this time the unglamourous task of No. 33 Staging Post at Masirah continued. Operational and transport aircraft were flying to and from the war against the Japanese, and the routine tasks of maintenance, rectification and refuelling had to be carried out by the dedicated ground crews. Only one accident is recorded. On 26th June a departing Mosquito pulled up into a loop and disappeared into low cloud. It reappeared pointing downwards too steeply and flew into the ground. In the 1980s a Merlin engine was discovered in rough ground between the airfield and the east coast.

At the end of May another 244 Squadron Wellington was lost on operations. An engine failed and the aircraft was unable to maintain altitude on the other one. It was suspected that the oil was to blame. The aircraft and all six crew were lost. There was a prolonged search by five of the squadron aircraft in the dull monsoon weather but nothing was found. Two of the searching aircraft had the same problem but struggled back to Masirah on one engine. One of these was faced with a night landing, and when taxying in there was a loud explosion and the other engine seized solid. The whole Squadron was immediately grounded. The engines were stripped down and examined in detail but no fault could be found. It appears that the engine fitters could have been suspected of sabotage, but eventually the cause was found after oil samples had been sent to AHQ: the oil had been tampered with at Bahrain. New engines were brought in by a Halifax Mk VIII which had a freight pannier in place of the bomb bay. It brought in four of the Bristol Hercules engines on each delivery. The air tests were protracted and boring, nine-hour flights within a short distance of the airfield. Later, in August, another 244 Squadron Wellington was lost. The cause is not known but it crashed on the island of Socotra killing the crew of six.

One of the 244 Squadron Wellingtons was detached to Riyan, near Mukalla, for famine relief. The crops had failed in the heavily populated Wadi Hadramaut the previous year. In normal circumstances the many expatriate Hadramis working in Africa and the Far East would have ensured a supply of food to their families, but this was not possible now due to enemy submarines. So the British military stepped in and, in spite of the War, made a heroic effort to relieve the famine. Until this time there had been no lorries, all inland transport being by camel train. Aircraft were the most immediately available transport and the Aden-based squadrons were heavily involved. In spite of the enormous endeavours by all concerned about 10,000 people died of starvation. It could have been much worse.

The grain was brought by sea to the port of Mukalla, and by truck from there to RAF Riyan some miles to the east, where the aircraft assembled. The Wellington had a hatch in the floor, and this was removed so that the sacks could be dropped through the opening. The flights were highly alarming, with the sacks being dropped to the floor of the wadi from 150 feet. On each side were cliffs which were about 1,500 feet high. There were two feuding tribes in the Wadi Hadramaut and no truce had been called during the famine. The tribesmen would sit behind rocks and snipe at their enemies, and any passing Wellington, which provided additional in-flight entertainment.

The 321 Squadron records written in English for the RAF are not usually very informative. The squadron base was at China Bay in Ceylon with detachments still in South Africa and the island of Socotra. The comments on Socotra are even more scathing than on Masirah. In April 1944 the Dutch had the following to report on their Masirah detachment of four amphibious Catalinas:

> The food position is unsatisfactory. Fresh vegetables and eggs are not available, and the food provided is insufficient. During 10 days of the current month no bread was available. The water situation is also very unsatisfactory. During the day drinking water is practically unobtainable. The water for other ranks' baths is turned on at 1500 hours and there is always a long queue waiting. When our men, as frequency happens, have to work on aircraft at this hour and therefore go to the bath house a little later, there is no water left.

The records written in Dutch for the Netherlands authorities are much more illuminating. The author asked his friend Freek Zijl to translate them, and the result is so charming that it is reproduced here with only the spelling and punctuation cleaned up for the sake of clarity.

> The Dutch became also situated by the British and were brought under British command. Soon after the incoming of the flyboats the 321 Squadron also put some amphibians in. Masirah showed lots of equals with Socotra, it existed for a great part of sandy hills, but there was a little bit more plants grown. The live-standard were more favourable as specially because of the Americans which shared with their British and Dutch brother-in-arms their

overwhelming supplies. The big advances of the supply traffic with the in and outcoming aircraft to the Far East frequently American cabaret-groups travelled, which were on tour along the American troops. These groups didn't let the temporary inhabitants of Masirah down, and gave during their stay one or two nights open air performances. In this context some of the famous movie stars as Betty Grable, Bob Hope, and Nelson Eddy brought much enthusiasm on this bare and deserted place. The Dutch pilots' flight programme was not less busy than anywhere else in the squadron. Here it was that as well as the South African the Suez Canal convoys passed, and it was the Dutch Catalinas which must accompany them to Karachi and Bombay. Not only the German but also the Japanese submarines were operational in this area, and gave them hands full of work.

There was also the weather as a big enemy. There could be days of low hanging clouds over the Arabic Sea which could bring back the sight to only a few hundred metres. In that case you could only fly on radar and the Dutch were also brought in at day time. In addition it could between June and September in this area be very rough weather. Within a few hours the wind could come from another direction and also changing of windforce. This meant that the utmost effort was demanded from the navigators in the search for convoys or the base camp.

An emergency landing on the Arabic coast was a harsh adventure because the arabs which swarmed around in those areas were of a dangerous and bandit kind. The chances of getting away alive were not particularly big. It was therefore regulation that every crew member must be armed during the flight, and every plane had an in Arabic written recommendation letter with the request to help and protect the strangers. Especially in the surroundings of the Gulf of Oman north of Muscat was known as dangerous. Here there were lots of whimsically shaped bays. More often the Allied pilots must conclude that a hunt for enemy submarines lead to nothing because the enemy searched for protection in one of these bays in which they could come very close to the coast. After a while they discovered that the submarines in these areas were supplied of oil and gasoline by bandited Arabs, and later the tracks in the sands showed what had happened. Then the procedure was that an official letter of the Allied authorities was sent to the Sultan which requested them to get a close inspection, but reality in secret was playing on the same side with the bandits. This because the Germans paid high amounts of money for these illegal helps, which made it possible for them to continue operations far from home.

The biggest terrifies of Masirah was formed by the sandstorms which a few times in a year did occur on the site. When this happened there was over the whole island a layer of sand and dust which sometimes reached a height of 400 metres and blocked the sun. Sometimes it was so terrible that men could not see the next barrack which was about 30 metres separated to another. During the walkover the Dutchman consistently must beware of

321 Squadron at the Top Camp during the Second World War.
The amphibious Catalina PBY 5As carried Dutch national markings, and all
personnel were Dutch (Photograph: via Andrew Thomas)

not being hit by empty gasoline-tins or even drums which then with an amazing noise sometimes thrown around the campsite. In the barracks the sand was several centimetres on the tables, chairs, beds, and suitcases, and this continued as long as two or three days.

There was indeed some severe weather during the summer monsoon of 1944. During one three-day period an unremitting gale washed away a 10,000-gallon fresh water tank at Ras Hilf. The water ration for the RAF was decreased to three-quarters of a service water bottle per day. However, rations included two bottles of Australian beer per day. Some personnel shaved in beer!

In the First World War Maconochies tinned meat and veg was so disgusting that the British soldiers reportedly fired them at the Germans. Later in the Second World War Maconochies M & V was superseded by compo rations, introduced into the British forces by the author's father. Unfortunately the energy rations – sweets and chocolate – were stolen by the dockers, together with the cigarettes.

When the Air Officer Commanding visited Masirah he was given the standard Maconochies meal. He was not much impressed, and arranged a weekly flight of fresh food from Karachi. This was a popular move. Cigarettes, however, were always plentiful and very cheap at the equivalent of 1½p for a packet of 20.

Starting in February 1944 there was considerable official correspondence about securing the use of the Masirah airfield after the end of the War. Those involved were the Consul at Muscat, the Resident at Bushire (who later moved the Residency to Shiraz in mid-1944), the Colonial Office, the India Office in London, the Government of India in Delhi and the Secretary of State for India. The Air Ministry saw Masirah as an important post-war asset and wanted unrestricted use of the airfield. It was comparatively cool in the summer, easy to defend and was not liable to be disrupted by tribal disputes. An outright purchase of the whole island was the favoured option, preferably linked to the return of the Kuria Muria islands to the Sultanate. The purchase of the island had certain legal complications dating back to the previous century, but they were not insurmountable. The Sultan had already granted the oil rights to the Iraq Petroleum Company and this represented another legal problem. It was thought that the Sultan might be more likely to sell the island if the oil rights remained his. Nonetheless the purchase price would have to be sufficiently tempting to interest the Sultan. In August the Treasury stepped in and raised objections to the cost of purchasing the island. The only option left would have been a 99-year lease of the airfield. This had the disadvantage of leaving the local population under the jurisdiction of the Sultan instead of the British authorities. It was decided that no proposal should be made to the Sultan until the party line had been agreed and an opportune moment presented itself.

By November the Consul had broached the subject with the Sultan. The Sultan immediately rejected the idea of selling the island. Even if he regained the Kuria Murias, he did not like the idea of losing sovereignty over Masirah. Evidently it was not an opportune moment to discuss this matter with the Sultan who felt that he had been badly let down by his trusted friends, the British. The Consul reported that the Sultan resented a recent deal with the Iraq Petroleum Company concerning the concession at Duqm. The Sultan thought that he had been badly advised by the British over this deal with a predominantly British company. So the British Government abandoned the idea of purchasing the island and instead settled for a 99-year lease. This was not actually granted until 1950.

During the rough seas of the monsoon the crews of the Miami rescue launches at Umm Rusays were called out on a couple of rescue missions and were kept busy with practices. During transits between bases life could become eventful. Take, for instance, the transit of Miami 2541 from Salalah to Masirah during the summer monsoon. At Salalah it was pounded by the south-west monsoon, tied to a buoy off an exposed beach. There was some shelter from the small headland of Raysut, but it was obvious that the vessel could not remain there in those conditions. On 9 August it was ordered to Masirah where there would be more sheltered water at Umm Rusays.

She set off in a heavy following sea, and all day the weather deteriorated. Eventually the skipper and first coxswain were alone on the bridge. The rest of the crew were battened down below to stop the launch filling with water as the waves broke over her. At dusk they reached the Kuria Muria Islands, moving into the lee of the largest of them, Hallaniyah Island. Here they dropped two anchors and prepared to ride it out. They were there for a week, running short of fresh water. The skipper prohibited washing and shaving, and the crew even tried reconstituting dried vegetables in a mixture of fresh water and sea water. Mixed with Maconochies the crew voted the experiment a failure. The Gulf of Aden Pilot mentioned a well and a tiny population on Hallaniyah, so three of the crew attempted to go ashore in the dinghy. They took with them a .303 rifle and a Sten gun, not knowing who they might meet. The dinghy was overturned in the heavy surf, the weapons were lost, and the crew lacerated on the rocks. Luckily the dinghy was undamaged and was pulled ashore by the wet and battered crew. Before looking for the well one of the crew signalled the skipper who was back on the launch, using semaphore, to inform him of the situation. The skipper ordered them back to the launch immediately, and was evidently extremely displeased at the loss of the weapons, as such a loss was a serious offence. (The skipper of a high-speed launch was a junior commissioned officer, the only officer on board.)

When the weather had moderated a little the skipper decided to risk a departure. The heavy following sea slammed the rudders and the port rudder arm broke. The launch could turn only to the right. The connecting arm was removed and the launch crept back to the lee of Hallaniyah Island. In those conditions, it would have been unwise to continue with only the starboard rudder serviceable. The shortage of water could develop into a life-threatening situation. Necessity is the mother of invention. A very large shackle was

One of the Miami High-Speed Rescue Launches off Umm Rasays. Later 2541 was
driven onto rocks at high speed at night off the north beach
(Photograph: George Chambers)

repeatedly heated on the galley cooker and gradually bent straight over the course of a day. One eye was then cut off, the end sharpened to a tang, and the other eye filed into a square. In this way a new rudder arm was manufactured and 2541 ventured out once again.

A few hours later the cliffs of Ras Madraka passed by on the left without being recognised. The skipper should have identified this prominent headland, but in his defence it must be pointed out that the Miamis had no logs to show speed or distance covered. There had been a speed calibration at Aden over a measured mile using different power settings. But now, with the shortage of water and fuel, the Miami was lightly loaded and travelling faster than expected. The launch maintained her easterly heading for another 40 miles before the error was realised. At Ras Madraka she should have turned onto a much more northerly heading. A serious situation was developing. The launch now had insufficient fuel to reach Masirah, little food and two gallons of water for the crew of ten. Dusk was approaching. Radio bearings were no use for fixing her position because all the beacons were in a straight line. The sea was rough. The skipper swung round onto a more northerly heading and increased engine power to the limit for sustained cruising. He hoped to reach some area shallow enough to anchor for the night, and to be able to fix his position by landmarks. He found a sheltered bay as the light was fading, but had no idea where they were.

A couple of hundred yards inland from the beach there were signs of habitation, barusti palm frond shelters and canoes, etc. Three crew members rowed ashore in the dinghy and found a fisherman. With gesticulations, place names and pointing, a rough position was established.

The following morning a signal for help was sent to Umm Rusays. From there 2649 arrived with two barrels of petrol, some water and some beer. When it had been transferred the two launches set out for Umm Rusays. One of 2649's engines had to be shut down due to a very common fault: a hole had been burnt through the crown of a piston. This slowed her down, so 2541 took her in tow. The two cautiously negotiated the Masirah Channel, swinging the lead for depth soundings. Both safely reached the haven of Umm Rusays.

At Umm Rusays the crews of the three high-speed launches lived and slept aboard, but came ashore to eat in the large mess/cookhouse building. The poor diet had resulted in many septic sores and boils. Not long after its arrival 2541 was on the move again. This time to Muscat with a wireless operator for the Political Agency and a medical officer to help with a large programme of vaccinations. This time the voyage was uneventful except for backfiring from the engines which necessitated resetting all ninety-six valves.

The programme of vaccinations was for inoculating the native labourers who were awaiting shipment to Masirah. The vaccine was flown to Muscat in the Fairchild Argus but before landing at Bait al Falaj the vaccine was to be parachuted directly into Muscat to save time. Unfortunately the vaccine container became detached from the parachute when it was thrown out of the aircraft, and all the vaccine bottles were smashed when the container hit the ground. After refuelling at Bait al Falaj the Argus returned to Masirah for more vaccine. This was successfully delivered to Muscat by the Argus which again refuelled at the Bait al Falaj landing ground. Unfortunately the Argus crashed on take-off, but the pilot and his passenger (the Clerk of Works) were uninjured and were brought back on Miami 2541 On the return voyage it became apparent that the steering was somewhat erratic. An investigation soon revealed that the port rudder had fallen off, no doubt a legacy of its rough passage up from Salalah. The following month high-speed launch 2541 took a salvage party to Muscat to recover the aircraft. They stayed there for a couple of weeks and returned on 2541 with some parts from the aircraft. After their vaccinations in Muscat, 1,324 native coolies arrived at Masirah by dhow to replace the previous party who had been there for six months.

Some of the RAF lads had been at Masirah for some considerable time, so a programme of leave was arranged. Every week five airmen were to be taken to the RAF leave centre at Ser Amadia in the hills of northern Iraq, and another five to Nathaniya in Palestine. Some of the men had had no leave for two years and the Miami crews had been cooped up together for nine months. The scheme started in September, but within a month the Ser Amadia leave centre was closed. So only five per week went on leave to Palestine. Arrangements were therefore made to repatriate those who had been at Masirah for the longest time. Two Dakotas flew them out but one of them crashed on landing at Aden, killing four 244 Squadron aircrew and five from the Marine Craft Unit at Umm Rusays.

Up at the Top Camp Wg Cdr Hankin, OC 244 Squadron, thought that a sea survival exercise would keep people occupied and interested. Evidently there were not enough U-boats to do this. So it was arranged for a Catalina to take some of his aircrew and land them in the ocean to the east of Masirah. Here the hapless Wellington aircrew were cast adrift in a rubber dinghy. As the Catalina disappeared from view a very large shark arrived at the dinghy and began to investigate it. It swam around it, and under it, and rubbed its back on the underside of it. The aircrew in the dinghy became very occupied and interested. The hand-cranked 'Gibson Girl' transmitter was urgently brought into use, its balloon carrying the aerial aloft. Back at Umm Rusays 2541 set out on its rescue mission, homing in on the 'Gibson Girl' transmissions, but not realising the desperate plight of those in the dinghy. When the launch arrived at the dinghy the survivors went up the scrambling net like scalded cats. The launch crew thought it a huge joke; the aircrew did not. After this the survival exercises were conducted close to base in the Masirah Channel.

On 11 December another exercise was organised by Wg Cdr Hankin, to test the Wellington's ASV radar at night. He wanted to know whether it would show a surfaced U-boat. Above the surface a high-speed launch was about the same size, so 2541 was sent out to simulate a U-boat. The exercise was off

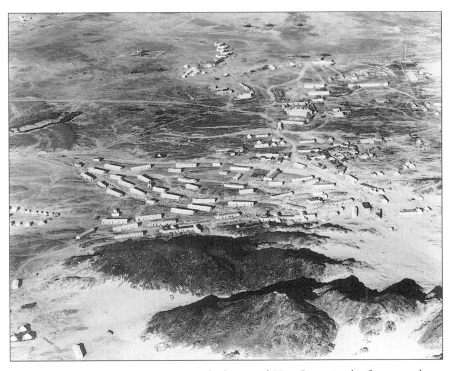

RAF Masirah, December 1944, with the Petrol Tin Camp in the foreground
(Photograph: Public Record Office)

the east coast of Masirah under cover of complete darkness on a moonless night. The Wellington successfully found the launch without any difficulty and the exercise was finished by midnight. The new skipper of 2541 returned at top speed and close inshore. The crew knew about the reef off the north beach, but evidently the skipper did not. There was considerable anxiety amongst the crew as the launch raced blindly through the inky darkness off the north beach. The only light visible was the single aircraft beacon. The first and second coxswains were on the bridge and voiced their misgivings to the skipper, but were told to mind their own business, while the rest of the crew became preoccupied with self-preservation, shutting watertight doors and starting the bilge pumps. Such precautions were totally inadequate because, when the launch hit the reef, the bottom was torn out. Fortunately no one was killed or injured by the impact.

The next day Miami 2738 was recalled from Ras al Hadd to assist with the salvage of the wreck. It arrived at 2.30 a.m. on the 13th, but its crew had little sleep and they spent the day refloating the wreck and taking it to a barge where it was moored. It was not until ten days later that 2738 attempted to tow the wreck to Umm Rusays, but the attempt was abandoned as impractical after only twenty minutes. Parts were salvaged off the wreck for the next week, but then 2738 had to return to Ras al Hadd to take the Consul back to Muscat. En route to Muscat the crew saw the Muscat state launch and realised that it was dead in the water, drifting with its engine broken down. 2738 took it in tow to Muscat and returned to Ras al Hadd the next day. Here the Miami was delayed by rough weather and had to shelter in Khor Jarama for some days before returning to Masirah, where the slow task of salvaging the wrecked 2541 recommenced. Empty 4-gallon tins were inserted into the flooded compartments and slowly the wreck began to ride higher in the water. When working in the flooded compartments the salvage crew hoped that no moray eels had taken up residence. After ten days the wreck was judged to be sufficiently buoyant and 2738 towed it slowly to Umm Rusays. Here it was beached and more equipment was removed, including the engines, but the hulk itself was obviously beyond economical repair.

The skipper, who was also the Officer Commanding 214 ASR Unit, lost two years seniority and was posted back to the Mediterranean. The crew were envious and wondered whether they would be posted back to civilisation if they wrecked a high-speed launch.

In December 1944, the last of the Dutch amphibians of 321 Squadron was withdrawn back to its base in Ceylon. The 244 Squadron Wellingtons were enough protection against the small number of U-boats and Japanese submarines which remained.

The year ended with storms even more severe than a year earlier. On 23 December, and at 2 a.m. on 27 December, there was torrential rain at the Top Camp. The petrol-tin huts were on comparatively high ground in the general area of the present dhobi (laundry), but even so they were 6 inches deep in water. Lower down the wireless cabin was flooded to a depth of 4ft, so all contact was lost with the outside world. For outside communication a Catalina flew up from Umm Rusays and anchored off the jetty at Ras Hilf. The airfield was a lake. There was more rain during the day on the 27th, and also on the 28th and 29th. Seven miles of railway track were damaged. Some people slept on tables in the Airmen's Mess until the floodwater subsided. A rum ration was authorised on the evenings of 27th and 28th. Gradually life returned to normal, the base being back on the air on New Year's Day, and the airfield dried out a few days later. Grass grew, much to everybody's surprise, and the staff of Station Headquarters hung out their records on string to dry in the sun. This provided an air of gaiety to the station, like one of His Majesty's ships bedecked in flags 'dressed festive overall'.

The track from Umm Rusays was washed out, as it had been a year earlier. All manner of unwelcome creatures emerged from their flooded burrows: scorpions, snakes, camel spiders, and at Umm Rusays the dreaded whip scorpion. Nobody knew what it was. A local fisherman was invited in to identify it. His hasty retreat was more eloquent than words. At Umm Rusays the threadbare tents and the palm-frond roofs of the buildings had given little

Buildings constructed of 4-gallon petrol tins at the 'Top Camp'.
Top: 1944 (Photograph: Tommy Hazell); *Middle:* After heavy rain, Christmas, 1944
(Photograph: Arthur Banks); *Bottom:* The Roman Catholic Church, 1944
{Photograph: Tommy Hazell)

protection against the rain. Life ashore was miserable, and the crews of the Miamis stayed aboard. The vessels were able to resupply Umm Rusays by sea until the track had dried out.

1945

In February there was another show by American entertainers passing through, and two British ENSA concert parties. The Hudson taking one of the ENSA parties to Salalah suffered a hydraulic failure shortly after take-off and returned to Masirah. Unable to lower its undercarriage, it had to make a belly landing, the spectacle providing additional entertainment. No one was hurt but one of the concert party had to have a sedative to help him regain his composure.

In April another retrieval was required from the north of the island. An iron barge had broken loose from its moorings and had drifted off. One of the Miamis was sent to bring it in, but could not find it. Two days later the Miami carried out another search and this time located it, but it was in very shallow water and the launch was unable to get close enough to get a tow line onto it. The following day it was found in deeper water and towed slowly back to Umm Rusays where it was anchored. A couple of months later it was taken a mile south of Umm Rusays but broke loose and ran aground on a rocky headland a few hundred yards south of the jetty. In the mid-1990s it was easily recognisable but is now no more than a pile of skeletal rust.

Also in April the Sultan paid a three-day visit to the island while he was en route to Salalah for the monsoon period. He was taken to sea in Miami 2738 which towed a splash target at the end of a long tow line. A 244 Squadron Wellington gave a demonstration of depth-charging the splash target. The Sultan spent the nights on his dhow which was considerably more comfortable than any building made of petrol tins. He dined in the Officers' Mess, and on one occasion with the BOAC staff in their buildings halfway to the jetty.

Later in the month an American C-46 transport aircraft crashed into the sea to the west of Ras Hilf. Miami 2738 searched the area without success and the following morning was led to the submerged wreck by a 244 Squadron Wellington which could see it from the air. Unfortunately there were no survivors, all the aircrew having perished in the wreck. It is believed that the bodies were not recovered.

The RAF Levies were finally withdrawn in February, being taken by dhow to Jiwani for guard duties there. At Masirah they were replaced by two companies of APL, the Aden Protectorate Levies. The APL guard at Masirah was to last for a number of years.

During the early months of 1945 the war in Europe was drawing to a close. Only two allied ships were sunk in 1945, so the anti-submarine aircraft were

The visit of His Highness Sultan Said Bin Taimur in April 1945.
With the Station Commander, Wing Commander B.P. Young OBE.
(Photograph: Tommy Hazell from the 244 Squadron archives)

gradually withdrawn and disbanded. In February the 209 Squadron detachment at Umm Rusays was withdrawn, and in May all the remaining Catalina detachments were also withdrawn. These were from 259, 265 and 212 Squadrons. Also, on 1 May, 244 Squadron disbanded. The aircraft were flown to Aden by the aircrew and the groundcrew followed in Dakotas. There were now no Masirah-based aircraft other than the station Beechcraft which had arrived some months before. It was a small twin-engined communications aircraft of American manufacture. A week later Germany surrendered. The Americans pulled out of Masirah on 7 June. It was a much shorter route for their aircraft to island hop from the United States across the Pacific to the war in the Far East. For the British it was still a shorter route across the Middle East to the Far East, and No. 33 Staging Post at Masirah was maintained. The war against the Japanese showed every indication of being protracted and extremely costly in lives.

After the Americans' departure from Masirah the RAF planned to move into their accommodation. The Quonset huts were luxury compared to the petrol-tin huts which were to be abandoned. Rust was already taking its toll of the sand-filled tins and the buildings were beginning to crumble away. But unrecorded difficulties were apparently encountered and it was not possible to move into the American camp immediately. It took five months before the airmen could move into the American enlisted men's accommodation, and

A 244 Squadron Wellington depth-charges a splash target towed by a Miami
High-Speed Rescue Launch
(Photograph: Tommy Hazell from the 244 Squadron archives)

eight months before the officers and SNCOs could move. By this time a new
RAF Officers' Mess had been built and a start had been made on replacing
the American desalination plant which had deteriorated due to corrosion. The
new desalination plant was built next to the American plant and protected
from corrosion inside a tall building known as the Giraffe House.

It was in 1945 that the railway reached its furthest limits. There were extensive
sidings to the fuel dumps along the north beach, and on the western shore as
far south as the village of Hilf. There were also many sidings at the off-loading
area at the jetty and to its north towards Ras Hilf. There were 12 miles of
track and five locomotives which were kept busy offloading huge quantities
of fuel, oil and food before the summer monsoon of 1945. There were
American-built underground petrol tanks under the concrete hard standing in
front of the watchtower (air traffic control). This was served by a spur of the
railway running through the camp in front of the line of Quonset huts. As a
matter of interest, the Masirah railway was the only railway in the Arabian
Peninsular at that time. Until the First World War there was the Hijaz railway
built by the Turks for bringing pilgrims south to Mecca. The Hijaz railway
also had military uses, so it was destroyed by Lawrence of Arabia who planted
his 'tulips' under the track and ambushed the Turks. In modern times the
Saudis have built a railway from Riyadh to the Gulf coast.

In August two more Masirah-based aircraft joined the Beechcraft. These
were a Vickers Warwick and a Wellington adapted for air/sea rescue. They were
a detachment of 294 Squadron at Basra. The Squadron also had Walrus amphibious aircraft but these were more suitable for the calm waters of Basra and
Bahrain and Sharjah where the Squadron also had detachments. The Masirah
Wellington was old and well worn, and the Warwick was an unsuccessful

heavy bomber. It was an enlarged version of the Wellington but its development was plagued by problems and many lost their lives during development flying. As an air/sea rescue aircraft it carried an airborne lifeboat which could be parachuted to survivors. There is no record of any such rescue from Masirah and both aircraft were unserviceable for most of the time. There were four officers on the detachment, fifteen groundcrew and ten NCO aircrew. One flight sergeant pilot was killed when he fell off a lorry. The detachment was finally withdrawn after eight months when the Squadron disbanded.

In October 1945 there was a water survey of the island to discover whether the RAF station really needed to rely on the expensive water produced by the desalination plant. The first fact to emerge was that deep boreholes could not be used. Sea water would percolate through the decomposed igneous rock and replace any fresh water which was abstracted. The local population had excavated shallow wells at the mouths of the major wadis, and such wells were the only available source of fresh water. Several locations were capable of yielding 10,000 gallons per day providing they were not pumped at a rate greater than 1,000 gallons per hour. The water was perfectly fit to drink and more than sufficient for the needs of the airfield. The needs of the local population were minimal because few had returned to the island. The entire indigenous population numbered no more than about 300. One nearby well was supplying 600 gallons per day to the coolie camp but the quality of the water was marginal and it was not capable of supplying any more without a further deterioration.

There were practical difficulties in supplying sufficient potable water to the airfield. The best wells near such places as Haql and Sur Masirah were up to 25 miles from the airfield. The pumping stations would need to be secure and visited regularly. Gravity tanks would need to be constructed in the hills and many miles of pipe would be required. These would need to bridge wadis so that they were not ruptured by flash floods. As the island's population returned there may not have been enough water for them, and they would be highly likely to hack open the pipes if they were so minded. A prolonged drought could leave the airfield without water, so a desalination plant would in any case be required as a back-up The expense and practical difficulties were too great so it was decided to continue with the secure and convenient desalination plant.

Also in 1945 a new powerhouse was built close to the petrol-tin camp. The building still survives and is in good condition; the hardwood roof rafters seem destined to last for ever. The only other wartime buildings to survive to the present time are the clothing stores (then the food store) and two Nissen huts adjacent to each other. These had been erected in May 1944 by the RAF lads themselves. One was the NAAFI store and the other was a cinema, the projection room being built on to the end. The projection room is still there. These two Nissen huts were later the railway workshops.

Umm Rusays was not abandoned after the Catalinas had departed in the first half of 1945. The Miami high-speed launches remained there due to the large number of transit aircraft passing through. These were combat aircraft as well as transport aircraft taking men and supplies to the Far East. It was a severe monsoon that summer and the seas were too rough for the crews to sleep aboard the Miamis at Umm Rusays. They came ashore at night and slept in the tents which flapped and tore in the howling wind. Sport was encouraged but there was no cinema at Umm Rusays. It was difficult to maintain enthusiasm in the absence of any real work. During the summer monsoon of 1945 it appears that there was still a Miami at Ras al Hadd but probably not at Raysut.

In August 1945 the atom bombs fell on Hiroshima and Nagasaki and suddenly and unexpectedly the War was over. However, the requirement for air transport was undiminished. The forces in India and the Far East still had to be maintained until they could be brought home. Air-sea rescue launches were still needed at Masirah.

The Miamis periodically required overhauls at Aden, and their crews also returned there after a tour of duty at Umm Rusays. In September 1945 it was time for 2649 to return from Aden to Umm Rusays with a new crew to relieve 2738. Also on board were some personnel for the Marine Craft Unit at Umm Rusays. It was plain sailing to Mukalla where a very battered ship's lifeboat brought out burmails of 100-octane aviation gasoline. If this was the fuel usually used it is small wonder that the Hall-Scott Defenders had holes burnt

1994. Survivor from the past.
At RAFO Masirah (Photograph: Ann Richardson)

through their pistons. At Mukalla the crew were initially not allowed ashore because thieves were having their left hands cut off in the market place. This is the punishment specified under the Moslem Sharia law. There is very little thieving. For a second offence the thief has his other hand cut off which makes it extremely difficult to commit a third offence. The crew did not go ashore that day and spent the night on board.

Mukalla was a very picturesque town, particularly when viewed from the sea. The buildings were gleaming white against the background of rugged hills. The following day the crew were invited ashore for a concert in the grounds of the Sultan's palace. Two large groups of children were marched in, first the small boys dressed in white and then the small girls dressed in

1994. Survivor from the past. At Umm Rusays (Photograph: Ann Richardson)

purple. These orphans had been rescued from the Hadramaut by a British sergeant on famine relief. Their parents had all died of starvation. The band was then marched in and seated in front of the dais on which were the seats for the Sultan and his entourage. After they had arrived the concert started. During the performance the orphans sang songs to the audience.

After the concert the crew were able to visit the suq for shopping, returning to the launch in the late afternoon. They sailed through the night and arrived at Salalah the following day, dropping anchor in the shelter of Raysut Bay. The skipper was rowed ashore in the dinghy to arrange for refuelling, and was met by a jeep of the Sultan's Army. The soldiers were armed with antique Martini-Henry rifles. At first the crew were not allowed to disembark but later two American jeeps arrived with clearance from the Sultan himself. The American jeeps also contained two of the Sultan's soldiers to ensure that the visitors did not stray from the track to the American camp, where the crew enjoyed the best of American hospitality. That night they stayed on their launch and were amazed to see Salalah lit up like the Blackpool illuminations, which was possible due to the generators given to the Sultan by the Americans.

The following morning the crew topped up their fuel tanks and stowed six full burmails in the well deck to be sure of having sufficient fuel to reach

Masirah. Obviously they had heard of the ignominious arrival of 2541 a year earlier. The Miami sailed early enough to reach the lee of a Kuria Muria island in daylight and transferred the fuel from the burmails to the fuel tanks. There was no semi-rotary hand pump, so the fuel transfer was by syphoning through a rubber tube. This entailed crew members sucking the bottom of the petrol tube until there was a sudden rush of petrol. At best this would result in a mouthful of petrol and at worst a throatful which happened to the coxswain who lost his voice for quite some time but luckily suffered no permanent harm.

The transfer of fuel by this method took a long time, so the Miami remained at anchor for the night. The early start the following morning should have allowed them to arrive at Umm Rusays in daylight, a necessary precaution for navigating the Masirah Channel. However, not long after leaving the Kuria Murias the starboard Hall-Scott Defender showed signs of distress. Evidently it found the aviation gasoline just as unpalatable as the unfortunate coxswain. Soon the engine had to be shut down. Then it proved impossible to run the port engine on the fuel in the starboard tank. Next the bridge and wheelhouse steering failed. A jury rudder was rigged and it was found that there was just enough fuel to reach Umm Rusays. However, Miami 2738 was making its way from Masirah to Aden and was on hand to take 2649 in tow. Six hours later the tow parted so both launches had to make their way independently to Ras Madraka where they sheltered for the night. They set off again at 6 a.m. the following morning at slow speed and kept in visual contact with each other. Eventually they arrived at Umm Rusays at 3 p.m. and tied up to the Munro buoys. After a promising start the passage from Aden had proved as eventful as usual.

The crew of 2649 was ferried ashore and made welcome by the crews of the other two Miamis and the Marine Craft Unit. Beds were allocated in the 'Tamboos' (tents) but some of the crew chose to sleep aboard. It was now the Marine Craft Unit which was responsible for the refuelling and maintenance of all craft, but the Miami crews also helped in rectification. The starboard engine required no more than a top overhaul. There was a hydraulic system for the steering, and a pipe had split. All the hydraulic oil had therefore been lost. A new length of pipe was fitted and the system refilled. The problem with the starboard fuel tank was also easily rectified: it was simply a blocked filter.

There were now three dogs at Umm Rusays: Judy, Nelson and Micky. There were also two lorries, a 3-tonner and a smaller 30cwt. (For younger readers unfamiliar with imperial measurements, the lorries could be loaded to about 3,000 kg and 1,500 kg respectively.) They brought supplies from the Top Camp and burmails of slightly brackish water from the well at Dawwa for the shower which was rigged up, using a perforated 4-gallon petrol tin. There was a fair number of coolie labourers from Muscat to carry out the menial tasks, and to prevent pilfering by the local fishermen there were askaris (native guards).

'Tiffin' was the meal at 1 p.m. in the Mess. The crews would row ashore for this, and again be back in the Mess in the evening for beer or minerals and a game of darts.

The impending visit by an Air Marshal caused some anxiety. Most of the lads wore only shorts and sandals and urgently needed haircuts and shaves. Most of the uniforms were eventually located in kitbags in the well-deck bilges of the three Miamis. The coxswain of 2649 had some clippers and two cut-throat razors with a strop and honing stone. By the time the Air Marshal arrived all the lads were correctly dressed, shaved and had short back and sides.

At the end of November it was time for Miami 2515 to sail from Aden to Masirah. She reached Salalah safely and after refuelling set out for the Kuria Muria Islands in the late afternoon – not a good time to start the passage if the dead-reckoning navigation did not allow for the currents. Darkness fell and 2515 raced through the night. South of Mirbat the lookout suddenly saw breakers ahead, but too late. The launch ran onto a sloping rock at about 25 knots and shuddered to a halt. The bow was high and dry but the stern began to sink. The wireless operator managed to send an SOS before the batteries were submerged in sea water – 2650 at Umm Rusays responded to the SOS but its starboard engine broke down and it had to return to Masirah. The closest Miami was then at Mukalla – 2646 which had an unserviceable generator and batteries which would not hold a charge. Her wireless operator had joined all the dry batteries together so that he could receive messages, but he could not transmit. He heard the SOS from 2515 and the order from Aden to sail

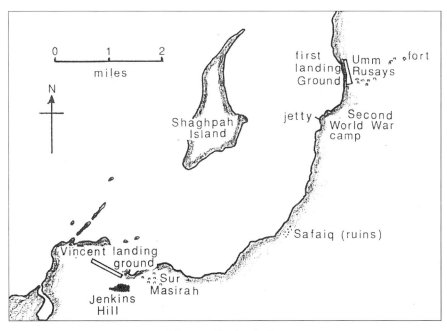

Map 14: Shaghpah Bay

to the rescue. Somehow the crew managed to start an engine by 2 a.m. and carried out some rectification en route. The launch reached Salalah during daylight but had to refuel there, using buckets. When she eventually reached 2515 they found her being harassed by local arab boats. The crew on the wreck had no weapons other than a signal pistol.

A Royal Navy tug left Aden together with another Miami which was carrying floatation gear. They arrived a few days later and managed to salvage 2515 which was slowly towed back to Aden.

Then on 30 December a message arrived from the Top Camp that an ENSA party of entertainers had arrived. They were to be picked up at the jetty at the Top Camp and brought to Umm Rusays by two Miamis. There were young ladies in the party, so it was rumoured, and Umm Rusays became highly charged with speculation and anticipation. Nothing like this had happened before. What should be done about toilets for them? And what about the desert lily?

The two Miamis were under the command of one officer, the skipper of the leading launch. The other launch was to follow exactly in its wake through the treacherous Masirah Channel. The ENSA party embarked at the Top Camp, and there were indeed young ladies. To give them a thrill the launches opened up to full power and raced down the channel. When they were nearing Umm Rusays a dhow under sail cut across ahead of the leading Miami, obscuring the skipper's view of the lead-in markers. Giving way to sail, the skipper swerved right to go behind the dhow's stern, and shuddered to a stop – he was stuck fast on a sandbank. The coxswain of the following launch also went hard right

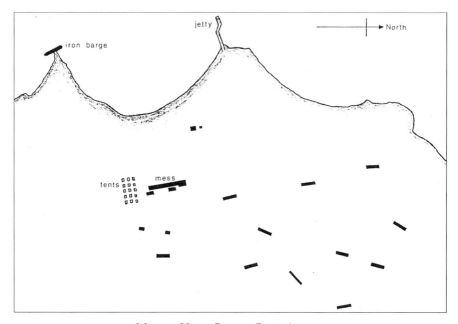

Map 15: Umm Rusays Camp in 1945

154

Gas masks were adapted for use under water
(Photograph: Charles Meacock)

behind the dhow, and even further right to miss the leading launch. He had
had the foresight to throttle back, so hit the sandbank at a slower speed. Both
launches were stuck fast, but fortunately it was a rising tide.

By reversing and pushing with boathooks the launches were soon freed and
crept back to their moorings at low revs, although it was obvious from the
vibrations that not all was well with the drive shafts or propellers. The ENSA
party were rowed ashore. The lads were overawed by the presence of the young
ladies, and were on their best behaviour for the performance. The desert lily
was very definitely not in use until the ENSA party had departed – by road
in the 3-tonner. This was a less comfortable journey, but safer.

Next came the investigation of the damage under the waterline. The crew
of 2649, like all the Miami crews, were masters of improvisation. Two gas
masks were adapted for underwater use, air being pumped down from hydraulic
priming pumps. These were large cylinders with taps at the bottom which
controlled the flow of air. A fitter and deckhand went down to inspect the
rudder, propellers and P brackets, and they reported that one propeller and
its shaft were bent. At high tide a cradle was slipped under the launch, and
at low tide the bent shaft and propeller were removed and replaced by spares
kept at the base. While high and dry on the cradle the launch was painted
and had antifouling applied below the waterline. Within a tide the Miami was
serviceable and back on its mooring. It was shortly after this that a small
slipway was built about 100 yards south of the jetty.

1946

In January 1946, in the aftermath of the War, Miami 2649 was sent on detachment to Ras al Hadd. Here, next to the airfield, was a jetty in the deep-water bay of Khor al Hajar. A mooring had been laid so there was no need to lie at anchor. There were no other launches or marine craft, only a few fishing houris belonging to the small local community, who would sell fish cheaply to the crew of the Miami who did their own cooking. Only the skipper ate ashore, at the Officers' Mess at the airfield. The airfield was kept busy by transport aircraft staging through. None crashed, so the crew of 2649 led a placid life fishing, exploring the local area and the large deserted fort. Once a week a jeep would arrive at the jetty with the mail.

One day the coxswain, Charles Meacock, was fishing alone on the launch. He noticed a warm wind spring up, and in his experience this spelt trouble. Khor al Hajar was an open bay, and no place to be during rough weather, so he rowed ashore and alerted the skipper and the rest of the crew who were in the canteen. They hurried back to the Miami, started the engines, cast off, and moved up the coast to the narrow entrance of Khor Jarama. By the time they arrived there was a steep following sea which was lifting the square stern and burying the bow. The stern was slammed this way and that so that it was difficult to steer accurately down the narrow twisting fjord. At the entrance they had noticed two dhows on the horizon which were obviously in trouble.

By skilful use of rudder and differential throttle the coxswain brought the Miami safely into the calm waters of Khor Jarama. With a sigh of relief they dropped anchor, and thankfully started a brew up. Some hours later the smaller of the two dhows also arrived in Khor Jarama and dropped anchor. From the activity of its crew it appeared that all was not well, so the skipper and coxswain of 2649 rowed the dinghy across to investigate. Previously the skipper had been involved in road construction in the Hadramaut, working with Arab labourers and consequently was fluent in Arabic. The crew of the dhow told him that the larger dhow had been driven onto the rocks at the entrance to Khor Jarama. The skipper and coxswain rowed back to the launch, started engines, raised the anchor, and cautiously negotiated the fjord again. The gale was unabated. At the entrance to the khor the crew of the larger dhow had somehow freed her from the rocks and were rowing a houri to tow her in. The rest of the dhow's crew were bailing out the water entering the gaping hole in the bow. The houri was in danger of being swamped so the Miami turned about and threw a line to the dhow, taking her in tow. They safely negotiated the narrows, and made for the sandy beach at the south of Khor Jarama. Here the Miami increased power, accelerating towards the beach, and slipped the tow at the last moment. She swerved away and the dhow continued straight ahead and beached with the gaping hole up on the sand.

The Miami dropped anchor, cut engines, and the skipper and coxswain rowed across to the beached dhow, very much hoping that they had done the right thing. They had. The owner of the dhows was effusive in his thanks. The hole was soon repaired and the dhow was refloated on the high tide the following day. In the evening the whole crew of 2649 were invited to the large dhow for a feast. There was a mountain of rice, large sections of goat, and gravy. The skipper understood the etiquette so was able to prevent any breach of traditional good manners. The coxswain reports that there were sheeps eyeballs buried in the rice. The author has been told by an authoritative source that Moslems are not permitted to eat such offal, and eyeballs are included only when Europeans are present. Sometimes this is due to the mistaken belief that they are a European delicacy, but more often it is due to the Arab sense of humour. The Arab hosts exchange glances and scarcely discernible smirks as their embarrassed guests try every ploy to avoid giving offence short of actually eating the eyeball. Charles Meacock reports that the sheep's eye was 'a luxury which as coxswain I was obliged to indulge. I managed to palm it into the pocket of my khaki drill jacket undetected I hope!' It is the author's guess that he was closely observed.

Afterwards there were dates and coffee but of course no alcohol. It was the early hours of the morning before the crew returned to 2649.

The following morning the gale was still blowing so 2649 remained in Khor Jarama. Some of the dhow's crew came across to be treated for mild ailments, further cementing the relationship. When the wind moderated 2649 was able to return to Khor al Hajar where she was more readily available if an aircraft ditched in the sea.

A little later the Sultan's motorised dhow entered Khor al Hajar to pay the Ras al Hadd labourers in Maria Theresa dollars. The agent and his crew came aboard 2649, watched the filter and oil changes on the twin Hall-Scott Defenders, and were shown around the launch. They were startled by the explosive start of the 650-horsepower engines. There was a return visit to the Sultan's dhow which was in beautiful condition. Later 2649 embarked on a test run to Muscat but after a short distance the starboard exhaust coughed black smoke, so the launch returned to Khor al Hajar where it was found to be only a minor fault. There was no further opportunity to visit Muscat because the launch was recalled to Masirah.

A month or so later two Miamis, 2538 and 2649, were sent from Umm Rusays to Ras al Hadd to help dispose of surplus ammunition which was no longer required now that hostilities had ceased. The CO of the Top Camp went on one of the Miamis. At Ras al Hadd boxes of ammunition were loaded onto the launches and taken out to deep water some miles offshore where they were dumped over the side. That night at the airfield the surplus ammunition was being used in spectacular fashion. A fire could be seen from the Miamis, with pyrotechnics and wild fusillades of rifle fire; it was a disturbed night's

The Jetty at Umm Rusays.
Top: The fuel dhow and a Miami moored up alongside at high water
(Photograph: Alan James)
Bottom: Immediately before the final departure of the Miamis when Umm Rusays
was abandoned (Photograph: Charles Meacock)

sleep for the crews on the two launches. Next morning the two crews motored their Miamis home to Umm Rusays at high speed.

The airfield at Ras al Hadd remained open as a staging post until March 1947, but there is no mention of the dead Norwegian seaman being moved. Perhaps his body is still there. In 1949 there was some correspondence about erecting a lighthouse there and the LT *Nearchus* visited to investigate the possibility. There is high ground in the vicinity and at that time it was not practicable to build a lighthouse which was tall enough to be viewed from a wide arc. It was not until 1969 that Wimpey civil engineers erected an unmanned light tower 41 metres high with a revolving light. Like the crew of the LT *Nearchus*, the civil engineers received a most hospitable welcome from the Ras al Hadd villagers who were living in extreme poverty, and who had not seen Europeans for twenty years.

When the two Miamis returned to Umm Rusays they found preparations for disbandment. One sad task was to dispose of the unit's three dogs. Four or five of the lads took them inland on the 15-cwt lorry to shoot them. They were turned loose, the lads opened fire, but they missed. The dogs could not believe what was happening, and bolted so the lorry set off in pursuit but the dogs soon disappeared from view.

Another task was to burn the hulk of 2541 which had been wrecked at night on the rocks off the north beach. The superstructure burnt, but lower down the hulk was sodden with wet rot, seaweed and barnacles. At the base documents were burnt and the three Miamis fully fuelled and victualled, departing for Aden in line astern. A short time later the Marine Craft Unit departed, the seaplane tenders, bomb scow, etc., being loaded onto ships as deck cargo. It was the end of the story of Umm Rusays, the story which had started so long ago in 1931 when the two Southampton flying-boats of 203 Squadron and Major Fowle on HMS *Penzance* had arrived on their first tentative investigation.

A series of vertical air photographs taken in 1960 shows a total of fourteen structures at the abandoned base, the largest being the mess hall and kitchen. Only one building remains today. The photographs also show the jetty at the same place as the present substantial mole which was built in the 1980s. The wrecked Bisley can be seen on the sandbank halfway across to Shaghpah Island, and the large iron barge can be seen on the beach a short distance to the south of the jetty. In the village the mosque is in the same place as the present breeze-block mosque, and the large fortified house a short distance to its south-east appears to be in an advanced state of disrepair. There is no sign of the corner markers or white circle of the original landing ground which had been condemned by Flt Lt Teddy Nuttall. The southern end of this original landing ground was between the mosque and the beach.

After VJ Day in August 1945, No. 33 Staging post at Masirah was busier than ever. British Forces in India and the Far East were being flown home for 'demob' and the Gulf route via Sharjah and Bahrain was being used up to its maximum capacity. To ease the strain the South Arabian route was also used to fly the troops home. It was not therefore possible to repatriate the staging post personnel, and this led to some discontent. Some of them had been there for three years which they considered quite long enough.

By April 1946 the load had eased and the shorter route via the Gulf was all that was required, so RAF Masirah was reduced to skeleton manning for 'care and maintenance' only. The CO was a junior officer and in addition there were ten airmen and nineteen civilians, plus a small number of Aden Protectorate Levies. There was a weekly supply flight by a Wellington of the Aden Communications Unit, but Masirah proved unexpectedly popular with a number of civil airlines. The airfield was used regularly by Dakotas of Indian Overseas Airlines and Ethiopian Airlines as well as Handley Page Haltons of the Lancashire Aircraft Corporation, Airspeed Consuls of Chartair and Skyways' Yorks. BOAC maintained its Lodestar service but considered that the runways were not suitable for the York aircraft which might be used. To handle the other traffic a number of BOAC staff were drafted into Masirah, their duties including the operation of the direction finding (DF) station.

After the Second World War new air agreements for civil and military aviation were negotiated with the Sultan. Before the War the files of the British Political Agent at Muscat contain some 6,600 pages on aviation matters. It is remarkable that Sultan Said bin Taimur appears to have handled the whole of the Omani side of this complex correspondence himself. During the Second World War the Sultan co-operated closely with the British authorities in the defence of the area, making it quite clear that these facilities were for the duration of the War only. At the same time he drew up regulations for British personnel in the Sultanate in order to avoid possible misunderstandings and conflict with the local population. Once the War was over he insisted on the prompt implementation of the agreed withdrawal arrangements.

In 1946 the British and French governments prepared a draft agreement on the facilities required for their military aircraft on long-haul routes to the Far East, and in particular for emergency landings. When the text was shown to the Sultan he was adamant that French military aircraft would not overfly his territory. He wrote in English to the British Consul:

> As far as we can make out the matter has been clarified but just to make it more clear and to avoid any misunderstanding we should like to point out that it is understood that the French military aircrafts shall not fly over or land in our territories as they have not got the right to do so.

Sultan Said bin Taimur certainly knew his mind. Salalah and Masirah were limited to a maximum of fifty British personnel in normal times, and up to 150 in times of emergency.

CHAPTER IV

The Lonely Outpost

1947

FOR MASIRAH THE SECOND WORLD WAR did not end on VJ day when the Japanese surrendered – there was the heavy commitment of trooping flights in early 1946, so 1947 was the first clear post-war year. With the station consigned to care and maintenance there was little to enliven or stimulate the few personnel on this moribund outstation. There were just enough British personnel to raise a cricket or soccer team if everybody played, but there was no one to play against. There were no ENSA concert parties; the buildings, stored items and vehicles were falling into disrepair due to the lack of care and maintenance and in February BOAC withdrew its service. Captain Tony Spooner writes:

I lived in Cairo and flew as a captain on No. 5 Line. The line had about nine twin engined Lockheed Lodestars and a solitary DC3 Dakota, which was used mainly for freight.

Nigel Pelly, my affable and rotund Flight-Captain, sent for me. Between us we had just formed the BOAC cricket team and I was expecting to take part in a discussion whether or not to open the innings with Hillary. He was the BOAC Middle East Manager and had let it be known that he wished to have a game. Nigel was a stickler for protocol and was all for sending him in first.

I was wrong. It wasn't about cricket at all. 'Tony, old boy,' he announced, 'I have just been given the order to wind up all our stations on the South Arabian route. We have to get everything out and cart it all to Karachi. I want you to take the Dak down there and shift everything moveable.'

The South Arabian route was one which the RAF had opened up at a time when it seemed likely that the Germans would soon be in Cairo. It was an alternative way of getting to India by way of Aden and various hastily constructed new airfields along the south coast of Arabia.

From Aden it went to Riyan, near Mukallah, thence to Salalah and Masirah Island. After that it hopped over Ras al Hadd and the Gulf of Oman to Jiwani and finally into India (later Pakistan) at Karachi.

Each airfield was about 300 miles from the last and by far the biggest of these outposts was Salalah. None of these airfields were, in 1947, equipped for night flying and the schedules that BOAC had been flying included a night stop at Salalah in both directions. There was some sort of hutted accommodation for the Lodestar crew and up to fifteen passengers.

'How long will I be away?'

'Don't know, old chap, just keep going until everything is carted away.'

Within a day or two I had arrived at Riyan by way of refuelling at Port Sudan. It did not take long to pick up what little possessions BOAC had there and I was able to get to Salalah for the first of many nights to be spent in that desert silence. At Salalah BOAC had a radio station and some kind of met office too. It might even have boasted an ATC unit, but I believe that this consisted entirely of an old aircraft altimeter from which the local rep would give us our QNH prior to landing.

All in all there was quite a lot of stuff to move to Karachi – quite a few people too. Not that we had any seats for them. Soon, thanks to a very helpful BOAC rep we were running a daily service between Salalah and Karachi and the Dakota was packed to the roof most of the time. On all these journeys the aircraft was up to (at least) its maximum permissable take-off weight. Part of the freight was a large radio mast which had been cut up into suitable lengths. We had no means of accurately weighing the sections. There was not so much freight to take out of Masirah, and only about four people. But being so heavily loaded at Salalah we often had to call in at Masirah for fuel, not wishing to stop at Jiwani or Jask. At the latter place an earlier schedule BOAC flight to Karachi had stopped to refuel, only for the crew to be held to ransom by the locals.

From time to time we had to spend the night in Karachi where my co-pilot and I had found an ancient and rather faded grand hotel. It was here that we met the famous geologist who we were to take to Salalah. The Sultan was engaging him at some vast fee to survey his territory for oil. The geologist was a wonderful man, way past 60 I believe. He had spent all his working life in the sub-continent and had made many discoveries. The only snag was that he was almost stone deaf and all conversations had to be carried out in the 125 decibel range. I recall an occasion in the lobby of that lofty hotel.

'Have you ever found any gold in India?'

'What was that?'

'DID YOU FIND ANY GOLD?'

'Any what?'

'ANY GOLD. GOLD, GOLD. G-O-L-D?'

By then the entire lobby had been hushed into silence and a dozen dusky figures showed obvious interest by edging closer.

Actually, it was silver, not gold, that caused us much bother. BOAC, as an act of friendship, had decided to present the Sultan with a splendid silver gift, a model of a Lodestar. This did not please the Indian Customs men at all. There was an embargo on the export of all precious metals. BOAC was quite determined that the Sultan must have his gift, and that I should be the means of transporting it to Salalah. Almost every time we went to Karachi there would be further discussions with Customs. In the end we smuggled it out.

It was on our final missions that we cleared out Masirah. This insignificant strip of bare and barren sand had become an important RAF staging post. It had decent runways and the very first underground refuelling tanks that I had ever seen. Normally we were refuelled by bowsers or, as often as not, by a line of natives carrying on their heads four gallon petrol tins, which, under the personal supervision of the First Officer, would be emptied into the tanks via a chamois leather filter. Hydrant refuelling out of the hard standing was unheard of.

The island of Masirah was completely uninhabited, apart from the RAF. It had no vegetation of any kind. It never rained there. It did, however, contain about 30 palm trees. Each of these had been named by the RAF. It was the kind of station where it greatly helped if one was half crazy before one arrived. Why otherwise should each palm tree have been given a girl's name? Also the personnel went around almost naked. Not at all Halton or Cranwell! The only pastime that I heard of was riding on the backs of giant turtles. The heat was always 100°F and the humidity about the same. I don't know what crime one had to commit to be posted to Masirah but it must have been a fairly serious one.

In February the station operations record book contains the following dismal statement:

> Two dhows arrived from Aden at the beginning of the month bringing goats, sheep, firewood and dates. Most of the goats died en route and the rest are in poor shape.

These supplies would have been for the APL soldiers as the Aden Communications Unit Wellington brought food for the British personnel.

1948

In early 1948 the Wellingtons of the Aden Communications Unit were replaced by DC-3 Dakotas which were a more suitable aircraft for the RSM (Riyan Salalah Masirah) resupply flights. All three stations were still on care and maintenance, as was Hargeisa in British Somaliland which was another wartime airfield. The CO at these stations was a junior officer on a three-month detachment from the Aden Communications Unit. The airmen were there for six months. Also at Aden 8 Squadron was flying Hawker Tempest fighters, but the Squadron did not have enough spare officers to man the route stations. The three-month tenure of the COs was not long enough for any of them to address the mounting problems. Les Bulmer was CO of RAF Masirah for four months in 1948 and writes:

On my arrival my predecessor took me for a ride on the railway and showed me the fuel dumps. There was supposed to be 2,250,000 gallons of 100 octane aviation petrol, most of it left over from war time and all of it in drums. Apart from one dump of 80,000 gallons which was relatively new, nothing remained of the other dumps but bits of rusty metal sticking out of the sand. No one would take responsibility for writing the whole lot off. Later in my stay a sergeant from the RAF Police arrived to investigate the apparent loss of a 4 lb bag of flour which we could not account for one month. While he was there I mentioned the stock of fuel we were supposed to have, and reckoned that the actual useable stock was probably 100,000 gallons, if that. Two weeks later a flight lieutenant and a sergeant from the police arrived to find out what I'd done with over two million gallons of petrol. They spent nearly two weeks on the island making drawings of the northern coastline and calculating whether it was possible for the Arabs to have brought in dhows and pinched the lot from under my nose. Actually, I think they only came up to Masirah to enjoy a couple of weeks holiday. I never heard anything further and, as far as I remember, the missing fuel was never written off during my subsequent two years in Aden.

There was a medical officer who left as I arrived. He was not replaced, so the occupants of the Officers' Mess were myself and the AMWD engineer who looked after the power house, desalination plant and railway. He had about 20 Adenese mechanics and clerks etc. There were also an RAF Regiment squadron leader and a pilot officer who were in charge of the 130 APL. There were also some Arab APL officers but they did not live in our mess.

There were about fifteen RAF personnel, and about the same number of Omani labourers from Muscat who lived in the old RAF petrol tin camp. This was disintegrating and most of the roofs were missing. The Wali also lived here. There were no locals from Masirah working on the station, and none of them lived anywhere near.

There were a couple of disused concrete and steel reservoirs at the north-west corner of the coastline, and a steel jetty just to the south. The sea water for our desalination plant was piped up from a well on the east coast. Unfortunately baby turtles kept falling into the well which was only a few yards from the sea, but I never heard of baby turtles clogging up the desal plant.

Near the north-east corner of the island there was a monument to commemorate some seamen who had been killed there earlier in the century. Close by was the skeletal remains of a Blenheim – or more probably a Bisley of 244 Squadron. I had the feeling that it had been returning to base and hadn't made it. It was certainly not the best of places to put it down since it was sitting on rocks above the beach.

Our pride and joy was the runway lighting system, the only one among the Aden route stations. It had been developed by AMWD and consisted of a series of the old style green lampshades buried along each side of the runways with the bulbs sticking out of the top. The control tower had a large hand-wheel to switch from one runway to the other. Whenever an aircraft did a night landing (on runway 25 in the summer when I was there) I had to get him to back track to the intersection. When I judged him to be there I had to switch to the lights on the other runway so that he could taxi south to the hardstanding. The runways, of course, were rolled sand and there was no perimeter track.

We had about 30 MT vehicles but they were kept in the open and rusted away, particularly the radiators. For a while we had an American ambulance which was a runner, but the crash tender had to be parked on a slope for a push start. I always hoped (and prayed) that if anyone was contemplating a crash landing they would give me sufficient notice so that we could get our emergency services up and running. The only other serviceable vehicle was a Coles crane. Luckily the AMWD had a reliable 15 cwt. lorry.

There was a large hangar full of Wellington spares. Not only bits and pieces but whole wings and a tailplane. There were also a fair number of one man inflatable rubber dinghies which we used as surf boards. The hangar caught fire while I was handing over to my successor. It was thought to be caused by an old Very cartridge blowing up in one of the dinghy packs. There was some anxiety that acetylene cylinders close to the dinghy packs might go up and take the hangar with them, but all was well in the end. Even the crash tender made it to the hangar. The Omani cook gave the alarm when he saw smoke pouring out of the hangar from the Officers' Mess window and ran over to SHQ to inform my successor. Not wishing to interrupt what the new CO was doing he waited patiently until he was free and then announced 'Sahib, the hangar's on fire.'

Nearby was a tall building which looked like a parachute packing workshop but housed our food supplies. My predecessor claimed that it had once been full of American tinned chicken but this had all been consumed. However, the Officers' Mess cook, an Omani, had his own secret supply and we continued to enjoy American chicken throughout my stay on the island.

The power station had two diesel generators with a smaller one which was having a complete overhaul while I was there. One generator carried the full load of the camp but when the MF radio beacon was switched on all the camp lights went dim. So we only had the beacon on for short periods when aircraft were arriving or leaving. There were five radio masts but three of them had fallen over because the stays had rusted through. We managed to rig up a short wave aerial to one of the masts and thus had contact with Salalah who relayed our messages on to Aden.

June 1948 brought M.V. *Bray* and a whole lot of problems. I received a signal from Aden saying that a M.V. *Bray* would be calling at Masirah for refuelling. She was to be supplied with 3000 gallons of petrol of an octane we didn't have – something like 85, I believe. To arrive at the correct octane figure I was instructed to use a mix of two-thirds low octane (motor spirit) and one third 100 octane aviation spirit. It was left up to me how I did it, since those who had issued the orders had never been to the outstations and had no idea of the problems involved.

I had no idea how big the *Bray* would be – I was thinking in terms of a small cargo liner. Nor did I know when she would be arriving, except that it would probably be within a week of receiving the signal. I just hoped that they would have some means of coming ashore because we had no boat, and anything of any size couldn't get alongside the jetty because of the reef which runs around the northern tip of Masirah and lies about 50 yards or so off the end of the jetty. The prospect of shunting some 90 barrels of fuel by rail to the jetty and then transferring them by small boat to the ship was not one I was particularly keen on, but I couldn't see any other means of doing it. It was going to take a long time and I hoped that the crew of *Bray* knew what they were letting themselves in for.

About a week after receiving the signal, we were enjoying our usual afternoon swim on Ocean Beach when a large motor yacht appeared close in (she was actually a converted wartime motor torpedo boat) and was obviously heading round the top of the island for the jetty. There was a bit of a panic to get back to the airfield, grab a radio operator, an Aldis lamp and battery, and hare off down to the jetty. By the time we got there she was anchored beyond the reef – they had, at least, realised it was there.

Fortunately they had an inflatable and some of the crew came ashore to discuss how they were to refuel. They were also short of food and asked if we could help out. The skipper reckoned that he could clear the reef at high tide and get alongside. This would give him about three hours to refuel before he would have to leave while there was enough water to get back over the reef. We arranged to have the fuel and stores ready for him next day by about late morning when he expected to come alongside.

I returned to the airfield to organise the transfer of petrol drums to the jetty. I still thought we should be pushed to get 90 barrels of fuel aboard in three hours if all he'd got was a hand pump. Then I had an idea. In the MT compound was a trailer bowser with a capacity of around 3000 gallons which was used as a static tank to hold fuel for the vehicles. I got one of the MT mechanics to check the contents of the bowser and, lo and behold, it contained 2000 gallons – just the amount we wanted. All we had to do was to fetch up 1000 gallons from the 100 octane dump by train and pump it into the bowser. The two mechanics spent the rest of the day pumping the contents of some 30 drums into the bowser by hand. They were a bit knackered by the time they'd finished.

The problem then was how we were to get the bowser down to the jetty next morning. The only thing with enough power to tow it was the Coles crane which, fortunately, was in working order. Works & Bricks assured me that the jetty would take the weight, so early next morning we set out with two of the MT section gingerly driving the crane while I was alongside in the Works & Bricks 15 cwt. keeping an eye on the tow bar. We made it after a slow and nail biting journey. *Bray* came alongside at the appointed time and refuelling was comparatively simple. She was being delivered to Aramco in the Persian Gulf and the crew were British, mostly amateur sailors from all walks of life, who had taken time off work for a bit of an adventure.

We gave them what food supplies we could spare and sent them on their way. I suppose they made it to their destination. The ambulance was not there for emergencies but was the one vehicle that worked at that time and we used it to ferry the crew up to the Mess for a drink. A few drums wouldn't go in the bowser so these were hand pumped into the *Bray*'s fuel tanks after the bowser was emptied.

I complained afterwards to Aden about the amount of hassle their order had caused – they had no idea what was involved. Fortunately, there were no aircraft due over this period so the whole station could concentrate on the operation, but I had no wish to make a habit of it. My protest may have born fruit because some time later I received another signal from Aden to say that another boat (can't remember its name) was heading towards Masirah and I was not to refuel it. I wasn't sure what I was supposed to do with a boat which looked likely to arrive on my doorstep with not enough fuel to go anywhere else. It did arrive unexpectedly and, once again, I hared down to the jetty with Aldis lamp and operator. She was cruising up and down off the jetty right on top of the reef – a good job the tide was high. We warned him to stay clear – he was obviously unaware of its existence. I then told him of the orders I had received from Aden but asked him to come ashore so that we could discuss what to do and I would contact Aden. He declined, or couldn't, I don't know which, and signalled that he was going on to Bombay, We wished him God Speed and he departed. I have often wondered if he made it.

Towards the end of 1948, or possibly in 1949 after I had left, there was a new arrangement for filling the CO post at Masirah. The Comms Unit had provided the officer but most of us had already done our stint at the outstations so Headquarters turned to the RAF Regiment officers of the APL. In my time the CO of the APL squadron was a squadron leader but came under the jurisdiction of the OC Masirah who could be a flying officer or flight lieutenant who of course was junior in rank. When I later flew up the route in the RSM I was somewhat surprised to find that the CO was an APL squadron leader complete with wife. As he had no experience of air traffic control one of the Comms Flight's warrant officer pilots had been sent to carry out these duties. The squadron leader obviously didn't think it proper for him to share the Mess with an NCO so he had a partition erected across the middle of the bar/anteroom, with a door in one corner. The warrant officer and the NCOs in our crew were banished to the far end. It was not very popular with any of us. I often wondered how his wife managed to fill her days.

Bill Rogers was the wireless fitter who arrived at Masirah at about the same time as Les Bulmer arrived as CO. He writes appreciatively of the Indian Overseas Airlines DC-3 which contained a gorgeous girl as air hostess and always left a box of fruit, mostly mangos, pineapples and limes. The hostess, like the rest of the crew, was British but dressed in an Indian-style outfit of silk maroon top with a white neckband and white silk trousers. The effect was quite charming. The six-monthly supply ship was the SS *Velho* which had a Greek captain and a Scottish engineer. Much of the cargo was drums of petrol, but also live goats for the APL. Both were offloaded onto dhows which took them as close inshore as possible. Both were then tipped into the sea, the goats to swim ashore. At night the goats were kept in a corral of empty fuel barrels, and by day they were allowed to graze under the watchful eye of a shepherd. Bill writes:

> We had a visit from an air commodore and I was driving him down to my transmitter station in the petrol bowser, which was the only vehicle which would start that day. He asked me how long I had been there and I replied 'Ten months'. I was recalled to Aden soon after. I didn't really want to go back, I was quite happy at Masirah.

1949

The number of aircraft passing through seems to have increased in 1949. Dakotas of Ethiopian Airlines were regular visitors and from Addis Ababa there was also a Saab Safir belonging to Count von Rosen. An American Church Mission aircraft passed through, as did aircraft of the Iraq Petroleum Company. Surprisingly, in view of the Sultan's embargo, there were also eight French Air Force Dakotas and Junkers 52s from French Somaliland.

The following excerpt appeared in the *Sunday Empire News* on 27 November 1949:

> Even today piracy has by no means disappeared. One tragic incident startled Masirah only a few months ago. A party of pilgrims bound for Mecca

chartered a native sailing dhow and set out from a port on the Arabian mainland. There was little food and water aboard, and the passengers were soon reduced almost to exhaustion. Then the captain, backed by his crew of toughs, demanded more money and refused to continue the journey until the passengers paid up.

When, a few days later, the dhow came abreast of Masirah he forced the passengers ashore there and headed for home, leaving them on the edge of a wilderness of sand and scrub.

Five of the passengers died. After three weeks of appalling hardship five others managed to cross Masirah and reach the RAF station. One of them, a woman, had a broken arm. The RAF fed, clothed and housed them, gave medical aid, and got up a subscription to which all the personnel contributed, including the native levies from the Aden Protectorate who make up the island garrison. After five days the stranded pilgrims were flown to Aden – and continued their journey to Mecca.

The article also contains the following fanciful item:

Nature is full of surprises there. Take the sporadic volcanic eruptions. They give out neither smoke nor lava, but merely a chalky white substance that nobody on the island is able to identify.

1950

The Wali Camp is mentioned for the first time by Gerry Lukes who was at

1950. The six-month supply ship, the tramp steamer SS *Velho*
(Photograph: Gerry Lukes)

1950. Taking empty fuel drums to a dump
(Photographs: Gerry Lukes)

Masirah in 1950. It was a collection of shanties the other side of the black hills at the back of the station. There was a brackish well there which was the site of the village of Hilf which had been burnt down by the British Political Agent in April 1943. The name 'Wali Camp' implies that the old RAF petrol-tin camp was no longer habitable and that the Wali and the labourers had moved out.

Gerry Lukes reports that the CO had been posted in from Malta, so presumably there were still insufficient aircrew officers at Aden to man the route stations. He also mentions the two cannons which were found and taken to the Officers' Mess where they were mounted outside the entrance. The cannons were found near the monument and the wreck of the Bisley. Local

Bringing the fuel drums ashore from a dhow
Top: Rowing them ashore in 1950 (Photograph: Gerry Lukes)
Bottom: Swimming them ashore in 1952 when no other method was available
(Photograph Bob Bolton)

fishermen said that they were taken there a long time ago from Sur Masirah, but this does seem unlikely. They would be too heavy to move, even by camel; and there seems to be no reason to move them to this uninhabitable spot. So perhaps the cannons came from a ship which was driven ashore and wrecked near the monument.

In September an Indamer charter aircraft spent five days at Masirah after bursting a tyre. There were six crew and twenty passengers including three women and three children. They seriously depleted the station's rations but the new faces made a pleasant change. Just before Christmas six Brigands of 8 Squadron, together with two Valettas full of ground crew, spent the night at Masirah, en route from Habbaniya to Aden. The total number of visitors was fifty-six which was about the maximum the station could accommodate. It was certainly enough for a station which was supposed to be on care and maintenance, although the number of British personnel had now increased to seventeen.

1951

In March there were thunderstorms with heavy rain, the first rain since 1946.

On the morning of 16 July a distress transmission was received from the tanker *British Character*. A seaman on board was suffering from appendicitis and his life was in jeopardy; he urgently required a surgical operation. The ship's lifeboat was out of commission so the tanker's skipper requested that a craft from RAF Masirah should come to the ship and take the seaman ashore. RAF Masirah had no boats of any kind so a local dhow was hired. It sailed to the tanker but the seaman had already left for Masirah on the ship's lifeboat which had been repaired. The two craft had crossed but not seen each other in the poor visibility of the south-west monsoon. By the next day a team of three medical officers had arrived from Aden and performed the operation for a perforated appendix. The seaman was still dangerously ill so he was flown to Aden where there were better medical facilities.

There was now a serviceable Bedford lorry on the station. It was used to empty the latrines (there were still no flush lavatories) and then hosed down with sea water before being used to collect the rations from the RSM supply aircraft.

In October Jack Sharing arrived from Aden and writes this comprehensive account of his time at Masirah.

> The station consisted of a small cluster of low buildings which appeared to be randomly scattered on the south side of the main runway which was aligned on 070°/250°. The runway itself was rolled sand. There were a few other buildings dotted around in the middle distance, all looking rather forlorn and derelict, the largest being a rusty old hangar. My billet was in one of the Quonset huts which had been divided into two rooms with their own entrances at each end. I shared my room with the medical orderly, and the room at the other end was shared by the airframe fitter and engine fitter. We even had our own entrance porch complete with a castor oil plant which looked rather undernourished. It was not common

The Aden Protectorate Levies
(Photograph: via Bill Corser)

for airmen to be billetted together in pairs for reasons which might seem obvious today but were not then.

As the radio operator my duties were to ensure that the wireless station was manned and to operate the HF/DF facility for incoming and outgoing aircraft. The wireless station was manned by two Arab operators from the Aden Protectorate Levies who handled most of the point to point work. I usually looked in two or three times each day to see that all was well. The link with Aden and the other route stations lasted from 0630 hours to 1830 hours on six days a week. Traffic consisted mainly of met reports, routine open messages, encrypted messages and aircraft flight plans. The two APL operators were good and did most of the work. Occasionally I would stand in for them if they needed time off for religious ceremonies, etc. They were good workers and their morse was accurate which was, I thought, very commendable considering that they were working in a foreign language with a foreign script. I learned a lot about the Arab character and their way of thinking from Ali and Mohammed, and we became good friends. The APL lines were surrounded by rolls of barbed wire and on the whole there was little mixing between the RAF airmen and the Arab soldiers. However, I did visit the APL lines sometimes and will not forget the monkey which they had brought with them from the Aden Protectorate. It had been caught stealing so they had chopped off a hand in the Moslem manner. I felt really sorry for it. It spent its whole day chained to a post. Presumably they fed and watered it occasionally but it always looked so pathetically sad whenever I saw it.

The met readings were taken by the Indian Meteorological Officer. Apart from the temperature, surface wind and atmospheric pressure etc. he also released a hydrogen balloon five times a day, following it by theodolite to plot the upper winds. The point to point link to Aden closed down after he had sent his last report at 1800 hours each evening.

The station headquarters was immediately in front of the hardstanding on which the visiting aircraft were parked. Above the SHQ was the air traffic control tower, an imposing structure in timber and glass with an aerial mast on its roof. The control tower appeared to sit on the roof of the main building but it was actually supported on a trestle which was partly in front of the building and partly through it. A verandah ran along the front of the building facing the airfield giving it a rather elegant appearance. An outside ladder with hand rails climbed through the roof of the verandah up to the control tower.

Beside the SHQ building was the wireless building, and between the two was the point to point receiving aerial mast, about 30 feet high. The other end of the wireless building was used by the met officer for his equipment. Near the mast was a signpost pointing to Aden (939 miles), Mauripur (the RAF staging post at Karachi), Colombo (in Sri Lanka, as it is now called), Bombay, the South Pole, and London.

Behind the SHQ (looking from the airfield) were the officers' accommodation huts with their Mess over to the right. Behind the officers' accommodation was a long building which housed (left to right) the NAAFI, its entrance hall, a games room with a snooker table, the cinema, the cookhouse, and the Airmen's Mess. [Author's note: the foundations of this building could still be seen in 1998 in line with the clothing store to its south-east.] To the left of this building was the line of airmen's accommodation huts with the railway running in front of them. The railway was for taking barrels of aviation petrol to a concrete ramp to the left of the SHQ building. Labourers rolled the barrels up the ramp and tipped the contents into a sink hole down to the four underground storage tanks which were, I think, of 2500 gallons capacity. The aircraft were refuelled on the hardstanding directly from these underground tanks without the need for a bowser. [Author's note: The aircraft hardstanding still survived in 1998. It is the large rectangle of concrete immediately to the south-east of the fuel bowser shelter and still has the aircraft picketing rings in recesses in the concrete.]

Behind the NAAFI/Airmens' Mess was another building with a verandah all the way round it. This was Station Sick Quarters. To the left and slightly behind this was the APL compound. More towards the black hills at the back were the AMWD offices, power station and desalination plant. Behind this was the old wartime camp made of four gallon petrol tins. [Author's note: this was the area in front of the laundry in 1998.]

The days passed slowly, and I enjoyed every minute of them. I had an

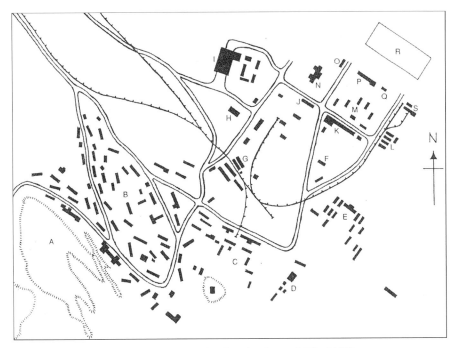

Map 16: RAF Masirah after the Second World War

Key:

2-ft gauge railway

Vehicle Track

A   Low dark hills

B   Petrol tin camp (Abandoned except for Wali and labourers)

C   Air Ministry Works Directorate

D   Water Desalination Plant – originally the American plant to the south, later the RAF plant in the 'Giraffe House'

E   Aden Protectorate Levies

F   Station Sick Quaters

G   Two Nissen huts which have survived to the present day

H   Tall stores building

I   Hanger full of Wellington spares

J   Stores which has survived to the present day as the clothing and stationary store

K   Airmens' Mess, NAAFI, cinema, and later Sergeants' Mess

L   Airmens' Billets. Quonset huts

M   Officers' Accommodation. Quonset huts

N   Officers' Mess. A small annex to the north survives to the present day

O   Signals

P   Met, SHQ, Library. Air Traffic Control Tower

Q   Aircraft servicing and refuelling equipment

R   Concrete hardstanding for aircraft

S   Fuel tanks with underground pipes to hydrant refuelling on the hardstanding

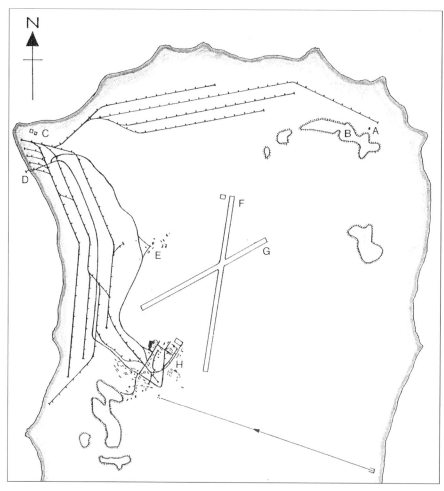

Map 17: RAF Masirah after the Second World War

Key:

Vehicle Track	———————
2-ft Gauge Railway	⊢–⊢–⊢–⊢–⊢–⊢
Salt Water Feed Pipe	————→

A   Monument
B   Brady's Beacon
C   Reservoirs (disused)
D   Jetty
E   BOAC
F   Runway 01/19
G   Runway 07/25
H   RAF Masirah

extremely light work commitment, unlike most of my fellow airmen who had to put in a full day's work. The MT team, for example, had an impossible task to keep the fleet of ageing miscellaneous vehicles in running condition. All the vehicles were left over from the Second World War, some of them American. There was a 15 cwt Ford pickup, a Bedford 4 wheel drive 3 tonner, an Austin ambulance, a Chevrolet 3 ton lorry which had been resurrected from the scrap heap, the station fire engine, a Coles crane, two or three water bowsers and of course the railway locomotives and their rolling stock.

As the airfield was at the north end of the island it was bounded on three sides by sea. But we didn't swim, due to sharks, barracuda, sea snakes, moray eels, stone fish and all the other creatures which could poison you or bite bits off you. Some of the boys built a raft by lashing together a couple of old aircraft drop tanks, and they had a great time trying this out around the jetty. I fished off the jetty and walked to the hills which were within reach. The hill above the monument had a red light on top of it to warn aircraft arriving at night.

For fishing we used nylon line and hooks purchased from the NAAFI – no rod. You just put a weight on the end of the line, baited the hook with a bit of dried fish, swung it round your head and let it go as far as possible. Often the tackle got caught and lost in the coral. The best place to fish was off the end of the jetty. Once I saw a dark shape flash by in the water. There was a sharp tug on the line, then nothing. When I pulled in the line the bait, hook and weight were all gone. That puts you off swimming.

The best beach lay on the east coast and it was here that we were fascinated by the loggerhead turtles as they came in to lay their eggs after sundown. The struggle these large creatures endured to climb up the shore to above the high tide mark; their tearful efforts to excavate the nest with their rear flippers; the laying of about 100 eggs; the subsequent covering up of the nest and the return to the sea all took a very long time. It was a very emotional experience for us who had not had the advantage of prior knowledge through TV wildlife documentaries. We knew little of these things and it was a greatly revealing experience to learn about life at first hand. Sadly I never saw the young turtles hatch and begin their great struggle for survival.

During the day this beach was a different place. We might see a small group of local fishermen netting the inshore fish. In addition to their catch of sardines there was often a dogfish or even a small barracuda in the net, which simply reinforced our view that the sea was for the fish and not for the likes of us! In some places there were ghost crabs, about the size of a hand, and standing up on elevated legs. In one part there were so many that they formed a moving circle round you as you walked along, always facing you and with eyes aloft on stalks. Their burrows were just above the high tide mark, each marked by a cone of sand which they had excavated out. It was like being in an alien place. I was thankful that they were timid creatures

RAF Masirah, 1958.
The top photograph was taken from a Single Pioneer of 78 Squadron in transit between Aden and Muscat during the Jebel Akhdar War. The building below the Air Traffic Control Tower was demolished by the cyclone on 13 June 1977.

(Photographs: Terry Scott Collier)

and didn't like to come any nearer than a few feet. One minute you would be walking through a colony of them, and then you would go a few more yards and there would be none.

Walking was really my favourite pastime. I was sorry that we were not allowed to stray very far from the camp area, for the rest of the island was always there, luring, beckoning and begging to be explored.

Occasionally there would be a recreation run out to Sur Masirah, but this did not happen very often. One day the CO together with the APL CO decided to mount an expedition to explore the hills to the south of Sur Masirah. We set off in two vehicles with cameras, water bottles, etc. At Sur Masirah the CO and the medical orderly dispensed some medicine to the locals, and then we split into teams and took to the hills. Our team first walked south, then eastwards, crossing right over the island to the eastern shore. Then we walked north for a while, then west across the island back to the vehicles at Sur Masirah. We were on the lookout for gazelle but saw none, and I suspected that there were none on the island. In fact apart from the occasional snake, lizard and scorpion we saw no animal life at all. It was about the hottest day I had experienced and really quite uncomfortable in the wadis. I was sorry when the time came to return to camp and I looked forward to repeating the exercise another day.

Mention of snakes reminds me of my very first day at Masirah, the day after I arrived. As I walked to the DF cabin I saw this snake scuttle across the ground and disappear under the cabin. The cabin was raised above the ground by a few inches to allow the cables to pass underneath and into the cabin through a hole in the floor. I had been told that the most common snake on the island was the silver krait, a small snake with a deadly bite unless quick treatment was at hand. As you can imagine, I entered the cabin cautiously, had a good search round and then switched on the set. I did the whole of that watch with my feet on the seat and my eyes glued to the hole in the floor. The next day I sealed up the hole.

There was a bit more interest on the days that the RSM Valetta arrived from Aden. We had a look at the passenger list to see who was on it, and we got to know some of the crews quite well. In fact I still correspond with one air signaller. The aircraft were at Masirah overnight so we often met the crews in the NAAFI in the evenings. The NAAFI was the centre of most activity after work, with darts, dominoes, snooker and card games. The RSM usually brought a film which was shown a couple of times. Sometimes a couple of us would go to the wireless room after dinner and listen in to the hams on the amateur radio bands. Reception was good and we enjoyed listening to the chat from all around the world. I could receive All India Radio and the BBC World Service on the radio in my billet.

In November 1951 a US Navy Liberator was with us for almost a week. It was on a photographic survey which took it away on very long flights, but

I've no idea where it was going. It had a crew of ten so we got to know many of them. It came back for a shorter visit just before Christmas.

Although we knew we were a long way from our home base in Aden we never felt forgotten. On one occasion a services entertainment party arrived. There was a female singer, a magician, a juggler/fire eater and comedian. It was greatly appreciated. Christmas 1951 brought the usual festivities, not helped by the fact that the NAAFI was closed for the period. Some of the lads built a bar in the entrance hall and stocked it with goods which had been bought from the NAAFI. On Christmas morning we held a crazy football match in fancy dress with crutches etc., and dinner was served by the CO. The cooks had excelled themselves. No one worked harder than our cooks and the day to day food at Masirah was always first class.

1952

Sometime in early 1952 a flight of four Shackletons made the long and somewhat hazardous direct crossing from Aden to Negombo in Ceylon (now Sri Lanka). The route stations were asked to maintain watch and provide DF for the aircraft. The flight was uneventful until just before the point of no return when one of the aircraft developed an engine fault and had to turn back to Aden. A second aircraft accompanied it. I stayed on watch the whole time until they were safely back – a total of fifteen hours. I was quite shattered at the end but felt that I had done my bit. When they were 800 to 900 miles away I was able to give class A bearings which is an accuracy of plus or minus two degrees. This was remarkable and due to the lack of local interference. HMS *Flamingo* put into the Masirah Channel for four days to give the crew a break. We were invited aboard to sample some naval hospitality. A boat met us at the jetty in the evening and took us out to the ship. The crew had been saving their rum ration for the occasion so we all finished up extremely happy and hoarse after going through the whole repertoire of air force and naval bawdy songs. A night or two later we invited them ashore to share an evening with us in the NAAFI and we all had what was known as 'a reet good time'.

One morning we awoke to a strange noise to find we had been invaded by a swarm of locusts. They were everywhere but thankfully they could not get into our billet. I was reluctant to venture outside and stayed under cover as long as I could. The Arabs, on the other hand, were delighted. They ran around catching the insects which were about the size of fat dragonflies, stuffing them into jars and eating them alive. After a few hours the swarm had passed by and our castor oil plant had been stripped of its leaves. Some years later I read that this had been a very large swarm which had originated in

East Africa. Part of it had travelled the length of the South Arabian coastline and into Oman.

After six months I managed to get a three month extension to my tour, but eventually the time did come for me to return to Aden, and from there to be repatriated to the UK. For me spending nine months at Masirah was the experience of a lifetime and I often think back to those days in which I felt totally relaxed and at peace with myself. Maybe time has coloured my memory a little but I know that my two years national service influenced the rest of my life.

The supply ship, the SS *Velho*, was now in her last year of service to Masirah. The station operations record book for April 1952 included the following:

At 0830 on Sunday 6th April the six month supply ship, the SS *Velho*, anchored 300 yards off the jetty. Unloading commenced half an hour later and was completed by midday on the 8th. Facilities available for the operation were the unit air sea rescue launch and a large motor boat brought up by the *Velho* plus a dozen locally hired sailing dhows, one Coles crane, the diesel-engined train, five 3-ton trucks, an abundant supply of labour comprising RAF airmen, Aden Protectorate Levies and native technicians and coolies. The principal items off-loaded were: the No. 2 Squadron Aden Protectorate Levies, 330 sheep and goats, six month's supply of hay, six month's dry rations for approximately 180 men and 40 tons of AMDGW stores. Back-loading began at 1400 hours and by 1700 hours was complete. This comprised 203 empty POL drums and the remainder of the dry rations brought by the *Velho* on its previous visit. At 0600 hours on the 10th the ship left for Salalah.

During that month three dhows arrived with 638 burmails of gasoil and 344 of petrol for the MT. The aviation gasoline had arrived during the previous two months on a total of eleven dhows carrying 2,756 burmails. There was apparently some loss of aviation gasoline from the tanks under the aircraft hardstanding. When this was investigated it was discovered that the leak was in the underground pipes to the storage tanks. These had to be dug up and replaced. The US Navy again applied for permission to base its Liberator at Masirah from 15 September to 15 December for further photographic surveys. This would require an extra 7,000 gallons to make up a total of 20,000 imperial gallons of aviation gasoline.

HMS *Flamingo* called again in September and the SS *Velho* came on her last visit in October. This time she was not used for changing over the whole APL Squadron – some of the changeover was by air.

The supply of fuel and oil by dhow was not proving to be entirely satisfactory. In November two dhows arrived from the refinery at Bahrain with fuel and oil for both Masirah and Salalah. However, the dhowmasters refused to sail on to Salalah, and pitched Salalah's burmails into the sea. Somehow the RAF managed to retrieve all of them. Later in the month another dhow arrived with 600 burmails of gasoil. The dhowmaster was told to take them on to Salalah, but he refused. There were now 895 burmails at Masirah which should have been at Salalah. The trader Khimji Ramdas was approached to see if he could help. He could. He hired five dhows to take the burmails to Salalah.

There were few changes to the situation at RAF Masirah for some years to come, but elsewhere events were beginning to unfold. These events would ultimately result in Shackleton aircraft being detached to Masirah for bombing operations.

In 1952 a fleet of Aramco oil trucks unexpectedly arrived at Buraimi which is on the northern border of Oman. Some of the Buraimi villages belong to Oman but most of them were part of the Sheikdom of Abu Dhabi. Aramco was the American oil company operating in Saudi Arabia, and these trucks contained a posse of Saudi police with their leader Turki bin Ataishan. He announced to the local inhabitants that he was their new governor and that they were now the subjects of King Abdulaziz ibn Saud. The nearest Saudi border was over 100 miles away. The Saudi claim on the Buraimi oasis was based on the temporary armed occupation by Wahibi tribesmen from the Negd area of what was later Saudi Arabia, and which had ended about ninety years earlier. In historical terms the claim was extremely thin, but Buraimi was important to the Saudis because it was the gateway to the potentially oil-rich area to the south of the Hajar mountains.

The Saudi police established themselves in the Buraimi villages and embarked on a programme of massive bribery. The Sultanate villages were quickly subverted but the Abu Dhabi governor, Sheikh Zaid, stood firm and earned himself a place in the Guinness Book of Records for refusing the world's most handsome bribe – a sum equivalent to £30,000,000 was mentioned.

Some Aden Protectorate Levies were flown in, and the Sultan assembled a rabble of several thousand loyal tribesmen on the Batinah coast opposite Buraimi. The British Government viewed this development with some misgivings. There was little doubt which side the Americans would take, and British colonialist aggression would be condemned in the United Nations. As the Sultan's rabble was about to advance the British Consul General arrived hot-foot from Muscat. He strongly advised caution and a low profile, and the Sultan's hand was stayed at the eleventh hour. His rabble dispersed and the Sultan returned to Muscat. Instead of an offensive the Saudi garrison was to be besieged. The intention was not to starve them out – they had plenty of money to buy food – but to throw around them a cordon sanitaire to isolate them from the rest of the human race.

1953

The Trucial Oman Levies (as they were then named) piquetted Buraimi, and armoured cars of the RAF Regiment were shipped in from Habbaniya. AHQ

Levant then had responsibility for the area. Also from Habbaniya the Vampires of 6 Squadron were detached to Sharjah for short periods, and carried out the occasional 'flagwave' over Buraimi. This, of course, drew protests from the Saudis. The Valetta which brought the ground crew was used to drop leaflets on the Muscat and Oman villages of the oasis, urging the inhabitants to remain loyal to their Sultan. But the Saudi money spoke louder. The 6 Squadron Vampires were damaging the sand runway at Sharjah so their detachments ceased. Instead the Meteor FR 9s of 208 Squadron were detached for short periods from their home base in the Suez Canal Zone, but they were never used in anger. The bulk of the air effort was by maritime Lancasters of 37 and 38 Squadrons at Malta. They were detached to Bahrain for the reconnaissance of the supply routes from Saudi Arabia to Buraimi along the southern part of Trucial Oman, later called the United Arab Emirates. Later the PR Lancasters of 683 Squadron were diverted to this task, and so were the Valettas of the Aden Communications Unit and the Ansons of the newly formed 1417 Flight at Bahrain. It was an incredibly boring task. The search of the supply routes was protracted, costly, and fruitless.

On the ground the fifty-strong Trucial Oman Levies were quite inadequate for their task, so gangs of discharged Aden Protectorate Levies were rounded up in the backstreets of Aden, paid handsomely to enrol in the TOL, and freighted up to Sharjah. Most of them had been dishonourably discharged, and they had learnt no more honour in the backstreets of Aden. At Buraimi these louts discovered a profitable sideline in selling their ammunition to the locals. The CO determined to put down this lucrative trade, so he drove to the outpost in his Land Rover together with his Jordanian RSM, an RAF medical officer, and a visiting REME sergeant who came along to see the fun. All but the REME sergeant were shot dead. The mutineers then melted away, but were picked up by Sheik Zaid's men. They ended up in the grim prison of Fort Jalali in Muscat.

Incarceration in Jalali was feared throughout Oman and the mention of its name to an Omani could bring conversation to a dead stop. It was built by the Portuguese in the sixteenth century, a grey fortress on a crag of black rock in Muscat harbour. As the heat of the day built up the encircling black hills reflected and contained the unbearable heat, and the stagnant fetid air stank of rotting fish and sewage. The silent fastness of Jalali was connected to the Muscat sea front at low tide by a filthy strip of beach, and entry to the fort was up vertiginous steps to the blockhouse which jutted precariously over the sea. A row of massive cannons pointed into the bay through arches in a wall. On the other side there was a blank stone facade pierced here and there by barred windows. The ordinary prisoners were permanently shackled with ponderous iron bars between their ankles. The more important ones were kept in perpetual solitary confinement. The water ration was tiny, and in the leaden heat there was an atmosphere of forlorn despair.

On another occasion two British soldiers arrived in Buraimi at night and blundered into the Saudi stronghold. The gates closed behind them and it was some time before anyone realised that they were missing. A severely worded ultimatum was then sent to Turki, who allowed it to expire by a conspicuous margin before releasing the two bewildered lads.

1954

After a couple of years everyone was getting bored with the Buraimi Incident. It was agreed that the whole matter should go to arbitration at Geneva. There was to be a military withdrawal, including aircraft, leaving only fifteen personnel of each side at Buraimi. The Aramco oil trucks had lain unused for so long that Turki and his police had to be driven to the Saudi border by the TOL.

At Geneva the Saudis attempted to bribe the members of the tribunal, while at Buraimi Saudi aircraft were flying in additional personnel. Eventually the British Government lost patience and unleashed the TOL who swooped at dawn in October 1955. The Saudis were rounded up and flown out by the following morning. There were a few minor skirmishes but a low-flying Lincoln of 7 Squadron, Bomber Command, added just the right measure of menace to discourage resistance. The Buraimi Incident was over.

It was not only the Saudis who were interested in the prospects of oil in Oman – a British Company, the Iraq Petroleum Company, was also interested but due to political difficulties an approach from the north was not feasible. A beachhead on the south coast was the only practical way into the interior. The first length of coast to be considered was immediately opposite Masirah, but this was rejected because it was low-lying land and liable to flood. The next to be considered was the bay immediately to the south of Khaluf in the Ghubbat Hashish. A Royal Navy survey ship investigated and found the bay to be unsuitable. The next length of coastline to be considered was the wide Sauqirah Bay to the west of Ras Madrakah. The Sultan favoured Khor Gharim but said that he would have to send someone to investigate the tribal situation before giving his permission.

Eventually the spot chosen was Duqm, between Ras Madrakah and Khaluf to its north. By the beginning of 1954 the camp was well established with three desalination plants allowing two gallons of fresh water per man per day. There were about 300 soldiers recruited from Muscat and Aden with a training officer on loan from the Aden Protectorate Levies. There was an LCT (landing craft tank, or in other words a craft for landing tanks) which brought supplies from Aden, and a small airfield had been laid out about five miles from the camp. Local fish was available outside the period of the summer monsoon, and it was possible to buy goats locally. Geological parties had surveyed the area as far west as the border with Dhofar which ran north from Ras Sharbatat inland to Mughshin. In Dhofar an American company had the oil prospecting rights.

The area to the west of Duqm did not look particularly promising and the company's attention switched to an area 200 miles to the north near the Jebal Fahud. It would be a major undertaking to establish a drilling rig there and would take about a year before drilling could begin, the target date being at the end of 1955.

1955

In May 1955 Colonel Gerald de Gaury secured the right to prospect for minerals along the Batinah coast and on the island of Masirah. Oil, gas and coal were excluded, the prospecting rights being mainly for metal ores. The rights lasted for two years. Gerald de Gaury had been an officer in the British Army and in the Foreign and Political Service of the Government of India in the days of the British Raj. His speciality is not known but he appears as a passenger in Vincent pilot Donald Cromar's log book in the mid-1930s.

Gerald de Gaury's main interest seems to have been in copper ores between Sohar and Buraimi, and on Masirah. He had delved into the old India Office records and found the report of Assistant Surgeon Carter who had investigated the copper on Masirah in 1846. He took a sample home to the UK but found it difficult to interest any prospecting company. At that time copper prices were high and the prospecting companies had found vast deposits of high grade ore elsewhere. Gerald de Gaury submitted over-optimistic reports about the quantity and quality of the Masirah copper ore, and the interest of prospecting companies. His two years expired and he applied for an extension. This was refused in a somewhat icy letter from Neil Innes, the Sultan's Minister for External Affairs.

By the end of 1955 the Iraq Petroleum Company was ready to begin drilling at Fahud. The company's thoughts turned to the supply route and the route of any pipeline to the coast if oil should be found. Due to the south-west monsoon Duqm was not a convenient beachhead for supplies, and for the same reason it would not be a good location for an oil terminal. The company looked north for a supply route and route for the pipeline. As indicated earlier, there were political difficulties which should now be explained.

Muscat and Oman was still a medieval land. There were no tarmac roads anywhere in the Sultanate, no electricity or piped water, no telephone or postal services, a single school and no hospitals other than the American missionary hospital at Muscat. Contact with the outside world was by sea, but south of the Hajar mountain range Central Oman was isolated by the sand sea of the Rub al Khali. Here the tribesmen were untouched by the outside world. Theirs was a land of barren hills and plains scoured by wadis which would flood after the occasional torrential storm. Mud villages and date groves took advantage of every source of water, including man-made underground tunnels introduced by the ancient Persians. Forts and watchtowers dotted the landscape, eroded by the winds and rains of centuries. The tribesman wore the traditional dishdash, a long white garment. Around his waist was an ammunition belt for the Martini-Henry, a half-inch calibre smooth-bore breech loader, which was carried on his shoulder and held by the barrel. He was barefoot, and around his head was a shawl wound into an untidy turban. On his belly was his *kunja* (dagger) in its ornate scabbard. He was darkly bearded and, in later life, grizzled by the merciless sun.

In 1737 Ahmed bin Said, the Wali of Sohar, slaughtered the remaining Persians who were occupying the Batinah coast. Ahmed later became Imam (a spiritual title) and founded the dynasty which rules Oman to this day. The title of Imam should have been by election, but Ahmed's successors made it hereditary and assumed the title of Sultan. The tribes of the interior (Central Oman) then began to elect their own imams from among the more pious of their sheikhs. For a century and a half there was an Iman of Oman and a Sultan of Muscat and Oman. Sometimes the Sultan called himself Imam, and sometimes there was no Imam in the interior. There were times when Sultan and Imam co-existed in the greatest harmony, the Sultan recognised as titular overlord while the Imam was the spiritual leader of the interior. In 1913 many of the tribes in Central Oman rebelled against the Sultan's authority and fought a fairly successful war against him. It was concluded by the Treaty of Sib. This ambiguously worded treaty pledged the Sultan not to interfere in the internal affairs of Central Oman.

In the early 1950s there was harmony. The Imam was wise, just and respected. Sultan Said bin Taimur was a benign autocrat, but obsessed by the debts that he had inherited from his father. He radiated a confident authority and easy charm, speaking perfect English, Hindi, and of course Arabic. Said bin Taimur had all the qualities expected of a sultan of the Old School. When the Saudis occupied Buraimi in 1952 it was the Imam who provided his Sultan with most of the unruly warriors who assembled on the Batinah coast. Unfortunately the Imam died before the Saudis were evicted. Turki's bribes secured the election of a puppet Imam by the name of Ghalib bin Ali. Ghalib was a colourless man but had local backing. His younger brother, Talib, was active and ambitious. Also backing Ghalib was Suleiman bin Hamyar, who had a thoroughly nasty reputation and who was Sheikh of the Jebal Akhdar region. Another prime backer was Sheikh Saleh bin Issa from further east in the province of Sharqiya. The four of them were the leading lights in the proclamation of an independent Imamate. Perhaps they expected the Saudis to respect their independence.

The Sultan contemplated the situation with some displeasure. In spite of the Treaty of Sib he had no doubt that he was the legitimate sovereign ruler of the heartland of Oman.

At the end of 1955 the Sultan embarked on a remarkable journey across the desert from Salalah. With a handful of Dodge Powerwagons and a few retainers and Bedouin guides he navigated across the trackless wastes to the oil camp at Fahud. Here he joined his Muscat and Oman Field Force and advanced on Nizwa, the Imam's stronghold. It was a personal triumph. Suddenly the inhabitants found their Sultan in their midst, magnificently dressed and holding court with a haughty disdain. Not a shot was fired. The Imam abdicated and returned to his village. Sheikh Suleiman came to pay his respects and swore his loyalty. In the Sharqiya the news reached Salah bin Issa who thought it prudent to slip quietly out of the country to Saudi Arabia. Talib also fled and took refuge in the formidable fort at Rostaq. Here he was besieged by the Sultan's Batinah Force. One dark night he slipped away, creeping through the encircling piquets and escaping to Saudi Arabia where he joined Saleh.

Meanwhile the Sultan continued his drive to Buraimi where the Saudis had recently been expelled. Here he had a friendly meeting with the Sheikh of Abu Dhabi who ruled most of the oasis villages. He then continued his royal progress through the hills and down the Batinah coast to Muscat. His Highness Said bin Taimur, Sultan of Muscat and Oman, was the undoubted ruler of all his hereditary lands.

But where was the Imam Ghalib? Where was his brother Talib? Where was Saleh? Where was the repulsive Suleiman? None of them was safely incarcerated in the grim Fort Jalali in Muscat.

1956

By May the drilling rig at Fahud had reached a depth of 4,000 feet. Although smears and traces of oil had been found, there had been no strike. The company was not too disappointed, for the ultimate depth had been planned at 12,000 feet. Work was held up when the casing split. By the end of October the drill bit was down to 8,700 feet and it looked very much as if the well would be a dud. Nevertheless drilling continued and a track to the capital area was established via Izki and Fanjah.

In Egypt the Americans withdrew their funding for the Aswan High Dam. This was a project which was important to Colonel Nasser, President of Egypt. He looked round for an alternative source of money and nationalised the Suez Canal which belonged to Britain and France. Britain and France attempted to reclaim it by military force because they did not want this vital waterway to be controlled by a pro-Soviet dictator. When the British and French forces were well on their way down the canal their advance was halted by the

Americans with threats of economic sanctions. The British and French handed over to a United Nations force and the United Nations force handed it back to the Egyptians who blocked the canal by sinking ships in it. Anti-British propaganda inflamed the Middle East (except for Sultan Said bin Taimur) and even the Omani labourers at Masirah went on strike.

CHAPTER V

The Jebal Akhdar Campaign

1957

CENTRAL OMAN is dominated by the impregnable massif of the Jebal Akhdar (the Green Mountain) which is the most substantial part of the Hajar mountain spine. The greeness of the mountain is not apparent. The Jebal Akhdar is grey. Its highest point is nearly 10,000 feet and there is a plateau at 6,000 feet where there are a number of villages. The village of Saiq lies in a depression full of orchards, vineyards and fields. At nearby Sharaija the terraced fields are stacked down, tier below tier, descending 1,000 feet into a huge bowl at the top of a gorge. The walls of the jebal are mile-high slabs thrusting up abruptly. The slabs are smooth, and between them are steep-sided wadis, spectacular clefts cut into the mountain. A few of them have donkey paths which lead up to the plateau. A handful of men could command each route up the mountain. The plateau is a fortress. To the east the mountain drops steeply to a valley through which the oil company drove its trucks from Muscat to Fahud. Below the southern wall of the mountain the towns and villages are enclosed in a valley, hemmed in to the south by black barren hills. To the east is Nizwa which is between the black hills and an enclosing spur of the Jebal Akhdar.

There is plenty of surface water in the wadi at Nizwa, and extensive date groves. There is a great round fort built over a rock, its walls many feet thick. It is infilled so that it is solid for three quarters of its height. Inside is a warren of passages and rooms, and two wells to an underground water supply. On top are two 20-ft vertical shafts, oubliettes down which prisoners were lowered to end their days in darkness and squalor. Eventually the corpses would be hauled up feet first.

A mile or two south of Nizwa is the village of Firq, pinched between the crab claw of hills. It is the gateway to Nizwa and the valley area south of the mountain. South of Firq are wide sandy plains punctuated by the occasional ridge.

After his bloodless victory in 1955 the Sultan left a small garrison of his Muscat and Oman Field Force on the plain south of Firq. They surveyed a scene of pastoral innocence, but their intelligence was poor. Young men were

189

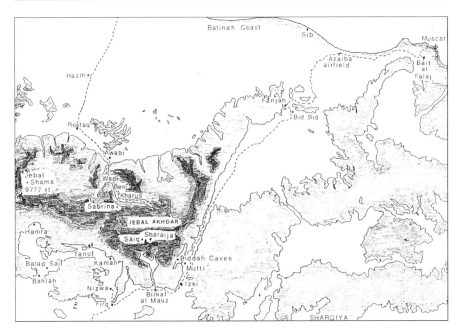

Map 18 & 19: The Jebal Akhdar Campaign

quietly leaving for Saudi Arabia where Talib was recruiting and training his Oman Liberation Front.

Talib's plan was for a two-pronged rebellion to erupt simultaneously in the Nizwa area and in Saleh's Sharqiya. Talib would lead the uprising on his home ground, returning from Saudi Arabia by dhow. The rebellion in the Sharqiya would be led by Saleh's brother Ibrahim, but Ibrahim was a born loser. At the appointed time, in April 1957, he unsuccessfully attempted to foment rebellion among a disinterested population. He did not know that Talib's dhow had broken down and that the uprising had not started in the Nizwa area. The Muscat and Oman Field Force paid him a visit and persuaded him to go to Muscat to discuss the matter with the Sultan. The Sultan flung him into Jalali without further ado. Sheikh Suleiman was invited to Muscat as a precaution, but there were no grounds for imprisoning him. He was virtually under house arrest, detained at the Sultan's pleasure.

Talib arrived later by dhow with a few score of his armed followers. He landed undetected on the Batinah coast and made his way to his home town of Balad Sait. He summoned his brother and told him he had been reinstated as Imam. The banner of revolt was unfurled, the white banner of the Imam.

The news reached the Muscat and Oman Field Force who thought they ought to drive from Firq to Balad Sait to see what was happening. At one point the track twists up through a rocky pass. Conscious of their line of communication (and line of retreat) it was arranged that the loyal Abriyin tribe would occupy the high ground and secure the pass against ambush. Thus reassured the Muscat and Oman Field Force set out for Balad Sait in their Land Rovers. It was an uneventful 20-mile journey, and sure enough the Imam's white flag flew over Balad Sait. The Muscat and Oman Field Force assembled their screw guns and settled down to the task of breaching the town walls. The screw guns were archaic – Kipling had written of them. At Balad Sait they soon ran out of ammunition. Back in Muscat the commissariat then discovered that the only remaining ammunition was in the Imperial War Museum in London. So the bombardment continued with mortars and machine guns. Battle raged for a week.

The news of the battle reached Suleiman in Muscat. The malevolent old lecher got into his motor car (the only one in the interior) and drove to his home territory. On his way home he came across a Land Rover full of wounded soldiers being taken to hospital from the battlefield. He killed them all, sparing only the driver, Abdul Karim, who was wounded but able to continue the drive to Muscat with the dead bodies. Suleiman's domain was not only the Jebal Akhdar but all the surrounding villages up to the outskirts of Nizwa and here he rallied his tribes to the Imam's cause.

The Muscat and Oman Field Force were now in hostile territory, they had not taken Balad Sait, and behind them were Suleiman's armed villages. They withdrew, but the loyal Abriyin were not holding the pass. The track threaded through hostile villages where every man's hand was turned against them. They were ambushed and harassed, and their Land Rovers unexpectedly encountered landmines. It was a massacre.

Some died among the waterless rocks in the blistering heat, some were captured, and some were killed out of hand. A few escaped, some melting away into the villages and some being led back over the hills by their British officers. For all practical purposes the Regiment was destroyed, the wounded Colonel evacuating the few survivors to the oil camp at Fahud.

The remainder of the Sultan's army was not large or strong enough to repeat the triumph of 1955. The Sultan had lost control of Central Oman together with its potential oil reserves, so he called on the British Government for help.

The British Government reacted with uncharacteristic speed and resolve. The Sultan would be given immediate assistance to defeat the rebels before international condemnation could get into top gear, but minimum force was to be used.

Sir Bernard Burrows in Bahrain was the Political Resident Persian Gulf and had political responsibility for the area. He consulted the Commander, British Forces Arabian Peninsular, whose headquarters was at Aden. Experience in the Aden Protectorates indicated that air power alone might quell such a rebellion, so this was the basis of their plan. After the surrender of the rebels the Sultan's Army, strengthened by the Trucial Oman Scouts, would move in and occupy the area. The Foreign Secretary said in the House that no British troops would be used.

At short notice four 8 Squadron Venoms were flown from Aden to Sharjah on 20 July. The groundcrew and equipment followed up in a Valetta belonging to 84 Squadron which had recently been reformed at Aden. Sharjah was far from ideal as an operating base. The airfield was on a low-lying salt flat a few hundred yards inland from the creek. On the inland side of the airfield were dunes and sparse scrub. The 6,000-ft runway was of hard sand, continually rolled to preserve the surface. The Venom had a characteristic nose-up attitude on the ground, its low jet pipe pointing slightly downwards. While taxying the aircraft raised a plume of sand, while on take-off the aircraft destroyed the runway, raising huge dust clouds and blowing away slabs of rolled sand. This had been known since the beginning of the Buraimi Incident when the 6 Squadron Vampires arrived from Habbaniya, but nothing had been done to eliminate the problem. The only way to preserve the runway was to stop the Venoms using it for take-off, so they had to take-off on a narrow semi-prepared strip on the far side of the runway which was kept as smooth as circumstances would allow. After each take-off the following Venom would have to wait for the dust to clear before the pilot could see the take-off strip.

The Venom was a single-seat jet fighter developed from the Vampire but was a much better aircraft in every respect. It had four 20mm cannons which fired explosive and incendiary shells, and could carry up to eight rockets. These rockets had explosive heads weighing 60lb which were useful for destroying tanks, buildings and small ships etc. Although the Venom was capable of dive-bombing it never did so in the Aden Protectorates or Oman due to the distances to the targets which required extra fuel in underwing tanks. These tanks were carried on the same mountings as bombs. If there was any bombing to be done it was carried out by Lincolns and later by Shackletons which were primarily maritime patrol and anti-submarine aircraft. Both had four piston engines and were developed from the Lancaster heavy bomber of the Second World War.

Dominating the airfield at Sharjah was the fort which had been built by Imperial Airways and was now used by International Aeradio who operated the airfield. The RAF were in old huts covered in peeling white plaster. Everywhere corrosion was evident; scattered around were piles of empty burmails. The only source of fresh water was the ancient distillation plant known affectionately as Betsy. She produced only enough water for drinking and was a static version of Stephenson's 'Rocket', the boiler and tall funnel squatting beside an open-ended hut with a rusty roof of corrugated iron. The condensed water squirted vertically up from a pipe running down the centre of the hut, hitting the rusty roof, and falling suitably cooled to the floor where it was drained away. The whole amazing process was accompanied by much wheezing and gurgling, hissing steam emerging from random fractures.

Brown salt water ran in the bath and shower house, staining and corroding the fittings. The salt water soap formed a scum which was difficult to remove. Outside on a ledge stood two burmails, one containing water and the other apparently containing black maple syrup. Actually it was oil. Drip by drip the mixture of the two fed a remarkably fierce fire known as a hydro-burner which was used for heating the salt water.

The decayed sleeping accommodation had torn flyscreens and large air ducts from the noisy air-conditioning plants outside. There was no temperature adjustment between 'on' and 'U/S'. The Mess was as squalid as the rest of the camp, the poor food being served by two unwashed Iranians in grubby grey nightshirts. RAF Sharjah was a slum.

Since January 1957 half of 42 Shackleton Squadron had been detached to Aden from its home base at St Eval in Cornwall. At Aden it had replaced a flight of ancient Lincoln bombers which had been disbanded. By mid-year the detachment was proving somewhat irksome for the families in Cornwall and it was therefore decided to form an Aden-based Shackleton squadron. This was to be 37 Squadron which was based in Malta and under threat of disbandment. It was reduced in strength to five aircraft which were flown to Aden via Iraq.

The sudden military involvement in Oman brought more units to the area. The Cameronians took over the garrison duties at Sharjah and Buraimi to release the Trucial Oman Scouts. The four Shackletons from the 42 Squadron

The Jebal Akhdar Campaign
The Blackburn Beverley. 'A warehouse with wings, piloted from a window in the roof' (Photograph: Aeroplane Monthly)

detachment in Aden flew into Bahrain. At this time the 37 Squadron Shackletons were passing through Bahrain en route to their new base in Aden. One of the 37 Squadron Shackletons was commandeered as a spare for the 42 Squadron detachment at Bahrain. The unfortunate 37 Squadron crew continued to Aden as passengers in a Valetta. The Shackletons at Bahrain were soon joined by two Abingdon-based Beverleys which had been detached to Aden. The Beverley was a huge, slow-flying, transport aircraft, a warehouse with wings, piloted from a window in the roof. More 84 Squadron Valettas flew up from Aden. The Pembrokes of the resident 1417 Flight at Bahrain were used for visual reconnaissance of Central Oman, monitoring movement and checking on the flags flying from the forts and watchtowers. The Sultan's red flag was conspicuously absent, the white flags of the Imam showing that the entire area was under rebel control.

On the day after their arrival at Sharjah the 8 Squadron pilots were picked up by one by the Shackletons and flown over the rebel-held area to familiarise them with the local geography. There was doubt about the actual location of the villages, the 1:500,000 air maps showing many of them miles from their true positions. The Shackletons photographed the forts and towers so that their construction and strength could be assessed. On 22 July the 8 Squadron Venoms joined a Shackleton in the rebel-held area where it was dropping warning leaflets near the Izki fort which had been chosen as a Venom target. The procedure was repeated the following day when the Shackleton and Venoms both dropped leaflets at the great round fort at Nizwa. The Venoms could drop leaflets from their split flaps.

The Venom attacks began on 24 July 1957. On successive days they rocketed the forts at Izki, Nizwa and Tanuf, with ten or twelve sorties on each fort. By this time Meteor FR9s of 208 Squadron had arrived from Malta and took low-level oblique photographs for damage assessment. These showed that the

The Jebal Akhdar Campaign
An 8 Squadron Venom firing a rocket (Photograph: Jerry Baxter)

attacks had been reasonably successful but the rockets had punched holes through the walls rather than knocking them down. Some walls were breached but none of the forts were completely destroyed. The great round fort at Nizwa withstood the attacks which only cratered the thick walls.

On 27 July a further six Venoms of 249 Squadron arrived at Sharjah from their home base at Nairobi. They were given a day to settle in, and then all six of them attacked the fort at Birkat al Mauz together with the four Venoms of 8 Squadron.

The Shackletons provided top cover for the fighters, but their bombing was limited to the small 20-lb anti-personnel bombs. The 500-lb and 1000-lb high-explosive bombs were considered to be too indiscriminate. The air action did not seem to be having the desired effect so the Shackletons dropped more leaflets threatening intensified air action. One of the Shackletons was briefed to drop leaflets into the inside of the fort at Firq as for some reason it was important that the leaflets did not fall outside the fort. So the leaflets were rolled up inside empty tins and dropped through the chute at very low level. As it passed over the fort the Shackleton was raked from nose to stern by small arms fire. One round narrowly missed the signaller who was observing in the tail cone. One of the other rounds entered the nose where there were three people, but it only damaged an intercom box. One of the people in the nose was Group Captain Harry Bufton, the Senior RAF Officer Persian Gulf, who was based in the small RAF headquarters at Bahrain. He was slightly injured by a piece of flying metal, but it was only a flesh wound. Many bullet strikes

The Jebal Akhdar Campaign.
Shackletons over the Jebal Akhdar (Photograph: Jerry Baxter)

were found on the aircraft after it landed, one bullet being found in a tin of sweets in the survival rations. They were lucky that nothing vital was hit and that no one was seriously injured.

Both Venom detachments rocketed the fort at Firq on 30 July, also setting fire to some vehicles. The following day the attacks were switched to the fort at Bahlah, and on 1 August the attacks were on the ex-Muscat and Oman Field Force camp at Firq, some tents nearby, and the impregnable Nizwa fort. A few red flags began to appear, probably to prevent further rocket attacks rather than as a display of genuine loyalty.

The Shackletons then dropped leaflets into an area which had been 'proscribed', while Venoms and Shackletons patrolled the area in which no movement was allowed outside the villages. The rebels, numbering about 1,000, withdrew into the area bounded by Firq, Tanuf and Bahlah.

Mounting these air operations presented considerable difficulties. Apart from the poor maps the aircrew were not familiar with the territory and the visibility is very poor at that time of the year. At Sharjah the fuel was floated ashore in burmails, and was soon all used. A further ship load was despatched, but further supplies had to be flown in. The Beverley had only recently entered service, and it was said that its tropical trials had been carried out in Libya in the winter. Bahrain in July was a different matter. The Centaurus piston engines had never been used in such slow aircraft, and it was believed that the large propellers were not well matched to the engines. Problems with the oil system resulted in a very poor serviceability. An unserviceable Beverley could not be left with a full weight of freight aboard, so the sweating Air Movements personnel wasted their time unloading aircraft.

One of the Beverleys failed to take-off at Ibri: it overran the end of the runway and hit a tree, damaging a propeller. A new propeller was flown to Ibri and the change was carried out there in primitive and difficult conditions. After several more unsuccessful attempts to take-off it finally succeeded and returned to Bahrain where it continued to have difficulty taking off, and was flown back to Aden for the fault to be identified. The floor panels in the freight bay were lifted to see if tons of sand had collected there, but this was not the cause. Eventually the cause was found to be a split in the rubber seal between the tailplane and the elevator which had made it difficult to raise the nose on take-off.

The rebels did not surrender when their forts were rocketed and their area proscribed, therefore the Sultan's army and the Trucial Oman Scouts could not occupy the rebel area. There were only two alternative courses of action. Firstly the operations could be abandoned and the area left in rebel hands. The second course of action was chosen, to send in British troops in spite of the Foreign Secretary's assurance to the House. The Cameronians were flown to Fahud in Valettas and Shackletons, while the 15th/19th Hussars with their Ferret armoured cars were also brought up from Aden. The 8 Squadron detachment was temporarily withdrawn to Aden, leaving the 249 Squadron detachment at Sharjah. However the detachments returned three days later, on 5 August.

The advance on the rebel area was to be from two directions. To the south-west the Cameronians gathered at Fahud and advanced towards Firq, joining the Trucial Oman Scouts and the Sultan's Northern Frontier Regiment at the well at Awaifi. Together they were known as Carter Force after Colonel Stewart Carter commanding the Trucial Oman Scouts. The TOS had been much improved since the days of the Buraimi Incident, and Stewart Carter exemplified the new image. Ferociously moustachioed, he was a large man, every inch a colonel of the most predatory kind. With his beaked nose, and hunched at the wheel of his stripped-down Land Rover, he looked like a huge bird of prey. His Scouts had adopted the red headdress of Glubb Pasha's Arab Legion, folded into a triangle and held in place by a circular rope around the head.

From the opposite direction Haugh Force advanced from Bait al Falaj, the HQ of the Sultan's forces near Muscat. Frank Haugh commanded the Muscat Regiment, a small unit used mainly for ceremonial purposes. By including a detachment from the Training Depot Haugh Force mustered only about 100 men. Lorries were hired from an Indian contractor and the expedition drove off. After Bid Bid the track ran through a wide valley, the Wadi Sumail, under the eastern wall of the Jebal Akhdar. Here they met up with a wild horde of loyal tribesmen led by Sayid Tariq, the Sultan's half brother. They were also in hired lorries and together they advanced cautiously south, in a state of continuous surprise at the lack of opposition. After halting at dusk a lone figure appeared from the south, a wizened gnome with eyes of impenetrable gloom astride a small grey donkey. A messenger from Talib? A fugitive? An apparition? He said that he had been visiting friends, and no, he had no news. On being pressed he admitted there was some business of a rebellion, or so he had heard. Nothing you could call news. He expressed no interest in Haugh Force, and as he climbed aboard his donkey to resume his journey he tossed out, as casually as one mentioning the time of day: 'I met Suleiman bin Hamya at Mutti. He is well. He has six hundred men and says he is going to slaughter you all tonight. God is great.' He bobbed away down the track towards Bid Bid. Haugh Force manned its stone barricades, strengthened its piquets, and the officers fortified themselves with whisky.

Next morning a reconnaissance patrol probed south towards Mutti. A low brown hill appeared to have white bushes on it. The bushes vanished, to be replaced by puffs of grey smoke. These were followed, first, by a remote 'pop' and then a whirring sound like monstrous beetles winging overhead. Then there came the whip-crack of high velocity bullets. The patrol was under attack. The 8 Squadron FAC called in the Venoms which swooped low over the rebels to intimidate them. Were they fleeing, panic stricken? No, they were standing up in their sangers waving their weapons and cheering in derision. It was time for the serious business. The Venoms dived again and the low brown hill sparkled with flashes as the cannon shells struck home. No one was hurt, but that was enough. Haugh Force continued south. There was resistance around Izki and the Shackletons moved in with bunches of 20lb anti-personnel bombs. The advance was held up for two days before Haugh Force broke through. Actually they did not want to break through too soon and enter the rebel heartland before the arrival of the much stronger Carter Force.

Carter Force began its advance on the night of 6 August, stopping short of the village of Izz. It had been flying a white flag, and after a short night's rest the advance continued in open formation. Closer to Izz the advance halted and Major Jasper Coates had the unenviable task of going forward in his vehicle to negotiate. He displayed a very large and very red flag. Jasper Coates was one of the Sultan's contract officers, a retired Group Captain who had previously been the Senior RAF Officer Persian Gulf. He later formed the Sultan's Navy. He first features in this book in the mid-1930s. As Jasper Coates motored slowly towards Izz Anthony Shepherd was admiring his bravery when the Colonel told him to follow and report back events on his radio. When the village came within sight it could be seen that no white flags were flying, but no red ones either. Some dignitaries emerged bearing palm leaves and some off-red flags. They were followed by about fifty well armed tribesmen and some women peered inquisitively over a wall. Jasper sat on the ground and started to parley with the emissaries. Anthony Shepherd's Landrover was engulfed by a swarm of inquisitive small boys. The armed tribesmen watched expressionless, and some picked their noses. Time passed and it grew hotter. At long last the parley finished and Jasper returned to Carter Force with a few of the village elders. The advance on Firq continued.

On the outskirts of Firq the village of Radat was equally disinclined to make an issue of it, and again a few ancient burghers produced a red flag to demonstrate their total commitment to the Sultan's cause. Carter Force was unconvinced, and the advance continued more cautiously on foot. This was well justified when accurate sniper fire started from the date groves and buildings of Firq. The Venoms were called in but it was impossible to pinpoint the snipers so the advance halted.

On each side of Firq the hills closed in, more snipers hiding there behind boulders and in clefts. It was stalemate. Then back down the trail plumes of dust heralded the arrival of the Ferret armoured cars of the 15th/19th Hussars, like Blücher arriving in the nick of time at the field of Waterloo.

The following day was spent probing and planning the next move. It was decided to take the eastern ridge that night, and the rest of the day was spent softening it up. The FAC (forward air controller) used Venoms and Shackletons against the ridge, the Shackletons using their twin 20-mm front guns. Unfortunately the belt feed was convoluted and prone to jamming, so it was too risky to use HE ammunition. Ball ammunition was used, but there were long pauses while the guns were being cleared. The Shackletons also carried fifty-two 20-lb anti-personnel bombs which were made of tightly coiled wire. After hitting the ground they were designed to bounce to head height before exploding. The Shackleton crews had not been trained for forward air control, but by good fortune one bombing run did straddle a party of rebels escaping up a gully. The author was a passenger on this aircraft and the FAC was his previous squadron commander on a Venom Squadron in Cyprus.

That day 8 Squadron mounted six sorties, and the squadron F540 notes: 'A large fortified building being used by snipers was destroyed by rockets at request from the ground.'

The Cameronians put in a slick night attack and had taken the ridge before dawn the next day. By tradition Arabs did not fight at night, so the rebels were taken by surprise and retreated after the briefest resistance. The TOS and NFR advanced through Firq on foot, but there was no resistance. Led by the armoured cars, Carter Force drove on towards Nizwa in a cloud of dust. There was still no resistance, and the great round fort stood bland and silent. The rebels were fleeing north on foot, plainly visible to the Venom pilots who picked them off with cannon fire; there were many casualties. Later what remained of Tanuf fort was demolished with rockets.

Haugh Force and Carter Force met at Birkat al Mauz, and the press were there for the historic meeting. The *Daily Telegraph* reporter asked a Cameronian soldier if it had been a hard battle at Firq. 'Battle? Battle?' he replied, 'I've had better fights in Sauchiehall Street on a Saturday night.' Before the British intervention few people had even heard of Muscat and Oman, and the publicity provided a fascinating story in an antique land. *Time* magazine provided this gem:

> Who is the Sultan of Muscat and Oman?
> Is he a 'yes man' or is he a 'no man'?
> Is he a pro- or anti-status quo man?
> Is he the noblest, like the Roman?
> Or is he abominable, like the snowman?

In Nizwa forty prisoners of the Muscat and Oman Field Force were found and released, and some of the Regiment's weapons and equipment were recovered. There was much of interest in the great round fort, such as cannon balls and landmines lying in an unusual juxtaposition. The rust was scraped away from a cannon to reveal that it was made in Manchester in 1611. Sayid Tariq, the Sultan's half brother, was appointed Governor of the area and received the surrender of Nizwa by its elders. The Imam, his brother Talib, and Suleiman the Horrible were not numbered amongst them. Where were they? The elders' trembling fingers pointed north, their aim elevated noticeably above the horizontal.

It was impossible for the Cameronians to follow them up the Jebal Akhdar in that temperature – you could fry an egg on the wing of a Land Rover; the logistics of supplying water during the climb would have been an insurmountable problem. The TOS had not been trained in mountain warfare, the Sultan's army was too weak, and the few donkey tracks were easy to defend. At the foot of the jebal the forts at Balad Sait and Ghumr were demolished by Venom rockets, and the substantial fort at Izki was destroyed by demolition charges. Sayid Tariq selected sheikhs of dubious loyalty to press the plungers, ensuring that the events were covered by an adequate photographic record. Sayid Tariq was shrewd and uncompromising with the rebels but he was a cultured gentleman of dignity and gentle charm. He had been educated in Germany, liked Beethoven, played a good hand of bridge, and spoke English well.

The Cameronians were withdrawn quickly before political condemnation became too embarrassing. Part of the TOS took up garrison duties at Izki, the rest returning to Trucial Oman. The transport aircraft at Bahrain dispersed to their bases, one of the Beverleys suffering an engine failure at Masirah on its way back to Aden. The 42 Squadron Shackletons went home to Cornwall and the Venoms of 8 Squadron returned to Aden. The Venoms of 249 Squadron remained a little longer before returning to Nairobi. The Sultan's Forces built a new camp at Nizwa to replace the one destroyed at Firq. The 15th/19th Hussars remained for escort duties with their Ferrets, later replaced by the 13/18th Hussars and finally by the Life Guards.

The rebels licked their wounds on the 6,000 foot plateau of the Jebal Akhdar and the Sultan's forces wondered how to dislodge them. Jasper Coates, the retired group captain, had some ideas. Almost as soon as Nizwa was in the Sultan's hands Jasper disappeared from view, re-emerging a day or two later looking dusty, slightly shaken, but with a glint in his eyes. He had led a gaggle of assorted tribesmen up a ravine into the jebal. With blood-chilling war-cries and guns blazing the enthusiastic mob had charged into the mouth of the gorge. But as the rock walls closed in the sunlight was eclipsed to gloomy shadow. The war cries floated back in melancholy spectral echoes. The tribesmen were spooked and melted away.

Jasper then tried a more subtle approach. He went alone up another ravine to locate the rebel piquets. He spent the night a rock or two below a nest of rebels, listening to them talking and cooking their meal. Next morning he strode back down again. He then appointed himself regimental donkey man, having found a peculiar sympathy with those charming animals. He enlisted a squadron of donkey-boys and a number of sturdy jebal donkeys, almost as big as mules. They became known as Jasper's Horse. Jasper's donkeys adored him, and he tended to them like a shepherd. He had a complete sailmakers kit including huge curved needles, lumps of beeswax, a monster thimble, and yards and yards of sailcloth and cotton. He hewed himself a new walking stick, knobbly as a highlander's, and had his own private brand of malt whisky sent to him by the case from its obscure Strathspey distillery. Jasper Coates was a memorable man.

From Carter Force and Hough Force the disparate elements of the Sultan's contingent coalesced into a reasonably coherent whole under the benign colonelcy of Colin Maxwell who had joined the Sultan's army quite by accident while on his way to Borneo or somewhere. This was at the time of the Buraimi Incident. He had that indefinable sympathy with Arab soldiers which owed nothing to The Seven Pillars of Wisdom. He was large of girth and arthritic of hip and was unable to play a forward part in scaling mountains. However, he planned and encouraged the operations and became the bedrock of the Sultans's army. He was Deputy Commander of the Sultan's Armed Forces during the subsequent Dhofar War and was still a valuable adviser when he died in the 1980s.

There were several more reconnaissance forays up the ravines by Philip Allfree and his soldiers, Sayid Tariq's tribesmen and Jasper's Horse. There were sudden confrontations with rebel piquets, the antagonists first blinking at each other in disbelief and then bolting for cover, followed by an exchange of fire. It was clear that no route up the jebal was ever undefended.

On 25 September there was the most daring foray of all. It was up the Wadi Tanuf and led by Philip Allfree who was misdirected up tortuous and ill-defined tracks. On one wrong track they were fired on, but retreated and found the correct track. With his soldiers and FAC he made his way up to 8,000 feet to the edge of the mountain where it fell away steeply to the north towards the sea. The way to the east to the main rebel area was barred by a cliff topped by twin peaks, later known as Sabrina, which will feature again in this campaign in the fullness of time. Allfree's vanguard came under fire from this cliff, and binoculars revealed a multitude of turbans among the rocks. From up behind came Sayid Tariq's hundred odd tribesmen. A Shackleton was at hand and Allfree decided that it was worthwhile taking on the rebels. The FAC directed the Shackleton onto the cliff where it opened up with its twin nose cannons. After firing about fifty rounds both cannons jammed and the Shackleton left the scene. After a long wait a pair of Venoms arrived from Sharjah and again the FAC described the target. The Venoms attacked and their cannons opened up with a hellish clatter. But they had misunderstood the FAC's directions and the cannon shells exploded near Allfree's position with flying shrapnel, rock splinters and volcanic clouds of dust. No one was hurt. The evening was now well advanced and there was just time before nightfall to withdraw to Jasper's camp where donkey loads of food, bedding, water and whisky awaited.

Clearly it was not going to be easy to take the jebal. In AD 1265 it had been taken by the Persians, but it had reputedly cost them 15,000 of their 20,000 men and had never been invaded since then. To the outside world the Jebal Akhdar was unknown territory, the only European to have been there being a Royal Marine officer in 1870. None of the great Arabian explorers had been able to gain access.

For political reasons the British Government did not want to become involved in a major campaign to capture the jebal, and any smaller involvement was to be kept secret, which would be almost impossible if a British infantry battalion was used. Towards the end of October four 8 Squadron Venoms were sent to Sharjah but used only for a firepower demonstration on the jebal. Then two of them returned to Aden. There were no further 249 Squadron Venom detachments at Sharjah, the Squadron having re-equipped with Canberra B2 bombers at Akrotiri in Cyprus. For ten days the pair of 8 Squadron Venoms rocketed a slab of rock just below the plateau. Although it provided entertainment for the rebels it was of course insufficiently threatening to result in their surrender. The pair of Venoms returned to Aden on 5 November, staging through Masirah, and from there making the long non-stop flight to Khormaksar.

The Sultan's army was again reinforced by the TOS for an attempted invasion of the Jebal Akhdar on 15 November. To cover this 8 Squadron sent seven Venoms to Sharjah and 37 Squadron sent some Shackletons to Bahrain, but the plan was wildly optimistic. It involved two troops of the TOS piquetting hilltops near the plateau while 100 of the Sultan's Northern Frontier Regiment climbed between them up the Wadi Kamah. Behind them would be loyal tribesmen rounded up by Sayid Tariq, the Sultan's brother; coolies and donkeys would bring up water, food, blankets and warm clothes. The operation was doomed to failure, and it was indeed a fiasco.

The following report by the 8 Squadron FAC is in the squadron F540 which is held by the Public Record Office:

No trouble was experienced during the initial part of the climb up the 6000 ft Jebal Akhdar. The first feature, 'Black Rock', where trouble was expected, was attacked by Shackletons of 37 Squadron using 20 lb fragmentation bombs and an unopposed advance was recommenced immediately. Four sorties of 8 Squadron Venoms, each carrying 8 rockets and 600 rounds of 20 mm cannon, attacked the next hostile feature, 'Pinnacle Hill'. All rockets and cannon were usefully placed on target. After the Venoms had ceased fire the column advanced, but at a slower pace due to the very hard going. It was at this point that opposition was experienced as the force came under the fire of rebel snipers on the upper slopes. One pair of Venoms was called in to rocket and strafe the hill but firing continued. A Shackleton of 37 Squadron dropped ten 20 lb fragmentation bombs with little effect. In spite of the firing the advance continued and the column reached the top of 'Pinnacle Hill' where a halt was called to reform the troops. During this halt six sorties of Venoms rocketed and strafed the slopes ahead of the force and attacked targets on the top of the jebal. A further 500 yards advance was made under fairly sustained but inaccurate fire. It was obvious now that the objective would not be reached by nightfall due to the slow progress, so it was decided to make camp at that point. A supply drop was effected by Pioneers of 78 Squadron, but almost half of the supplies were lost down 3000 ft ravines flanking the route. During this time six sorties of Venoms continuously rocketed and strafed the slopes and the summit of the jebal but it was not possible to see the result.

One Shackleton crew was a little too enthusiastic in pressing home its attacks. The underside of the aircraft was damaged by shrapnel from its own bombs which had been dropped from an unsafe height. The aircraft Captain was in trouble with higher authority, and so was the Squadron Commander who was also on the aircraft.

Unfortunately the column was unable to secure the waterhole on which the success of the operation depended. Indeed there was some doubt about whether there actually was a waterhole. An air photograph had shown a black blob at the bottom of the wadi which looked as if it must be a rock pool. It was later discovered that it was indeed a rock pool, but at the bottom of a cleft which was so precipitous that it was completely inaccessible. Jasper's Horse could bring only enough water to support a retreat if the operation was unsuccessful. The plan was for the hundred men of the Sultan's army, and the loyal tribesmen, to replenish their water supplies from the black blob and continue up to the main rebel area on the 6,000 foot plateau. There the loyal tribesmen would fan out, loot and sack a village or two, and drive out the rebels.

When the rebel firing first started the coolies supporting the TOS piquets raced helter-skelter back down the jebal, and so did the coolies supporting the main centre party.

The NFR commander had no radio contact with his forward troops or with the TOS piquets, so the 8 Squadron FAC acted as a clearing house for information as well as directing the Venoms on to rebel positions. The forward troops had to spend a cold night up the mountain with no blankets or warm clothes, no water and no food.

The following morning the ground force commander decided to await a delivery of water and rations before pressing on. However, the coolies could not be persuaded to make the long climb back to the hostile fire. Then it became apparent that the ground force commander's second in command was missing. Nobody knew where he was. After dark he had walked down a few hundred yards to discuss something with Jasper Coates, and sample the product of the Strathspey distillery. On his return he had strayed from the path and walked up further than the leading troops, attracting a volley of fire from the rebels. During his descent he went over the edge of a precipice into the deep wadi bottom. The following morning the ground force commander, Philip Allfree, walked down to Jasper's Horse to see if his second in command had arrived there the previous night. Sayid Tariq was there, with a Bren gun over his shoulder. He dispersed his tribesmen in a search, and a Pioneer of 78 Squadron searched the wadi bottom. Nothing was found and after several hazardous and unrewarding hours the force commander decided to withdraw his troops back down the mountain. It was a reluctant decision, but there was nothing else that he could do.

To continue from the FAC's report:

> While all this was taking place the 8 Squadron aircraft had been rocketing and strafing the slopes ahead since first shooting light in preparation for an advance. After the decision to withdraw they provided continuous cover and consequently not a shot was fired by the rebels, while the ground forces descended the jebal. During the operation 32 sorties were flown by 8 Squadron. Communications were poor and it was not always possible to use the donkey conveyed BF 201 VHF set.

The second in command was not dead having survived his fall down the slope in the middle of the night. He later gathered his wits and walked down the mountain alone. When he reached the foot of the mountain, tattered and dehydrated, he was luckily found by friendly tribesmen.

1958

All the time young men were slipping away from villages such as Balad Sait, Izki and Mutti and making their way to Saudi Arabia where Saleh was busy collecting cash and weapons. Trained rebels and supplies were infiltrated back into Central Oman by various routes, and Royal Navy frigates assisted by searching suspicious dhows. None of the arms smugglers or rebels were ever caught.

There was one particularly audacious resupply. Saleh infiltrated forty young toughs who originally came from his Sharqiya province. They landed at Sharjah and travelled overland from there. They refrained from sabotaging the Venoms perhaps because the HQ of the TOS in Sharjah town was too close for comfort, but they hired pack animals and made their way individually through the mountains and across the border to the Batinah coast. They had with them four heavy machine guns, thirteen Bren guns, three radio sets and boxes of ammunition and mines. On the Batinah coast a large lorry had been hired and positioned on the open road at a rendezvous. It had to remain there for some days so the driver feigned a major breakdown by removing the front axle and convincingly spreading it around in pieces. The passengers lolled around under trees or cooked rice. This was a common enough spectacle on that road and nobody paid any attention. Nobody noticed that as the days went by the number of passengers increased and that they were all healthy young men of military age. Their baggage and belongings were wonderfully sprouting up around them like mushrooms in the night. After a few days all the rebels had arrived, the lorry was reassembled and was driven off towards the jebal, its occupants disguised as the Sultan's soldiers. At Rostaq it was challenged but drove on regardless. Later it passed an army Land Rover and everybody exchanged friendly waves. A few miles further on at Awabi, there was another army outpost where it was again challenged. This time it was fired on, but it kept going and escaped up the steep-sided Wadi Beni Kharus into the confines of the Jebal Akhdar. There was no line of escape and it was trapped; the army followed in hot pursuit. The lorry stopped for long enough for the rebels to lay a few landmines behind them in the shingle of the wadi bed, and then continued to where the donkeys and their handlers were awaiting their arrival. The army blundered straight into the landmines and had to return to Awabi with their casualties. At the head of the wadi the supplies were loaded onto the donkeys and carried up the steep northern escarpment of the jebal. The lorry was then set on fire and destroyed.

Back at Awabi the army requested the Pioneer for casualty evacuation. The sun set and darkness enveloped the mountain alongside the airstrip. Eventually the Pioneer arrived and found the runway marked out by vehicle lights. There are more hills to the north and it is not an easy approach. On landing the Pioneer overran the short runway and crashed into the Land Rover belonging to Colonel David Smiley, Commander of the Sultan's Armed Forces. The pursuit of the gunrunners had not been a success.

The Pioneer belonged to 78 Squadron at Aden which maintained a small detachment at Bait al Falaj, HQ of the Sultan's Forces. The Pioneers had a

A 78 Squadron Pioneer climbing steeply after take-off, its wings covered with
aerodynamic extravaganza (Photograph: Gerry Baxter)

remarkable short field performance, their large wings being covered in aerodynamic extravaganza. However, their tailwheel configuration and high nose
attitude were a distinct disadvantage when landing in a stiff crosswind, while
their Alvis Leonides engines were unreliable in that climate of heat and dust.
The ferry flights between Aden and Bait al Falaj were low-speed sagas, and
the pilots were old and bold.

Talib's men became bolder, laying mines by night on the tracks near Izki
and Nizwa. The mines were quite small, containing about 5lb of explosive,
but this was enough to blow a wheel off any vehicle and injure the occupants
if sandbags were not laid on the floor. Larger mines caused more of a problem
later. The Americans refused to stop supplying them to Saudi Arabia, and by
the end of the campaign 150 vehicles had been destroyed. The villages of Tanuf
and Mutti were suspected of helping the rebel minelayers so both villages were
laid waste by loyal tribesmen and the Sultan's forces. But still the mining
continued. This was a major problem for the oil company which was supplying
the camp at Fahud by road from the north. The company attached a flail to
the front of a bulldozer, but the contraption did not work. In trials it flailed
backwards and forwards several times over a known mine before finally
exploding it. In November the company found that Fahud was a dry well and
moved the entire camp to another location 80 miles south to Ghaba. The
track to it was still via Izki and the mining forced them to use an ancient
Avro York transport aircraft for some of the resupply.

The Sultan still spent the summer months at Salalah but the mining prevented him from travelling by road through Central Oman. He therefore sailed to Duqm where he disembarked and drove overland from there to Salalah.

The Sultan acquired two 5.5-inch medium guns from Aden which he located at Kamah. The entire plateau area was within range, and they must have caused some feeling of insecurity. Talib replied by making mortar attacks on the gun positions and on the army camp at Izki.

After an absence of a few months a new Venom detachment of three aircraft was sent to Sharjah in March 1958. For the first ten days the Venoms bided their time, waiting to make their first appearance in response to a rebel ambush. It was a boring wait in the squalor of RAF Sharjah but eventually there was an ambush and the Venoms caught the rebels in the open as they escaped up the jebal north of Nizwa. It was worth the wait to make a dramatic entrance like this. Four days later there was another rebel ambush, this time at Mutti where a steep-sided wadi runs into the jebal. It was the TOS who were ambushed and pinned down, their company commander being killed. The Ferret armoured cars came to the rescue and the Venoms were scrambled. On arrival the Venoms killed eight rebels and went on to attack some huts on the side of the jebal nearby. These were thought to contain landmines, and a further fifteen rebels were killed during this attack – the Venoms were proving their worth. There was another similar ambush at Mutti a few months later when a Royal Marine sergeant was killed and two others wounded. This led to a permanent army outpost being established there.

The Venoms targets were mostly known ambush positions, paths, and a valley known as the Inner Circle which lay behind the first ridge of the jebal around its south-east corner. Two more Venoms joined the original three but serviceability was appalling. One was written off when its main undercarriage hinge split open during a landing; another almost failed to take off when its jet pipe split open; a third collected a ricochet cannon shell in the engine; and a fourth had a burst fuel tank. Another three Venoms arrived at Sharjah for another army operation, and at the same time two Shackletons of 42 Squadron arrived at Masirah from their base in the UK.

In Aden the 37 Squadron Shackletons were kept busy by trouble in the Protectorate and only three could be spared for the campaign in Central Oman. The 42 and 37 Squadron Shackletons were detached to Masirah, so this was the first time the station had been engaged in aggressive operations since the Second World War. Plenty of fuel and bombs had been laid in and the strength of the station had been increased to about thirty-six RAF personnel. There were now two officers, the CO and the adjutant, both on six-month tours from the Aden squadrons. The number of APL had been reduced to about sixty, and the APL officers were all Arabs who lived in the APL compound. By mid-April the Shackletons were bombed up and ready for the army operation, but for some reason only four of them participated.

The plan for the operation was for the Sultan's Northern Frontier Regiment to advance up the Wadi Kamah as they had done during the fiasco of 15 November, but this time they were to retreat back overnight, tempting Talib's rebels to follow. The rebels would then be attacked from the air in the knowledge that the NFR were safely clear of the area. The plan was apparently the idea of the RAF HQ at Bahrain. On 15 April the piquets and the main party climbed conspicuously up the wadi and passed the evening noisily. There was no doubt that they were noticed by the rebels because part of the main centre party started a firefight with one of its piquets. Fortunately no one was hurt, but during the night a soldier dropped a Bren gun which sprayed a few bullets around. A donkey handler was shot through the hand, a donkey was hit, and a Royal Marine corporal was seriously wounded. Sadly he died before reaching hospital.

In the early morning it became clear that all was not going according to plan. The NFR found that climbing up the mountain by day was easier than climbing down by night and they were not clear of the area by 0700 hrs when the air attack was due to begin. The four Venoms from Sharjah and the Shackletons from Masirah orbited. Eventually the area was clear and the four Shackletons in loose line astern lumbered in, each dropping a full load of fifteen 1,000-lb airburst bombs in quick succession. There were five hang-ups but fifty-five bombs fell on target in the confines of the upper wadi. It was a really remarkable sight. The waiting Venoms immediately moved in, rocketing and strafing everything in sight, but it was feeble compared to the opus magnum of the Shackletons. However, the rebels had not followed down the mountain as planned and remained above as interested spectators. It was a great display for them and the soldiers below, an awe-inspiring spectacle. As a rebel-killing exercise it was a failure.

After the operation the 42 Squadron aircraft returned to the UK and one of the 37 Squadron Shackletons returned to Aden, but the other two remained at Masirah for another week. Their targets were mostly rebel supply routes and, like the Venoms, they were not permitted to attack the villages.

A single 37 Squadron Shackleton (WL 800) returned to Masirah at the beginning of May and stayed for nearly two months, although there was a change of crew. WL 800 was a sweet-running aircraft which flew in perfect trim. On most of the sorties a full load of bombs was carried and the twin 20mm cannons in the nose were in constant use. The ancient water channels, aqueducts and dams were attacked to break down the agricultural system so that the rebels could not rely on local produce. Most of the rebel resupply was at night, so the Masirah Shackleton started bombing at night. Then delayed-action bombs were used, liable to explode at any time. Some bombs, of course, were duds but the rebels had to regard them with suspicion for some time in case they were delayed-action bombs. On 28 June the Shackleton carried a full load of fifteen 1,000-lb bombs because it was believed that a rebel ammunition and landmine storage dump had been identified in a cave. WL 800 then returned to Aden, but other single Shackletons of 37 Squadron replaced it at Masirah for a further three weeks until the detachment was withdrawn to Aden on 23 July.

Four days earlier 42 Squadron had arrived at Aden because of the political situation in the Middle East. There had been a revolution in Iraq and the royal family and prime minister had been murdered. The British Government expected trouble all over the Middle East, and there was a risk that the new regime in Iraq would attempt an invasion of Kuwait.

When the 42 Squadron Shackletons arrived in Aden on 19 July they found the airfield jammed with aircraft and there was a shortage of accommodation and other facilities. About four of the aircraft were sent to Sharjah in preference to Masirah. Both airfields were about the same distance from the Jebal Akhdar, but Sharjah had more accommodation and was closer to Kuwait. At Sharjah there was a shortage of spares and there was none of the heavy servicing equipment normally regarded as essential. The weather at Sharjah in the summer is debilitating with high humidity and temperature, and no breeze. For three weeks the 1,000-lb bombs were hand-winched into the bomb-bays. Two of the aircraft were held on standby for Kuwait but the others were used for bombing missions over the Jebal Akhdar, many of them at night.

At the beginning of September 42 Squadron was allowed home to the UK and was replaced by four Shackletons of 228 Squadron. The first 228 Squadron bombing mission from Sharjah was on 13 September. Venoms could appear suddenly and catch the rebels in the open, but Shackleton bombing missions could not achieve surprise. First a smoke flare was dropped to assess the wind, and after this had been observed the aircraft flew away to the start point of its bombing run, a pedantic affair at about 8,000 feet above the ground. All this gave the rebels plenty of time to take cover.

When the targets were dams and aqueducts, etc., the lack of surprise did not matter. There was one particular dam which had withstood persistent bombing, but 228 Squadron managed to breach it. There were also targets of opportunity. 'Ray' Raymond-Barker writes:

> One day we found a field containing a dozen donkeys. We made several bombing runs and presumably killed some of them. Then we found ourselves being fired on by a machine gunner using tracer bullets. One hit the gun mounting in the nose, just missing Flt Lt Harry Harvey. The fact that it hit the gun mounting stopped it, luckily, otherwise its line of flight would have taken it right through the first pilot's chest – I was the first pilot! It certainly made me feel a lot better – not quite such a big bully. I've always loved donkeys!

It should be pointed out that the donkeys were beasts of burden used for bringing supplies up the jebal.

The Squadron was also committed to the defence of Kuwait, and one of the detachment's tasks was to fly the 8 Squadron groundcrew from Sharjah to Bahrain and back every two weeks. Kuwait had been an independent sovereign state since the sixteenth century, and never part of the Ottoman Empire. A treaty had been signed with Great Britain in 1899, guaranteeing Kuwait's independence. This became more important in the 1930s when oil was discovered, and even more important after the Second World War when oil production increased significantly. The oil revenue was coveted by the neighbouring states which posed a serious threat to Kuwait's independence. In 1958 the principal threat was from Iraq. The Venoms from Sharjah operated from Bahrain on one day every fortnight on the Longboat exercises which were amphibious invasions of the island of Halul. Live ammunition was used, the island being uninhabited except for one terrified lighthouse keeper. In this way the Army, Navy and RAF practised the procedure for the liberation of Kuwait in the event of invasion.

During the whole Jebal Akhdar campaign there were 429 Shackleton sorties, 1,540 tons of bombs were dropped and 7,000 rounds of 20mm cannon fired. The Venom detachments at Sharjah continued throughout the summer of 1958, 8 Squadron flying a total of 1,315 sorties during the campaign compared to 163 sorties by 249 Squadron. Together they fired 3,718 rockets and 271,060 rounds of 20mm ammunition. Up to the present day the plateau remains littered with shrapnel and cartridge cases.

At about this time a musical selection from the film *High Society* was heard revolving around RAF Sharjah. This unusual phenomenon brought personnel outdoors to see what was happening. The sky-shout Pembroke was announcing its arrival from Cyprus where it had been shouting discouraging messages to the EOKA terrorists. It was called psychological warfare. The aircraft's passenger door had been removed, and in its place a battery of four loudspeakers pumped out the decibels; the Greek tapes had been erased and the bad news was now in Arabic. There was another sky-shout Pembroke at Bahrain with loudspeakers fixed to the wings. The flying Prophets of Doom winged their way to the plateau villages to cast despair over the rebels, who sent down an emissary with a neatly typed complaint about the quality of the reproduction - it was difficult to hear the propaganda. After only a few sorties of inaudible gloom the rebels tired of this novel form of entertainment and on 16 September replied with a .5 inch machine gun, hitting the Bahrain Pembroke. One bullet severed the elevator cables and passed between the knees of the audio techician. Another severed the aileron controls. A third hit the port engine oil reservoir. The engine seized almost immediately. The loud speakers were jettisoned and the Pembroke managed to clear the edge of the plateau and landed at the airstrip at Firq, the pilot flying the aircraft on the trim controls. The crew withdrew to the officers mess at Nizwa to await the arrival of the rectification team. The rebels came down the mountain with a machine gun and shot up the disabled aircraft but hit only the fin and rudder. Wisely neither sky shouter went to the jebal again. Rectification took over a month before it could be flown back to Bahrain.

The Venom detachments continued until 3 October, the primary aim being to deny food to the rebels. Their goats were strafed and the dams and water channels were rocketed. The terraced fields at Sharaija became barren, and the plantations of fruit trees and grapes withered. Regrettably the ancient agricultural system was systematically destroyed by the Venoms and Shackletons. The aircraft did not attack the villages but these too were being battered by the Sultan's 5.5-inch guns. Better intelligence helped to pinpoint the rebel positions and the caves used for accommodation and storage. Group Captain Harry Bufton, the Senior RAF Officer Persian Gulf, personally flew the Venom and Shackleton pilots on conducted tours in a Pembroke of 1417 Flight. It was an alarming experience to be flown through the valleys in coarse pitch, the Group Captain preoccupied in pointing out some passing target – often the Venom and Shackleton pilots were more interested in the terrain which lay ahead.

Absolute secrecy was maintained throughout the period, and the press and radio were oblivious of the operations. One news hound caught wind that something was afoot and visited Sharjah for some days. To deny him access would have been highly suspicious. The ammunition and rockets were hidden, and the Venoms flew training sorties. The S Ad O remained his constant companion so that he could speak to no one in private. Eventually he departed with apologies for the interruption that he had caused – he knew full well what was going on, but he had not a shred of evidence on which to file a story.

He may well have noticed the extraordinary number of Venoms in the scrap compound – corrosion had taken its toll and there had been a number of crashes. A 249 Squadron Venom had flown into the ground doing a beat-up on the airfield, but the other wrecks were all 8 Squadron. There was an unexplained fatal accident during an air test in June 1958. At the end of August a Venom flew into the plateau while strafing goats, the pilot being killed. The cause was never discovered, but he made no transmission. He may have been shot but it is more likely that he misjudged his round-out. The rebels buried him under a cairn of stones and removed the guns and ammunition from the aircraft, but the guns were too bent to be of any use. After the war was over an RAF padre conducted a burial service and the body was cemented into a horizontal crack in a low cliff nearby. It is inconspicuous and marked only by a raised cross in the concrete. Owen Watkinson's body remains there to this day in what has become known as Venom Wadi. Some of the remains of the aircraft lie scattered around to the present day.

Two weeks after this crash there was another fatal accident at Sharjah. One of the Venoms had been well overdue for its return to Aden but it had been plagued by a series of unserviceabilities; the aircraft was in an appalling condition. One of the Rhodesian pilots on the Squadron remarked that he

Owen Watkinson's grave in 2002 on the right painted white
with the engine in the foregronud.
(Photograph: British Embassy Muscat)

would fly it to Khormaksar in return for a DFC. However, there was a young
pilot in Aden who had recently arrived from the Hong Kong Venom Squadron.
He was sent up to Sharjah in a Valetta to fly the Venom back. He took off
from Sharjah and two minutes later he was dead – his aircraft dived into the
ground and he ejected too late. The crash services sank into the soft sand and
it was the casual observers who arrived first on the scene.

The Venoms were grounded while a board of inquiry tried to discover the
cause of the accident. While the board sat three of the detachment pilots flew
to HMS *Bulwark* because her Sea Venoms, Sea Hawks and Skyraiders were
about to start operations over the Jebal Akhdar. The 8 Squadron pilots flew in
the observer's seats of the Sea Venoms to familiarise the naval pilots with the
area. The operations lasted only two days, then two oil tankers collided in the
Gulf of Oman, HMS *Bulwark* abandoned her operational commitment and
made her way towards the scene of the collision. A helicopter was used to put
a boarding party on the larger of the two tankers, the *Melika*, which was towed
to Muscat where Royal Navy helicopters took the injured to Masirah and from
there they were flown to hospital. One of the injured died at Masirah and was
temporarily buried near the monument. The Royal Navy never restarted their
air operations over Central Oman, and the 8 Squadron pilots returned to

Sharjah. The Venoms had been cleared to fly again but the detachment was withdrawn from Sharjah a few days later, and there was no further 8 Squadron participation for nearly a month.

At the end of October four Venoms returned to Sharjah for a week's detachment. They were led by none other than George Elliott, the Squadron Commander, who was always full of surprises. He surprised the rebels by leading a night attack on their campfires. It was a surprise too for the detachment pilots who had never trained for night attacks.

Soon after this the rebels negotiated for a truce. Life had been hard for them and they wanted a period free from attack to build up their strength. They had a two-week respite, but their terms for an end to the war were unacceptable. During this lull in the fighting the 228 Squadron Shackletons moved from Sharjah to Masirah. The CO at Sharjah was a squadron leader, but Masirah was a smaller station where the CO was a flight lieutenant, there were fewer facilities and less accommodation. 228 Squadron was accommodated in tents, and the runway was marked by a line of oil along one side.

For a time there was some doubt about whether the Venoms could continue to use Sharjah. The Sheikh of Sharjah was being subjected to pressure from Cairo, and in any case was not on friendly terms with the Sultan. Masirah was the alternative, and the Squadron contemplated this switch with some pleasure – it was an equal distance from the Jebal Akhdar and it was in a better state of repair. However, the Shackleton detachments occupied all the spare accommodation, and there was one serious disadvantage for the Venoms: the rolled coral of the runways had a sharp texture which lacerated their high-pressure tyres. Perhaps it was fortunate that the Venom detachments were able to continue at Sharjah.

The approaching cool weather of the winter provided an opportunity to take the jebal from the rebels. Grandiose plans were submitted by HQ BFAP in Aden. They included two British infantry battalions with supporting artillery, and a powerful air offensive by the RAF and Royal Navy. Even on the scale projected there was no certainty that the operation would be a success, and the plan was turned down by the Cabinet in London on 3 October 1958.

An alternative plan was submitted. It envisaged using the SAS and appeared to offer a reasonable prospect of success as well as the ability to keep the operation secret. The SAS were involved in the Malayan Campaign but were due to return to the UK towards the end of the year. The plan was approved after the Colonel of the 22nd SAS Regiment had secretly visited Central Oman in late October.

On 18 November 'D' Squadron of 22 SAS left Malaya in the utmost secrecy, travelling without emblems or badges of rank in two RAF transport aircraft. They staged through Sri Lanka and landed at Masirah. In all there were eighty officers and men led by Major Johnny Watts, and in a single night they consumed all the beer at RAF Masirah.

The cover story was that they were flying to Khartoum via Aden. The two RAF transport aircraft returned to Singapore from Masirah, and a single Beverley from 84 Squadron flew up to Masirah from Aden. It took the SAS to the unmanned Azaiba airfield which was between the sea and the present-day Seeb International Airport. From there they were driven to a tented camp near the fort and airfield at Bait al Falaj outside Muscat. After five days they were driven to Tanuf, three of their vehicles being destroyed by landmines en route. At the insistence of the SAS Colonel a field surgical team was established at Nizwa and two Sycamore helicopters were brought up from Aden inside Beverley transport aircraft. After reassembly they were kept at Nizwa for casualty evacuation.

At 2100 hrs on 28 November 8 Squadron was ordered to send a detachment to Sharjah as soon as possible. By the following afternoon there were five Venoms and pilots at Sharjah, together with the Squadron Engineering Officer, twenty-six groundcrew, and spares for three months.

'D' Squadron of the SAS was organised into four troops. Two of them probed the sloping slabs of the Jebal Akhdar above Tanuf and Kamah. One of the helicopters was hit by a rebel heavy machine gun while it was reconnoitring for a reasonably level patch of ground on the mountainside above Tanuf. Level ground for casualty evacuation was not easy to find, but luckily the helicopter was not badly damaged and nothing vital was hit. An SAS corporal was shot dead by a sniper on the slopes above Tanuf and the rebels then launched a determined attack on the NFR and the 5.5-inch guns at Kamah. The attack was backed by heavy mortars and the defenders nearly broke but just in time the Ferrets of the Life Guards arrived and beat back the attackers. On 1 December the SAS took the initiative. A rebel cave had been identified on the side of the jebal but it was difficult to approach without being seen. One troop moved up on it by night, taking a long route round to keep in dead ground, and by morning they were within 200 yards of the cave entrance. The Venoms took off before dawn to rocket the cave, and the SAS opened up with FNs, Bren guns and a 3.5-inch rocket launcher. Even under such withering fire the rebels did not surrender. Twenty of them were killed, the two-man crew of their mortar being killed by a Venom rocket as the SAS withdrew under fire.

The other two troops of 'D' Squadron went to the north of the mountain to where the Muscat Regiment was camped at Awabi. An officer of the MR had discovered an unguarded track from the village of Hijar to the top of the jebal. The SAS exploited this discovery, climbing to a thin neck of land on the skyline at 7,000 feet. This thin neck of land, known as the Aqbat al Dhofur, dropped steeply on each side into the Wadi Tanuf to the south and the Wadi Beni Kharus which led to Hijar and Awabi to the north. There was no easy access to the plateau because it was well to the west. It was, in fact, a route used by the ancient Persian invaders. It was a steep and arduous climb.

At the top of the track a platoon of the Muscat Regiment dug itself in while the SAS probed forwards towards the plateau. They got only 3,000 yards, as far as a cliff jutting upwards across the ridge line. There was a rebel outpost in the caves in this cliff, and it was rapidly reinforced as the SAS tried to work around it. Two troops of the TOS strengthened the camp at the top of the Hijar track and they were soon joined by a troop of NFR and twenty Life Guards who carried up eight of their Browning machine guns. This high and barren ridge was rapidly becoming the focus of attention of both sides. It was bitterly cold with 60 m.p.h. winds and driving rain, and sometimes enveloped in cloud; there was hail and even snow, the temperature at night being below freezing. The rebels brought in 3-inch mortars and a heavy machine gun which they used to good effect. On one occasion forty rebels tried to overrun the SAS position, but the SAS held their fire until the rebels were within 120-150 yards, then opened up with their FNs and a Bren gun. Five rebels were killed and another four died of their wounds. The rebels' cliff became known as Sabrina due to the two rounded hills at the top, and was named after a well-developed lady in the entertainment world. From Sabrina the rebels shouted down in English, 'Come up, Johnny, and fight'. On 27 December the SAS came up and fought – they put in a night attack, scaling the cliff with ropes and coming to close quarters with the rebels in their caves. There was a wild mêlée in the darkness, with bullets, grenades and insults flying between the combatants. The rebels fought back stubbornly until the attack was called off. Five rebels died but by good fortune the SAS had only one minor casualty from a grenade splinter.

The 228 Squadron Shackletons from Masirah were bombing pinpoint targets in support of the SAS when the weather permitted. But the detachment was unexpectedly withdrawn back to the UK on 14 December and replaced at Masirah by a single Shackleton, once again WL 800, of the Aden-based 37 Squadron. It flew daily sorties over the Jebal Akhdar (except over the three days around Christmas) and never dropped less than ten 1,000-lb bombs and fired up to 600 rounds of 20mm ammunition on each sortie. The targets were mostly on rebel positions above Tanuf and on the plateau around Saiq. The aircraft was not withdrawn to Aden until 9 January 1959.

1959

An officer in the garrison at Izki had climbed the first ridge of the Jebal Akhdar at night. By dawn he had reached the top of the ridge to look down into the Inner Circle to see if he could spot any rebel mining parties. What he saw was a number of men emerging from some caves at the bottom of the valley. These were the Biddah Caves, and evidently the rebels were in residence.

On 1 January all the available Venoms took off before dawn with the maximum eight rockets per aircraft. By sunrise they were at the plateau where they fell into long line astern at low level. They flew off the eastern edge of the plateau 5,000 feet above the Biddah caves and dived on them, each aircraft in turn releasing all eight rockets in a single dive. It was the first time that this target had been attacked.

Also on 1 January 1959 two Shackletons of 224 Squadron departed from their base at Gibraltar, followed by another pair on the following day. They refuelled at RAF El Adem on the Libyan coast, RAF Khormaksar at Aden, and flew on to Masirah to join the 37 Squadron Shackleton. For a couple of days there were a formidable five Shackletons at Masirah, before the 37 Squadron aircraft returned home. The 224 Squadron detachment numbered 18 officers, 19 Senior NCOs and 46 groundcrew with an officer on loan from the Technical Wing at Gibraltar. There were a total of five crews for the four aircraft, plus a 37 Squadron pilot who acted as a guide until the crews were familiar with the targets.

In addition another thirty-five personnel were drafted in to strengthen RAF Masirah. They included an air traffic control officer, a National Service medical officer and a small party whose sole task was to keep the desalination plant running. The Coles crane on the jetty should also have received more specialist attention because it kept breaking down, and on one occasion somebody cut an oil line to sabotage it. At one time there were three supply ships lying offshore waiting to unload. One of them had been there for three weeks and demurrage charges were mounting up.

Sitting solidly on the open spaces of the airfield the Shackletons brooded gloomily over the local scene as the groundcrew busied themselves with preparation. Bombing up was done with hand-winches and refuelling was by bowser as the hydrant refuelling on the hardstanding was no longer in use. Due to the number of extra personnel tents were used for accommodation, as they had been on previous large Shackleton detachments. The Shackletons' targets were the same as the Venoms: Sabrina, the upper slopes above Tanuf, the plateau and the Inner Circle, particularly the Biddah Caves inside the first ridge near Izki. On 15 January all four Shackletons took off two hours before dawn for a saturation attack on the Biddah Caves at sunrise. In line-astern formation they dropped forty-five 1,000-lb bombs in one bombing run, although the results of this attack, and the similar Venom attack two weeks earlier, were never discovered.

Meanwhile donkey columns climbed the steep Hijar track and six 84 Squadron Valettas from Bahrain supplemented the resupply when the weather permitted. The first drop was nearly a disaster. It was an air drop of mortar bombs and twelve of the seventeen parachute canopies failed to open properly. The mortar bombs fell among the troops and exploded on impact, but by incredible luck no one was injured. Pink parachutes dotted the ridge line and served as shelters from the weather. When the weather permitted the Venoms gave close air support at Sabrina where the strikes were directed by the SAS officer, Muir Walker, who was usually known as 'Red Rory', but for some inexplicable reason the troopers called him 'Black Abdul'. On occasions cloud capped Sabrina and the Venoms made low-level attacks through the rain at cloudbase. This meant pulling up into cloud after the weapons had been released, and letting down out of cloud to the south. Other targets were rebel positions on the plateau and in the Inner Circle, and rebel piquets on the lower slopes. During dusk strikes on Sabrina on 6 and 7 January the Venoms killed approximately seventeen rebels.

The bad weather also affected Sharjah but the Venoms were still returning with only 40 gallons of fuel, enough for only a few minutes flying. There was no point in having any more, there were no diversions and the manual homer could not be used for an instrument let-down. The underwing tanks were always filled and this allowed the Venoms about forty to forty-five minutes in the operational area. It rained at Sharjah in mid-December and the flood water grounded the aircraft for some days. There was no drain-off from the low-lying airfield, the drying process being simple evaporation. There was another storm on Christmas Day which kept the aircraft on the ground until the 29th, although it did not really dry out properly until the 31st. When it began to rain again on 16 January the detachment commander (the author) evacuated the aircraft before the airfield again became unusable. The Venoms flew to Masirah and attempted to operate from there for a few days without their ground crew. Some operational sorties were flown but it took a long time to turn round the aircraft, the arming being particularly tedious because the Shackleton armourers were not familiar with the belt feed to the cannons. The Venoms returned to Sharjah on the 19th, going via Tanuf where the 8 Squadron FAC directed them onto a target. He was a Rhodesian who had shaved his head for the New Year's Eve fancy dress party at Khormaksar and had put himself out of circulation until it grew again. His call sign was Goldilocks.

It became clear that 'D' Squadron had met their match at Sabrina and could progress no further. They had not expected to meet rebels of such high calibre, and no doubt the rebels were surprised to encounter a unit like the SAS. Some other route to the plateau would have to be used, and a strengthening of the SAS presence would be required as well. 'A' Squadron were also returning from Malaya and it was agreed that they should join 'D' Squadron in Central Oman. Lt Col Tony Deane-Drummond, the CO of 22 SAS, joined the new Tac HQ which had formed at Nizwa. 'A' Squadron of the SAS under Major John Cooper flew in to Masirah in two Hastings transport aircraft on 12 January, and two days later replaced the one remaining troop of 'D' Squadron at Sabrina. The 'D' Squadron troop walked down the south face of the mountain on the night of 19 January, a difficult and dangerous walk, and joined the rest of the Squadron at the foot of the mountain at Tanuf. The stage was set for a first-class dust-up.

On 16 January another five Venoms flew up to Sharjah, increasing the detachment to ten aircraft. Two returned to Aden five days later leaving eight aircraft.

It was well known that the Arabs did not like fighting at night and the SAS determined to exploit this chink in their armour. The final assault on the Jebal Akhdar was planned for the night of 25/26 January 1959 but was delayed 24 hours by further bad weather. Talib must have expected an assault but did not know where it would be, and Tac HQ kept him guessing. 'D' Squadron carried out offensive patrols from Tanuf and drove the rebels from some high ground which they were using as an observation post. A company of NFR made an attack in the same area while another company of NFR mounted an attack from Izki. 'A' Squadron of the SAS supported by the TOS made a night attack on Sabrina capturing it in the early hours of 24 January. Having been awake all the previous day and fighting all night, 'A' Squadron withdrew for a meal in the morning. Leaving one troop behind at Sabrina the rest of 'A' Squadron marched all that day and night, arriving at Tanuf in the early hours where they joined 'D' Squadron. They slept well that night! The TOS and the troop of SAS were left behind at Sabrina to disguise the withdrawal. Talib was kept guessing by these barbs being thrust in from all directions, as any of them could have developed into the final assault.

A hundred donkey handlers had been gathered to support the final assault and four of them were given a confidential briefing which included details of the route to be taken. They were warned on pain of death not to pass on this information. Talib heard the news twelve hours later, but this was the best deception of all – in fact, none of the known routes was used.

On the night of 26 January the SAS scaled the bare slabs on the eastern side of the Wadi Kamah. At the same time there were noisy diversionary attacks by the SAS troop and TOS at Sabrina and at Tanuf and Izki by the Sultan's Northern Frontier Regiment. Talib and Suleiman with a hundred of their rebels had hurried to the defence of Sabrina where they believed the blow would fall, while at the same time reinforcing the defence of the Wadi Tanuf where the donkey handlers had said the assault would be. The actual route chosen afforded little cover, and at the edge of the slabs the SAS had to descend down the steep cliffs to the next slab. During their climb the SAS encountered only two rebels with a .5-inch Browning machine gun which had been too heavy to move. The two rebels were asleep in their cave a short distance away. They were left to sleep on with three SAS guards watching over them; the SAS guards killed the rebels in the morning.

At 3 a.m. the SAS were behind schedule. At first light they would be below the plateau and overlooked by the rebels; with no cover this would be disastrous. The alternative was risky but there was really no choice, so they cached their rucksacks and continued with only their weapons and a small quantity of ammunition. They raced for the plateau and just made it by first light. First there was Peter de la Billiere, a very short distance ahead of Johnny Watts. Peter de la Billiere was later the most decorated officer in the British Army and was knighted after commanding the British Forces in the Gulf War of 1990/91. Johnny Watts later became Chief of the Defence Staff in Oman, retiring as Lieutenant General Sir John Watts. Behind them were the dismounted Life Guards with the machine guns off their Ferrets, a company of the NFR and 'Goldilocks', the 8 Squadron FAC who had been in the Rhodesian SAS and had also operated against the Chinese terrorists in the Malayan jungle.

Behind them were the donkey handlers with their specially imported Somali donkeys and a collection of fifty irregulars who were distinguished only by red armbands. Only fifteen of them made it to the top, and the small Somali donkeys were unequal to their task. The only SAS casualties were when a stray bullet set off a grenade carried by an SAS trooper. Three of the SAS were badly wounded and were evacuated by helicopter the following morning. During the evacuation rebel mortar bombs exploded all around the helicopters, fortunately without damaging them. Two of the wounded SAS died a couple of days later but the third made a complete recovery.

In the half light before dawn the rebels woke up to discover that the SAS had arrived. The rebels opened fire with mortars and machine guns but were soon silenced by a Venom strike and the 5.5-inch guns. Throughout the entire daylight period there were only fifteen minutes when Venoms were not available at the jebal, but they were not needed again. Resistance evaporated. Three Valettas dropped 30,000lb of supplies, again with the bonus of the pink parachutes which could be used as tents. Some of the rebels may have thought that paratroops were being dropped. Their leaders were at Sabrina, miles away, so most of them thought it prudent to escape before being rounded up. Sayid Tariq together with Colonel David Smiley arrived on the plateau by helicopter, where they joined Colonel Tony Deane-Drummond who had climbed the jebal not far behind the leading elements of 'D' Squadron.

Meanwhile, on the northern side of the jebal, another force embarked on the long climb under Major Jasper Coates, one of the Sultan's contract officers. This remarkable man had with him a hopelessly inadequate platoon of the Muscat Regiment, but between them they shepherded two hundred loyal tribesmen up the north face of the jebal. This rabble arrived on the plateau two days later having taken the surrender of seventy rebels. They disarmed the rebels and embarked on an orgy of pillaging and looting all over the plateau. Donkey trains of weapons and loot went back down to Al Hamra. They were the same loyal Abriyin tribe which had failed to secure the pass when the Field Force was massacred on the retreat from Balad Sait.

Unfortunately Talib, Ghalib and Suleiman slipped away to the Sharqiya and from there to Saudi Arabia. The remainder of the rebels surrendered and were well treated. Patrols over the jebal yielded a rich haul of weapons and correspondence which incriminated many who had professed to be loyal to the Sultan. An 8 Squadron Venom pilot (the author) joined an SAS patrol and located the cairn of stones where the rebels had buried Owen Watkinson.

On the plateau near Saiq an airstrip was laid out for the Pioneers of 78 Squadron. The Sycamores returned to Aden inside Beverleys and all the other aircraft returned to their bases; the British troops returned to the UK and the TOS returned to Trucial Oman. The last of the Venoms returned from Sharjah to Aden on 24 February 1959. The 224 Squadron detachment at Masirah gradually reduced in numbers, the last aircraft returning to Gibraltar on 8 March. After the capture of the Jebal Akhdar the Shackletons patrolled the jebal to discourage any further outbreak of hostilities, and carried out reconnaissance over the Sharqiya. The surplus bombs, all dating from the Second World War, were dropped live into the sea off Masirah. It was all over. Details of the operation were released to the press but it was old news and excited only passing interest. On the jebal the Sultan's Forces built a fort near the airstrip at Saiq and embarked on the long task of helping to restore the agricultural system and the villages which had been shattered by the Sultan's guns. In his book *Muscat & Oman – the end of an era* Ian Skeet states that Saiq had been 'blasted by the RAF'. This is not true as the RAF was never allowed to attack the villages. He also states that Tanuf, at the foot of the jebal, was destroyed 'by the rockets of the RAF'. Certainly Tanuf fort was rocketed, but not the village which still lies in ruins. Amid the devastation the mosque alone is untouched – clear evidence that the village was destroyed by demolition charges.

Later in the year the newly formed Sultan of Oman's Air Force received two Pioneers and three armed Piston Provosts which were based at the airfield at Bait al Falaj.

Mines continued to destroy vehicles. They were the larger anti-tank mines rather than the smaller mines which had been used earlier. At first it was assumed that they were old mines which had been planted before the victory on the jebal, but as time passed and vehicles continued to be blown up it became increasingly obvious that new mines were being laid. It was a worrying development. The Sultan's army became desperate to capture a mine-laying party, but success eluded them.

On one occassion the Minister of the Interior, Sayid Ahmed bin Ibrahim was on the British India ship *Dwarka* when a bomb exploded under his bed; fortunately he was not killed. Another British India boat, the *Dara* blew up, caught fire and sank off Dubai with the loss of several hundred lives. An airliner disappeared on its approach to Sharjah and all were killed. There were explosions around the capital area of Muscat and sabotage to an aircraft of the newly formed air force. Gradually the Sultan's intelligence network was developed and expanded. Names and information became more significant, and it became increasingly clear that it was not the work of a single organisation but an amalgam of educated expatriate citizens and Arab nationalists who were working to overthrow the Sultan. Talib supplied the bombs and mines and arranged for them to be smuggled in and planted. It was not until 1962 that the network was broken when a dhow was captured off the Batinah Coast. It contained arms and mines, two hard-core rebels and ten others. Interrogation led the security forces to thirty other rebels and the seizure of more material. Talib's network collapsed. This was the final end to the Jebal Akhdar Campaign which had begun seven years earlier when Saudi money had ensured the election of the Imam Ghalib bin Ali.

In spite of the dry well at Fahud some of the consortium still regarded it as a promising site. Shell and the Gulbenkian interests returned to Fahud and drilled another well only 400 yards from the original dry hole. They struck oil in 1964, and also at Natih and Yibal. Commercial exports started three years later when a 36-inch pipeline had been laid to a terminal on the coast west of Muscat.

But back to Masirah. The station had had a hard time supporting the Shackleton operations during the Jebal Akhdar War. There had been a huge resupply of bombs and fuel. At high tide the Coles crane on the jetty transferred them from dhows to the railway flat trucks, and these were hauled to the dumps by diesel locomotives. Often the bombs and burmails bounced off the flat trucks and had to be retrieved. Accommodation and meals also taxed the station resources.

CHAPTER VI

The New RAF Masirah

THERE WAS A CASE for strengthening the infrastructure at RAF Masirah, particularly in view of the new RAF route to the Far East. Earlier the route had been down the Gulf to the RAF staging post at Mauripur outside Karachi; the new route was via Gan, one of the Maldive Islands to the south-west of Sri Lanka. The first aircraft had landed at Gan in August 1957, and Masirah was the closest RAF staging post to it on the route from the UK. The Sultan granted a 99-year lease on the Masirah airfield in 1959, the annual rent being £15,000. There were a number of clauses, for instance: 'No flag of any sort will be flown over the camp or aerodrome (this does not include apparatus for showing the direction of the wind)'. And 'No church, mosque or similar place of religion will be built but there is no objection to normal religious services being held ... Any church or mosque built without permission will be removed.' And 'No one will be permitted beyond the leased area without the permission of Your Highness's representative. This does not apply to the foreshore in the immediate vicinity of the leased area to which the personnel in the leased area shall have free and unrestricted access for all purposes.' The forces permitted were the Aden Protectorate Levies and the Royal Air Force and the air forces of Canada, Australia, New Zealand, the Union of South Africa and the Federation of Rhodesia and Nyasaland.

In May 1959 two French sailors arrived unexpectedly from a passing ship, to exhume the body of the seaman who had died following the collision of the two tankers. Fortunately they knew where the body was buried, because the CO did not.

The detachment of the Aden Protectorate Levies was a collection of soldiers specially selected by their officers in Aden. They were a hotchpotch of malcontents and wasters, and their officers wanted to be rid of them for six months. At Masirah they mutinied in 1959, and stoned the huts of their Arab officer and sergeant who were taking refuge inside. The mutiny was put down by an RAF party armed with Sten guns and a revolver. The four ringleaders were identified but there was nowhere to lock them up, so they were kept under guard and flown back to Aden on the RSM schedule the following day.

1960

At the beginning of 1960 RAF Masirah was virtually unchanged since the end of the Second World War, but by the end of the year there had been some obvious improvements. Thirteen aluminium Twynham huts had been built and some Quonset huts had been moved from the APL compound to other locations on the station. The official record makes no further reference to the APL so it is assumed that they had been withdrawn. Accommodation was still extremely tight because by December 1960 the station strength had increased to 6 officers, 19 SNCOs and 110 airmen. The CO was now a Squadron Leader and the station had become self-accounting. There was a manual telephone exchange and a new airmen's dining hall had been built. The main runway, 07/25, had been lengthened and for recreation there was a fibreglass boat. Sea swimming was now permitted and water polo was a popular sport. During the monsoon there was an attempt to use one of the old reservoirs at Ras Hilf as a swimming pool. Due to the increase in the number of personnel the desalination plant was only just keeping pace with consumption, and well water from Dawwa was used in the showers. About 2,000 gallons per day were brought to the station by two old bowsers which had both been officially scrapped.

In March an Argonaut of East African Airlines made an emergency landing due to an engine failure and the fifty-three passengers spent an uncomfortable night at Masirah before being moved on the next day by another Argonaut. There was another unscheduled arrival in June when an RAF Canberra, flown by an all-Australian crew, made an emergency landing. A very smart red Heron of the Queen's Flight passed through Masirah en route to India and Pakistan for the Queen's visit to the sub-continent.

At the beginning of the year 38.4 mm (nearly 1½ inches) of rain fell on one day in April. The airfield was flooded and unusable for five days. It rained again on three days in May and once again the airfield was unusable.

The local population had by now mostly returned from the mainland, and it was no longer necessary to bring in labourers from Northern Oman. The local labourers had been promised a pay rise in April, but by June they had not been given the extra pay, so they went on strike. Luckily the dispute was soon amicably settled. Contact with the locals was made much easier by Norman Ghalib who worked as a clerk in the orderly room. He was bilingual and acted as interpreter. His father was an Arab seaman from Yemen and his mother was English; he had been brought up in North Shields and had a strong Geordie accent. He had worked at Masirah for many years and four years previously had had his knuckles rapped for supplying RAF materials to one of the local fishermen who was building a boat.

The SS *Eletric* was a small tramp steamer of 4,963 tons, and 390 feet in length. She was on passage from the Portuguese colony of Goa on the west coast of India bound for the East German port of Lübeck on the Baltic Sea with a cargo of iron ore. In the foul weather of the south-west monsoon she ran aground on a reef off the north beach of Masirah on 12 August. Somebody at RAF Masirah noticed this small addition to the local scenery, and the CO thought that he ought to do something. An Aldis lamp was taken down to the north beach and used to signal to the master to enquire what help he needed. The master was singularly uncommunicative and would only give the ship's name, which is usually misquoted as the SS *Electric*. The master did, however, transmit a distress signal which was received by the tanker *Ras al Ardh* which was three hours steaming away. The visibility was only 3½ miles but Captain Moar of the *Ras al Ardh* finally located the *Eletric* by radar. By this time it was dark. The *Ras al Ardh* launched a rescue boat which made a hazardous journey to the *Eletric* where it was waved off by the master who considered conditions too dangerous for a rescue. The weather remained bad when the rescue started again next morning. From Captain Moar's log:

> Radio contact was made with the *Eletric* at 0500 hours. I requested the master to use his own boats but he replied saying that they were unsuitable … Our motorboat left and proceeded to the wreck, returning towing two boats. As the weather conditions were unsuitable for recovery by derrick, these two boats were cast adrift after piercing their buoyancy tanks and hulls. Our motorboat was recovered at 1107 hours and the vessel resumed passage at 1136. The crew of the *Eletric* are fit and well.

The rescued crew were put ashore at Suez eight days later. Personnel of RAF Masirah used their fibreglass boat to go to the wreck and board her to prevent pilfering until salvage operations could start. There was an attempt to tow the wreck off the rocks, but in heavy weather she regrounded and broke her back just forward of the bridge. Later the bow section sank, and the wreck remained in this condition for another seventeen years until it broke up and disappeared during the cyclone in June 1977.

Shortly before Christmas the contractors, Costain, arrived at RAF Masirah, presaging a further expansion of the station.

1961

Ships containing heavy plant for Costains arrived in January and were unloaded onto a Z craft, a small flat-bottomed landing craft which could be unloaded at the jetty or beached for large vehicles to drive ashore. The Z craft had sailed under her own power from Aden but had an extremely rough passage and had suffered some considerable damage. Amongst the cargo on the Z craft were four go-karts which had been obtained by the Station Commander. Luckily they were undamaged and a thriving club was formed the following month when a race track had been prepared. Also in February Viscount aircraft of PIA arrived with Costain's Pakistani labourers, and construction of the new runway began. It was on an alignment of 17/35, 2,750 yards long, and just 20° off the old north-south runway of 01/19 which had some low hills in line with it to the south. The new runway had clear approaches and would be capable of a further extension if it was ever needed. It took all year to build and was ready for use on 28 December when it was used for the first time by the AOC from Aden flying his own Canberra. A new signals station was also built, and Costains levelled a new football pitch and laid an asphalt tennis court as a gesture of goodwill.

As during the previous year, there was heavy rain in April and again the airfield was unusable for four days. Flooding caused a power failure so there was no communication with the outside world, but even with six inches of water in the airmen's kitchen the CO reported that an excellent meal was produced, although an airman at Masirah at the time is considerably less complimentary about the general standard of the food. After the flood there was serious discontent among Costain's Pakistani labour force. RAF personnel formed a riot squad armed with pickaxe handles, but fortunately never had to use them.

By 1961 the 1899 treaty between Kuwait and Great Britain was no longer appropriate to Kuwait's new stature in the world. In June the treaty was replaced by an Exchange of Notes which acknowledged the friendship between the two countries and pledged the British Government to come to the aid of Kuwait if the ruler should ever request it. A week after the Exchange of Notes had been signed Iraqi troops moved south to the Kuwait border. At Aden 8 Squadron had been re-equipped with Hunters and there was another fighter squadron in Kenya. This was 208 Squadron which was also equipped with Hunters. Both squadrons immediately flew to Bahrain, and from there Kuwait was just inside their radius of action. Two Shackletons of 37 Squadron followed them up from Aden, and two Canberra Strike squadrons flew from Germany to Sharjah. Army and naval units converged on the area, and after a few days the Sheikh of Kuwait did indeed request assistance from the British Government. The Hunter squadrons and army units moved to Kuwait itself, and naval forces moved up to be offshore at Kuwait. A large number of transport aircraft were involved and the short-range aircraft from Aden had to refuel somewhere. The weather at Salalah is often dank and gloomy at that time of year, with low cloud and drizzle; Masirah was a better staging post.

After a few weeks the threat to Kuwait subsided and most of the British forces were withdrawn. One of the two Hunter squadrons, or at least part of a squadron, remained at Bahrain and rotated with the other squadron every month or two. Masirah was often used for refuelling during the changeover, but night stops were not encouraged due to the lack of accommodation. A

Shipwrecks – 1960–1

Top and Middle: The SS *Eletric* off the north beach
(Photograph: Top, John Fordham; Middle, Jeff Mellor)

Bottom: The *World Jury* east of the south point of the island (Ras Abu Rasas)
(Photograph: John Fordham)

The 'Masirah State Railway'
At the jetty in 1961. The six-monthly supply ship is in the background. The crane
has transferred a load of barbed wire from a dhow to the flat wagons
(Photograph: Ted Newell)

new wooden accommodation block was built in line with the airmen's Quonset huts, but camp beds had to be used by personnel in transit. In July six Javelin fighters staged through Masirah on their way to the Far East where they were to re-equip a squadron in Tengah, Singapore.

If heavy rain in April was an echo of the previous year, so was a shipwreck in August. On 24 August the *World Jury*, a tanker of 20,235 tons, ran aground in mist just to the east of the south point of the island. She had been built in 1955 but this was her first voyage to the Gulf from Durban. Assessors arrived by air on the following two days and they, together with many station personnel, pioneered a route to the south point. In the station operations record book the CO notes that the RAF were inspired by visions of salvage rights and a photographic scoop. At the wreck there was heavy surf and it was not possible to reach the ship which was a few hundred yards offshore. There is no mention of how the crew left the tanker, but all thoughts of immediate salvage were dispelled due to the force of the monsoon seas. It was not possible for the RAF to put a guard aboard the tanker to prevent pilfering so the CO wisely entrusted this task to Sheikh Khamis bin Hilal who was still Sheikh of Masirah. The Sheikh was delighted by the opportunity this presented, and the relationship between the Sheikh and the RAF improved considerably. There had been some hard words a month previously when the Sheikh had banned

RAF transport from leaving the leased area. This had resulted from a mis-understanding, and in any case the Sheikh did not have the authority to impose such a ban. Only the Wali had this authority.

By the end of the monsoon the *World Jury* had been badly damaged and salvage was no longer possible. Over the following monsoons the ship gradually began to break up until eventually by the mid 1980s only one small part, believed to be the engine, was visible above the surface. Even that has now disappeared from view. Until the RAF departed the south point of the island was always called World Jury instead of Ras abu Rasas.

There had been no improvement in the supply of desalinated drinking water on the station, and at one time the station had reached the limit of the drinking water reserves. However, the washing water supply was improved when some 2,899 gallon tanks were taken to Dawwa and elevated above the well. Pumps were left to run to fill the tanks, and thus the water bowser could be quickly filled by gravity on its visits.

1962

In January the well at Dawwa was found to be slightly infested with Bacillus coli. It was immediately treated, but it was not until April that the water was found to be absolutely clear. By May the station was abstracting a record amount of washing water from Dawwa which was a most valuable resource. Without it everyone would have had to wash in sea water, with salt-water soap, which would have inevitably resulted in skin complaints.

The building programme on the station continued throughout the year. The bulk fuel installation was started at Ras Hilf and more domestic accom-modation was completed. A new power house and desalination plant was built close to the old petrol tin camp and was completed in April. The building was, however, only a shell as the generators and plant had not yet been delivered. Again a Z craft sailed up from Aden to help with the unloading of heavy items.

On the sporting side the go-kart club went from strength to strength, winning both race meetings against Sharjah. Volleyball started but soccer was still the main sport. Sea swimming became popular again once the weather warmed up but stopped during the rough seas of the summer monsoon. Expedition training down the island, with desert survival, was a new activity; teams walked up to 16 miles.

In May the first large jet transport aircraft landed at Masirah – a Comet 4 of RAF Transport Command with the C-in-C himself on board. The following month forty different types of aircraft visited Masirah, including the first Argosy transport aircraft ('the Whistling Wheelbarrow'). These aircraft were to become frequent visitors when they entered squadron service at Aden with the newly formed 105 Squadron. But for the time being the RSM schedule was either a Valetta of 233 Squadron at Aden or a Dakota of Aden Airways. These arrived daily from Monday to Friday. In addition to the RSM there was the BSM (Bahrain Sharjah Masirah) schedule which arrived about twice a week. The aircraft were Pembroke light transports of 152 Squadron which was based at Bahrain. There was also a Beverley BSM which arrived on Wednesdays, being either 84 or 30 Squadron aircraft. On one occasion a Beverley of 34 Squadron passed through on its way to the Far East containing the Pioneers which had formed the Sultan of Oman's Air Force three years earlier. These well-worn aircraft were on their way to 209 Squadron at Seletar for a third career. At Bait al Falaj the Sultan's Pioneers were replaced by the more rugged and dependable Beaver which had won an excellent reputation in service with the British Army Air Corps as well as with bush pilots in Canada.

Hunters of 8 and 208 Squadron continued to stage through Masirah en route between Aden and Bahrain. In September seven aircraft were flying to Aden, but four of them were delayed and made the first night jet landings at Masirah. The threat to Kuwait's independence appeared to have subsided and the Hunter detachments to Bahrain were now little more than routine training. There was now only a flight of Hunters at Bahrain to cover the Kuwait commitment and the Shackleton detachment had been reduced to a single aircraft. The Beverleys of 30 Squadron returned to their base in Kenya, but the aircraft continued to be used for tasks around the Arabian Peninsula.

1963

In January the Secretary of State for Air, The Right Honourable Hugh Fraser MP, arrived in a special Comet 4. The purpose of his visit was to present the station badge which had recently been approved by the Queen. The central motif was a loggerhead turtle and the motto was 'AL-'ITIMAD 'ALA AL-NAFS' written in Roman script. The translation from the Arabic means 'The reliance is on oneself'. Correspondence about the design of the station badge had been continuing for some months. The original central motif had not been approved and the suggested motto 'Perseverance' had already been allotted.

There was a violent storm and tornado in February. A visiting Valetta was damaged and spun round on the ground, and 29mm of rain (over an inch) fell in twenty minutes. It is the only recorded tornado at Masirah.

The weather was again foul the following month when the duty wireless operator was alerted by an incoming signal shortly after midnight on the night of 8/9 March. The signal was from London and read:

Master of tanker *Caltex Wellington* lying east of Masirah Island 17 hours steaming from Muscat and 74 hours steaming from Aden reports that there is possible acute appendicitis case on board. Casualty Officer at Weston-super-Mare (Somerset) advises landing patient at first opportunity.

The master had no idea that there was an RAF station on Masirah, and he did not know of the American mission hospital at Muscat. The tanker was loaded and on her way from the Gulf to the Suez Canal, so naturally the Master decided to continue to Aden through heavy seas. For six hours RAF Masirah attempted to contact the tanker by radio, but without success. Wireless stations had been informed that the patient could be landed at Masirah and that an aircraft was available there to fly him to hospital in Bahrain.

This aircraft took off at dawn to search for the tanker, but without success. There was a strong wind and heavy swell with rising dust which reduced visibility to as little as 400 yards. The aircraft continued on its scheduled flight. A 30 Squadron Beverley inbound to Masirah also searched the area, but again without success. Confusing and contradictory signals were being received by Masirah. One from Mauritius stated that the tanker was in contact with Masirah; another from London stated that the patient had improved and the tanker was continuing to Aden.

The following night the RAF at Bahrain managed to contact the tanker which turned about and headed back towards Masirah. Half an hour later the Masirah Z craft put to sea with the Medical Officer on board but they were unable to make radio contact with the tanker to arrange a rendezvous. The master of the tanker had no detailed charts of the inshore waters of the area and was therefore unwilling to come close to land, but due to the heavy swell it would not have been possible to transfer the patient in the open sea. Already heavy timbers had been torn off the Z craft's loading ramp.

In sheltered water just to the north of the island a British Ellerman Line ship lay at anchor. She was the *City of Khartoum*, a general cargo ship delivering contractors' supplies. The Z craft approached her, and although it was the middle of the night Aldis lamp signals alerted somebody. Using Morse code the Z craft Aldis lamp was used to inform the *City of Khartoum* of the situation. She was able to contact the tanker by radio and guide her in to a safe anchorage.

The Z craft came alongside the tanker at 2.30 a.m. and the medical officer climbed aboard to inspect the patient, Bharat Singh, who was indeed in urgent need of medical attention. He was lowered into the Z craft in a stretcher. It took seventy-five minutes for the Z craft to return to Masirah where another difficulty became apparent: it was low tide and the Z craft could not approach the beach over the reef. Aldis signals were exchanged with the waiting ambulance, and an airman took a boat out to the Z craft. In this way the patient and the Medical Officer were brought ashore in the dark.

The crew of the 30 Squadron Beverley had been alerted, the runway flarepath was illuminated, Air Traffic Control manned, and the Fire Section was standing by. The patient was on a saline drip in the Station Sick Quarters and when all was ready he was again taken to the ambulance. At this moment another radio signal arrived stating that the mother of one of the airmen had died. After a few minutes delay the airman and the patient were airborne for Bahrain.

The airman was transferred to a UK-bound aircraft and the patient underwent a successful operation in the Government Hospital in Bahrain. It had been an eventful thirty-three hours since the initial signal had arrived at Masirah. This was not a unique incident – a few months previously a seaman on a passing ship was haemorrhaging, had been taken ashore on the Z craft and flown to hospital in Bahrain.

In November there was a tragedy. One of the firemen was out on the Z craft and decided to swim ashore, but did not realise the strength of the current and was swept away. By the time he was picked up it was already too late, he had drowned. There was no medical officer on the station at the time, so instructions were radioed from the MO at Sharjah. Resuscitation continued for many hours, but it was all to no avail. The CO was not empowered to pronounce the man dead, so a doctor had to be flown in from Bahrain. He took the body back with him to Bahrain where the funeral took place.

The building programme continued through the year. Some of the new power house sets arrived before the summer monsoon, individual items weighing as much as 13 tons, so some ingenuity was required to bring them ashore. The Z craft was of course used for this, and also to bring water ashore from the visiting ships. The quality of some of this water left much to be desired.

The magnificent Super Constellation of PIA was much admired when it arrived with additional Pakistani labour for the contractor, Costain Mothercat. Mothercat was a Lebanese company with useful local contacts. Near the new power house and desalination plants a new laundry was built and completed in July. It was known as the 'dhobi', an Urdu word. A new hangar was started and by November it was being sheeted. A new ATC tower was started in November and at the same time the last of the four generators was being installed in the power house. The following month saw the completion of the Bulk Fuel Installation at Ras Hilf. There was an undersea pipe to a mooring offshore, and the first attempt to pump fuel ashore was from the tanker *British Birch*. The attempt was a failure – the ship moved and pulled the pipeline which parted and fell into the sea. Bad weather then prevented a further attempt for a while, but the second attempt was a success, much to everybody's relief. A second tanker was needed in order to fill up all the tanks. This was the *Clyde Prospector* which moved in after the *British Birch* had finished discharging. The age of the burmail was over.

Although the building programme was progressing well there was still insufficient accommodation on the station. In October six Canberras of 73 Squadron arrived for an exercise from Akrotiri in Cyprus. The officers had to be accommodated in tents, so the situation had changed little from the days

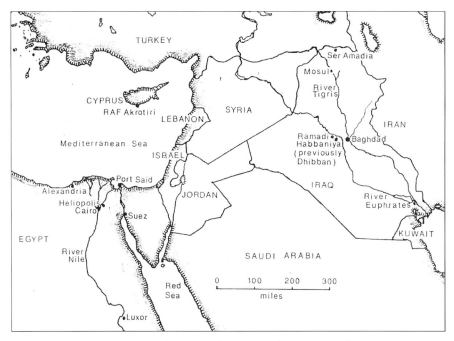

Map 20; After 1956 when RAF Akrotiri opened

of the Jebal Akhdar War five years previously when the Shackleton detachments had to be accommodated in tents. The building programme still had some way to go.

The go-karts had been great fun but due to fair wear and tear, as well as the inevitable bumps and scrapes, only two were still runners. They could be used for familiarisation but not for serious racing. Fortunately the Command Central Fund came to the rescue and expenditure for four new go-karts was sanctioned at the end of the year.

1964

In January the very last RSM Valetta visited Masirah. From now on the schedule from Aden would be by 105 Squadron Argosies as well as the ancient Dakotas of Aden Airways. RAF Khormaksar at Aden was the busiest and most crowded station in the RAF. There were now three Hunter squadrons there, each of twelve aircraft. The most recent of them was 43 Squadron which had recently joined 8 and 208 Squadrons; there was also 1417 Flight which had four reconnaissance Hunters. There were 233 Squadron which had six Valettas; the ten Argosies of 105 Squadron; 26 Squadron which had seven Belvedere helicopters; and also three Sycamore helicopters on the Search and Rescue Flight. 37 Squadron was now down to four Shackletons and 78 Squadron had eight Twin Pioneer light transport aircraft. 84 Squadron had six Beverleys, but the other Beverleys of 30 Squadron in Kenya were also frequent visitors. Altogether there were nine Squadrons and two flights at Khormaksar with a total of eighty-four aircraft. There was also, of course, Aden Airways. Back in 1956 there had been only the Aden Communications Unit and 8 Squadron with its Venoms.

Masirah had been given a generous grant for four new go-karts, but they never arrived. Without them the club was not viable and closed down in February. The club had been a popular recreational facility and the reason for the cancellation of the four new go-karts cannot now be discovered. The CO's comments in the operations record book are circumspect, perhaps because copies are sent to Command Headquarters.

The Bulk Fuel Installation at Ras Hilf seems to have been renamed the Ocean Fuel Terminal. It was later called the Petroleum Supply Depot, another change of name for no apparent reason. Whatever its name, 23,000 gallons was successfully pumped from it to the new power house storage tanks. There was noticeable progress in the building of the 'New Masirah'. Construction of the Water Sports Club started at Ras Hilf, and the officers and SNCOs moved into their new accommodation and messes in September – a great improvement. The two cannons were brought across from the old Officers' Mess, and so was a joke which dated back to the 1950s. The old Officers' Mess had a door marked 'TV Room', and visitors going through it found themselves outdoors. An outside door in the new Mess was also marked 'TV Room', and gullible visitors seen going through it were expected to buy a round of drinks. The handover of the Airmen's Mess was delayed until November due to problems with the electricity cables.

There was still no airfield boundary fence so donkeys, camels and goats roamed at will. They had to be rounded up and placed in a compound before any take-offs or landings. The RAF Police were particularly wary of one particular camel which was bad tempered and showed a vicious streak. Its owner was told of the problem but said that it was a gentle and benign animal, and sadly misunderstood. He was invited to remove the animal himself, but when he attempted to do so, the camel killed him. Everyone was stunned. No one realised that a camel was capable of this.

Lack of security fences around the fuel storage areas and bomb dump was a worry for the CO, and the distillation plants and generators were also vulnerable to sabotage if anyone were to become so minded. Fortunately the locals were not interested in causing damage. However, three of them helped themselves to a 60/40 methanol mix under the impression that it would serve as an alcoholic beverage which the RAF seemed to enjoy. Two of them died.

In November a Hunter of 43 Squadron crashed into the sea shortly after take-off and the pilot was reported as 'missing believed killed' because his body was never recovered, in spite of Royal Navy divers working ceaselessly to locate the wreck in difficult and dangerous conditions.

Casualty evacuation from passing ships was becoming quite routine. In December another seaman with a burst appendix was picked up from the tanker *British Eagle* and flown to hospital. To accomplish this a Beverley had to fly from Aden to Sharjah to pick up the Medical Officer, take him to Masirah to give the patient emergency treatment, and then fly them both to Bahrain.

Although the fuel was no longer arriving in burmails the narrow-gauge railway was still in occasional use up to the end of 1964. It was a useful way of moving heavy engineering equipment from the jetty. However, maintenance of the track and rolling stock was a drain on resources and it was easier to use road vehicles, so the railway system was abandoned and left to decay.

1965

In February another seaman was taken off a passing ship, this time the MS *Toronto*. The Z craft was again used and the patient was quickly transferred to a waiting Pembroke. The Arabian Sea appeared to be conducive to appendicitis. The Z craft had now carried out more rescues than the high-speed rescue launches in the Second World War.

The Station Commander wrote with some pride of the 'New Masirah' which was nearing completion – it would be the most modern and well-appointed base in the Middle East. During 1965 the Medical Section moved into the new Station Sick Quarters beside the Sergeants' Mess. The southern aircraft parking area was finished, but the northern one was not built until 1970. Air Traffic Control moved from the old Second World War watchtower into the new ATC building. There was now an athletic track and pits for the high-jump and long jump; there was a cricket pitch with practice nets; and behind the officers' accommodation a new nine-hole golf course was laid out. Since the greens could not be green they were oiled to keep them smooth and called 'browns'. Desert survival courses were held down the island for personnel from other units as it was not safe to carry out this training in the hinterland behind Aden.

There were now nearly 180 RAF personnel on the base, including 181 Signals Unit which arrived in January. There is little mention of the unit in the official records but it would appear to have been equipped with the cumbersome Type V radar from Aden which had been replaced by more modern equipment. At Masirah the Type V radar was used to watch over air-to-air refuelling operations between Bahrain and Gan.

There were now more lorries and Land Rovers and these allowed personnel to venture further down the island and camp for the night as far as *World Jury*. On one occasion the Z craft took a fishing party down to the wreck of the *World Jury*. There were Falcon sailing dinghies and a powered *sambuk*, a

The locals in a festive mood. Dancing at a wedding in 1965
(Photograph: Peter Wickenden)

wooden Omani fishing vessel. Fishing was a popular pastime and barracuda steak became a favourite item on the menu. Crayfish could be bought cheaply from the local fishermen who did not eat them because they were bottom-feeders. Due to the plentiful air transport the crayfish were exported to other RAF bases and even reached the UK in sufficient numbers to be included in the buffets at summer balls in the officers' messes. This was a profitable sideline for RAF Masirah, and as the trade built up the crayfish were referred to as 'mariners' in RAF signals. It should be pointed out that the profits were paid into the PSI non-public fund and not pocketed by individual entrepreneurs.

The enhanced facilities at Masirah allowed Canberra bombers from Cyprus and Germany to stage through on their way to the Far East for exercises. A powerful non-directional radio beacon was installed and this was a valuable aid even for long-range aircraft overflying Masirah en route between the Gulf and Gan. The Hunter squadrons from Aden began to arrive for exercises at Masirah. It is assumed that the Clelland air-to-ground weapons range had been brought into commission by this time, but it is not mentioned in the official record.

In April an RAF Police Land Rover encountered a party of men who did not look like Omanis. Several shots were fired at the Land Rover, one of them hitting the windscreen and narrowly missing the driver. This was totally unexpected, and the unarmed police quickly withdrew from the area. It was assumed that the intruders were a party from a Pakistani fishing vessel who had landed illegally and wanted to avoid arrest by the authorities.

On Christmas Day the small 500-ton Liberian freighter *Naomi* went aground on a reef at the south of the island, just 800 yards to the south-west of the south point. The ship was bound for Bombay with a cargo of sugar. The weather conditions were ideal and it is difficult to see how such an error could have been made.

1966

On New Year's Day the tug *Orinoco* arrived to haul the *Naomi* off the reef, but she was stuck fast. So the Greek skipper and Turkish crew were taken aboard the tug which returned to Bahrain. The Sultan claimed ownership of the abandoned wreck, but in spite of his orders the local dhow owners embarked on an orgy of plunder. The Station Commander visited the wreck on 9 January and found fifteen local craft alongside the *Naomi*, removing her fittings and the uncontaminated sugar. Armed guards of the Sultan's army were then put aboard and, to quote the official record: 'The remainder of the cargo and equipment was subsequently removed under the local control of Sheikh Khamis bin Hilal.' For some years the ship's wheel hung in the Officers' Mess at RAF Masirah.

In 1960 the whole island had been covered by high-definition vertical air photographs. They showed, for instance, every detail of the Second World War base at Umm Rusays and even the semi-submerged Bisley halfway between Umm Rusays and Shaghpah Island. These photographs were used as the basis for the first accurate map of the island. This was to a scale of 1:50,000 and was published in 1965. Apparently the village of Samar did not exist in 1965 because it is not shown on the map, nor is the village of Shaghaf, although it was mentioned in the 1934 survey.

The photographs were also used for a water survey by Major F. Moseley RE who flew from Masirah as a Bisley pilot of 244 Squadron during the Second World War. Evidently Frank Moseley and his sponsors were not aware of the water survey carried out in October 1945. Using only the air photographs Frank Moseley came to the same conclusions as the 1945 survey, and his provisional report recommended that some thought be given to constructing covered reservoirs near the mouths of the major wadis. These could hold the enormous volume of water from flash floods, water that would otherwise go to waste in the sea. Such reservoirs would be expensive to construct, but the desalination plants were currently costing £10,000 per week which was a great deal of money in those days. Then W.O. Seaman visited Masirah and tested the salinity of the shallow wells near the mouths of the major wadis. The salt concentration was between 1,000 and 3,000 parts per million which was too saline for British servicemen except for washing purposes. In April Frank Moseley visited Masirah before submitting his final report which was essentially the same as his provisional report, but he now knew that the Masirah well water was not fit for drinking.

On the station a salt water swimming pool, 25 metres in length, was constructed alongside the tennis courts. A new indoor cinema was completed and, with this and the new Operations and Communications Centre, the New Masirah was essentially complete and remained virtually unchanged for the remaining ten years of the RAF tenure.

The crayfish trade continued to flourish. They were bought for one shilling each (5p) and sold for two shillings and sixpence (12½p). In exchange coconuts and bananas were brought in from Salalah by the aircrew, and fresh fruit, mostly oranges, arrived from Cyprus 'by hand of pilot'. These were sold by the PSI but the NAAFI objected and attempted to have the fruit charged as cargo at air freight rates. The unofficial arrangement was allowed to continue when it was pointed out to the NAAFI that the tennis balls from Aden, which they were selling, were arriving under the same unofficial arrangements.

Halfway to the jetty the Khimji Ramdas shop, in the old BOAC buildings, had for many years been selling supplies to the local community. The shop was within the leased area so when the price of the goods became unreasonably expensive the Orderly Officer and the Medical Officer would carry out a hygiene inspection and condemn the perishable stock unless the prices were lowered. The supplies were brought across the desert by Land Rover and Bedford 3 tonners to Nuqdah on the mainland opposite the north of Masirah; the sea crossing was by dhow and even by houris which was quite hazardous.

The ships bringing in supplies were now Royal Fleet Auxiliaries. Many of the crew were Chinese and one of them fell ill and died in the Station Sick Quarters. There was only a Moslem burial ground on Masirah, and the other Chinese would not allow the body back on board. Apparently he had to be buried where he died otherwise his soul would wander the earth and perhaps haunt the ship. This was a totally unfamiliar problem for the Station Commander who sought advice from Aden. It was not a problem faced every day by RAF staff officers at headquarters but eventually the correct procedure was discovered. The body was buried at the end of the sand runway and a saucer was broken over the grave.

One of the Pakistani workers violated the daughter of a local sheikh. The Pakistani was reportedly a mullah, a holy man who should have had better morals. The Sheikh's sons caught the Pakistani and 'cut him badly with their swords'. The report is discreet about which particular parts of the Pakistani were cut. The sons were then rounded up and taken to Muscat in chains for trial. While awaiting trial they were caned every morning just to let them know that they had not been forgotten. At the trial itself the judge decided that the sons' reaction was perfectly reasonable in the circumstances and acquitted them. When they returned to Masirah there was great rejoicing, with wild fusillades fired into the air.

During August the station was involved with the withdrawal of British troops from Zambia. They had been flown there following Rhodesia's unilateral declaration of independence. The withdrawal of the troops via the Gulf took two weeks, and during that period Masirah was open for a full twenty-four hours on nine of the fourteen days. There were 128 aircraft movements and over 100,000 gallons of aviation fuel was issued.

Earlier in the year there had been some teething problems with the new water desalination plants. Evidently these problems were difficult to rectify because in November there was a grave shortage of fresh water. Bowsers were no longer collecting well water from Dawwa, and the showers and basins were connected to the salt water supply. Fresh water was turned on for only two hours each day. It was a most inopportune time for any visiting squadron to arrive for an exercise, but that is exactly what happened: the Lightnings of 5 Squadron arrived with their accompanying Victor tankers for an uncomfortable detachment.

1967

The British Eastern Relay Station

In March 1967 material began to arrive at Masirah for the construction of the Diplomatic Wireless Station, later called the British Eastern Relay Station (BERS). Its function was to rebroadcast the BBC World Service in English and in the local languages in that part of the world. It was to be manned by about a dozen British Foreign Office personnel and a number of Pakistani employees.

The original relay station was near Berbera on the north coast of the protectorate of British Somaliland, which began broadcasting in 1960 but following the independence of Somalia in 1963 there were political difficulties. The relay station was ordered to evacuate Somali territory, so it moved temporarily to an RAF site at Aden. The plan was to dismantle the station at Berbera and ship it to a new site on Perim Island. Perim is a small island about 3 miles long and 1½ miles wide at the entrance to the Red Sea about 100 miles west of Aden. The Red Sea is only 15 miles wide here and Perim is a couple of miles off the Yemen (later North Yemen) coast but close to the border with the then Aden Protectorate. Like the enclave of Aden, Perim was British Crown territory and not part of the Protectorate. It had originally been a coaling station for ships using the Suez Canal, and a telegraph station.

At Berbera Harry Henseler had been left behind to dismantle the station and have it shipped out, but the new Somali regime charged him with sabotage and threw him into prison. The British Consul was powerless to intervene and enlisted the help of the American Consul who was more acceptable to the new regime. The American Consul travelled from Mogadishu to Berbera to intercede, and after four days Harry Henseler was released.

Due to the lack of indigenous people Perim was a secure operating base, and in spite of its small size and bleak landscape the engineers were content with their lot. A small airstrip enabled people to visit Aden for shopping and a change of scenery. In Aden and the Protectorate the independence movements were turning against each other and the British, but Perim was considered to be secure against sabotage. It was therefore an unpleasant surprise when the station was totally destroyed on 31 March 1966, but it was not sabotage. A Deltic diesel generator, an engine of a truly bizarre design from the first British diesel locomotive, had self-destructed and there was a huge conflagration which destroyed the entire station. The telex reached Crowborough on 1 April. It was appreciated as an excellent April Fool, but perhaps in questionable taste.

At this time the political situation in Aden was looking distinctly uncertain, so the Perim Island station was not rebuilt. The Sultanate of Muscat and Oman was a more stable and friendly regime and a site close to RAF Masirah provided a secure environment with good communications by air. For good radio propagation a low-level site next to the sea was required, and the site chosen was the eastern end of the north beach. Site preparation by Costains began at the beginning of 1967. While the building was in progress the British personnel were accommodated in the RAF Officers' and Sergeants' Messes, and some of the RAF lads found gainful employment by moonlighting in their spare time. In late 1968 or early 1969 transmission began on 1413 KHz, and later other frequencies were added. In 1976 work had begun on a new HF site, then, on 13 June 1977, the cyclone struck when work was almost complete. Like the fire on Perim Island it was a disaster, but all this will be described later.

The BBC has a number of relay stations around the world, and the Overseas Service had acquired an enviable reputation for impartial reporting. Although it is funded by the Foreign Office no politician is allowed to slant the news. Whenever there is a crisis the world listens to the BBC, and knows that it is being told the truth. It is a valuable service which Britain performs for the benefit of the world.

Before the cyclone the British families lived comfortably enough in light-weight accommodation, and the UK BERS Club was functional rather than luxurious. The Pakistanis had their own separate accommodation and club but were not accompanied by their families.

Powerful radio transmitters certainly use plenty of electricity, and the BERS generators used a prodigious quantity of diesel fuel. BERS had a row of its own tanks at the RAF Bulk Fuel Installation. The mighty diesel generators were awesome – and deafening. BERS was self-sufficient for fresh water which was produced as a by-product from the generators' cooling water. In the transmitter hall electricity was handled in industrial quantities which, to the uninitiated, was quite unnerving.

Transmission in English began in the early morning for a short time and again after 5 p.m. As an introduction a closed loop of tape played a recording of the Bow Bells, followed by the tune of Lilliburlero and a voice announcing that it was the BBC Eastern Relay Station broadcasting on 1413 KHz. Greenwich Mean Time was then announced. With split-second timing the Pakistani controller switched from the recording to the transmission from London with the Greenwich time signal and the world news. The medium-wave transmissions reached as far as Sri Lanka, India, Pakistan, Iran and the Gulf States It was, and is, an impressive operation. Unfortunately the British public are not permitted to listen to the interesting and informative programmes, except in the small hours in the middle of the night on Radio 4, because the service is funded by the Foreign Office and not by the licence fee. It is regrettable that British taxpayers are denied reasonable access to the excellent service which they have paid for.

In November 2002 BERS moved from Masirah to a site on the mainland near al Ashkirah which is between Masirah and Ras al Hadd. Even back in the days of the RAF tenure the powerful transmissions from BERS had imposed some operational limitations on military aircraft, and this was exacerbated when the HF site was brought into commission. However, the broadcast on 1413 kHz did provide a splendid radio beacon for the aircraft's automatic direction finding, but of course this was only during the limited periods of the broadcasts.

CHAPTER VII

RAF Masirah – The Last Ten Years

1967

ALTHOUGH IT IS NOT MENTIONED in the official record a new jetty was built by the contractors Wimpey in 1967, a short distance north of the Second World War jetty which carried the railway track.

Work was started on a new station headquarters building. It took some time to complete, and in the meantime SHQ remained in the building which had been underneath the wooden air traffic control tower. This building was finally demolished, like so many others, by the cyclone of 13 June 1977.

In March there was torrential rain once again. It was impressive even by Masirah standards, totalling 170mm which is over 6½ inches. It caused the usual domestic disruption, and of course the airfield was flooded. To improve the weather forecasting in the region the Meteorological Section began using radio sonde balloons which transmitted meteorological information as they ascended. They were assembled and inflated in a tall building to the east of the new paved runway. Occasionally the balloons fell to earth further down the island, the remains of the equipment mystifying those who happened to come across them.

In June the station once again proved its worth as a staging post on the Far East route. Thirteen Lightning fighters of 74 Squadron, together with their Victor tankers, staged through Masirah en route to RAF Tengah in Singapore. Before the Lightnings arrived at Masirah rotary hydraulic arrester gear had to be temporarily laid across the runway. At the beginning of the month there had been the Six-Day War between Israel and Egypt. The decisive Israeli victory had inflamed Arab passions, and the Lightnings had to fly non-stop from Cyprus to Masirah.

During 1967 those at RAF Masirah were very conscious of events in Aden. Britain had been attempting to prepare the colony and protectorates for independence as the South Arabian Federation. The APL had been renamed the Federal Regular Army, and later the South Arabian Army. However, rival terrorist groups were disrupting the process, fighting each other and the British who were unable to hand over to a stable and responsible regime. Progressively the RAF squadrons were disbanded or moved to the Gulf, and the headquarters moved to Bahrain. Those at the RAF Riyan staging post moved to Masirah.

Even as late as 22 June the *Daily Mail* reported this triumph of wishful thinking over reality:

> The symbol of Britain's rôle in the Middle East has changed from Gezira to Masira ... El Gezira was an exclusive sporting club in Cairo ... Masira is an island off the South Arabian coast 40 miles long and 10 miles wide where Britain rents an airstrip from the Sultan of Muscat and Oman for use as a staging post for the Far East. Now Masira is destined for a more important rôle. It is to be the new home of the British V-bomber force which, Mr George Brown announced on Monday, will protect Aden after independence next year. From Masira British V-bombers will probe deep into the desert on the lookout for an attack on the new South Arabian Federation from President Nasser's Egypt. The contrast between this tiny island, the first of the island bases on which the Government's cut-price East of Suez policy relies, and the comforts of the old Gezira Club could not be more marked.

The original date for the withdrawal from Aden was to be early in 1968, but due to the difficulty in maintaining control it was brought forward to the end of 1967. The final date for the evacuation of the very last British personnel was 29 November. The Royal Navy was then in close attendance with the aircraft carriers *Albion* and *Eagle* together with their support ships. For some

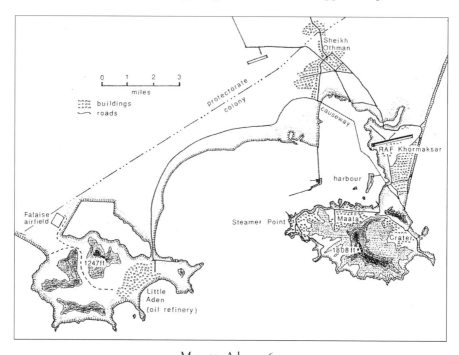

Map 21: Aden 1967

weeks before the final evacuation 8 Squadron had been based at Masirah rather than Bahrain or Sharjah which were crowded with aircraft from Aden. The Gulf bases were also extremely busy with trooping flights back to the UK. Also, Masirah was closer to Aden if 8 Squadron's Hunters needed to be recalled for operational reasons. At this time 208 Squadron was at Bahrain but also prepared to return to Aden if necessary. These Hunters exercised by flying to Masirah at night and returning before dawn.

Aden had been a British possession for 128 years, and of the forty-nine years that the RAF had been in existence, it had been in Aden for forty-eight. The last few years at Aden had been extremely difficult and few were sorry to leave. There was a short farewell ceremony at RAF Khormaksar, the only territory still under British control on 28 November. The High Commissioner and the Commander-in-Chief inspected a joint services guard of honour as the 1417 Flight Hunters flew overhead on their departure and disbandment. A solitary verse from the National Anthem was played, and as the High Commissioner mounted the steps of his aircraft, the Royal Marine Band from HMS *Eagle* struck up – not 'Auld Lang Syne', but 'Fings Ain't Wot They Used to Be'.

After the withdrawal from Aden the Carrier Task Force arrived at Masirah. 600 Royal Marine commandos set up camp on the island, and every day other personnel were brought ashore for R & R (rest and recreation). There were inter-unit sports and social gatherings in the NAAFI and Messes. The evening partying was often interrupted by night flying by the *Eagle's* Buccaneers, Sea Vixens and Gannets.

1968

After the withdrawal from Aden RAF Masirah came under the Commander Air Forces Gulf at Bahrain. Already there had been a Supplementary Statement on Defence Policy which, while detailing nothing specific, clearly implied a British military withdrawal from Singapore and Malaya, and a weakening of the forces in the Gulf. Even in 1968 there was simply not room in the Gulf for all the squadrons which had been based in Aden.

37 Squadron disbanded, its Shackletons returning to the UK.

21 Squadron disbanded, its Andovers, Twin Pioneers and Dakotas being mostly reallocated to other units.

105 Squadron disbanded. Its Argosies had provided Masirah with the RSM Schedule from Aden.

Of the three Hunter squadrons, only two remained: 43 Squadron was disbanded while 8 and 208 Squadrons became based at Bahrain.

84 Squadron's Beverleys returned to the UK and the Squadron was re-equipped with Andovers at Sharjah. By this time Sharjah had a concrete runway. The Twin Pioneers of 152 Squadron had been at Sharjah for some

time, but they were phased out, leaving only the Squadron's Pembrokes at Bahrain.

The Wessex helicopters of 78 Squadron had mostly been brought up from Aden on HMS *Fearless* and HMS *Intrepid*, although one or two flew up via Salalah and Masirah. The following year one of them flew to Masirah to lift a sick crew member from the tanker *Argosy*. The patient was flown to the new modern hospital at Dubai which is only a few miles from Sharjah.

The protection of Kuwait was the primary role of the Air Forces Gulf, but there was a serious shortage of transport aircraft for flying in the Army and its vehicles, due to a lack of parking space. There were no Beverleys and no Argosies other than a small detachment from the UK. Masirah was mostly supplied by the 84 Squadron Andovers at Sharjah, the fresh food coming from Lebanon.

At Masirah the only incident of note was a fire on one of the supply ships, the 6,000 ton SS *Dapne*. The RAF assisted as much as possible in extinguishing the fire and pumping out a hold which had become flooded.

In July a Defence White Paper announced the withdrawal of British forces from the Far East (except Hong Kong) and from the Gulf. The withdrawal was to be in 1971 but RAF Masirah and RAF Salalah were to be retained. Later in 1968 Salalah ceased to be an independent command and became the 'RAF Detachment Salalah', coming under the Station Commander at Masirah.

1969

For some years the Light Bomber Wing at RAF Akrotiri in Cyprus had occasionally been sending its Canberras to Masirah to provide the crews with navigation experience and to use the Clelland Range on the island. However, in January all four Canberra squadrons were disbanded and replaced by two V-bomber squadrons. These Vulcans of 9 and 35 Squadrons became regular visitors to Masirah over the next few years. Usually the detachments were of three or four aircraft and lasted about ten days. They used the Clelland Range but also flew low-level navigation routes over the Sultanate, which was encouraged by the Sultan who wanted to demonstrate to the population that the RAF was at hand and could carry out operations in the country should it become necessary. At low level the size and noise of the Vulcans made their presence very obvious. These detachments were known as Island Rangers. In June there was also a detachment of Lightning fighters from 74 Squadron in the UK. This was to exercise the reinforcement of the Gulf air defences which would be needed if there was a further Iraqi threat to Kuwait. It is not known why the Lightnings continued on down to Masirah from the Gulf, although it should be noted that Masirah was a secure base, well away from any potential hostilities further north.

Up until this time the Station Commander at Masirah had been a squadron leader, but it was becoming obvious that the post ought to be upgraded, not least because there were other squadron leaders under him. The first wing commander Station Commander arrived in April.

It was suggested that the Masirah railway could be reopened as a recreational facility and so it was handed over from the MPBW (the Ministry of Public Building and Works) to the station in January 1969, but a considerable amount of work was required, The whole system had been derelict for four years, the locomotives and wagons rusting and the track washed away in many places by flash floods. A realignment of the track was necessary because it ran across the western end of the sand runway, and a detour of 200 yards was required. One of the two locomotives was resurrected and the detour of the line was completed in May. The repair of the track was completed, and seats were attached to the flat wagons. It became known as the Masirah State Railway and an afternoon service to the Water Sports Club started in July. But towards the end of the year the whole venture was hit by what in modern parlance has become known as a 'double whammy': heavy rain washed away some of the ballast on which the track was laid, and it was announced that the sand runway was to be extended 200 yards to the west, right across the track. The last train ran on 19 December.

1970

However, the Masirah State Railway volunteers were not easily discouraged. A new detour was surveyed, and it was estimated that three-quarters of a mile of new track would be needed which was available from parts of the system which were no longer used. The new detour was far from ideal, embodying sharp bends and a steep gradient up to the terminal on the base. Work started in the New Year and progress was better than expected so that the Masirah State Railway was back in business by the end of March.

The year 1970 was to be known as the Year of the Rains at Masirah. A total of 1.6 inches fell on 12 and 17 January and the airfield could not be used for the rest of the month. There was more rain at the end of February, and at the beginning of March there was a further inch, with yet another inch of rain at the beginning of June, and over two inches at the end of August. These storms damaged some buildings and the railway track bed was washed away in some places. Paradoxically there was water rationing in August due to urgent work on the desalination plant. The locally employed civilians went on strike for several weeks at this time, but the reason is not recorded in the official record.

The local population was rising rapidly, being estimated at 2,100, 900 of them being under 12 years old. The strength of the RAF was 12 officers, 56 SNCOs and 185 airmen. In addition there were British civilians working for the MPBW which was responsible for water, sewage, electrical power and the maintenance and repair of buildings etc. The length of the tour of duty for servicemen at Masirah was one year, unaccompanied by families of course. By this time recreational facilities had further improved and there was an ambitious plan to sail two Osprey sailing boats around the island. It was an expedition which could easily have ended in failure, and even perhaps disaster. The two Ospreys set off in October accompanied by a safety boat and a land party in a 3-ton lorry. It must have been a considerable relief to the Station Commander when all returned safely from the circumnavigation.

Elsewhere in the Sultanate there was an important development. On 23 July His Highness Said bin Taimur, Sultan of Muscat and Oman, was deposed by his son Qaboos in a palace coup. The old Sultan had become a recluse in his palace at Salalah, fearful of the improvements which oil wealth could bring to his subjects. The 29-year-old Qaboos was like a breath of fresh air. He had trained as an army officer at the Royal Military Academy Sandhurst and had then served briefly with the Cameronians in Germany. After this he was incarcerated by his father in a house in the palace grounds at Salalah. He was virtually unknown to the people and had never been to Muscat in his life. He was an only son, and the only hope of salvation for the people. He did not disappoint them. When he was appointed Sultan he had many problems to address: the Sultanate had stagnated for many years and there were communist guerillas trying to seize control in the southern province of Dhofar.

News of the new Sultan quickly reached Masirah and a local dhow owned by Khadim bin Rashid departed for Muscat. It was powered by a 25hp diesel and took thirty-three people to meet the Sultan. They told him of the wretched condition of the people and asked him for his help.

1971

On 24 April Sultan Qaboos bin Said visited Masirah for the first time, but there was little he could do immediately to alleviate the poverty and ill health of his subjects there.

The British forces were due to withdraw from the Gulf at the end of the year, and consequently Masirah would assume a greater importance. A new programme to upgrade the base had already been put into effect, and the northern aircraft parking area had been completed the previous year. In 1971 the main runway was resurfaced, the roads on the base were improved and the capacity of the fuel storage tanks was increased. This was achieved by jacking up some of the fuel tanks and welding extensions underneath. The old Officers' Mess became the Travaux Club for UK civilians.

A donkey fence was erected around the airfield. This was long overdue. It was quite ridiculous that the RAF Police had had to round up stray animals before it was safe for aircraft to land or take-off at what was now a major staging post. At night it had not been easy to see whether stray animals had returned to the airfield. In November the airfield was particularly busy when the aircraft carrier HMS *Eagle* and the commando carrier HMS *Albion* were operating near the island. Twenty-two different types of aircraft were turned around that month.

The donkey fence caused a little extra difficulty for the Masirah State Railway because a gate in the fence had to be opened and closed on every journey. The MPBW warned that if the gate was ever left open or damaged the railway track would be cut. Another difficulty for the railway was a new signals unit which was to be built across the track a short distance from the jetty, so another detour of the track was required to take it behind the signals unit.

The withdrawal of the RAF from the Gulf continued slowly during 1971. In July the supply depot at Sharjah closed which was an advantage for those at Masirah because it meant that the fresh food was flown in directly from Cyprus in the RAF's new C-130 Hercules transport aircraft. Also in July the first Hercules arrived from Lyneham in the UK on what was to become a regular schedule.

At Bahrain 84 Squadron disbanded and all but two of its Andovers were flown home to the UK. The two remaining aircraft were transferred to 46 Squadron which was an Andover squadron at Thorney Island in the UK. These two aircraft were flown from Bahrain to Masirah at the end of September and became a permanent detachment, the first aircraft to be based at Masirah since the Warwick and Wellington in 1945 and 1946.

The final withdrawal of the RAF from the Gulf occurred during December. The last squadron to leave was, appropriately, 8 Squadron which had been based in the Arabian Peninsula since shortly after the First World War. Sharjah closed on 14 December after twenty-nine years of occupation and Bahrain closed the following day. Aubrey Rickards, who was killed at Khor Gharim in 1937, was the first RAF officer to live at Bahrain. The following year Jasper Coates acquired the land for the RAF and marked out the landing ground. It was considerably smaller than the 13,000 ft (4 km) runway subsequently used by the scheduled Concorde service.

Now there were no RAF stations in the Gulf so Masirah, Salalah and Gan became the responsibility of Headquarters Near East Air Force in Cyprus.

A few days later, on 20 December, a huge storm dumped 4 inches of rain on RAF Masirah. The railway track was once again washed away in many places and it was not repaired until the beginning of June the following year.

1972

In March the post of station commander was once again upgraded, this time to the rank of group captain, reflecting Masirah's increasing importance as a

A lady of the Wali Camp. Such face masks are still worn to the present day
(Photograph: David Barton)

staging post to the Far East, and as the parent station for RAF Salalah which was supporting the Sultan's forces in the war against communist guerillas in Dhofar. This kept the two Andovers busy as they were also used for search and rescue, and casualty evacuation. On one occasion they were joined by a Hercules to search for a Caravelle of Sterling Airways which had disappeared on a night approach to Dubai. The wreck was located in the hills to the east of Dubai, and all 112 occupants had been killed.

Masirah was proving to be a popular venue for RAF exercises. The Vulcans from Cyprus were still coming on their Island Ranger flights and making their presence known over Oman. Phantoms came on exercise from the UK together with their Victor tankers for air-to-air refuelling. A hundred new posts were established on the station, and the RAF Regiment was conducting trials on the Clelland Range.

With its new modern buildings and facilities RAF Masirah presented a neat and well-ordered appearance to the visitor, a far cry from the days of Petrol Tin Island. Yet the living conditions of the burgeoning local population had not improved and they still lived in hovels made of anything which lay to hand. At the Wali Camp it was mostly old burmails and bits of packing case, but further down the island it was palm fronds. The modest oil revenues of the Sultanate had many claims elsewhere, not least the cost of the Dhofar War. However, the Government did establish a school at the Wali Camp.

Although RAF Masirah appeared to be in good condition to the casual visitor, the living conditions were not always comfortable for the resident servicemen. They had no air conditioning, which would have been much appreciated at certain times of the year, and the desalination plants were a constant source of trouble. For much of the time the showers were connected to the salt-water supply and salt-water soap had to be used. Skin complaints were common. It was a great relief to all when, after a long period, the desalination plants were restored to full working order in July and everyone could wash in fresh water. The desalination plants had the capacity to produce 45,000 gallons of fresh water per day, and a week's supply was kept in storage. On expeditions down the island the RAF were able to take containers of fresh water to the local population there and each of the locally employed islanders was given 4½ gallons per day.

1973

The next phase of the Masirah Development Programme began in 1973. Airmen's accommodation blocks with ninety-one single rooms were built and another fourteen single rooms for the SNCOs. Opposite the Officers' Mess another block was built with five single rooms and four suites. Immediately to the west of this, just inside the boundary fence, air-conditioned Twynham huts were built for aircrew in transit. The only other air conditioning on the

A typical shanty in the Wali Camp during the RAF tenure
(Photograph: Gerry Baxter)

base was in the Air Traffic Control tower and the large building nearby, which housed the Operations and Communications Centre. The Station Headquarters building was extended, and some temporary portakabin accommodation was also brought in. During the shipping season there were three supply ships each year and there was a constant stream of small tankers which moored up a short distance off the jetty, an inefficient way of keeping pace with the station's voracious appetite for fuel. It was therefore decided to establish moorings for much larger tankers in deep water off the north beach opposite what was now called BERS – the British Eastern Relay Station. Mothercat, the Lebanese construction company, carried out undersea blasting for a submarine oil pipe from the new moorings. The pipeline surfaced close to the entrance to BERS, and was routed above ground to the storage tanks at Ras Hilf.

The bomb dump, between the station and the jetty, contained an embarrassing number of 1,000-lb bombs which were deteriorating, and no one was quite sure how to dispose of them safely. Finally it was decided to blow them up on the island. The spot chosen was a mile or two south of the airfield, just to the west of the present-day track to the BERS south aerial farm. Just to the north of low rounded hills (on which there are pre-historic burial mounds) there are still craters where the bombs were detonated.

Bulk meat and dry goods were delivered by the Royal Fleet Auxiliaries *Bacchus* and *Hebe* during the shipping season, and an almost daily supply of fruit and vegetables arrived on 70 Squadron Hercules from Cyprus. The standard of catering was high and Masirah's home-baked bread together with barracuda steaks and crayfish were popular items on the menu.

Women had never been allowed to spend the night at RAF Masirah, the accommodation and showers etc. being completely unsuitable. But in June 1973 the MMG – the Military Mission to Garrisons – was opened, a canteen and shop run by two widows, Dorothy Cook and Grace McShane. They moved into what had been the Travaux Club and before that the Officers' Mess. They lived next door in what was called Rose Cottage, and dispensed tea and sympathy to young airmen far from home.

1974

Games of ludo and scrabble etc. could be played at the MMG and tea and sympathy was required when the Turks invaded northern Cyprus in July 1974. RAF Akrotiri became preoccupied with its own security and the safety of British dependants, residents and holidaymakers on the island. Over 10,000 people were flown home to the UK. For some weeks there were no flights to Masirah, and the absence of mail from home was particularly keenly felt.

The RFA *Bacchus* delivered extra desalination units but they were not sufficient to stave off the inevitable water shortage during the summer. Actually it appears to have been the shortage of fuel as much as the desalination capacity which was the limiting factor. By careful husbanding and constant reminders and warnings the Station Commander managed to eke out his dwindling supplies of fuel to keep the desalination plants operating until the end of the south-west monsoon which marked the beginning of the shipping season. This

1974. The RAF at work
(Photograph: Peter Booker)

was the first summer for some years that the showers did not revert to salt water at some time.

After the summer monsoon had abated the new oil pipeline from the deep-water mooring was ready for testing. Like the first use of the narrow-gauge pipe, the test was not an unqualified success. The tanker moored up off the north beach, coupled up to the wide-gauge pipe, and started pumping. It may have been an unusually high tide, and as the tanker emptied it rose in the water. There was insufficient slack in the flexible pipe to accommodate the rise so pumping had to stop.

There were transit aircraft with interesting cargos, for instance to Woomera and Maralinga in Australia. The Sri Lankan Police Band passed through en

1974. The RAF at play
(Photograph: Peter Booker)

The RAF lads in a festive mood. A 'maasalaam' (farewell) party in 1974
(Photograph: Peter Booker)

route to the Edinburgh Tattoo, and gave a performance at Masirah while it was there.

At Salalah the Sultan's Air Force did not have enough of its Augusta Bell 205 Helicopters for all the tasks required by the Dhofar War so four Wessex helicopters were hired from the RAF together with their aircrew and ground-crew. They were delivered via Masirah in Belfast transport aircraft. A SOAF Caribou arrived at Masirah with a Land Rover for the Wali, and Strikemasters often refuelled in transit between Salalah and Seeb, the new international airport a few miles from Muscat.

In November there was the very last Vulcan Island Ranger from Akrotiri when four crews were detached to Masirah for low flying over the Sultanate. Shortly after this the two Akrotiri-based Vulcan squadrons returned to the UK.

The station pets should be mentioned. There were two gazelle and two dogs. Min was a small brown mongrel bitch who often rode in the CO's Land Rover. She was joined by Bundu, a large Omani saluki. During their time together they managed to produce a single offspring, a misshapen animal by the name of Cedric. The chameleons may count as pets since they are not indigenous to the island. They were brought up from Salalah where they are common in the Dhofar hills. They live on insects and some vegetation such as the black berries of the lantana plant and certain flowers.

1975

By this time the 46 Squadron Andovers had become known as Yimkin Airways, and the one serviceable railway locomotive was also known as Yimkin which is the Arabic for 'perhaps'. It was the name of the station's unofficial logo, a cartoon turtle with a leather flying helmet and goggles, and a dejected and care-worn expression. He appeared on T-shirts, the side of the locomotive, and anywhere else which seemed at all appropriate.

Due to the number of personnel now at Masirah it seemed a good idea to install a modern laundry. It was opened in 1975 and could wash more clothes faster than ever before, but it had an insatiable appetite for buttons and zips. The head dhobi wallah was Abdul Malik, and his problem was the combination of modern machinery and local labour. The new laundry was a failure.

SOAF kept some Beaver light transport aircraft at Salalah, but they were withdrawn from service in 1975 and ferried to Seeb via Masirah. They were quite small aircraft with a single piston engine and room for only a handful of passengers. One of the ferry pilots had not been given a satisfactory conversion onto the Beaver, and did not know how to fly for range (or in motoring terms, how to achieve the maximum miles per litre of petrol). He flew alone from Salalah with inappropriate engine power settings, consuming the petrol at a profligate rate. In spite of his shortage of fuel he embarked on the long sea crossing to the south point of Masirah Island but had insufficient petrol to complete the short distance to the airfield. He radioed Masirah that he was landing north of the airfield when he meant south, which caused some consternation because it is sea to the north. He landed on an ungraded track somewhere on the island and refuelled out of jerry cans which he had brought with him in the cabin. He then took off again and landed at RAF Masirah. After refuelling there in a more conventional manner he managed to fly the comparatively short distance to Seeb without running out of petrol. RAF Masirah informed HQ SOAF that the pilot's unusual actions had caused some anxiety.

1976

Dr Douglas Gow now has a practice in Australia, but in 1976 he was one of the two medical officers at RAF Masirah. He wrote to the author:

> Thank you for your recent letter. I am fascinated with your news about Masirah. Although I often think about the place, no-one here has ever heard about it (in fact Oman is beyond the geography of most Australians), so apart from about 3 millisecs on a news item during the Gulf War I haven't had any news at all.

You specifically ask about the health of the locals in my time there. Basically it was pretty appalling. My primary task was, of course, to look after the service personnel there, my secondary responsibility was to those at BERS including the Pakistanis, and I was told, although never officially, to do the hearts and minds bit with the locals. This produced some very tricky situations for me, solved often by my flight sergeant who was a wily young bastard. I became rather good at cooking the books to write off drugs and supplies as out of date about six months earlier than the expiry date, and transferring them down to the local clinic. We also got stuff which was time expired, or nearly so, from the hospital at Akrotiri at the whim of the supply people there. They often failed to supply us very well, never mind the hearts and mind supplies.

There were several major infectious diseases endemic on the island. Tuberculosis was one that killed a fair few of them. I have a strong memory (war story coming up) of my first day of work on the island. My sergeant RN came to me with a chest X-ray he had just taken of the local postmaster. It showed one lung completely whited out and the other with a fluid level about two thirds up the lung (in non-medical terms). This was very advanced TB, I guessed, and I declined to see him. That was the first step taken in my departure from accepted western standards of care. With hindsight, it was a pretty shrewd move as he dropped dead the next day at his dawn prayers! I believe if I had seen him and started futile treatment for his effusions he would still have died, but I would have been blamed for it.

My surgical colleague and I tried to organise a programme of anti-TB vaccinations for the locals, and I thought it would be polite to first inform the PMO at Strike Command about our plans. To our disappointment he gently told us to forget it. We brashly wrote again and asked why not, as it seemed a good idea to us, and wasn't going to cost the RAF anything. The Station Commander got a very brusque letter back telling him to get his young MOs marching in step or *he* would be asked to explain things. We also heard from the Consultant Adviser in Respiratory Medicine that what we planned was not 'good medicine'. Frankly, this may have been true in western society but we played by different rules out there, and there would have been a huge amount of good done for the majority of the locals, especially the young ones. But the Boss told us we would have to shelve the idea, and that was that.

It was a tricky question whether to start anti-TB drugs with the locals who had active TB. There was a fair chance they would default on the treatment (which was a series of painful injections) once they started to feel better. This would have encouraged the growth of TB bugs that were resistant to the current drugs. This is what has happened in the third world nowadays. However, we were often talked into treating various important locals, and our predictions about non-compliance were borne out.

Other infections were remarkably common. Ordinary infected wounds could be cured with simple penicillin because the locals had had very little exposure to antibiotics. But the Brits needed quite potent antibiotics for anything south of the knees. 'Flip flop toe' was a recognised clinical picture at Masirah and needed Flucloxacillin and daily dressings.

Other infectious diseases included cholera. There was an outbreak on the mainland at the time. Many of the simple childhood fevers were more of a problem than for a western child who would suffer no more than an inconvenience.

Malaria was a chronic rather than an acute problem for the locals. We often felt large spleens in the adults, and we assumed these were due to malaria. We were all supposed to take paludrine every day, but I reckon the doctors were the only ones who did, and I'm not even sure about the other doc! I certainly never saw a Brit with malaria.

Trachoma was very common, but I knew next to nothing about it then. I've seen it since in aboriginals. Looking back, that was something we could have done a bit about at very little cost to the service – assuming, of course, that the Consultant Adviser in Ophthalmology didn't veto it! I regret now not making more of an effort to find out about it, as just about everyone over forty was blind in at least one eye.

Infant mortality seemed to be about 30%. Certainly I became expert at introducing small tubes into the tiny veins of nearly dead babies. They were the ones who had become desperately dehydrated from gastroenteritis. Nowadays there are packets of salts made commercially to rehydrate these kids orally, but then we had to do it intravenously. We didn't have the right sort of fluids ready-made, so we had to mix our own and then re-sterilise the IV bottle before giving it to the babies. Many a night's sleep was given up by my nurses and medics to nurse these infants through the worst of their infections.

One of the causes of the chronic gastro in babies (apart from the general tack of hygiene) was the recently introduced belief that bottle feeding was a sophisticated modern alternative to breast feeding. Western advertising was to blame. There were two huge problems at Masirah – no bottles and no proper formula. The bottle problem was solved by a conch shell with the tip knocked off, and the formula was replaced by Nido which was some kind of powdered milk. The conch shell often had the remains of the original occupant still in it, and the Nido was totally unsuitable. It's not hard to understand why gastro killed lots of these babies. The formula producers have been castigated for many years now in the lay and medical press for encouraging artificial feeding in third world countries, but we saw it at Masirah before it became a fashionable topic for radical feminists.

We tried to organise baby care instruction for the mothers, but most of my blokes were unmarried, or at best they only had as much knowledge as their wives had given them – 'this end up, and don't drop it'.

On one occasion my colleague and I had to attempt a caesar on a local lady. There was no alternative. We produced a live baby and an anaemic but undamaged mother. I have often toyed with the idea of getting in touch with the Wali to see if the infant (Amira) survived the vicissitudes of growing up in Masirah, but it would only upset me if she hadn't survived. She would be twenty now.

The author wrote to his friend Bruce Watts at Masirah, asking if he could make some enquiries about Amira. She did indeed survive, and the author sent the details to Dr Douglas Gow in Australia. In his reply to the author Douglas Gow enclosed the following article which he had written light-heartedly for the Christmas edition of a medical journal:

Many years ago when the earth was young and so was I, the Queen, in the guise of a clerk at the Ministry of Defence, decided that she needed a new man in Oman. I was to report to the Medical Centre at Royal Air Force Masirah for duties as Senior Medical Officer and Anaesthetist. I knew where Masirah was, it was a desert island off the coast of the Sultanate of Oman. What did come as a surprise was the bit about anaesthetist, because spelling it was about the sum total of my skills in that field. The Queen had, of course, made plans to correct what she identified as the only deficiency in her loyal servant. Two months later I had done six weeks of anaesthetic training at the RAF Hospital Ely and spent a day at the Tropical Diseases Hospital in London. I also had five years of dental training compressed into two days. Her Majesty thought of everything.

So it was that I found myself in Masirah in November 1975 with only 273 days to go before returning to the bosom of my family. I started a 'gozhome' calendar and ticked off one day immediately.

In truth, life on the station was pleasant once you came to terms with not going home to Mum at the end of the day. But no-one else could either, so life revolved around the Mess. Gin was fourpence, and tonic was sixpence, so obviously one had to go easy on the latter. There was a bit of tape on the window in the bar that was said to represent the yardarm. As the weeks passed the tape was surreptitiously moved lower down the glass until it picked up so much fluff from the carpet that it wouldn't stick to anything. Then we abandoned it as a silly navy idea anyway.

Work had several aspects to it. First of all I had to play the officer with responsibility for a dozen blokes in my section. Several of them were considerably older than me, and my senior NCO had been in the RAF longer than I had been on earth. This made it difficult to act as patriarch. He 'kept me right', and we agreed to listen to each other's point of view and then do what he thought best. I had been round long enough to appreciate that flight sergeants know everything.

The clinical side of things was both fascinating and terrifying. You had to say to yourself 'You may not be very good, but you're the best for a thousand miles'. While neither geographically or factually correct, it was a great comfort to myself and my fellow Scot who was masquerading as a surgeon. His experience closely paralleled mine, although he had been on the surgical training scheme for three months. He therefore considered himself far better educated than me. I was to learn later in life that surgeons always think this. We shared the general practice work between us, and took turns at the local clinics, although a good deal of it was handled by my two RNs and two ENs. As SMO I had responsibility for the public health of the station. It ranged from the rubbish dump to the water in the swimming pool, the desalination plant and the laundry.

One day my sergeant nurse asked me to see a local woman who had been in labour for twenty four hours with no apparent progress. Of my many ignorances obstetrics was high up on the list. It figured prominently on my colleague's list too. We watched this poor woman for several hours and fondled obstetric forceps in the vain hope that we would be able to get them to articulate. It became clear that her only hope would be a Caesarean section. This posed some interesting challenges to both of us, not least because my colleague had never seen one, and that I had never gassed one. It was not the sort of op they let six-week-specials do for fun.

We overcame the majority of the problems. I found some donors by announcing over our radio station that everyone should immediately look at his identity card, and anyone with 'O negative' written across it should report immediately to the Medical Centre as he may have a rare blood disorder and would need a specimen taken for analysis. Within minutes four naïve and anxious young men arrived clutching their identity cards. I explained that we needed a large sample and left them to my RN to bleed. Meanwhile Paddy the Ratcatcher (the corporal environmental health technician) had stolen some perspex from stores. He cut it with the plaster saw and glued it together with ether to make an incubator. He then 'wrote off' the ambulance's oxygen regulator and fitted it to the incubator. He added a few coils of anaesthetic tubing around the inside to which we could attach either the hot tap, or more likely the cold one, to adjust the temperature in the incubator. The whole thing was screwed to a NATO standard litter and was still there and working well when I left a few months later.

I spent the time reading Lee & Atkinson's *Synopsis of Anaesthesia* and joined the thousands of anaesthetists around the globe who will always have a place in their hearts for Dr L. and Dr A. My colleague was sweatily looking through *Manual of Operative Surgery (Obstetrics)* and making imaginary slashes as it slowly dawned on him that this would be the biggest incision that he had made in his surgical career so far. Mum just went on screaming at two minute intervals.

I will spare you the details of the delivery, other than to say that it was prolonged. The possibility of having to resuscitate the baby had not occurred to me until after induction. Then I noticed the tremor in my colleague's hand was matched only by the one in his voice. This was when I discovered that we had no paediatric resus gear. Should you ever find yourself in a similar bind, be assured that an adult laryngoscope, Magill forceps and a urinary catheter are almost as good as the real thing. We had a live female of about five pounds, which was a bonus we never really expected, our unspoken aim had only ever been to save Mum.

We gave her all the blood we had, and tried to ignore the growing pool at my feet. (Why do theatres always slope towards the anaesthetist?) To our amazement she woke up with no more problems than our other forays into surgery had done. This is not to say it was a smooth, pain-free reversal of the miracle of anaesthesia, but it wasn't bad for a first attempt.

Both parents seemed delighted with their daughter. We kept Mum in the ward until the wound was pretty well healed as we were terrified of infection if she went back to the village. There were a few problems establishing feeding but my sergeant solved them. One morning I found him outside the patient's room doing press ups. When asked what it was all about he replied, 'Just expressed one breast, Boss, going back to the other now.'

Just before we rather reluctantly discharged our patient, our interpreter warned us that we would be formally presented with the infant, and we should give her back with a name and a small gift. This gave us time to think of a name that would be acceptable to both cultures, and to get along to the NAAFI store. We came up with 'Amira' and a little silver bangle, and duly went through the ceremony. I had a son of about 12 months at home and we rather fancied a daughter. It crossed my mind not to give her back, just to see the look on my wife's face when I returned from the desert with an infant, but reality prevailed.

Amira and her mother left my life that day, and apart from a couple of visits in the next month, I never saw her again. The RAF pulled out of Oman later so there was no source of further news, but I often thought about Amira. The infant mortality rate in Masirah was so high that it would be unlikely that she, a small caesar baby, would survive.

Then I had a letter from an Englishman who had served at Masirah in the Sultan's air force. He was researching for a book on the island and asked me about the sort of conditions we treated. I sent him a long letter with the details he wanted and mentioned the Caesarean section.

Last week's mail brought a letter from my UK correspondent. He enclosed a photograph of a tall pretty girl in black with her mother beside her. Amira sent a letter with the photograph. It is written in English. She is in Muscat studying to be a health educator. She returns to Masirah in November. Her letter begins:- 'To my Father'. My English correspondent remarked, in his covering letter, that he had always regarded medicine as a somewhat

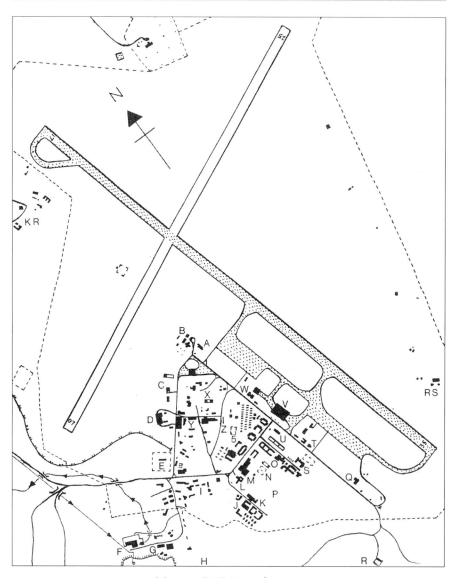

Map 22: RAF Masirah, 1976

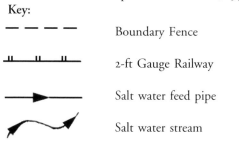

Key:

- - - - Boundary Fence

‖——‖——‖ 2-ft Gauge Railway

———▶ Salt water feed pipe

Salt water stream

Key to Map 22:

A   Fire Section

B   Air Traffic Control, Ops,
    Comcen, Met

C   Gas Plant

D   MT Hangar

E   Stables

F   Power station and Desalination
    plants

G   Laundry

H   Golf course

I   Department of the Environment
    ('Works and Bricks')

J   Officers' Accommodation

K   Officers' Mess

L   Medical Centre

M   Sergeants' Mess

N   Squash Court, Tennis Court,
    Swimming Pool (west to east)

O   Accommodation, Junior Ranks
    Mess, NAAFI, Cinema
    (north to south)

P   Sports Pitches

Q   Armoury

R   Small Arms Range

S   Ration Supply Depot. Movements
    Compound to the east next to the road

T   Movements Flight, Hunter
    Detachment Offices, Photo Section
    (south to north)

U   Station HQ

V   Aircraft Hangar

W   Air Publications and Forms Store.
    General Engineering workshops

X   Church, RAF Regt Flt (old SHQ
    & ATC Building) and fuel
    bowser shelter

Y   Supply Flight. Just to the north
    'Greystones', and the Lady
    Lampson Club in the old Officers'
    Mess

Z   Education Centre

5   Five-a-side football pitch. To the
    east, south and west accommodation
    for Junior Ranks and Senior NCOs

KR Khimji Ramdas and other
    civilian traders

RS Met. Radio Sonde balloon filling
    and launching site

gruesome way of earning a living, but now he understood why some people wanted to be doctors.

In March 1976 the RAF staging post at Gan was closed due to the almost total withdrawal of British forces from the Far East. In Oman the Dhofar War was over and the British forces were being withdrawn from Salalah. The reasons for retaining RAF Masirah were disappearing one by one. In July it was announced that RAF Masirah would close the following year. The number of personnel was reduced and the Group Captain Station Commander was replaced by Wing Commander Sam Boyce in August.

Towards the end of the year two geologists arrived at Masirah to have a last look at the island while it was still easy to do so. They were Frank Moseley and one of his post-graduate students, Ian Abbotts. Frank Moseley ERD DSc PhD MA BSc FGS had been a 244 Squadron Bisley pilot at Masirah during the Second World War and in 1966 had conducted a water survey of the island. This last visit was not a search for commercial minerals but an academic study of the ophiolite rocks.

Wing Commander Sam Boyce writes:

One evening I had been invited to have a fish and chip supper at BERS. Driving back to the Camp late in the evening I was just negotiating the bridge over the Masirah River (the outfall from the distillation plant which ran into the sea) when something caught my eye in the periphery of my vision. I stopped and backed off the road into the desert until the headlights illuminated a Land Rover on it's side with it's wheels pointing towards me. I carefully drove across the road and round the other side of the Land Rover where I found an arab sitting on the ground in an advanced state of inebriation. He was surrounded by dozens of cans of Carlsberg which had clearly burst out of their cardboard cases as he rolled the vehicle. He was clearly feeling no pain so I drove back as fast as I could and sent one of our doctors out to have a took at him.

The following day I sent for my provost officer, briefed him on the incident and told him to go and find out the source of this liquor. Not unexpectedly he reported to me after a week that his flat feet had been quite unable to find out anything at all, but I had a hunch and went down to the Royal Oman Police post in the village to see the delightful Mohammed, smart, ever-cooperative, trained at the Metropolitan Police College at Hendon and with an engagingly British sense of humour. I told him what had happened and said that I believed the Pakistani Mess was supplying this liquor to the locals. Would he look into it. Within two days he came to see me. He had dressed up one of his henchmen as a local fisherman and sent him up to the Pakistani Mess to inquire if he could purchase a crate of beer and how much it would cost. Just as I suspected, he was offered the beer there and then and asked to pay about five times the going rate. He pleaded that he didn't have enough money with him and would return later.

I sent for the Manager of the Pakistani Mess, walked up and down him for several minutes and then told him that his Mess was being watched. I told him that if I ever had so much as a sniff of this kind of activity again I would ensure that he and his disgusting profiteering friends would be on the next aircraft to Karachi on a one way ticket. All was quiet for some weeks thereafter until the Wali came to see me. He was, of course, the civil governor appointed by the Sultan. He was an engaging rogue with whom I always got on well, but he seemed ill at ease on this occasion. I inquired what I could do for him and he asked if I could get Bob Hankinson, my arabic-speaking officer, down to the office. This was quickly arranged and the Wali dismissed his own askar/interpreter.

'Now then Sheikh' I said. 'Tell me what's troubling you.'

He looked uncomfortable.

'It's a rather delicate matter,' he replied.

'Come on Sheikh,' I said. 'We're friends. You can talk in complete confidence in this office.'

He looked around the room shiftily.

'Well,' he said. 'My liquor supply's dried up. Can you help me?'

'Sheikh,' I said. 'You know I'm always anxious to help when I can, but you must also know that it's one of the Sultan's absolute conditions that we must never supply alcohol to his people.'

Of course he well knew this and it was a try-on, but we remained friends. It also neatly closed the loop in the saga which began with a pranged Land Rover in the darkness several weeks earlier.

Sam Boyce continues:

My father, Clayton Boyce, was a flying-boat pilot on 203 Squadron at Basra before the Second World War. He twice flew down to Sur Masirah to inspect the bodies of two aircrew who had been killed there, to see if they had dried up sufficiently to be taken to Iraq for burial. They anchored offshore and he said that on both occasions they were shot at by the locals. On one of the visits, while they were ashore, the clock was stolen from the aircraft. One day when that delightful old rogue Sheikh Khamis bin Hilal came to pay me a social call, we were talking of nothing in particular when I mentioned the theft of the clock from my father's aircraft. He immediately looked out of the window into the distance and said how good the weather was for fishing.

1977

Sam Boyce continues as follows:

I had to go back to the UK for a conference on winding up Masirah and selling it to SOAF. While I was there my father told me the story of the dead aircrew at Sur Masirah. They had been placed in a shallow cave wrapped in tarpaulin and it must have been an unpleasant task for all who were charged with inspecting the bodies. From my father's log book I see that he visited Masirah in September 1938 and in March 1939. Knowing about this crash Sam Key and I visited the village of Sur Masirah and found a goat pen there which was constructed, among other things, from a square section of corrugated dural with a window in it, together with an aircraft wheel with a balloon

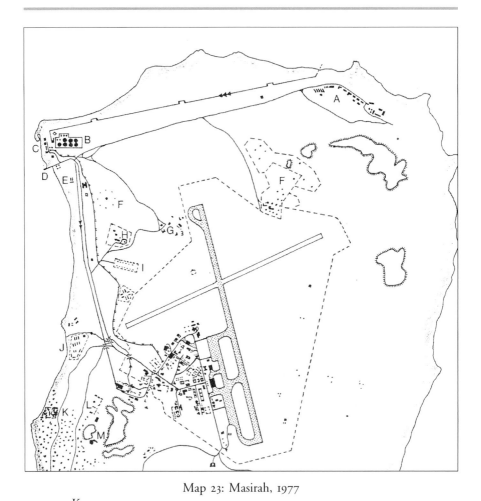

Map 23: Masirah, 1977

Key:

➤➤➤ Oil Pipeline	
Salt water stream	
Concrete	
➤ Salt water pipeline	
Narrow gauge railway	
- - - - Boundary fence	
Low hills of dark rock	

A BBC Eastern Relay Station

B Fuel Storage Tanks

C Water Sports Centre

D Jetty

E Police Dog Compound

F Aerial Farms

G Civilian Shops

H Explosives Area

I Bomb Dump (disused)

J Living Quaters for Desal./Power Station employees

K Desal./Power Station (left)

L Wali's Offices (north compound)

Village School (south compound)

M Civil Hospital

tyre. None of this threw any light on the crash site however. Some months later I was talking to a visiting SOAF helicopter pilot and mentioned all this. He was so interested that he insisted that we should fly there with him and comb the area which we did and found nothing. I then recalled Jasper Coates, a retired group captain and contemporary of my father, who had spent almost all his service career in the Middle East. Sam Key had known him during the Jebal Akhdar War and I gave him the task of tracking him down and writing to him. He found him somewhere in Yorkshire and sent him a 1:50,000 map and asked him to mark the crash site, which he did, and also sent pages of fascinating stuff about Masirah. The crashed aircraft was apparently a Vincent, probably from 8 Squadron.

Armed with this I contacted the helicopter pilot again. He flew us down to Sur Masirah and we went off and spent 30 or 40 minutes searching the area from the air. We found nothing. He then landed by Sur Masirah village and went off to talk to the locals with his Omani crewman. He eventually returned with the most ancient and smelly Arab I had ever seen and packed him into the front seat of the helicopter. The old fellow remembered the crash and took us unerringly to a shallow wadi where we landed. Sure enough, there were unmistakable signs of an oil fire and quite a lot of small bits of obvious aeroplane origin. He could not, however, tell us where the bodies were although Jasper Coates had told us that they were in a nearby cave. The plan to remove them was forgotten in the heat of war, and to the best of his knowledge had never been accomplished. We couldn't see any caves in the area and had to abandon the search for the bodies.

During the early part of the year the RAF withdrawal from Masirah continued its steady progress. Royal Fleet Auxiliaries were frequent visitors, taking away all that the RAF wanted to remove. The last train ran on 9 January with Wing Commander Sam Boyce on board and his CO's pennant fluttering in the breeze. The locomotive, Yimkin, on a small section of track, was deck cargo on the last ship. It was put on display at the RAF Cosford Aerospace Museum where it stood in the open for ten years. It was then formally presented to the Leighton Buzzard Narrow Gauge Railway where it can be seen to this day.

Sam Boyce continues as follows:

Quite early on in my tour at Masirah I had resolved to bring back a number of crayfish tails when we finally closed down the RAF presence there. We had always been able to obtain these through the crayfish combine run by Mohammed bin Khamis at prices which would have been the envy of any hotel in England. But the far better paid SOAF advance party had moved in and taken over both the Officers' and Sergeants' Messes some three months before we left. Mohammed, always with an eye to the main chance, raised his prices beyond the reach of our by then combined mess.

Around about this time Mohammed arrived one morning at my office and we exchanged the usual greetings. I asked after his father who was Sheikh Khamis bin Hilal, and we talked of various inconsequential things. However, I had been there long enough by then to realise that no arab ever came to see me to talk about the weather and eventually the purpose of his visit was revealed. Could he, he asked me, have one of the enormous metal-bound crates which littered the Station in which to keep the tools of his trade. I knew that these had not been included in the astonishing Dutch auction which disposed of those RAF assets which were not required to be shipped home, and equally I knew that they were not included in the list of things which we had been ordered to load onto the final RFA. They were gash and I realised this might be a trump card. I then said that I would like to take some crayfish home when we finally left and asked if he could supply them.

'Very difficult,' he said. 'Can I have the crate?'

'Very difficult,' I told him. 'They belong to my Queen and I can't just give them away.'

'Couldn't you write to her and ask if I could have one?' he asked me.

'I suppose I could but I'm really very busy and I just don't have the time to do that at the moment,' I replied.

He got up and left. However, he was back again in a couple of weeks to ask if I'd yet had time to pass on his request to the Queen and I told him I was still much too busy. This waiting game was repeated once or twice more before I told Mohammed that I'd written to the Queen on his behalf, but he should not expect an immediate response. At this juncture I again asked about the crayfish and was told that it remained very difficult. Thereafter, he came to see me almost weekly until I judged the time was ripe to say that I'd heard from the Queen who had very graciously agreed to let him have his crate.

'How much will it cost?' he asked.

'My Queen recognises your splendid work here and you will not have to pay anything. Now what about these crayfish?' I said.

His normally inscrutable face lit up.

'I think it can be arranged. How many crayfish would you need?' he asked me.

'I think about twelve dozen would be enough,' I replied.

'How much were you thinking of paying?' he asked.

'I wasn't really thinking of paying anything,' I told him.

He took his leave without another word. I'd played my trump card and had nothing left in my hand.

Some two weeks later my PA came in and said there were two arabs waiting to see me and I asked him to send them in. In came Mohammed Khamis with one of his team, each with a large sack over his shoulder which they then upended, discharging dozens of live crayfish onto the floor of my office.

Honour was now satisfied. I shook them both by the hand and they left. The Airmens' Mess sent someone over to collect the crayfish, they were cooked, wrapped, boxed and put into cold storage, eventually travelling back to England in the unpressurised hold of the last but one VC 10 and held in the Airmen's Mess freezers at Brize Norton from whence I collected them some ten days later. They lasted us almost a year by which time neither of us ever wanted to look another crayfish in the face!

RAF Masirah was being transferred to the Sultan of Oman's Air Force, and as RAF numbers thinned out so SOAF personnel arrived. The very last RAF aircraft, a VC10, left with the few remaining RAF personnel at 5.45 a.m. on 31 March. It was the end of an era. Petrol Tin Island had become a well-appointed modern station, and was the very last RAF base east of Suez. But it was to live on under new management.

CHAPTER VIII

The Sultan of Oman's Air Force

No. 1 squadron of the Sultan of Oman's Air Force (SOAF) moved to Masirah at the beginning of 1977 and has been there up to the present day.

SOAF was formed in 1959 shortly after the Jebel Akhdar War. Initially it consisted of three armed Piston Provosts which were new, and two well-worn Pioneers which had belonged to 78 Squadron in Aden. In command there was a Squadron Leader and six other pilots, all on loan from the RAF. The aircraft were serviced by six RAF engineers, but these were soon replaced by civilians of Airwork Services Ltd., a company which is still under contract.

After training in Aden SOAF moved to the Bait al Falaj airfield near Muscat on 10 August 1959. The natural surface runway was not in a good state of repair.

For a while SOAF was not engaged on active operations, being used for visual reconnaissance, casualty evacuation, as a taxi service and for checking on boatloads of illegal immigrants, etc. Then, in 1962, a minor rebellion started in the southern province of Dhofar, an area about the size of Wales and separated from the inhabited area in the north by hundreds of miles of desert. The main town of the province is Salalah where Sultan Said bin Taimur had taken up permanent residence. The Salalah plain stretches 15 or 20 miles each side of the town and up to 10 miles inland from the sea. Behind the plain, rolling downland rises to about 2,000 feet above sea level. It is covered in grass, bushes and trees due to the south-west monsoon of the summer months. At this time of year there is low cloud, poor visibility, drizzle, and no more than a light breeze. The sea is rough and surf pounds the beaches. Each side of the Salalah plain the hills rise higher, some covered in dense bush and others, in a rain shadow, are stark, craggy and barren. All these hills were collectively called 'the jebal' and this was the stage where most of the Dhofar War was acted out. It was sparsely inhabited by unruly warriors who are quite distinct from Omani Arabs. They are darker skinned, dress differently and speak languages entirely unrelated to Arabic. They were usually called 'Jebalis'. Their settlements were not large and few dwellings were permanent structures of stone.

Just inland of the highest ridges, at the watershed, the nature of the terrain changes abruptly from bush to wilderness as the flat land gradually slopes down towards the north. It is cut by steep-sided wadis winding inland in convolutions like the cuts in a jigsaw puzzle. This is the *negd*. Further inland the wadis become wider and shallower until they are no longer discernable, and eventually give way to the dunes of the sand sea.

The rebellion started in a small way and was directed against Sultan Said bin Taimur who had become a recluse in his Salalah palace. He showed no inclination to better the primitive existence of his subjects even when a modest oil revenue was in prospect. The rebels had a medley of old weapons which they occasionally used ineffectively against the army battalion which was resident in Dhofar. The rebels' pinpricks led to punitive retaliation by the Sultan which served only to recruit more Dhofaris to the rebels' cause. A political party was formed – the Dhofar Liberation Front. The Liberation Front began to receive active support from Saudi Arabia which sent supplies to the rebels and trained them in Dammam. In 1963 there were landmining incidents near Salalah so six ferret armoured cars of the 9th/12th Lancers were flown into Salalah by Beverley to assist the Sultan. In 1965 SOAF Provosts were detached from Bait al Falaj to Salalah where they were used in active operations in support of the Sultan's army. Just across the border, in 1966, the Royal Navy assault ship HMS *Fearless* landed the 1st Battalion of the Irish Guards who cordoned and searched the village of Hauf.

Over the border in Aden and the Aden Protectorates, there was serious trouble. Rival independence movements battled for supremacy which was finally secured by the leading terrorist group, the NLF. This organisation was supported by Egypt and Yemen, leading opponents of British rule. The British had planned to withdraw from the territory, leaving it in the stable and friendly hands of the proposed South Arabian Federation, but this was not to be and the territory was surrendered to the NLF. Respected sheikhs and loyal government servants were betrayed and left to suffer a brutal fate. Aden and the protectorates were renamed the Peoples Democratic Republic of Yemen, usually abbreviated to the PDRY. Its leaders embarked on a programme of mutual assassination. It was a hard-line communist state, and it formed a new terror organisation named the People's Front for the Liberation of Oman and the Occupied Arab Gulf, usually shortened to PFLOAG. It was sponsored by the Chinese, and later the Soviet delegations in Aden. Its terrorists infiltrated Dhofar, dominating and subjugating the Dhofar Liberation Front. They controlled all the jebal, the hilly area of Dhofar, but not the Salalah plain or town. Communist cells were established throughout the jebal to re-educate the tribesmen by a campaign of terror. Those unwilling to deny their religion had their eyes gouged out by red-hot knives or were brutally murdered. Their children were abducted and sent to the PDRY for indoctrination.

In July 1970 the Sultan was deposed by his son Qaboos in an almost bloodless palace coup. During the coup the old Sultan shot and wounded a sheikh who supported his son, and then accidently shot himself in the foot. He was evacuated from RAF Salalah and spent the remaining two years of his life in the Dorchester Hotel in London. Qaboos came to power in a frenzy of national rejoicing which has proved to be well founded. He is an excellent ruler.

It was hoped that the Dhofar rebellion would crumble, but unfortunately the communists' stranglehold was too tight. They were concerned with the spread of communism, not the welfare of the people. They were called '*adoo*' (enemy) by the other inhabitants of Oman, as the country was now named. Oil revenues enabled the young Sultan to strengthen his armed forces and begin a massive programme of civil aid and development which was extended to the hill country of Dhofar when his army had established permanent outposts there. These outposts showed the benefits of the Sultan's rule, and gradually the *adoo* tribesmen began to rally to the Sultan's cause. Many of them joined the Loyal Firqat which was composed of SEPs (surrendered enemy persons) who fought on the Sultan's side. It was a slow process, and almost the entire jebal was still in the hands of the *adoo*. As late as 1973 the *adoo* were firing 122-mm Katyushka rockets and 75-mm RCLs from the hills into the Salalah airfield north of the town.

By this time the Piston Provosts and Pioneers had long since been replaced by Strikemasters and Beavers, and were permanently based at Salalah. They were now named No. 1 Squadron because other squadrons had been formed. The first Strikemasters arrived in 1969 and some of the original batch were still in service thirty years later. Also at Salalah there was No. 2 Squadron

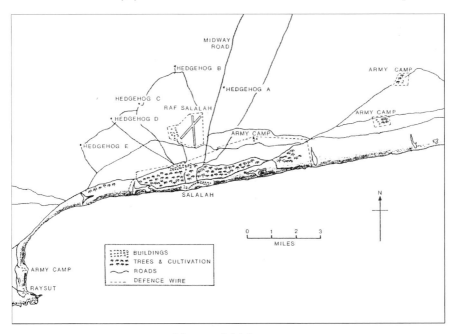

Map 24: Salalah, 1974

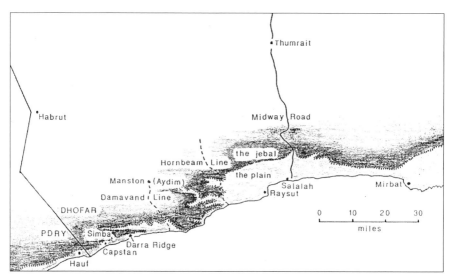

Map 25: Towards the end of the Dhofar War

with light and medium transport aircraft, Skyvans and Caribous. No. 3 Squadron was a helicopter squadron of AB 205s and 206s which was also based at Salalah. In Northern Oman the Bait al Falaj airfield had been abandoned and No. 4 Squadron with Viscount transport aircraft was based at the new Seeb International Airport where HQ SOAF was also located. The headquarters of the Sultan's Armed Forces (HQ SAF) remained in the fort at Bait al Falaj.

Between 1973 and 1975 the war gradually swung in favour of Sultan Qaboos. The Salalah air base was ringed by a substantial security fence with watchtowers. Between the airfield and the jebal there were five 'hedgehogs', which were machine-gun and mortar posts, one of them with artillery. Microphones were planted in the plain between the hedgehogs and the airfield, and were wired to the sound ranger which could instantly plot the position of a Katyushka or RCL launch. Artillery could be brought to bear and Strikemasters scrambled to attack the launch site before the *adoo* fled. Artillery shells and bombs could also be plotted by the sound ranger, and corrections given immediately. However, the sound ranger never had to be used because the army established five permanent piquets, the 'Dianas', on the jebal opposite the airfield. These denied the area to the *adoo* and the airfield was now safe from rocket attack. The Dianas themselves were not safe, particularly for the helicopters which resupplied them.

A tarmac road was built over the jebal from Salalah to Thumrait where a new modern airfield was being built in the *negd* 40 miles inland. The road was closely guarded where it wound its way up through the jebal, first by the Imperial Iranian Army and later by the Oman Gendarmerie and then the Jordanian Special Forces. The roadside guard posts prevented *adoo* ambushes

274

and had the additional advantage of inhibiting the *adoo* supply route to their eastern area of operations.

Further to the west, between Salalah and the PDRY border, a defensive line was laid down from the sea, up through spectacular barren mountains, to a point 27 miles inland. This was the 'Hornbeam Line'. Every three or four miles there was a permanently manned army outpost with commanding views, When completed the Hornbeam Line was a formidable barbed-wire barrier with landmines, and the *adoo* were unable to bring their camel caravans of supplies any further east. North of the Hornbeam Line was the open terrain of the *negd* where the *adoo* could not hide from the Strikemasters, and to the south the sea was patrolled by the Sultan of Oman's Navy (SON).

The PDRY border was 70 miles west of Salalah. In 1972 a daring helicopter assault established a permanent position for the Sultan's forces on two bald ridges only four miles east from the border. Known as Simba, it was supplied entirely by air. Even the water had to be flown in. Initially fixed-wing aircraft were used but it did not take long for the PDRY artillery and PFLOAG Katyushkas to zero in on the landing ground. After this only helicopters could be used. The position was constantly under heavy bombardment, but the army were well dug in and there were few casualties. Simba was at 4,500 feet above sea level, and the ground sloped steeply down to the sea in a series of cliffs, terraces and a jumble of huge rocks. The original intention was to gain an overview of the *adoo* supply route from the PDRY, but unfortunately the track was hidden from view in dead ground. Vehicles were not used on the *adoo* supply route as the terrain was completely unsuitable. Camels were used and moved at night so that they could not be seen from the air.

At Simba attempts were made to descend to another dominating feature overlooking the supply route, to be known as Capstan, but *adoo* opposition and landmines made it an impossible objective. Nevertheless, the garrison at Simba was maintained to prevent the PDRY claiming that the border was any further east.

RAF Masirah's role in the war was as RAF Salalah's parent station, supplying it and administering it. Due to the fear of *adoo* attacks RAF transport aircraft were not permitted to spend the night at Salalah, and it was too far to fly from Cyprus to Salalah and leave before nightfall. Masirah is a convenient 350 miles from Salalah, and the C-130 Hercules and Andover aircraft could make the return flight in daylight hours. RAF personnel at Salalah were responsible for operating Air Traffic Control, the fire service, and other basic needs which included the Officers' Mess until the beginning of 1974. After this the mess was run by SOAF. There was a NAAFI shop on the station, and the resident British forces included the RAF Regiment which was responsible for guarding the airfield, which included manning the hedgehogs. The Royal Artillery at the hedgehogs was known as the 'Cracker Battery', and it was here that the ZBD ('Zebedee') radar was located. The sound ranger was also manned by the British Army. There were British Army or RAF surgeons at 'MASH', the Field Surgical Team, and Royal Engineers were employed on a medley of tasks including civil development on the jebal. The SAS led the Loyal Firqat who co-operated closely with the Sultan's land forces during operations on the jebal.

The SAF headquarters for the area, HQ Dhofar Brigade, was located at the Salalah airfield but its other units were elsewhere. There were always two large infantry battalions of Baluch soldiers recruited from Gwadar by permission of Pakistan, to which the territory had been ceded. The other two infantry battalions were of soldiers recruited from Northern Oman. The Oman Gendarmerie manned the border post in the *negd* at Habrut. There was also the Oman Artillery with 25-pounder guns and 5.5-inch medium guns. The Armoured Car Squadron was equipped with Saladins, and there was Z Company with pink Land Rovers on which were mounted heavy machine guns. This was led by a Rhodesian soldier of fortune whose speciality was causing mayhem. The officers in SOLF (the Sultan of Oman's Land Forces), SON and SOAF were mostly British, about half being on loan from the British forces and the other half being ex-officers of British and Commonwealth Forces, on direct contract to the Oman Government.

In 1974 there were only about half a dozen SOAF Augusta Bell 205 helicopters and pilots at Salalah which was a totally inadequate number for the tasks they had to perform. These included helicopter-borne army assaults on to positions in *adoo* territory that were then temporarily occupied, resupply of these positions, and casualty evacuation. There was also the constant resupply of Simba and other permanent positions which did not have airfields. Imperial Iranian Army Bell 205 helicopters assisted with the resupply of Simba, and for ten months there was a detachment of four Wessex helicopters with their air and ground crews on loan from the RAF. There were also four or five Short Skyvans and a couple of ancient DHC Caribous which were used to supply the army outposts which had airstrips. Some of these airstrips on the jebal were absolutely diabolical.

In the *negd* between the Hornbeam Line and the border there was a small airfield called Manston which was used as a forward base for the helicopters flying supplies into Simba, and was built up into a large headquarters for the Iranian Brigade which the Shah sent to assist the Sultan. The short natural surface runway was extended to 1,000 metres of concrete and used by Iranian C-130 Hercules transport aircraft flying non-stop from Iran. The task for the Iranian Brigade was to establish another defensive line south to the sea. Due to inexperience and poor leadership they suffered at the hands of the *adoo*. In establishing their 'Damavand Line' their advance into *adoo* territory was hesitant and accomplished by a truly profligate expenditure of ammunition hosed off indiscriminately in every direction.

A whole book could be written on the Dhofar War but this short summary must suffice to set the stage for 1 Squadron's operations in the closing stages.

There were usually only about five or six pilots and Strikemasters at Salalah together with two DHC Beavers which were flown by the same pilots, but the Squadron also operated in Northern Oman.

In the far north of the country the mountainous Musandam Peninsula juts into the Straits of Hormuz. It is a land of fjords, huge wadis and lofty barren mountains. The principal town of the province is Khasab where the garrison of the Oman Gendarmerie lay on the eastern side of the wadi. There were a number of low buildings, the inevitable parade ground, a white fort, a natural surface airstrip and an aircraft parked behind the Officers' Mess. There were three mess members: the CO, the Civil Aid Officer, and the pilot. For three weeks out of every four the aircraft was a 1 Squadron Beaver and on the fourth week it was a 3 Squadron helicopter which was able to visit sites where there was no airfield. The Salalah-based pilots took it in turns to come to Khasab. There were five airfields in the province, the closest being Bukha which was just round a headland from Khasab and was no more than a five-minute flight from Khasab, but there was no road. There were a few vehicle tracks around the town and a few miles inland, but no land communication with the rest of the province or the rest of the Sultanate. The 1 Squadron Beaver pilot was kept busy and could fly over a hundred flights during the three weeks. This was often in rough conditions when there were thunderstorms, or downdrafts and curlovers as strong winds tumbled over the mountains.

The Beaver was a single-engined light transport aircraft with the classical configuration of a tailwheel undercarriage and high wings above the cabin. It was incredibly tough and the cockpit instruments and controls were more reminiscent of the cab of one of the army's more indestructible vehicles. It could take five passengers, but not at Khasab because there was a spare mainwheel and jack in place of the two rear seats. It was designed for bush flying in Canada and was also used by the British Army Air Corps where it was regarded as satisfactorily soldier-proof. At Khasab the pilot was responsible for refuelling from burmails, looking at the dip-stick and pumping up the tyres, etc. If the wind threatened to increase he tied the aircraft down, roping it to screw pickets so it did not blow away.

Elsewhere all the SOAF aircraft were serviced by civilians of Airwork Services Ltd. At Seeb they carried out the more thorough inspections and servicing of the Strikemasters as well as the more frequent servicing of the ejection seats. So there were quite frequent ferry flights between Salalah and Seeb. There was always a 1 Squadron pilot at Seeb who was there for two or three weeks 'R & R' (rest and recreation), but was usually kept fairly busy. He met new pilots at the civil air terminal, arranged their accommodation and arrival programme, and flew with them in the Strikemaster to convert them to the aircraft and ground-attack role. There was an unmanned air-to-ground weapons range near the present-day satellite tracking station. There were forward air control (FAC) courses for officers of the Sultan's Land Forces. During these courses they learnt to use the hand-held SARBE radio to talk Strikemasters onto targets on the ground, and there was live practice when the 1 Squadron pilot arrived in an armed Strikemaster to attack simulated targets in the uninhabited areas where the training took place. In those days there were no tarmac roads in the interior, and few graded vehicle tracks. The Seeb Beaver was therefore a popular mode of transport, ranging far and wide with army officers, medical teams and visiting journalists, etc., all of which represented a serious interruption to the pilot's social life at the SAF Beach Club.

There were two more Beavers at the Squadron's home base at Salalah, and these provided additional interest and variety for the pilots. They were used for taking army officers, civil aid workers and medical teams, etc. to airfields on the jebal and in the *negd*. They also flew the Brigade Commander and his staff on reconnaissance sorties over territory on which they planned to mount a helicopter-borne assault or a major advance into *adoo*-held areas. The Beavers were also used by the squadron Ground Liaison Officer to take photographs for his target folders. The Beavers dropped leaflets and flew what were known as 'Hawkeye' operations. These Hawkeye sorties were with the bilingual intelligence officer and a newly surrendered *adoo* who was prepared to betray those who had recently been his comrades. The SEP would aim two pointers at a hitherto unknown *adoo* position, and two other pointers fixed in parallel would indicate the position to the intelligence officer. He then pointed out the position to the pilot who called in the Strikemasters and directed them onto the target. It was a nasty surprise for the *adoo*.

Sometimes a Beaver was used at night, cruising high above an area where the *adoo* were thought to be present in some strength. The Beaver was an Aunt Sally, plainly visible with its navigation lights, landing light and anti-collision beacon all switched on, but above the range of anti-aircraft fire. In the back of the Beaver the hatch had been removed from the floor and the squadron's Ground Liaison Officer (the 'glow') sat astride the hole with powerful parachute flares stacked up around him. These he threw down through the hole in sticks of three, and further sticks of three when they had burnt out. The brilliant parachute flares and the illuminated Beaver gently circling in the night sky must have presented a weird spectacle to the *adoo*, but it was like a red rag to a bull, and they could not contain their excitement. They went crazy, firing all their available weapons at the tempting target. What they did not realise was that a blacked-out Strikemaster was also present, out of earshot, its pilot noting the position of the muzzle flashes in the illuminated countryside. Suddenly two 500-lb bombs would explode in the midst of the muzzle flashes. Night bombing without the Beaver was never very successful because it was difficult to read the map or see the ground in the dark.

The Strikemaster's standard armament was two 7.62-mm machine guns in the fuselage, and under the wings were two 500-lb bombs and sixteen Sura rockets in four tiers of four each. One bomb was usually fused for a groundburst, preferably in a confined space like the bottom of a wadi, and the other fused for an airburst over open ground where the shrapnel and blast would cover a wider area. It was not advisable to drop one of these bombs closer than a kilometre to 'own troops' because the blast could cause nausea and disorientation. The British 540-lb MC (medium capacity) bomb was the best, but the Squadron also used the Spanish 250-kg Expal bomb, and the Pakistani 470-lb bomb which was not entirely satisfactory because the tail fins sometimes fell off. Some years later these Pakistani bombs were taken out of service when one of them exploded just after it had been dropped from a SOAF Jaguar.

The Strikemaster was a beefed-up version of the Jet Provost which the RAF used as a training aircraft, but it was a much better aircraft than the Jet Provost, with a more powerful engine, more fuel, more batteries and faster limiting speeds, etc. It was a side-by-side two-seater but at Salalah it was usually flown with only one seat. Like most of the aircraft at Salalah they were dispersed singly around the airfield in blast-proof shelters made of sand-filled burmails to protect them from RCL and Katyushka rocket attacks. The domestic and working accommodation on the station was also protected by walls of sand-filled burmails. The squadron crewrooms were in the solid old BOAC accommodation built during the Second World War, but the sleeping accommodation was recent and Jerry-built.

During daylight hours there was always a pair of Strikemasters on standby on at least the 'green' state of readiness which meant that the aircraft could be airborne within ten minutes of the scramble bells ringing. These bells were extremely loud and sited anywhere on the station where the pilots might be. If there was an army operation in progress the standby pair would be on 'red' in the crewroom wearing their 'Mae West' life-saving jackets. They would be airborne within four minutes. In addition there was a backup pair on 'green'. There would be a scramble whenever any army position was under attack by *adoo* mortars, RPG 7s, RCLs or rockets. This was usually at Simba or one of the piquets on the Hornbeam Line, or most likely during an army advance into *adoo* territory. If it was a helicopter assault the Strikemasters would often give 'top cover', circling above the helicopters which were very vulnerable to *adoo* small arms fire if they were at low level. The SOAF Commander, Group Captain Les Phipps, frequently visited the Squadron from his office in HQ SOAF. He flew operational sorties in the Strikemaster and would put himself on standby during his visits. He kept himself current on the Beaver as well. The SOAF Commander of Salalah also flew with the Squadron.

When the Operations Officer sounded the scramble bells the pilots and Airwork groundcrew would jump into their 'scramble wagons' (the Mini Mokes were the best ones) and race to the assigned aircraft which had been prepared for start-up. All other aircraft would vacate the area and Air Traffic Control would transmit the simple message 'Scramble East' or 'Scramble West'. Once airborne and heading in the right direction the pilots would receive more detailed instructions from the Operations Officer, and then from the position under attack. This could be on the multi-channel high-frequency radio. The leading Strikemaster would make a low-level run-in and pull up if it was important to give the *adoo* no prior warning of its arrival. The leader would fire a rocket at the *adoo* position, and if the army FAC transmitted 'on target' the second aircraft would drop a bomb. During rocket or dive-bombing attacks the other aircraft would make synchronised machine-gun attacks from a different direction. This was to distract the *adoo*'s attention in an attempt to prevent return fire.

Those not on standby would fly preplanned sorties of harassing fire and reconnaissance (HF & R) to search the *adoo* supply tracks in Sultanate territory and attack anything suspicious. If nothing was seen the aircraft attacked known *adoo* stores caves and waterholes where the camel trains rested up by day. Occasionally the Squadron flew similar sorties at night, but this achieved very little as map reading from the air was quite difficult, even in a full moon. The *adoo* must have doused their fires and switched off any lights when they heard the aircraft because nothing was ever seen. It was also difficult to harass the *adoo* during the south-west monsoon when low cloud shrouded the jebal in fog. Level bombing was tried, with carefully calculated timed runs from features in the *negd*. Direct hits on *adoo* positions were most unlikely, but they must have felt vulnerable and insecure when bombs dropped through the fog in their locality.

It was a great loss for the Squadron when the Beavers were withdrawn from service at the beginning of 1975. HQ SOAF decided that the safety factor of having two engines was of paramount importance, so a new squadron of BN Islanders was formed. For some reason they were known as Defenders when in military service. These became No. 5 Squadron. The myth of twin-engine safety was exposed when two of the Defenders had engine failures and were unable to maintain altitude on the other engine. One came down in a cornfield and the other in the sea with some loss of life. Beaver engines never failed. 1 Squadron had 1,000 sticky labels printed with the caption 'Bring Back the Beaver'. These labels found their way into the most inaccessible places, including inside every secret file in the headquarters and even under the lavatory seat in the Commander's residence. In response the Beavers were indeed reintroduced for a while, but were withdrawn again later in the year.

It was hoped to end the war after the monsoon of 1975. The new airfield at Thumrait was open for business and a large number of Hawker Hunter fighters had arrived there as a gift from King Hussein of Jordan. With them came a couple of Jordanian pilots and a stock of highly suspect Sura rockets. One of them exploded immediately after it had been fired by a Strikemaster, but fortunately it did not destroy the aircraft or injure the pilot. RAF loan service and contract Hunter pilots arrived from the UK to form No. 6 Squadron at Thumrait.

The final battle of the Dhofar War was to be a helicopter assault across a deep gorge to capture the Darra Ridge which overlooked the sea between the Damavand Line and Simba. This was to take place in October 1975, well after the south-west monsoon and after the holy month of Ramadan. It was a highly risky operation because it was known that the *adoo* now had surface-to-air missiles in Dhofar. These were SAM 7 heat-seeking missiles, although this information was withheld from the pilots; no exhaust muffs were fitted to the aircraft, and there was no change in the tactics to safeguard the aircraft and their occupants.

There were diversionary operations on the jebal to keep the *adoo* guessing where the final blow would fall. The first SAM 7 was fired during one of these – it blew the tail off a Strikemaster and the pilot, Roger Furlong, ejected and parachuted into *adoo* territory. The *adoo* were nearby in the bush. To be rescued by helicopter Roger Furlong had to run to a nearby hilltop but the rings in his leg restrainers were clinking together as he ran, so he discarded them as well as his map, white gloves, and the white writing pads on the knees of his flying suit. He activated his SARBE radio beacon and legged it to the nearby hilltop. The other Strikemaster climbed to a safe height and organised a rescue attempt. Another SAM 7 was fired at it, but missed. By chance there was a Simba resupply by SOAF helicopters at the time, one of them was fitted with a winch and had two pilots in it. It responded to the request for a rescue attempt which was highly risky. The whole incident was being observed by the Brigade Commander, Brigadier John Akehurst, who was on higher ground further north at an army position. Next to him was a major who urged him to call off the rescue attempt because of the risk to the helicopter. Two more SAM 7s were fired at the helicopter, but missed, and it was also under fire from a machine gun firing tracer ammunition. It was a hideous decision for the Brigade Commander, but he decided to let the rescue attempt go ahead. His decision would have been questioned had he called it off, and the helicopter pilot had disregarded his order and carried out a successful rescue. The helicopter homed in on the SARBE beacon, but there were too many bushes to allow it to land so the crewman used the winch to lower the hook. There was no rescue strop on the hook, and the winch jammed a few feet above the Strikemaster pilot so the helicopter descended further until Roger Furlong was able to engage the hook into the becket handles on his Mae West jacket. The helicopter was still under fire and took some hits, but slowly climbed out with Roger Furlong dangling underneath. The helicopter was heavily laden with troops from Simba, and as it slowly climbed away everyone expected it to be knocked out of the sky by another SAM 7, but none were fired. The *adoo* operator must have used all his missiles. The rescue was successful. The *adoo* did not take prisoners, and if Roger Furlong had not been rescued he would have been shot out of hand immediately after capture. The helicopter pilot was rightly decorated by the Sultan for this heroic action.

Later another Strikemaster was hit by a SAM 7, but although the back end of the aircraft was severely damaged it was not completely disabled. The pilot managed to reach Manston where he crash-landed. The aircraft was destroyed during the crash-landing but the pilot was uninjured. The same happened to one of the Hunters and the Jordanian pilot also survived the crash-landing at Manston. A total of about twenty-three SAM 7s were fired, but miraculously only two pilots were killed, the two crew of a helicopter.

One of the diversionary operations was an advance south from Simba towards the sea. A mine-clearing party went ahead and Capstan, the dominating feature below Simba, was occupied without opposition which was a surprise. Evidently the *adoo* knew that it was only a feint and had concentrated where the main attack was to take place further east. The Brigade Commander was at Simba to watch the feint advance and decided on a complete change of plan, bringing reinforcements to Simba and continuing the advance down to the sea. The logistics were flexible enough to accommodate this brilliant stroke of opportunism. Suddenly the *adoo* were cut off from the PDRY. There was still serious fighting further to the east, but there could be no resupply for the *adoo*, and no line of retreat to the safety of the PDRY. PDRY regular troops were cut off and had to make their way home further inland through the waterless wastes of the *negd* where they suffered terribly.

The seaside town of Hauf was just across the border in the PDRY. Above it in caves were extensive stores and artillery. For years the artillery and Katyushka rockets had been pounding Simba, and they were now stung into furious action against all the SAF positions from Simba down to the sea. To counter this the Sultan's 5.5-inch medium guns were brought in as underslung loads by Iranian Chinook heavy-lift helicopters. The Hunters were unleashed and allowed across the border to attack the stores and artillery above Hauf. They carried the same Sura rockets as the Strikemasters, but their 1000-lb bombs and 30-mm cannon were much heavier weapons, and their higher speed offered some protection against SAM 7s. Then the PDRY brought in heavier artillery pieces, and so the hard pounding continued. Many of the Hunters sustained serious damage and one of them was brought down. The pilot ejected out to sea off Hauf and took to his inflatable dinghy. Enemy guns opened up on him, and a boat was launched from Hauf to pick him up, but before it got to him a SOAF helicopter arrived and winched him up to safety. By this time the surrounding sea was dotted by machine-gun rounds fired from the shore. After a month the Sultan's artillery fell silent and the Hunters were called off their prey. Enough was enough. But the PDRY artillery bombardment continued for another four months until Saudi Arabian diplomatic pressure prevailed. Although the war was undoubtedly won there were still odd corners of *adoo* resistance. On Christmas Day 1975 Brigadier John Akehurst and his wife Shirley visited all the outlying army positions by fixed-wing aircraft and helicopter. When leaving one of the positions on the jebal the helicopter was hit by ground fire from an *adoo* AK 47, which caused serious damage and it had to make an emergency landing very soon afterwards. Few brigadiers' wives are shot down, and the story must have become the main topic at the wives' coffee mornings at Aldershot.

The Sultan was magnanimous in victory. An amnesty was declared and generous payments were made for any *adoo* weapons or ammunition handed in. There could now be a massive programme of civil development on the jebal where the Loyal Firqat ruled the roost.

The end of the war was a great relief for the pilots who had had a hard time in the closing stages. Their social activities had never been demure, but their pastimes and activities now became wildly and dangerously uninhibited, and it is remarkable that no one was killed. Exhibitions of low flying became ever more spectacular.

1 Squadron was a spent force as a ground-attack squadron – the Strikemasters were vulnerable in a SAM environment unless they attacked from an altitude that degraded weapons accuracy. They were slow and feeble compared to the Hunters, the heavy mob up the road at Thumrait.

But a new role was in prospect for the Strikemasters: they were a popular training aircraft throughout the world, and this was to be their future employment in SOAF. As pilots left the Squadron they were replaced by RAF-trained qualified flying instructors (QFIs). But when would it all start? And where?

A Strikemaster flying past Air Traffic Control at Salalah after the Dhofar War.
Exhibitions of low flying became ever more spectacular
(Photograph: Frank Milligan)

It seemed that RAF Masirah was the ideal home for the FTS, being an underutilised airfield now that the Dhofar War had ended. Seeb International Airport would not welcome early solo students amongst the big jets, and Salalah was ruled out by the south-west monsoon. Thumrait was a possibility, but with a lack of local ground features students could easily become lost. Also it was doubtful that the uninhibited behaviour of the Hunter pilots would be a beneficial influence on impressionable young Omani student pilots. HQ SAF suggested Manston (now called Aydim) but there was only a 1,000-metre runway at 1,500ft elevation.

Due to impending defence cuts HQ SAF said that the FTS (Flying Training School) could not start the following year, 1976. There was even a suggestion that the Strikemaster squadron would have to disband in July 1976. But then it was agreed that SOAF could indeed start an FTS, although not for another two years. Meanwhile students were progressing through the training pipeline – their elementary flying training was in Scotland and their officer training was with the RAF. On their return to Oman the first course would be ready to begin their Strikemaster training in June 1976. HQ SOAF did not know what to do with these students and nobody was planning the Strikemaster FTS.

In April 1976 an edict from the Palace stated that SOAF was to form a Strikemaster FTS at RAF Masirah in January 1977, but there were still two outstanding problems. Firstly, there was still no financial approval to purchase the instructional equipment which the Squadron would need to fulfil its new task. Secondly, the RAF had not given approval for the Squadron to move into RAF Masirah. In July 1976 it was announced simultaneously by the BBC and Radio Oman that RAF Masirah was to close on 31 March 1977. Suddenly a Strikemaster squadron at Masirah looked like an expensive option. Nevertheless, the decision was made to buy the base and operate it. The negotiations were between the experienced DS4 team of the UK MoD playing on home ground, and a single SOAF officer. The DS4 team were extremely pleased with the outcome of the bargaining, having obtained an unexpectedly high price for the base.

In August 1976 Frank Milligan arrived at Salalah to become the new Officer Commanding 1 Squadron. He was a QFI, his previous appointment having been as the officer commanding an RAF University Air Squadron. Fortunately he saw eye to eye with the FTS staff officer, and both worked hard and harmoniously to prepare for the Squadron's new role at Masirah. Unfortunately there was still no such co-operation from the financiers who had still not given any authority to purchase specialist equipment. The staff officer moved permanently to RAF Masirah in December 1976 to concentrate on the task in hand, abandoning his other job at SAITS. He was appointed CGI designate, but even had to buy his typewriter out of his own pocket.

The early months of 1977 saw a steady increase in the number of SOAF

The Augusta Bell 205 Rescue Helicopter
(Photograph: Bruce Watts)

personnel at Masirah. Unfortunately this did not include the vital MoD engineers who should have been learning how to operate the power station, the water desalination plant and the sewage system, etc. Some came, and were then withdrawn. The RAF kept their civil engineers as long as possible but a proper handover was not achieved. The MoD engineers arrived at the last possible moment.

Some of the Strikemasters arrived from Salalah as early as January 1977, but the final ferry flight was not until the second half of March; the Search and Rescue helicopter arrived on 28 March. The SOAF Station Commander arrived in February at about the time that the Officers' and Sergeants' Messes were transferred from the RAF to SOAF. There was an immediate and dramatic improvement in the food, but all the RAF were told to eat in their Airmen's Mess, although a few RAF officers did sneak into the SOAF Officers' Mess to have a decent meal.

There was a steady decline in the number of RAF personnel, and heavy equipment was shipped out on Royal Fleet Auxiliaries, the last shipment being on 14 March. The heavy equipment included 'Yimkin', the diesel locomotive. At a stroke this denied SOAF the use of the railway for recreation. At that time the SOAF personnel regarded this as a senseless and selfish act, but twenty years later 'Yimkin' survives at the Leighton Buzzard Narrow Gauge Railway.

It would not have survived at Masirah. However, the DUKW did remain at Masirah. This was a large amphibious vehicle of Second World War vintage and dubious reliability. It was to provide many anxious moments, particularly when members of the Sergeants' Mess tried to sail it round the island. The RAF left behind their fine grey gelding which had been presented to them by the Sultan, and the NAAFI shop also remained at Masirah for another three years. The RAF also left behind a Shackleton engine which was not discovered for another twenty years. An RAF C-130 Hercules crew spirited away the two ancient cannons which were mounted each side of the entrance to the Officers' Mess. It is not known whether this had been officially sanctioned by the RAF, but it certainly drew vigorous protests from SOAF, so the cannons were returned. The few remaining RAF personnel left at 5.45 a.m. on the very last VC10 aircraft on 31 March 1977.

CHAPTER IX

SOAF Masirah – The First Three Years

1977

THE SOAF OPENING CEREMONY was not until 1 April. The SOAF Station Commander had decreed 31 March a normal working day. He declared an 'open station', and the locals were free to come in whenever they wished. He did not realise what was going to happen: on 31 March the local population flooded onto the station in every available vehicle and removed everything that was not nailed down. While everyone else was at work a single officer attempted to stem the pillage, turning back vehicles loaded high with furniture and carpets, etc. The soft pornography from the airmen's accommodation was obviously popular. When the heavily loaded vehicles were turned back they simply left the station by the other exit near the armoury.

On 1 April the SOAF ensign was raised and the Station Commander led a flypast of eight Strikemasters in the figure '1' (1 Squadron). Then the Squadron Commander carried out an excellent and vigorous display of low-level aerobatics. After that the rescue helicopter carried out its display, hovering in front of the spectators and winching up a simulated survivor. Later everyone went down to the north beach to watch a firepower demonstration carried out by two Hunters from Thumrait which fired their cannons and salvos of rockets at the wreck of the SS *Eletric*. It must be admitted that their aim was not outstandingly accurate, and there must have been a number of shell-shocked fish in the general area. Nevertheless the display was satisfactorily noisy and afterwards the spectators had to duck when the Hunters beat them up.

On that day the station strength was 25 officers including 5 student pilots, 43 senior NCOs and warrant officers, and 11 Omani other ranks. A further 103 civilians were brought on strength during the month.

The station salt water swimming pool had to be drained and cleaned following the RAF's last night as the bottom was littered with broken glasses and evidently some substance had been added to the water. It must have been quite a party. After it was refilled the pool became popular with the locals and their children who used the showers in the changing rooms as a lavatory. No one would clean up the faeces, so eventually the changing room doors were locked but the smell wafted out. The 'open station' policy had its critics, not

The SOAF Masirah opening ceremony. Hunters attack the wreck of the SS *Eletric*
(Photograph: Frank Milligan)

least because the NAAFI shop was often absolutely full of locals shouting at the manager.

By this time 1 Squadron and Station Operations had moved into the vacated RAF comcen building next to Air Traffic Control. The Omani students continued their initial period of ground school while the flying instructors carried out staff continuation training. The first instructional flight was on 23 April, and the first student solo flight was on 8 May. Training was continually interrupted by presentations to VIP visitors, in Arabic by the students or in English by the Squadron Commander. Preparation and practice took a long time and continuity of training suffered. One of the visitors was the Commander of the North Yemen Air Force whose own pilot training had been in the Soviet Union. He gave a generous quantity of high-quality Yemen coffee to the station. It was decreed that the coffee should be shared out to all the SOAF bases, so Masirah was left with less than a quarter, which was stolen by the locals.

RAF Masirah had had no taxiway to the threshold of runway 17 – aircraft always had to taxi back up the runway and turn round at the loop at the end before beginning their take-off run. A busy flying training school should not have its main runway blocked by taxying aircraft. At SOAF Masirah one of the first tasks for the MoD Engineers was to grade a natural surface taxiway to the threshold of runway 17, and later grade a taxiway parallel to the sand runway.

Most of the flying instructors were on loan from the RAF, and all had volunteered in the full knowledge of their conditions of service, but when they had all arrived at Masirah the RAF reneged on the terms that had been agreed. The local overseas allowance (LOA) had been pitched sufficiently high to secure enough volunteers, but the RAF then decreased the LOA by £1,300 per year. This was worth a lot more then than it is now and represented perhaps as much as a quarter of their total income. The RAF's case was that LOA was for the purpose of maintaining a standard of living in foreign countries where the cost of living was higher than in the UK, whereas the cost of living at Masirah was very low because it was not possible to buy anything. The loan service officers countered this argument by pointing out that they had to fly to Seeb to do their shopping in the capital area – their LOA should therefore be the same as loan service officers at Seeb. The dispute continued for months with the RAF refusing to give way. The loan service officers suggested that they should be repatriated to the UK and be replaced by others who might be enticed by the lower remuneration. At the heart of the problem was the RAF's use of LOA as a hard-living allowance.

SOAF Masirah had not made a good start, but worse was to come. The following is a transcript from an audio tape sent home by the Chief Ground Instructor (CGI):

I don't know if it has been in the newspapers yet but we've had quite a dramatic time here at Masirah. It all started some days ago when we heard that there was a revolving tropical storm, a cyclone, off the coast of India and coming in our direction. It's not unusual at this time of year but they usually veer off to the right and go back towards India again. This one seemed to be coming rather closer than it ought to, and if it kept on coming it would be with us in three days. Everyone got quite excited but then the satellite photo showed that the storm had turned right and was heading up towards Pakistan. Everybody got all unexcited and thought nothing more about it. It got a bit cloudy actually, and we got some rain which got heavier and heavier. It really was chucking it down on the evening of the 12th of June. I was down working quite late in the office with Frank. I came back in the Land Rover with him and left the bike down there because there was so much rain. Round about 4.15 the next morning when it was still dark, I woke up and there was a terrific wind going on, and corrugated tin roofs flapping about. I had a look outside and it really did seem to be very stormy indeed. And it seemed to be getting a bit windier all the time.

About 4.30 Frank pitched up. He saw me looking at the storm and I saw him looking at it so called him across and he came in for a cup of coffee. I'm not sure how safe it was to venture out because it really was a howling gale.

The thing which had woken me up was in fact that someone's tin roof had come off and it was rattling against the end wall (I'm on the end here).

As we drank our coffee more roofs started flapping about. We could see the Mess from here and a bit of it's roof came undone and peeled back and then blew away. It was really very dramatic actually. The wind was really howling.

Frank went back to his room but I couldn't get to sleep. It seemed to be getting stronger and stronger all the time and I was just hoping that it would start being the same or even get a bit better, but it didn't. Anyway, round about sevenish or so I ventured out and keeping under cover I went down to Frank's room. Tim, the Air Traffic Controller, was there, so we all had a cup of coffee and wondered what we ought to do because it was time to go to work. We didn't think we ought to go because there was a whole load of bits of tin roof, etc. flying through the air.

It was really beginning to get quite dramatic at this time. The wind was about 80 knots now with gusts to over 100, and it was much darker than it should have been. It should have been quite light at that time. Anyway, we went across to the Mess to see if there was any breakfast. Half the Mess roof was off by this time. Every now and then a piece of roof went whizzing past down the road so we had to choose the right moment to make a dash across to the Mess. We had a bite of breakfast and while we were there, at about 8 o'clock, the wind suddenly dropped off to only about 20 knots or a bit more. So we set off in the Land Rover to have a look round the station to see that all was well, particularly the aircraft. They had all been put in the hangar, thank goodness. But most of the hangar roof was off, and quite a bit of the far wall. But there was very little damage to the aircraft, the wall and roof must have all gone outwards. The cockpit procedures trainer was in there on its wheels and had got blown around and bumped into some of the aircraft. Then we went to the squadron. My motor bike was in a kind of alcove at the entrance and although it was sopping wet and covered in sand it was okay. So I popped it entirely indoors. We had a look at Air Traffic Control and that seemed okay.

The wind seemed to be starting to get up again from the other direction. It was a bit worrying as we didn't know whether the storm had passed and that's why the wind had died off, but when it started to blow from the other direction we realised that we were in the eye of the storm – right in the middle of it – and this was confirmed later by a satellite photo that showed that the centre had passed slap over us. It's rather funny being in the eye of the storm. It must have been about 10 miles wide I suppose, and quite clear. There was a lot of cloud round to the north moving very fast but it was okay where we were. We couldn't see very much to the south because the vis [visibility] wasn't very good.

We went back to the Mess and the wind was now from the south and getting stronger and stronger. I heard later that the atmospheric pressure in the eye of the storm was 956 millibars which is very low. It had dropped 40 millibars since the previous day and 9 millibars in the previous hour. I thought

13 June 1977, after the cyclone
(Photographs: Sam Boyce)

the Mess would be the safest place so went there. Frank went to his room and was inside when the whole of his roof blew off. He heard it go and looked out of the downwind window. The complete roof didn't touch the next block at all, it went clean over the top. I went to the Mess because I

13 June 1977, after the cyclone. *Top*: The Supply Squadron hangar. *Bottom*: The Officers' Mess entrance (Photographs: Frank Milligan)

thought it was safer. There were a number of us there in the bar which is on the downwind side. The roof was off but the ceiling was still there, but then the ceiling panels started to fall down amongst us. There was just a tremendous roaring noise and something heavy was thumping up there above some ceiling panels. Torn roofing was flapping and scraping against the building. From what we could see through the windows (which wasn't very much because of the flying sand) it seemed that the station was being destroyed before our eyes. The patio was a shambles with all the trees blown down.

People were sheltering underneath tables and I set up some cushions in an upwind corner which I thought might be safe because really we thought that the whole building might be pushed over by the wind. The anemometer in the Met Section traces a kind of graph but the maximum reading is only 90 knots, and it went well over this in gusts. The estimate by the Met Officer at Seeb was 110 to 120 knots. That's up to nearly 140 mph. I suppose that's about the speed that bits of SOAF Masirah were going past the windows, but it was difficult to see out because the windows were plastered in wet sand. That's the windows on the east and west. There are no windows in the Mess facing into wind, but those that were in our accommodation just got blown straight in.

Eventually, after about three hours, the wind slackened a bit. Vic Mills, the Catering Officer, produced some sandwiches. He's known as 'Mr Meals' because that's how the Omanis pronounce his name. Then a couple of Hunters arrived and took photos of us. We had no communications, you see, no radio links, no signals with anybody since it all started. The lack of comms with us, I suppose, alerted people that all might not be well here. Later a Skyvan arrived with HF radio sets and we were soon back in contact with the rest of the human race.

After it had died down a bit I had a look round. The hanger was still standing and the aircraft were still okay. But none of the other hangers on the station survived. There is a big stores shed in the Supply Squadron and that had gone. MT were using the old wartime hangar and half of that had collapsed on top of the vehicles. The Air Traffic Control building which had been all right during the lull was not all right. It had stood up to the wind but great bits of timber had been flying through the air and broken the big plate glass windows at the top. It was still raining at the time and I got a bit wet. There is a small hanger which has disappeared completely. The power is off. I am running this on batteries. The fresh water – they've just got one of the plants going so that's okay.

The locals live in a shanty town over the hill, and of course it was completely wiped out there. The police station there is okay, and the hospital, but the power station and desalination plant is not too good I think. During the lull a couple of buses went down there to see if anybody wanted to come to the station, but they preferred to stay down there in the hospital and police station. The buses came back when the wind began to blow again. Pete Perry was driving the mini-bus and had the windscreen smashed as he was driving back, Mal Young and Mohammed Mubarik were in the 32 seater coach and got back as far as the MT yard. The wind was too strong to risk getting out of the coach so they pointed it into wind and sat it out there. It must have been quite exciting.

RAF Masirah's unofficial logo was 'Yimkin' the turtle which was retained by SOAF Masirah. This is the T-shirt design for those present during the cyclone of 13 June 1977

I don't know when I will be able to get this tape away to you. In case the news gets back to the UK first we asked whether it would be possible for someone to tell our families that we are all okay.

One of the facts not noted on the tape was the enormous amount of rain. During the 24-hour period there were 430.6mm which is 17 inches. This resulted in remarkably little flooding compared to the very heavy flooding in later years caused by lesser amounts of heavy rain. Perhaps the surface water was blown away by the wind.

The only fatalities were a local woman and her daughter who were with their goats down the island at al Qarin. They were never seen again and were presumably swept away by floodwater. Floodwater also washed out the narrow-gauge railway track which could never have been brought back into use even if the RAF had left the locomotive. Off the north beach the wreck of the SS *Eletric* broke up and virtually disappeared from view.

There is often a tidal surge associated with cyclones, but fortunately this did not occur at Masirah. If the eye of the storm had passed a few miles further south the sea would have been blown onshore. All the inhabited areas (except the air base) would have suffered catastrophic flooding with serious loss of life. As it was, only the very low-lying beaches, such as the north beach, were inundated.

The Sergeant's Mess was more badly damaged than the Officers' Mess or Airmens' Mess, but nonetheless the sergeants had a hot meal on the evening of the cyclone. The MoD engineers managed to repair the four main freezer units within eighteen hours and the remaining fridges within a week. Vic Mills fed the 700 inhabitants of the Wali Camp for two days.

In the Wali Camp the village school was damaged beyond repair, so a building was made available on the station. This was the old RAF Hunter detachment building which still had the emblems of the RAF fighter squadrons painted on the outside walls, and became the village school for many years.

On the station many of the American buildings from the Second World War were damaged beyond repair. This included the building which had been underneath the Air Traffic Control tower, the old RAF Officers' Mess and the large building which had been the Sergeants' Mess, Airmens' Mess, NAAFI and cinema. The bowser shelter had collapsed on the fuel bowsers. The church was damaged beyond repair and the magnificent bible which was kept there disappeared without trace. It was thought that this bible had arrived from Aden when the British left. The grey horse left by the RAF panicked during the storm and bolted, injuring himself as he escaped through the barbed wire fence round the paddock. When he was found he was so badly injured that he had to be destroyed.

At sea shipping weathered the storm except for the *Bukom Island*, a small ship 423 feet in length which was damaged and later sank.

The island wildlife suffered badly. Few birds survived and the turtles' nests were washed out. One bird, never before seen in Oman, was blown in from India. Dr James Perran Ross of the World Wildlife Fund was on the island at the time to investigate the turtles, but he naturally had an interest in all the wildlife. The heavy rain had flooded the burrows of the less socially acceptable members of the island's wildlife population, and they emerged to terrify the British. Scorpions were much in evidence, and the large and truly repulsive camel spiders caused shudders of disgust, becoming aggressive when cornered.

The British Eastern Relay Station was a disaster area. Work had begun on the HF site some seven miles south of the main site – this was wrecked. At the main site on the north beach transmission stopped abruptly during the 6 a.m. news broadcast when the corrugated roof of the power house became detached and fell into the building where it began to circulate at high speed. The power house engineer viewed the scene with mounting alarm. He shut down the diesel generators and made his way to the transmitter hall where Peter Lord had assembled everybody. They emerged later to a scene of devastation. Their lightweight accommodation had disappeared without trace and the masts measured their length along the ground. These included the three tall MF towers which Harry Hensler had erected and dismantled at Berbera, erected and dismantled at Perim Island, and erected again at Masirah. Amongst the debris and roofless buildings there was one paradox. After the cyclone had passed there was an 18-foot boat, not secured to its wheeled trailer, undamaged and in its original position as if nothing had happened. Although BERS was off the air other BBC relay stations strengthened their short-wave transmissions to cover the area. Four days after the cylone the news on the BBC Overseas Service included a report on what had occurred. Reportedly the cyclone had persisted for a week with 3,000 homeless and fifty dead. There was some anxiety that this news item might be broadcast in the UK, but, as requested, surely HQ SOAF had informed the families that everybody was safe, had they not?

They had not, and the news item was broadcast in the UK. One wife telephoned the BBC to ask if there were any British dead. The BBC did not know, and were not aware that they had a relay station on the island. Perhaps the misinformation was intended to obtain foreign aid which did indeed flood onto the island in Iranian C-130 transport aircraft. In the Wali Camp long queues formed for the free food and tents, etc., the locals rejoining the back of the queue time and time again giving the names of relatives who were dead or lived on the mainland. There was said to be enough rice to last the local population for two years, and a flourishing export trade started.

For the time being at least BERS was dead in the water. The Pakistani staff were sent home and the British held a farewell party a couple of weeks after the cyclone. Three of their staff were left behind to safeguard what was left, and lived in the SOAF Officers' Mess. The Foreign Office was undecided whether to rebuild BERS. The decision to rebuild came two months later, with more substantial accommodation and a storm shelter on the higher ground behind the site.

Opposite the airbase the mainland was virtually uninhabited, and the cyclone petered out as it made its way inland, probably the worst storm to hit Oman for at least 100 years. A storm struck Muscat in June 1890. There were 300mm of rain (12 inches) but there is no information on wind or pressure. On 16 May 1963 there was a cyclone out to sea south of Salalah. Shipping recorded the central pressure as 948 millibars. RAF Salalah had gusts of 80 knots and a total rainfall of 117.2mm (4.6 inches).

Soon after the cyclone at Masirah Omani servicemen and expatriate workers were flown in to clear up the shambles on the base. The first priority was to replace the corrugated metal roofs before it rained again. Only lightweight aluminium roofing was available, and this was hurriedly nailed onto the trusses. This was supposed to be a temporary measure, but in fact the temporary roofing was never replaced. To this day these lightweight roofs flap and tear whenever there is a moderate wind. The surviving RAF roofs are still sound.

A SOAF Police Training School had been officially opened on the day before the cyclone. It was housed in the large building which had been an RAF signals unit on the east of the road approaching the jetty. Everybody was needed for work on the base after the cyclone so training did not start for another two weeks. There was a passing out parade when the first course completed its training at the beginning of August, and in the following month six police dogs joined the school. Their kennels were on the other side of the road near the sea. Four Omani volunteers were trained as handlers and on National Day in November they were able to put on a display in the Wali Camp.

On the airbase life slowly returned to normal after the cyclone, but the first instructional flight with a student was not until 4 July. Working conditions were far from ideal and the Squadron found it difficult to carry out its instructional task without the equipment which was not forthcoming. In desperation the Squadron was secretly obtaining much of it from the Supply Officer at SOAF Seeb, and smuggling it back to Masirah without the knowledge of the Supply Staff Officer at HQ SOAF. Discontent about the LOA was a running sore amongst the loan service officers, and the airmail between Masirah and the UK was taking up to about ten days.

South of the island a ship had some serious problems and was in danger of sinking. The skipper purposefully drove her ashore on the mainland to the west of the south point of the island. The rescue helicopter lifted the crew ashore but the skipper was reluctant to leave, no doubt aware that the ship was in danger of being pillaged by locals, but eventually he also agreed to be taken ashore. SOAF personnel took possession of the ship and the SOAF ensign was hoisted. The deck cargo was timber and the holds contained farm machinery and blankets, etc. It was hoped that SOAF might benefit from this prize, but had to surrender the ship to the Royal Oman Police.

In October the station was given 15 minutes warning that a skyjacked aircraft would be arriving from Dubai. The instructions were not to communicate with it in any way, and to block the runways. Hastily all available vehicles were parked on the runways, but the aircraft never arrived. It landed at Aden.

The following month air conditioners were installed in the bedrooms. This was a very welcome development because during the early summer the

SOAF Personnel in possession of the ship which was driven ashore on the mainland opposite the south point of Masirah in 1977 (Photograph: Doug Gamblen)

temperature could reach 44°C. Up until this time the only sleeping quarters which were air-conditioned were the officers' Twynham huts which were built by the RAF for transit aircrew.

The Oman National Day is on 18 November, and in 1977 the main festivities were at Salalah. A maximum effort was required from the Squadron to provide a 'diamond 9' formation over the stadium. The Squadron was using only eight aircraft at Masirah, and ten aircraft were required so that a spare could be available for the flypast, so the extra aircraft were provided from Seeb where they were in storage. Enough pilots could be made available by banning leave and utilising the Station Commander and the two ground instructors. The ten Strikemasters flew to Thumrait to practice the flypast in co-ordination with formations of helicopters, Skyvans, Hunters and the Jaguars of 8 Squadron which had recently been formed. After four practices the flypast on the actual day went well and afterwards all the pilots were invited to the Sultan's reception in the garden of his palace. King Hussein of Jordan was also present.

In December a tanker moored up off the jetty. It was the first supply of fuel since the departure of the RAF, and therefore the first occasion on which the MoD engineers attempted to refill the large fuel storage tanks at Ras Hilf. The resupply was absolutely vital, not least for the production of fresh water. Fortunately all the fuel was transferred successfully.

The Concorde service from Bahrain to Singapore also started in December 1977. The Indian Government would not permit supersonic overflights because it feared a trail of broken windows and shell-shocked citizens, so a considerable detour was required to fly round the south of the subcontinent. The route to Singapore was over the Arabian desert, coasting out at Masirah, where the condensation trail could be seen streaking across the sky at incredible speed, but there was no sonic boom. Well after the aircraft had passed overhead there was a faint distant rumble which could only be heard away from the noise of air conditioners or traffic, etc. Everyone wondered what the fuss was about. Due to the long detour the Singapore service proved uneconomical and was withdrawn. Later the service from London to Bahrain was also withdrawn.

But Masirah did suffer a sonic boom from an altogether different source. The first pair of Jaguars to visit Masirah were given permission to make a low pass. Whether accidently or on purpose the leader allowed his Mach number to reach the critical figure which resulted in a strong shock wave. It was like an explosion, and quite devastating. Roof trusses shifted sideways, lights fell out of ceilings, and most serious of all, many of the heavy plate-glass windows in the Air Traffic Control tower were shattered.

1978

In January the Sultan made his first visit to Masirah since 1971, touring the station and seeing everyone at work. The student pilots gave a presentation on the work of the Squadron. Two of the No. 1 Course students had recently qualified to fly solo in formation, and this they did in a flypast for His Majesty. Then the Squadron Commander performed his usual vigorous display of low-level aerobatics.

Following the devastation of the cyclone the Sultan was paying for the Wali Camp to be rebuilt. The contractors were the Lebanese firm Mothercat, their camp being on the beach between the Wali Camp and the jetty. The new Wali Camp buildings were of simple breeze-block construction, each bungalow having its own courtyard. The original plan was to eliminate all the shacks and hovels of the old Wali Camp, but there were strong objections from their owners. So outside the area of the neat rows of new bungalows the old ramshackle dwellings were allowed to remain.

At the end of the month there was a report of illegal immigrants aboard a Saudi Arabian dhow. The dhow was also said to contain 1,700 sheep and goats. A Strikemaster located it near Duqm off the mainland coast and the rescue helicopter lowered a boarding party of four men. A month later there was another shipping incident when a seaman was badly injured having fallen from the rigging of a large tanker named the *Shatt al Arab*. In the late afternoon a description of the ship was received at Masirah, its position being reported as 100 miles north-east of the island. The helicopter was readied and the ground-crew prepared a Strikemaster, the Shell employees filling the underwing fuel tanks as it was going to be a long flight. The only Strikemaster pilot who could be found was a ground instructor who had not flown at night for over 2½ years; the helicopter pilot was a European from Hong Kong who had never qualified at night.

Both aircraft set off in a north-easterly direction. As dusk was gathering the Strikemaster found a tanker fitting the description, but a low flypast showed the wrong ship's name. On the horizon was another tanker further out to sea. There was still just enough light to read the ship's name which was indeed the *Shatt al Arab*. With all its lights on the Strikemaster circled the tanker while the helicopter homed in on its transmissions. At last the helicopter arrived; it was pitch dark with no moon. The tanker captain floodlit the deck area but there were so many masts and rigging lines that it was impossible for the helicopter to land, so it hovered above the masts and used its winch to lower the SOAF medical officer and a stretcher down to the floodlit deck. Dr Potdar, the medical officer, was on loan from the Indian Air Force.

After some time the injured seaman had been securely strapped to the stretcher and he and Dr Potdar were winched up to the helicopter. Both aircraft set off in the general direction of Masirah, but unfortunately the Masirah radio beacon was not working. With no moon it was inky black everywhere, and looking outside it was impossible to tell which way was up and which way was down. As the transmissions from Air Traffic Control at Masirah seemed to be getting weaker, the Strikemaster pilot suspected that his main compass had failed and that he was flying away from the airfield, so he switched on the light on his standby compass, but it did not work. No torch had been available before take-off; the alternative was definitely a low-tech solution. Undoing his straps he reached into a pocket for his cigarette lighter – the flame revealed that he was indeed going in the right direction. The two unqualified pilots returned safely to Masirah and the seaman's life was saved.

By the end of January it was becoming apparent that the students were making very slow progress through their pilot training. There were many interruptions caused by Moslem holidays, National Day practices and the preparation required for presentations to VIP visitors. Fasting during the Holy Month of Ramadan severely curtailed the students' flying, and there was none at all during their leave and long weekends. The number of instructors and groundcrew was insufficient for the task. Due to the education system in the Omani schools the students needed a course of mathematics and physics before starting their initial ground school, but there was no Station Education Officer. There was now only one ground instructor instead of two, and the number of flying instructors and groundcrew were also well below the establishment figure. The groundcrew were not Airwork employees as at other SOAF stations but were uniformed British contract Senior NCOs paid in Omani riyals. Like the contract officers, the sterling equivalent of their salaries had decreased considerably due to the rate of exchange, and promises to increase their salaries in compensation had not been honoured. The groundcrew were working with old worn-out equipment, and like the instructors they were working long hours when other personnel were off duty. Morale was low.

There was also an insufficient number of Strikemasters available. There should have been eight of them, but one had been away at Seeb undergoing a major modification and had not been seen for some time. When it did reappear the rest of the fleet would require the same modification. One of the aircraft at Masirah had no right-hand seat and could only be flown solo. Usually nearly half the Strikemasters were grounded due to a lack of spare parts. At Seeb there were another three aircraft in storage, but they were of an earlier mark with an entirely different cockpit layout, so although they could be brought out for National Day flypasts they could not be used for instructional flying. They also had no right-hand seats, a legacy from the Dhofar War when the aircraft were flown as single seaters.

Another course of students had already arrived and a third course was expected shortly. The Squadron Commander wrote a report on the situation, and forwarded it through the Station Commander to HQ SOAF. It was not possible to rectify everything immediately, but slowly these matters were addressed. More right-hand seats and spare parts were ordered from the manufacturers, and it was decided to modify the three aircraft in storage so that their cockpits looked the same as the other Strikemasters, although it was another four years before the last of these became available for use by students.

January 1978 was probably the low point in the Squadron's fortunes. The wife of a flying instructor suddenly died of a heart attack having been allowed to come to Masirah for a short family visit. A couple of months later the male

The MV *Sheba* on the rocks near the south point of Masirah in 1978
(Photograph: Doug Gamblen)

nurse in the Medical Centre also died. He was a wakeel (warrant officer), ex-Royal Navy and highly qualified. He was much respected and, for instance, carried out all the dental work with the equipment that the RAF had left behind. He also lectured the students on the dangers of drug abuse. Nobody realised that he himself was addicted to drugs until he was found dead of an overdose while away at Seeb for a weekend.

In May the Junood Club opened for the young Omani engineers. They had already completed their basic training at the Technical Training Institute at Seeb and were at Masirah for On The Job Training under the British SNCOs. The first SOAF inter-unit Swimming Championships were held at Masirah, and won by Masirah. The Gun Club began regular sessions of clay pigeon shooting, and two horses arrived on the station. Officially these were for the SOAF Police to patrol the security fence, and being official a groom and fodder were provided from service resources. Unofficially the horses were for recreational purposes. The station also benefitted from a free boat which arrived as an underslung load below the helicopter. This was the lifeboat of the MV *Sheba*, a small flat-bottomed ship of 433 tons which went ashore on the rocks near the south of the island. On 30 May, BERS was back in business, transmitting the BBC World Service on the medium wave and now living in their rebuilt accommodation and in their own Mess. By August No. 1 Course had completed all its Strikemaster training. SOAF Masirah was emerging from the doldrums.

The Squadron was also allowed to play with the Big Boys at Thumrait. Simulated strikes on Thumrait were mounted from Masirah, sometimes taking off before dawn and sometimes returning at night. The Squadron tried many ploys to avoid detection by the Thumrait radar, but were usually unsuccessful in making a simulated attack on the airfield without being intercepted. The flying instructors would fly in a layer of cloud or in the valleys of the jebal for as long as possible, and then fly low over the *negd* to the target. All too often they would look round to see a grinning fighter pilot a few feet away wagging his finger in admonition. It was all great fun.

At the beginning of November 1978 there was a warning of an approaching cyclone. If it had not been for the cyclone of the previous year no one would have been very concerned but as it was, that ordeal was deeply etched in the folk memory of the station. The weather continued to get worse, the sky darkening with a peculiar yellow tinge. The wind roared and, too late, the decision was made to fly the Strikemasters to Thumrait. The weather was so threatening that the groundcrew advised against taking the aircraft out of the hanger. The upwind hanger doors were kept closed, and the downwind doors opened. Against all precedent the pilots started up the aircraft inside the hangar and taxied out into the storm. Surprisingly it was possible to control the aircraft while taxying, and soon they were on their way to Thumrait. After landing, one of the SOAF BAC 1-11 transport aircraft brought the pilots back to Masirah.

They were unhappy to return in those conditions, but actually the weather was rapidly improving. They had left when the conditions were at their worst.

There was another cyclone scare four months later during the Moslem holiday of Eid al Haj. To make sure that there were enough pilots to fly the aircraft to safety two of the senior students were kept behind when the others had gone home. All the pilots had their overnight bags packed, but it was a false alarm and the cyclone moved away.

In 1978 the National Day celebrations were in the Capital Area and the Squadron flew to Seeb Airport a few days beforehand to practice with the Hunters and Jaguars from Thumrait. On the day itself all the aircraft started up at the appointed time but there was some delay in the proceedings at the stadium, so the aircraft remained on the ground with their engines idling. After some time the formation leader wondered what was happening and asked whether the pilots should shut down their engines. Due to the uncertainty of the situation he was advised to keep the engines running. Time passed and one of the nine Strikemasters became unserviceable so was unable to participate. The fuel level in the others was becoming critical, but then came the message that the aircraft could taxi out and take-off. The Jaguars were leading, followed by the Hunters, with the Strikemasters at the back. After a short time in the holding pattern the formation was called in, flying in from the sea to the stadium of the Royal Oman Police where the parade was being held. On the inland side of the stadium is a ridge of hills. The Jaguar leader was lower than during the practices, and the following formations were forced lower and lower to keep below the wake of the aircraft ahead. The last vic of three Strikemasters was down to the level of the stadium lights, and then had to pull up to miss the ridge of hills. This took them up into the jet wake and vortices of the aircraft ahead. It was extremely rough and the Strikemaster on the right was flipped over yet he managed to right himself quickly, but it was an anxious moment.

The Strikemasters' fuel was tight, but the Jaguar leader had been kept informed of the situation over the radio by use of the standard codewords. If he had returned to Seeb after the flypast all would have been well. However he decided to take everyone over the Capital Area. There was mounting anxiety among the Strikemaster pilots, particularly one who had built up a fuel imbalance of 300lb during the long waiting period on the ground. The engine will continue to run only if there is a fuel flow from both the left and right tanks. On the run-in to Seeb Airport one side had completely emptied, a situation which should have resulted in the engine stopping. He scanned the flat featureless terrain on the approach to Seeb Airport, planning where he could make a forced landing among the small bushes when the engine stopped, but unexpectedly the engine kept running, and when he landed, passing two aircraft with burst tyres, he had only 100lb of fuel, enough for only three minutes flying. The other Strikemasters fared little better.

Also in November 1978 Sheikh Khamis bin Hilal died, having been Sheikh of Masirah since the RAF first took an interest in the island. A new sheikh had to be chosen; tribal elders arrived from the mainland to join those at Masirah. Meetings and discussions were protracted as they had to be sure that they chose the right man. Groups of elders formed, and then broke up to reform different groups. Eventually there was general agreement and the new sheikh was announced – he was Sheikh Khalifa bin Khamis bin Hilal, son of the previous sheikh.

1979

A digger excavated a huge hole on the patio of the Officers' Mess and the officers themselves carried out all the rest of the work required for a fresh water swimming pool. Concreting, tiling, laying paving stones and building the changing rooms and patio walls had occupied the officers free time for some months. How could the use of 50,000 gallons of fresh water be justified? It was, of course, an emergency water supply which could be drawn upon in case of fire. The opening ceremony was in January 1979 during the visit of the RAF Chief of the Air Staff. It was thought that he should make the inaugural dive, but the weather was extremely cold and the CAS understandably showed some reluctance to take the first plunge. He was respectfully reminded

The fresh water pool at the Officers' Mess
(Photograph: Ann Rigby)

Boat building in the Wali Camp
(Photograph: Bruce Watts)

that his exalted position carried obligations as well as power, a point which he immediately appreciated. He went and put his swimming shorts on.

At the beginning of the turtle nesting season Dr Perran Ross of the World Wildlife Fund returned to Masirah having been on the island two years earlier investigating the turtles and training some of the locals to continue his work. He had taught them to tag the turtles and record the return of those which had been tagged. He had built numbered cairns to establish whether they returned to the same nesting sites on subsequent years. Unfortunately Dr Ross encountered some difficulty on this return visit which was believed to concern the temporary importation of his shotgun. His relationship with the relevant government department became strained, and he left earlier than planned. He has not returned to the island since then, and nor has anybody else from the World Wildlife Fund, now known as the Worldwide Fund for Nature.

After he had left, a huge number of fish died out at sea and were washed ashore on three miles of the east coast opposite the airfield where the foreshore was so thickly covered that in most places it was not possible to see the sand below the carpet of fish. This was a bonanza for the locals who moved as many as possible above the high-tide mark to dry in the sun. Dried fish are apparently prized as camel fodder, providing useful protein. The same unexplained phenomenon had occurred in August 1967.

During October Cedric returned to the airbase. Cedric was the single offspring of the two RAF dogs, Min a small brown mongrel bitch and Bundu a large Omani saluki. Cedric was a curiously shaped animal, a huge pair of jaws joined to just enough dog to keep the combination viable. He had a small brain and uncertain temper, and lived at BERS. Here he distinguished himself by some act of valour (probably due to stupidity) during the cyclone of June 1977. A metal plaque commemorating this hung in the UK BERS Club. However, the size of his brain and the size of his jaws were proving a great trial to all at BERS. He was put on trial for GBH, found guilty, and sentenced to death, but was reprieved when a soft-hearted SOAF Senior NCO took pity on him, and so Cedric started a second career at the place of his birth.

After the summer monsoon Masirah was visited for a month by the RAF Ornithological Society. They camped all over the island listing the birds passing through during the annual migration There were found to be a huge number of different species of birds, about 200, migrating between Africa and all of Asia including the Indian sub-continent. One great surprise was the discovery of a bat, the Common Noctule bat, not previously found in Oman or so far south in Arabia.

Towards the end of November a semi-sunken dhow was slowly towed to the SOAF jetty, its deck awash in the middle and with six other dhows in attendance. It had been making its way slowly through the Masirah Channel, swinging the lead. At night, south of Sur Masirah, it had encountered a shoal and backed out but unfortunately it reversed into another shoal and was badly holed. To keep afloat the crew had to jettison all the fish in its deep freeze The catch was being taken north for sale and was reputedly worth about 2,000 riyals (£3,000). At high tide it was inched to the side of the jetty, and at low tide was almost high and dry. The MoD engineers arrived with their crane, and the large diesel engine was lifted out. At the next high tide the dhow floated higher in the water and was slowly towed to the boat-builder's yard in the Wali Camp. It was heartening to see so much concern and genuine help being given.

1980

Weekend barbecues and camping down the island had become quite popular. On occasions the rescue helicopter was used to take picnickers to the grotto or to World Jury Bay at the south of the island. The new station commander, Gordon Browne, decided to establish a permanent facility down the island where people could spend the night in reasonable comfort, so he obtained a portakabin and laid a base for it near Ras Kaydah on the east coast, but transporting the portakabin was a problem as it was very big and there were no roads. In those days there were not even graded tracks, only the wheel marks where vehicles had previously been driven. A heavy-lift Bell 214 helicopter

Down the Island

Top: 'Bundu Bash'. An RAF Land Rover descends into Palm Wadi
(Photograph: RAF Masirah scrapbook at RAF Marham)

Bottom: A SOAF 'Camp Out'
(Photograph: Bruce Watts)

came from Seeb and was just able to lift the portakabin, its blades flogging the air as it slowly rose and laboured south.

At Ras Kaydah the cabin was furnished and provided with cooking facilities, crockery and cutlery, and there was even a shower; the beds had mattresses and bedclothes; there were curtains and hurricane lamps. The provision of all this caused considerable anguish to the Supply Officer who had been posted in from HQ SOAF, so it was kept securely locked when not in use.

The portakabin had been used only a few times before the locals broke in. Everything was stolen and the shower tray was used as a lavatory. The smell was terrible. The Royal Oman Police were informed but they failed to recover any of the stolen goods or discover the identity of the thief – the portakabin was never used again and gradually fell into disrepair.

CHAPTER X

Talons and Bladder Birds

O N 19 APRIL 1980 two black C-130 Hercules transport aircraft landed at Masirah and parked at the far end of Runway 25, the sand runway. Their national markings were so small and indistinct that nobody knew who they were, or where they had come from, or why they were there. A small camp mushroomed around the two aircraft. Two colonels of the United States Air Force came to live at SOAF Masirah Officers' Mess, and explained it all: 'Surveillance of the Soviet Fleet, sir.' No one was allowed beyond the runway intersection up to the American camp. The following day another two black C-130s arrived and parked with the others. Daily a C-130 of a more conventional colour appeared to be bringing in supplies from somewhere. On the 22nd three more C-130s arrived and parked at the American camp. Occasionally these visiting aircraft took off and returned some time later. 'Surveillance of the Soviet Fleet, sir.' There was a great deal of speculation at SOAF Masirah, and some doubt about the colonels' explanation.

On the afternoon of 24 April two large C-141 jet transports landed at Masirah. The colonels had asked to borrow two SOAF lorries and their drivers to remove the freight. The backs of the lorries were to be covered in canvas held up by frames. The following appears in the book written by Colonel James Kyle: 'Any fears that we had about the Omani truck drivers finding out about what we were doing were unfounded. It was obvious that they had no idea what we were doing and couldn't have cared less'. The Colonel was mistaken. One of the drivers was a bearded British flying instructor dressed for the part. He told his friends later that the concealed freight was indeed a surprise – it was people. He had never seen a more menacing bunch of yobbos. They were wearing black knitted caps, combat jackets, faded blue jeans and scuffed boots. Various sinister packages were held in harnesses about their persons.

Obviously something was afoot, and it was not surveillance of the Soviet Fleet. This was to be a story of courage and fear, disaster and national humiliation.

On 4 November the previous year a mob of several hundred Iranian students stormed the American Embassy in Tehran. After three hours the US Marine guards were overwhelmed and sixty-three Embassy staff were taken hostage.

The students demanded that the United States return the exiled Shah to Iran for trial.

The American armed services began to make plans for a military solution to the problem in case diplomatic pressure failed. The State Department showed no interest in assisting the military, there were no CIA agents in Iran, and the need for absolute secrecy increased the planning difficulties. A helicopter raid from Turkey was considered, but due to the distance the helicopters would need refuelling somewhere in Iran. There was a plan to parachute special forces into the area, release the hostages, capture the civil airport and fly everybody out. This plan was rejected. Ross Perot, a later presidential candidate, had earlier used surface transport from Turkey to release two of his employees from prison and spirit them out of the country, but there was no way that sixty-three American hostages and their liberators could merge into the local scenery and disappear. Nor could they fight their way out.

The best solution seemed to be a raid on the Embassy by Delta Force, an anti-terrorist unit like the British SAS. It was commanded by Colonel Charlie Beckwith who was its main asset; he was tough, extremely competent and certainly spoke his mind. The Embassy compound was 27 acres and contained fourteen buildings. There was an audacious plan to land C-130 aircraft inside the Embassy compound. The aircraft would contain Delta Force, and leave with them and the hostages. A trial was carried out with a C-130 bristling with booster rockets. In 1999 the film of the trial was broadcast on British television in the series 'Tested to Destruction' on ITV. The take-off was dramatic – multiple booster rockets around the rear fuselage fired the aircraft into the air after no more than two or three seconds. The landing was no less spectacular. Eight forward-facing doors behind the cockpit opened to reveal retro-rockets. They were intended to kill the aircraft's speed to shorten the landing run, and were fired automatically. But they fired too soon. The aircraft rapidly lost flying speed and flopped to earth where it broke up. The fate of the crew was not revealed, but there were no more similar experiments. Perhaps this was because the Iranian students erected poles in the Embassy compound to prevent any helicopters from landing. Any helicopters would have to land outside town, with Delta Force motoring in at dead of night.

The helicopters would have to penetrate Iranian airspace by night to avoid detection, but the distance was so great that the operation could not be completed in one night, and they would have to be refuelled somewhere in Iran on their way to Tehran.

The plan for refuelling the helicopters was to parachute 500-gallon rubber doughnuts full of fuel into the Iranian desert; pumps and tractors to gather the doughnuts together would also be parachuted in. Trials in the Arizona desert were not a 100 per cent success, and it took too long to gather the doughnuts and refuel the helicopters. A faster and more reliable method had to be devised: this was to actually land the C-130 tankers in Iran. Each tanker would contain two 3,000-gallon fuel blivets which looked like water beds. Three such C-130s, known as 'bladder birds', could refuel ten helicopters. The plan was to use US Rangers to capture a small Iranian municipal airport for long enough to complete the refuelling. These troops would land in the first C-130. But the plan appeared somewhat ambitious and was liable to alert the Iranians to what might happen the following night. So instead of an airport a flat part of the Dasht-e-Kavir desert was chosen, 530 miles from the south coast and 265 miles south-east of Tehran. The nearest town was Yazd 90 miles away. It became known as Desert 1.

It was essential that somebody should visit Desert 1 to assess its suitability and prepare it for night landings. It took some time to obtain presidential approval for such a visit. The reconnaissance was carried out by a Twin Otter aircraft which took off from somewhere on the western side of the Arabian Gulf. It was a moonless night and the aircraft landed at Desert 1 in complete darkness. It carried a small motorcycle to speed up the reconnaissance. The sand covering the hard floor was only 1 or 2 inches deep which seemed satisfactory, and samples were taken for analysis. A graded track ran north-east to south-west across the area, a minor road from Yazd to Tabas. Due to the ridges of sand at the sides of the track the landings and take-offs would have to be parallel to it. During the time that the aircraft was on the ground a total of four vehicles drove down the track, but none of the drivers noticed the aircraft or the motorcycle. A line of five battery-operated lights was laid beside the track which could be switched on by a radio signal from an aircraft. With this task completed the Twin Otter departed after just one hour on the ground. Originally Desert 1 was planned as a landing ground for spiriting away the Shah of Iran if there was no other means of escape. This is why it was alongside a graded track.

At Masirah there would be three EC-130 Bladder Birds for refuelling the helicopters at Desert 1. In addition there would be four MC-130 Talons which were basically people carriers specially adapted for low-level night insertions into hostile territory. One of them was a spare, and one of them carried three 500-gallon fuel doughnuts as well as passengers. A total of 139 passengers would be taken to Desert 1, most of them Delta Force, for transfer to the helicopters there. There was also the ground party and two former generals of the Shah's air force.

The helicopters were H-35 Sea Stallions, large twin-engined single-rotor helicopters, which had been resprayed in the same camouflage as the H-35s of the Iranian armed forces. There were eight of them on the aircraft carrier *Nimitz* in the Gulf of Oman, and the operation required at least six of them to be serviceable on their departure from Desert 1. They were to be flown by pilots of the US Marines, the original naval pilots having proved inadequate for the highly demanding task. The marine pilots were not a great improvement, so perhaps they were being asked to perform the impossible. All the pilots had difficulty in landing and taking-off in very dusty conditions. The downwash from the rotors whipped up a self-induced dust storm which prevented them from seeing the ground, or anything else outside the cockpit. It was not possible for the pilots to assess their height above the ground, or whether they were drifting towards some obstacle. It was even more difficult at night in the pitch dark with no lights.

In the USS *Nimitz* the helicopters had to be kept below decks to avoid detection by Soviet satellites or 'trawlers' shadowing the fleet. Consequently they did very little flying. Minor faults were difficult to rectify due to the difficulty in obtaining spares so two of the helicopters were robbed of their parts to provide spare parts for the others. Thus the two 'hangar queens' did not fly at all, and the remaining six helicopters were the minimum number required to depart from Desert 1 with Delta Force. So there was considerable anxiety about the helicopters, particularly after someone inadvertently activated the fire extinguishing system in the hangar which sprayed five of the helicopters with corrosive foam, but they were quickly cleaned and no damage could be detected. Eventually all eight helicopters became serviceable and declared to be in tip-top condition for the operation, although their condition was not absolutely tip-top because some of the secure radios could not be repaired in time. So in the interests of uniformity these radios were removed from all the helicopters, which left them without a means of communicating with each other, except by breaking radio silence on insecure radios.

The first aircraft at Desert 1 would be an MC-130 from Masirah containing the ground party. The remaining C-130s from Masirah would arrive an hour later when all the preparations had been completed. The helicopters would arrive 15 minutes after the last C-130. It would take 40 minutes to refuel the helicopters, and providing six of them were serviceable they would be loaded up with the assault troops and depart for Desert 2, the drop-off point for the assault troops. From Desert 1 it was a flight of 2 hours and 10 minutes to a position 4 miles north-west of Garmsar and about 50 miles to the south-east of Tehran. Desert 2 was a secluded wadi on the edge of abandoned salt mines in the foothills of the Elburz mountains. Here the assault troops would be met by two agents who had been infiltrated into the country and who would lead the assault troops to an even more secluded position five miles to the east where they would rest up during the following day.

After dropping off the assault troops the helicopters would depart for their own hide a few miles to the north-east. For reasons of security all this had to be complete before first light.

After the departure of the helicopters from Desert 1 the C-130s would take off and return to Masirah, their part in the operation finished. They would be short of fuel on their return to Masirah and would require air-to-air refuelling in the Gulf of Oman from KC-135 tankers based at Diego Garcia, an island in the Indian Ocean 2,000 miles south of Oman.

There had been some improvement in the hostage situation – ten of them had been released, lowering the total to fifty-three. Of these three were in the Iranian Foreign Ministry building which they happened to be visiting when the Embassy was stormed by the students. In addition there had been another six in the Canadian Embassy at the time. The Canadians had managed to smuggle them out of the country.

An agent named 'Bob' had been brought out of retirement and infiltrated into Tehran. He had provided a wealth of useful information, and through an Iranian contact he had obtained transport to bring the assault troops from their hide to Tehran for the second night's operation. There were six Mercedes lorries, a Datsun pickup truck and a Volkswagen bus kept in a Tehran warehouse, ostensibly for a construction project. 'Bob' had visited the football stadium on the other side of the road from the Embassy and assessed it suitable as a helicopter pickup point. Delta Force and the hostages would be extracted from here if it was not possible to fell the poles in the Embassy compound. There was another helicopter pickup point near the Ministry of Foreign Affairs for the three hostages there and the thirteen-man team who would release them. This team was composed of Special Forces troops, not Delta.

A short time before the operation a CIA agent was flying out of Iran on a commercial flight, and found that he was sitting next to a Pakistani cook who had been employed at the Embassy but had now been released. The cook said that all the hostages were in the chancery building. If true it would simplify the operation considerably. Charlie Beckwith kept an open mind, but said that if it was true the rescue would take only 30 minutes instead of 45. Later some doubt was cast on the story of the cook which was probably a cover story to protect the identity of a sensitive source.

At dusk on the second night the plan was for the Volkswagen bus and the pickup truck to arrive at Desert 2 near the rescue force hide. The pickup would take Charlie Beckwith on a reconnaissance in Tehran, and the Volkswagen bus would take the drivers and the Farsi speakers to collect the six Mercedes lorries. On the road between Desert 2 and Tehran there were two checkpoints, each manned by two Iranians. If there was any trouble the Iranians would be seized and put on the vehicles.

The rescue was due to begin at 11 p.m. The Volkswagen bus would go to the Ministry of Foreign Affairs, which was about a mile from the Embassy. The thirteen-man rescue team would scale the outside wall and enter through third-storey windows, eliminate resistance and free the three hostages.

The Datsun pickup truck would drive slowly down Roosevelt Avenue, the road outside the Embassy. The occupants would kill any walking guards and everyone in the two guard posts; this would be done with .22 handguns with silencers. Driving two abreast the Mercedes lorries would follow a little distance behind. Using ladders Delta Force would swiftly and silently scale the Embassy walls and drop into the compound. Those in the compound would be killed, and a large explosive charge would blow a hole in the Embassy wall. The assault on the buildings would then begin. The Iranian guards would be shot between the eyes and the hostages taken out into the compound. If the poles had been felled the first helicopter would pick up all the hostages and depart. If not, everyone would go through the hole in the wall and across the road to the football stadium where the helicopters would land and pick them up. There was adequate firepower at each end of the road to stop a mob overwhelming the rescuers. Overhead there would be an AC-130 Spectre gunship from Wadi Kena, near the Red Sea coast of Egypt. This was another type of C-130 with sideways firing cannons of 20-mm, 40-mm, and 105-mm calibre. The Spectre was a truly awesome weapon. Another Spectre gunship would be destroying the Iranian Air Force fighters at the nearby Mehrabad Airport, and a third would be in attendance at the Manzariyeh Airfield.

Manzariyeh was a disused airfield 50 miles south of Tehran, its asphalt runway a generous 2 miles long and 140 feet wide. It had been built by the Shah for viewing weapons demonstrations by his air force. The only buildings were a semicircular grandstand and a small caretaker's shack. The taxiway ran round behind the Shah's grandstand where there was a parking area. On the eastern side of the airfield was the main road from Tehran to the holy city of Qum. There was an Iranian Army Engineer unit somewhere in the vicinity, but otherwise the airfield was ideal for extracting everybody at the end of the rescue mission.

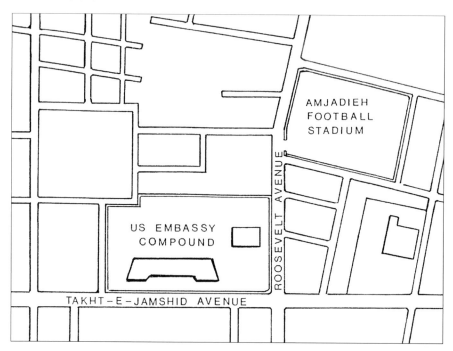

Map 26: The US Embassy at Tehran

During the second night the plan was to capture Manzariyeh Airfield by landing US Rangers in MC-130 Talons. These aircraft would also have to fly all the way from Wadi Kena in Egypt, and this of course would require air-to-air refuelling. No lights were to be shown and the four Talons would

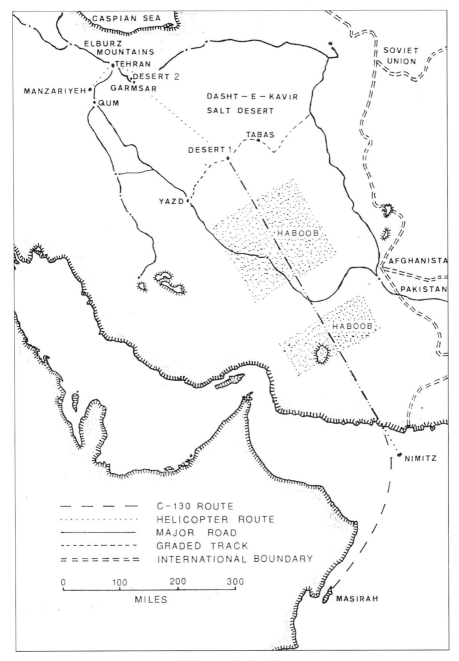

Map 27: April 1980

315

land in complete darkness. Actually their landing lights would be switched on, but completely covered in a special black tape which would be transparent to infra red but block out all visible light. This illumination was almost like daylight when the pilots were wearing night-vision goggles, but no one else would see anything. When the first Talon stopped, the freight door would open immediately and a jeep with a machine gun would roar out, closely followed by four motorcycles. Their headlights would be covered in the same black tape, and the driver and riders would be wearing night-vision goggles. Three more Talons would disgorge their Rangers and soon the airfield would be captured from a very surprised caretaker. One of the Talons would contain three 500-gallon fuel doughnuts in case any helicopter needed refuelling. This would only be necessary if any helicopters were shot down, and others had to make shuttles between Tehran and Manzariyeh.

Shortly before the arrival of the helicopters two C-141s would arrive from Wadi Kena, one equipped as a hospital and the other with airline seats. When the rescuers and hostages arrived from Tehran they would board the C-141s, together with the helicopter crews, and depart. The four Talons would then take off with their Rangers and depart to Wadi Kena together with the Spectre gunships. Due to the distances involved it would not be possible to fly out the helicopters which would be left behind at Manzariyah.

That then was the plan, but the operation itself did not run according to plan.

By 23 April all the C-130s had arrived at Masirah. One incident caused some light relief which helped to ease the tension. The old RAF boundary fence had deteriorated and was no longer animal proof, so goats, donkeys and camels wandered in at will, sometimes encouraged by their owners who could see that the airfield was not overgrazed. Whenever night flying was planned the SOAF police made a serious effort to round up stray animals, but early one morning a camel wandered into the American camp and woke the doctor with its cold nose and foul breath. The doctor's thrashing and yelling gave everybody a good laugh. Since the operation was to be launched at night the implications should have been obvious.

Shortly before the beginning of the operation there was nearly a serious breach of security. The presence of the C-130s at Masirah was reported to London by one of the Sultan's British generals who speculated that there was to be an attempt to rescue the hostages. Luckily no one leaked this information, and a State Department official was rushed to brief Mrs Thatcher and head off any comment on the report. The Americans were fanatical about security, covering their tracks and giving no hint of what was afoot. For instance, when the three EC-130 Bladder Birds arrived at Masirah from Diego Garcia their bladders were already full – to take on that much fuel at Masirah might have caused speculation. For special war missions the absolute maximum take-off weight was extended to a crippling 175,000lb. At Masirah the Talons were leaving at 180,000lb and the Bladder Birds at 185,000lb.

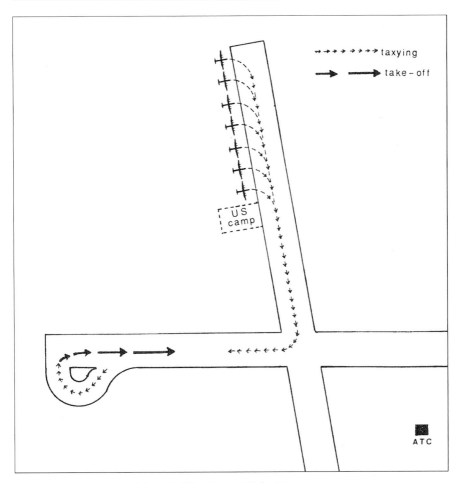

Map 28: The C-130 Night Departure

To those at SOAF Masirah it appeared that events might be beginning to unfold during the late afternoon of 24 April. A black C-130 started up and began to move as the light was fading. This was actually the MC-130 Talon which was to activate Desert 1. Its freight included a jeep, five Kawasaki motorcycles, a mobile TACAN beacon, secure satellite communications equipment, short-range radios, aluminium planking (in case the aircraft got bogged down in soft sand), and all the ground party including Farsi speakers and the on-site air force commander. Also on board was Charlie Beckwith with fifty-six members of his assault force together with the doctor and the two former Iranian generals who were there as advisers. It was a heavy aircraft.

Slowly and cautiously the overloaded Talon taxied down the sand runway, turned right at the intersection and made its way up to the loop at the north end. Then it began its ponderous take-off run. It was a very very long take-off run but it heaved itself into the air at the very end of the runway and cleared the boundary fence by a few feet.

An hour later the other C-130s followed. It was dark by then with little more than a half moon. Twenty-four turboprop engines droned in the darkness. Three curious SOAF officers went up the air traffic control tower; the control room was unmanned and locked; the runway lights were switched off and there was radio silence. The two USAF colonels were leaning over the balcony rails at the top of the tower. None of the aircraft was showing any lights. However, the pilots were probably wearing night-vision goggles and able to see everything better than the spectators. For them there was only the incessant drone of the engines with black shapes moving slowly through the darkness. The two colonels must have realised that the SOAF officers knew what was afoot, and that their probing questions were just a bit of fun:

'What's going on, Colonel?'
'Surveillance of the Soviet Fleet, sir.'
'It must be a bit difficult surveilling at night.'
'Electronic surveillance, sir.'
'Lot of aeroplanes, Colonel.'
'Big fleet, sir.'

The following is a transcript taken from an audio tape posted home by one of the SOAF officers:

They were taxying down the sand runway to the intersection and then turning up the main runway away from the tower. Three of them entered the runway and back tracked along it towards the far end. The others waited on the sand runway near the intersection.

There seemed to be some kind of hold-up with the third aircraft back tracking up the main runway. It stopped for quite a long time. About ten minutes perhaps. There must have been some kind of unserviceability they were trying to fix.

But the aircraft had taxied out in the wrong order, and the delay was probably caused by an attempt to rearrange the order without breaking radio silence.

Eventually he moved forward again to the loop, and the first one took-off. It was strange, just this black shadow in the darkness and very very heavy he must have been. After a minute or two the second one went past, seeming unnaturally quiet somehow and he took-off okay. Then the first one waiting on the sand runway moved forward and started to back track up the runway to the take-off point. This seemed wrong. We knew it was wrong when we heard the number three begin his take-off in the opposite direction. Without lights they couldn't see each other, and without Air Traffic Control they couldn't be told. We waited for a Godalmighty smash, but it didn't happen.

Somehow they saw each other at the last moment and there was the noise of a tremendous burst of reverse thrust from the one taking-off. Then we saw a cloud of dust with the noise of engines at full power. We thought one of the aircraft must have left the runway and gone into the sand, and the pilot must be gunning the engines to keep going and not get bogged down. Next morning we went out onto the runway to look at the wheel marks and see what happened. The chap taking-off was braking hard and left black tyre marks on the runway. The chap who was coming against him must have seen what was happening and went up to full power and went shooting off the side of the runway into the sand. At first they both swerved towards the same side of the runway, but the chap taking-off then went the other way. The wheelmarks in the sand are quite deep, and after a while he managed to get back onto the runway again. Amazingly he had not punctured any of his wheels by running over sharp corners of concrete or any runway lights. Lucky. But I don't think he stopped to have a look at his tyres.

Next morning when we had a look we measured the distance between the black tyre marks on the runway and the wheel tracks alongside in the sand. Even when they were furthest apart there was not even a wing span length between them. That means one wing passed over the top of the other without hitting it. Amazing good luck.

The chap who had been taking-off kept going down to the intersection and turned down the sand runway in the other direction to the ones who were waiting. And when everyone else had gone he went back up the runway and took-off. The last Hercules of all was in fact a stand by, and when the others had gone he just turned round and taxied back to the American camp.

It was well after 7 p.m Oman time when the last of the C-130s left Masirah. At the same time all eight helicopters took off from the USS *Nimitz*, even the two 'hangar queens' being serviceable. It may seem to be unbelievable incompetence, but someone had made a gross error in calculating the time it would take for them to fly from the *Nimitz* to Desert 1. It would actually take 50 minutes longer than the planned time. At the time of the helicopter launch the *Nimitz* was further south than planned and this further increased the time taken to fly to Desert 1. At this time of year the nights are shortening, and it had been calculated (using the erroneous helicopter flight times) that 1 May was the last date on which it would be possible to carry out the operation. It might appear that the Joint Task Force Commander should have exercised stronger control over his helicopters, but he was denied permission to visit them on the USS *Nimitz*. An air force general visiting naval helicopters could have excited speculation.

The helicopters were using both Omega and inertial navigation, but the Omega was proving unreliable and it is difficult to set up an inertial platform on a moving ship. The two systems were giving contradictory information, so they were pleased to see a single black C-130 overtake them. This was, of course, the Talon which had taken off an hour before the others. The helicopter formation lined itself up on the Talon's flight path knowing that they all had the same destination.

The leading Talon crossed the coast into Iran at 250 feet, but soon climbed to a more comfortable height. Practically all Iran is highland plateau with mountain ridges. The Talon's height of about 3,000 feet above the ground was safely below the Iranian radar cover and high enough to reduce the chances of being heard by a gendarmerie post. About an hour after crossing the coast it encountered some poor visibility for 10 or 15 minutes. It was not possible to see more than about a mile ahead of the aircraft, but by using the FLIR (forward looking infra red) the ground features showed up sharply again. Half an hour later the Talon encountered another area of poor visibility, known locally as a haboob. It is not a raging dust storm, just suspended dust particles in calm air. This time it took nearly half an hour to pass through it. There was a satellite communications radio on the aircraft, but it was not possible to use it to warn the following aircraft of the haboobs. The SATCOM was a recent development and so was in short supply, but the system did provide secure communications which could not be intercepted by hostile listening posts.

When the leading Talon passed out of the second haboob it was about half an hour's flying from Desert 1. When it was close the FLIR turret was lowered to illuminate the area with infra red. The major who had landed there in the Twin Otter was on board and helped to guide it in. His runway lights had been planted a month earlier, and when activated from the aircraft they worked perfectly. The pilot lined up with them for a surveillance pass at 1,000 feet to check out the area and look for vehicles and other obstructions. The time was 10.05 p.m. Oman time, 10.35 Iran time. There was a truck driving down the graded track alongside the five runway lights. The pilot pulled the aircraft round in a hard turn before overtaking the truck, and the driver would not have seen or heard the aircraft. He may have seen the runway lights but did not stop to investigate. On the second surveillance pass it could be seen that the runway lights were too close to the road at the touchdown end of the runway.

The aircraft made its final approach to land but the pilot allowed his speed to decay. The safety pilot called for power, but too late. The aircraft crunched down in a very very hard landing. The stowed freight bounced around and everyone felt sure that the aircraft was damaged. It shuddered and ground to a halt. In no time the roadblock team were out of the aircraft together with the ground controllers and Delta Force. Headlight beams were nodding up and down as a bus came bouncing down the track. The roadblock team and Delta charged into a blocking position, firing warning shots over the bus. A 40-mm grenade in front of the windscreen convinced the driver of the wisdom of stopping. It was only 50 yards behind the Talon. The bus interior lights were on and the forty-four occupants were conducted out and taken captive by Delta Force troopers. They were mostly harmless elderly people and children, and were instructed to sit on the shoulder of the road. One of them called out in English, 'Its about time you came, Yanks.' There was a plan for such an eventuality; the passengers would be put aboard the C-130s when they returned to Masirah. From there they would be taken to Wadi Kena, and from there to Manzariyeh where they would be dumped on the second night. The roadblock team moved out to 3 miles up and down the road. The combat controllers were laying another line of runway lights on the other side of the road, and the mobile TACAN beacon was being brought out of the aircraft and activated. It would home in the other C-130s and the helicopters from about 50 miles out.

WHOOMPAH! Down the track a fireball mushroomed. Around the aircraft heads swivelled and the American expletive was 'Holy Shit'. A petrol tanker had arrived at the road block, but the driver would not stop. Small arms fired into the engine proved ineffective so a small anti-tank missile was fired into the back. The result was spectacular. The driver jumped out of the cab and ran round to the back where a pickup truck was waiting. He jumped in and the pickup sped off back down the track. The roadblock team's motorcycle was outpaced and the pickup escaped. It looked as if the escape of the tanker driver would compromise the whole operation, but Charlie Beckwith viewed it with equanimity. With a backup vehicle like that the driver must be running contraband or drugs, in which case he would certainly not report to the nearest gendarmerie post.

The aircraft had been on the ground for 10 minutes and it was high time the arrival signal was sent out. The SATCOM was then found to have been smashed during the heavy landing. Charlie Beckwith should have had his own SATCOM on the aircraft, but it had been put on one of the other C-130s. The arrival code word had to be sent out on an insecure HF radio. The rescue mission was not off to a promising start.

By this time six KC-135 air-to-air refuelling tankers were airborne from the Indian Ocean island of Deigo Garcia. It was a long flight to where they were scheduled to refuel the C-130s on their return to Masirah. The other C-130s were in formation on their way to Desert 1. The haboobs had not been a problem and the navigation was straight forward. As they approached Desert 1 the crews were disturbed to see the burning petrol tanker. They had received the news that the first Talon had landed safely, but nonetheless the fire could signify a later disaster. The C-130s arrived at Desert 1 at the correct time and landed without incident. The lead Talon seemed none the worse for its heavy landing and departed for Masirah. After unloading another Talon left for Masirah. On the ground there were now the three Bladder Birds and the Talon containing the 500-gallon fuel doughnuts. The four aircraft were drawn up each side of the graded track and were ready to refuel the helicopters which were due to arrive soon after the last C-130, but the helicopters did not arrive. Charlie Beckwith used his SATCOM to contact Masirah and ask about the helicopters. He was told that there had been problems and the helicopters would be late. The agent at Desert 2 was advised of the delay.

The helicopter formation crossed the coast into Iran about 15 minutes behind the first Talon. They were 5 minutes behind schedule at this time. They flew inland very low, about 200 feet above the ground, because they had not been told that it was safe to fly any higher. They would have been below the Iranian radar cover at any height up to 5,000 feet above the ground. One hour and twenty minutes after crossing the coast a warning light flashed in one of the helicopters, indicating that there was a crack in one of the rotor blades. The marine pilot thought that it might indicate an imminent and catastrophic blade failure, and the helicopter had to land immediately to carry out an inspection. They determined that it was a genuine warning, collected all the classified material out of the helicopter, and climbed aboard a second helicopter which had landed alongside to rescue them. By the time it took off it was trailing behind the others by fifteen minutes. Subsequently it was revealed that the helicopter need not have been abandoned. The marine pilots were familiar with the marine Sea Stallions, but not with the navy ones that they were flying. The rotor blades on the navy Sea Stallions were of a different design and a genuine warning did not necessarily signify an imminent failure.

Two hours after crossing the coast some of the helicopter pilots saw the formation of C-130s overtaking them and flying parallel and about 2,000 feet above. It gave them confidence in their navigation, but it did make them wonder why they were flying so low. Then the helicopter pilots saw ahead what looked like a wall of talcum powder. This was the haboob, and soon they were in it. At low level it was very much worse than what the C-130s had encountered. Gritty sand was entering the cockpit and the temperature increased from 27° to 37°. Visibility was down to nearly 400 metres in places but they were able to see each other and maintain formation. Visibility improved again as they left the first area of dust, but soon they entered the next haboob.

This was much worse than the first one. The leader lost sight of the ground and could see only one other helicopter. He decided to do a U-turn and lead his formation out of it, and then think about what to do next. One helicopter followed him, the only one that could see him. After they left the haboob heading south they both landed in the desert about 300 miles from Desert 1. The leader used his SATCOM to inform Masirah that the two of them had landed. There was no way that he could talk to the rest of his formation and had no idea what they were doing. After twenty minutes on the ground they decided to continue to Desert 1. They took off and entered the haboob flying a little higher. The visibility was no better and the leader was totally unaware that the helicopter accompanying him was now suffering from a major emergency. One of its hydraulic systems had failed, the one that powers the automatic flight control system. During normal operations the pilot should land as soon as possible because any rapid and sustained movements of the flying controls would result in them locking. But on this vital mission the pilot decided to continue, hoping that the leak could be repaired at Desert 1.

Meanwhile the other helicopters were groping through the haboob further north, but one of them was in trouble too. The co-pilot was experiencing vertigo and two of the flight instruments had failed. These were the artificial horizon and the gyromagnetic compass. The standby artificial horizon was sticking in turns. The standby magnetic compass and the turn indicator were working but it takes skill and training to fly blind using only these instruments, and over long flights the intense concentration is tiring. Then the pilot lost visual contact with the helicopter he was following. He knew that all around him the air was full of invisible helicopters. So he descended to 50 feet above the ground but was unable to see it. They were still 145 miles from Desert 1 and ahead were two mountains nearly 10,000 feet high. The pilot had two options. One was to climb in the hope of finding better visibility – he might be able to see the horizon but he would not be able to see down to any ground features which would help with navigation. He also believed that this option would make him visible to the Iranian radar, so he chose the other option which was turn south and return to the *Nimitz*. His fuel was very marginal but he had faith that the *Nimitz* search and rescue helicopter could find them if they could not reach the carrier. He had no idea that any of the other helicopters were in trouble, and nor could he tell any of them what he was doing. The other helicopters that he had been with emerged from the haboob into clear air about half an hour later, and then realised that one of their number was missing. One of them turned back to search for the missing helicopter, looking along a ridge line for signs of a crash and searching the nearby terrain in case it had landed. It was, of course, a fruitless search and 10 minutes later the pilot resumed his flight to Desert 1.

So of the eight helicopters one had landed in Iran and its crew were on their way to Desert 1 in another helicopter; another had a hydraulic failure but was continuing to Desert 1; a third with flight instrument failure was returning to the *Nimitz* which it did in fact reach before running out of fuel. Only five serviceable helicopters could reach Desert 1. It had already been decided that it required six serviceable helicopters at Desert 1 otherwise the operation would be cancelled. Only two of the eight helicopters had kept going without any delays. They should therefore have arrived at Desert 1 about 15 minutes after the last C-130, but they were 50 minutes behind schedule due to the error in navigation planning. One helicopter was an hour behind schedule; another was 1 hour and 20 minutes behind; and the last two 1 hour and 30 minutes behind schedule. One more had been abandoned in the desert and one was returning to the *Nimitz* but unable to tell anybody.

At Desert 1 everybody waited and waited. The C-130s on the ground kept their engines running at idle in case there was any difficulty in starting them later, so they were consuming fuel all the time. Their fuel was running low and there were anxious calculations about whether they could reach the KC-135 air-to-air refuellers in the Gulf of Oman. The KC-135s could not loiter for too long in the Gulf of Oman without themselves running short of fuel so the standby KC-135s were launched from Wadi Kena to cover this eventuality.

At last the first two helicopters arrived at Desert 1, guided in by the burning petrol tanker. They had been briefed that there was no loose sand on the ground, and were therefore surprised by the dust whipped up by their rotor blades when landing. The first helicopter burst its nose-wheel tyres in a hard landing and had to hop up to its refuelling position behind a Bladder Bird. The helicopter tyres were too small for taxying through the two-inch deep sand and all of them had to hover taxi or hop to position behind the Bladder Birds. At last all six helicopters arrived at Desert 1 but all the pilots were mentally shattered by the ordeal of flying through the haboobs. Another helicopter burst its nose-wheel tyres in a hard landing.

On the ground all the helicopters and C-130s kept their engines running – there was noise, wind blast and blowing sand. It was a distracting working environment; none of the aircraft were showing any lights and there was no illumination; the moon was setting. One of the helicopters had to shut down to investigate its hydraulic failure. There had been a leak so the pump had run dry and seized and the only spare pump was on the helicopter which was returning to the *Nimitz*. There was some discussion on whether the rescue mission could go ahead with only five helicopters, but it was impossible. The General at Masirah was informed over the SATCOM, and soon Washington and President Jimmy Carter would know. The instructions from Masirah were to destroy the unserviceable helicopter and fly the others back to the *Nimitz*. The C-130s were to return to Masirah with the passengers that they had brought from there and the bus passengers were to be released. The burden of failure fell heavily on all those at Desert 1.

One of the Bladder Birds was desperately short of fuel and needed to leave for Masirah as soon as possible. Behind it were two helicopters which it had refuelled and would be sandblasted if the Bladder Bird taxied forwards to take off. The helicopters had to move out of the way, but they could not be taxied backwards through the sand. The first helicopter lifted off the ground to hover clear but was immediately engulfed in dust from the downwash and disappeared from view.

THWACK! Then there was a booming explosion. A fireball leapt 300 feet into the air. The helicopter flying blind had drifted forwards and sideways and had collided with the Bladder Bird. It came to rest on top of the C-130's wing centre section, silhouetted against the leaping flames. There were fourteen crew on the flight deck of the C-130, and Delta Force troops in the hold. The troops came leaping out of the side door of the hold which is four feet off the ground, some of them with their clothes on fire. The co-pilot made it down the stairs from the flight deck and exited from the door at the back of the hold. The two helicopter pilots got out onto the top of the C-130 and slid down the nose onto the ground, but the other three crew of the helicopter perished. Other crew members escaped from the C-130 but four were killed. There were many acts of heroism as burnt survivors were helped away.

One of the Delta Force troops had been asleep in the C-130 when the helicopter crashed into it. He woke up and joined the line of troops exiting the door. He assumed that the aircraft was airborne and adopted the free-fall position as he jumped from the door, landing spreadeagled on the ground. 'What were you going to do next, without a parachute?' he was asked. 'I don't know. I was just taking one problem at a time,' he replied.

Missiles, bullets and grenades were cooking off inside the C-130 with shrapnel flying in all directions. The three nearest helicopters were riddled with large holes ripped in the fuselage and external fuel tanks, as the crews scrambled clear to escape the shrapnel that was slicing through their helicopters. The SATCOM was used to inform Masirah of the disaster and the likelihood that many burns cases would be returning there.

One by one the C-130s were loaded up ready to leave for Masirah, the runway lights were removed and replaced by chemlites, and the whole site was cleared. Although ammunition was still exploding inside the burning C-130 the area was combed for wounded survivors. The helicopter crews had left classified material on board and asked to retrieve it. The On-site Commander refused, assuming it was codes which would be out of date in 24 hours, but actually it was the complete plan of the whole operation – they should never have brought all this with them. It was too dangerous to enter the helicopters to retrieve the material and there was nothing to use as demolition charges to destroy them. Using the SATCOM the agent at Desert 2 was advised that he would soon be compromised. The original plan was for him to leave from Manzariyeh on the second night, but now he would have to leave on a commercial flight. Being the Moslem weekend the booking offices were closed for two days and it is not known how he escaped from the country.

Two of the C-130s had left Desert 1 earlier, so there were now three to get away. On take-off the first two jolted through the sand embankments at the side of the graded road, but the aircraft did not seem to suffer from the sudden shock loading. By this time the petrol tanker had burnt out. With one more C-130 ready to leave the Air Force On-site Commander surveyed the scene of devastation. The two burning hulks looked like prehistoric monsters locked in mortal combat. The two shook with juddering explosions and red-hot shrapnel arced across the night sky. The shattered helicopters were leaking fuel which could ignite at any moment. One of them still had its engine and rotors running. There was one fully serviceable helicopter but this was being abandoned. The bus was sitting in the middle of the road, its passengers still squatting on the roadside embankment. The On-site Commander looked at his watch. It was 3.30 a.m. local time. Wearily he turned and entered the C-130. It had been a long night and it was a long four-hour flight back to Masirah.

The following is a continuation from the audio tape posted home by one of the SOAF officers:

The USAF colonels, Bob and Sam, said not to expect any of the Hercules to return until about three o'clock in the morning or a bit after. We went to the bar and had a drink or two and I went to bed with the intention of getting up at three-ish to see the first guy back in. But in fact I didn't wake up until three-thirty, got dressed and went down to the tower. Terry was there and said there had been some kind of disaster. They were expecting quite a number of injured people and burns cases.

When I went back at about four o'clock or so Watty was around and said: 'Hey look, how would you like to volunteer to drive an ambulance. They've got about forty burns cases and they can't deal with them all themselves. Potts and his crowd have jacked up our ambulances, and when it's confirmed we'll jack up the Wali Camp hospital as well. But we'll need English speakers to drive their ambulances.' John Merry, who is acting Station Commander, realised there might be casualties and had warned the Wali Camp doctor the previous evening. The Americans were actually not supposed to rely on us for anything at all except fuel. But apart from that they are self-sufficient in everything, including water, actually, which is extraordinary. They did borrow these lorries from us and we gave a Land Rover to Bob and Sam for backwards and forwards transit between our place and theirs.

I went up to the tower again shortly afterwards. There is no point in trying to sleep when there is obviously a drama happening. Only Sam was there and said the message he got was garbled. It wasn't forty people but only four who were injured and they were able to deal with that themselves.

A couple of C-130s had come back earlier and I had missed them. But the others came back much later than expected. The last one about sevenish I think, it was already light. He was on three engines with the fourth shut down and the propeller feathered. The last aircraft didn't return. We subsequently heard that it was lying burnt out in the Iranian desert with the crew dead, together with a helicopter which had flown into it while it was being refuelled.

After they got back in and taxied up to their place a couple of very large transports came in, C-141 Starlifters. They stopped at the intersection of the runways while people got on. We were naturally looking very interestedly from the tower to see exactly what was getting on and we didn't see anything which looked like fifty hostages. We were getting the impression by this time that the operation was a failure. Sam, up in the tower, wasn't saying anything, I think not even the surveillance of the Soviet Fleet was being mentioned at this time. Anyway the 141s had medical teams aboard and the four injured people on stretchers were loaded, and so were a lot of other people, not civilians. Then the 141s took off and disappeared. Nothing more happened until later in the morning, round about lunchtime, when it was announced on the news that the Americans had made an unsuccessful attempt to rescue the hostages in Tehran. It was only when it was on the news that Bob and Sam came clean and actually admitted that that's what they were doing, although I think all of us knew what it was that they were up to.

John Merry went up to the American camp for some reason with Colonel Bob and Colonel Sam. They were all a bit dejected up there, as well they might be, having I think with tremendous courage done this operation, and lost one of their Hercules with the people in it. The one that they lost was in fact the one which was taking off when it was suddenly confronted by the taxying aircraft coming the other way.

At lunch time when the news broke John and I were sitting in the bar, just the two of us. Then Bill Liddle came in. Sam and Bob were asleep in their rooms. And John said: 'Look, to hell with it, let's take down some cases of beer.' So each of us booked a crate of 24 cans each from the Mess bar and John and I put them in the Range Rover and drove down to the Americans. We dumped the cases there at their communications centre where some people were awake. John said: 'We are not supposed to speak to you but you will find a use for these I expect.' And we just drove away. There seemed to be a general convergence from the open sided tents where people were snoozing.

Many years later a book was written on the planning and execution of the operation. It was written by Colonel James H. Kyle USAF (Ret.) who was involved from the start and was the On-site Air Force Commander at Desert 1. The following appears in his book:

As we were talking we spotted a small lorry coming down our flight line. It seemed to have come from the other side of the airfield, where several British airmen employed by the Sultan of Oman's Air Force were billeted.

The lorry bounced to a stop in front of our maintenance crew tent. Two men got out, set two boxes down, and jumped back into the truck, which sped off in a cloud of dust.

A couple of loadmasters walked over to the boxes, looked at them, and then came hauling them to the operations tent on the double.

As they drew near, one of them yelled, 'Hey, you guys, look what the Brits brought us – two cases of cold beer. And there's a note written on the outside of the case.'

A knife came out and the flap was cut off the case and handed to Lieutenant Colonel Roland Guidry, commander of the Air Force Special Operations unit, which had lost the five airmen in the fire. A spokesman told the colonel,

'Your unit bore the greatest loss – this should be yours to frame.'

As far as we were concerned, no greater tribute had ever been paid by the military service of one country to that of another.

The handwritten note simply said: 'To you all, from us all, for having the guts to try.'

The note, written in John Merry's handwriting, is proudly displayed on the briefing-room wall of the 8th Special Operations Squadron, Hurlburt Field, Florida, along with mementos of the Son Tay North Vietnam raid and the Grenada action.

The name of Colonel Kyle's book is *The Guts to Try*.

CHAPTER XI

SOAF *Masirah* – The Next Ten Years

1980

IN EARLY DECEMBER the return of the Boeing 707 Freighter was awaited with some interest. It was bringing in supplies for the contractors. On its previous visit the crew were unable to shut the freight door, so they had to open a hatch and use a handpump which wobbled loose and fell off its mountings. The aircraft was in an appalling condition and the SOAF engineering staff wondered where it could have obtained a Certificate of Airworthiness. Emblazoned on it was the logo of a prominent local airline, but apparently it was on hire from a well-known British airline which is still in business. On this next occasion the aircraft had no auxiliary power unit so while it was being unloaded one of its engines was kept running to supply electrical and hydraulic power. It then sprang a massive leak from its hydraulic pump, so the Captain had to hurriedly shut down the engine before the hydraulic oil caught fire. The aircraft now contained no spark of life, and although unloading continued there was no way of starting any of the engines. Masirah had no compatible ground power unit so a Skyvan from Salalah flew to Thumrait where a suitable ground power unit was loaded, and then flew it to Masirah. It was unserviceable. The SOAF engineers had to determine what was wrong with it and eventually the faulty part was identified. Time was now critical so the replacement part was flown from Thumrait in a Hunter, but it was the wrong part – there was still no way to start any of the aircraft's engines. Meanwhile the SOAF engineers had done their best to rectify the hydraulic leak. The Captain of the aircraft had used his HF radio to contact his home base and tell his organisation of the problems; he was told that he must leave Masirah that evening to start his next task the following morning. If he failed his British airline would be bankrupted and put into the hands of the official receiver; the entire airline staff would then be unemployed.

Someone remembered an unusual way of starting a jet engine which had been tried successfully during the Korean War – it was worth a go. A Strikemaster was towed out and placed so that its jet pipe was pointing towards the intake on one of the Boeing's engine pods. The Strikemaster's engine was started and its power was gradually increased. Slowly the Boeing's engine windmilled, and with more power from the Strikemaster the Boeing's engine began to increase its revs. Unfortunately the Strikemaster's jet pipe was much lower than the Boeing's engine pod which was rocking alarmingly left and right. It looked as though the entire engine pod might break off, but that did not happen. The Boeing's Captain was able to restart the engine, and once it was running there was enough electrical power to start the other engines. It soon became apparent that the hydraulic leak had not been cured so that engine had to be shut down again and the leak investigated. On this occasion the leak was successfully stopped. Soon the Boeing was climbing away into the evening sky, but the SOAF engineers were not happy with what they had seen. The Boeing had bent fan blades where a bird had been ingested into an engine, there were missing rivets and signs of a previous fire in one of the engine pods which was cracked. This Boeing freighter never returned to Masirah, much to everyone's relief.

On another occasion a DC8 bringing equipment to BERS was stranded on the airfield, unable to start the engine which supplied the electrical power to start the other three engines. The first engine did not use electrical power to start, it used a compressed-air turbine which relied on compressed air bottles in the aircraft. These were fully charged, but to guard against over-pressure there was a safety disc which was designed to burst. This had deteriorated and ruptured, and the aircraft did not carry a spare. Ever prepared to improvise, the SOAF engineers made a replica disc from the bottom of an Amstel ash tray. It worked perfectly. The badge of RAF Masirah bore the motto 'Al-'itimad 'ala al-nafs' – the reliance is on oneself. It would also have been an appropriate motto for SOAF Masirah.

1981

Iranian C-130 freighters and their crews served SOAF until the Shah was deposed. Then the Royal Saudi Arabian Air Force stepped in to fill the gap with a single C-130 and its crew. It was with some pleasure that SOAF received the first of its own C-130s in the first half of 1981, originally with an American crew while SOAF crews were trained. SOAF BAC 1-11s continued to serve Masirah, and their airline-style seats were certainly more popular than the sideways-facing paratroopers' seats in the C-130s.

In May thirty-five Omani ambassadors visited Masirah. Oman had been advancing so fast that the ambassadors were brought home to familiarise themselves with all the latest developments in their own country. In their overseas posts many of them had been told that Masirah was now an American base. After their visit to the island they could refute such allegations with absolute assurance.

Towards the end of June forty contractors' representatives visited the air base. Their firms were interested in tendering for the main contract to upgrade the base which was to be a major undertaking. On the day of their visit the south-west monsoon was at its most horrible – the wind howled and the air was dirty with sea spray and driving sand. They enquired anxiously if the weather was always like this, and were only partially reassured when told that it was never any worse. The successful tender was won by the British firm Taylor Woodrow working in conjunction with the American firm of Towell, which had been established in Oman for many years.

1982

Four years previously 1 Squadron was labouring under severe disadvantages, but by 1982 the situation had markedly improved. There were enough Strike-masters available and enough ground engineers and flying instructors which allowed an extra three months of specialist training at the end of the fourteen-month basic phase. Students who had been selected to fly fighters were introduced to the type of flying which they would be taught later on the 6 Squadron Hunters at Thumrait. There were also one or two Defenders (BN Islanders) on 1 Squadron for further training of those students who had been selected to fly these aircraft on 5 Squadron at Salalah.

Wind-surfing was becoming a popular sport at this time, particularly among the 1 Squadron instructors and students. Masirah was the best SOAF base for this sport and for many years the wind-surfing championships were held on the island.

Taylor Woodrow Towell, the contractor for upgrading the airfield, employed a large number of expatriate workers who would have swamped the Wali Camp if they were accommodated nearby. So the contractor's camp was built at the site of the old flying-boat base near Umm Rusays. There was a number of large dormitories and other buildings on the inland side of the road where they built their own cinema which survived for many years after the contractor had left. Just one building from the Second World War now survives, the contractor having demolished the others. There were some large 'people carriers' to take the workers to the airfield and back. These were articulated vehicles, tractor units towing long trailers covered in wire mesh to stop the workers falling out. The track between the airfield and the contractor's camp was widened and smoothed with rolled silt which hardened after being dampened. The surface did not corrugate, as on other graded tracks, and high speeds were possible – and usual. At the contractor's camp a stone mole was built over the top of the Second World War jetty which was extended out to relatively deep water and was wide enough for vehicles to pass in each direction. Supplies were brought in on three flat-bottomed ships – *Masirah 1*, *Masirah 2* and *Masirah 3* – all of about 1,000 tons displacement.

At the airfield the main runway was extended in length in both directions, with a paved parallel taxiway. While this work was in progress 1 Squadron continued to use the runway, sometimes landing over the top of the workers, sometimes landing towards them with no runway barrier, and sometimes both at the same time. An additional hazard was open trenches at the sides of the runway where cables were being laid for the new runway lights. This was a particular danger at this time because the Strikemasters were experiencing transitory wheelbrake failures which could not be reproduced later and which could not be rectified because no one knew the cause. The wheelbrakes are not only for stopping the aircraft but are also the only way of steering it on the ground. On one occasion a solo student had one of his wheelbrakes fail during his landing run and he left the side of the runway at high speed, but fortunately there were no open trenches at that time.

The building programme in the Wali Camp and on the airbase required plenty of limestone which was quarried from an outcrop known as al Hadri, a couple of kilometres south of the BERS HF site. For the Wali Camp project water for the concrete was obtained from shallow scrapes at the end of the Wadi Firay between Shinzi and Rasiyah. There were a couple of small camps for construction supervisors on the north beach, and a contractor's work camp was built above the ocean coast immediately to the east of the threshold of runway 35. There was a fire here in the paint storage area on the night of 5 November when arson was suspected but never proved, and due to the date any culprit was thought likely to be British. Someone was also interfering with the valves which controlled the bulk fuel storage, but again no culprit was discovered.

Due to the terms of service, poor pay and substandard living accommodation it was difficult to recruit sufficient British contract SNCOs. Omani engineers were being trained at the Technical Training Institute at Seeb and coming to Masirah for on-the-job training. Most of them did not enjoy Masirah, particularly the separation from their families. They were leaving SOAF before becoming fully qualified and productive, lured away by better-paid jobs in more congenial surroundings, so the effort of training them was largely wasted. Inevitably Airwork Services Ltd provided many of the aircraft engineers, and they became a permanent presence at Masirah. Two of them were lucky to escape with their lives at the height of the south-west monsoon in June. They had gone down to the Water Sports Club and taken out a sailing boat when there was no one else present, but were unable to sail it back against the wind and tidal rip, and had to spend the night tied up to one of the channel marker buoys.

A couple of months later the Squadron was lucky not to lose one of its Strikemasters. The instructor and student had just taken-off when the engine stopped. Above a certain height and speed it is possible to turn the aircraft quickly and land on the runway in the opposite direction, but the aircraft had

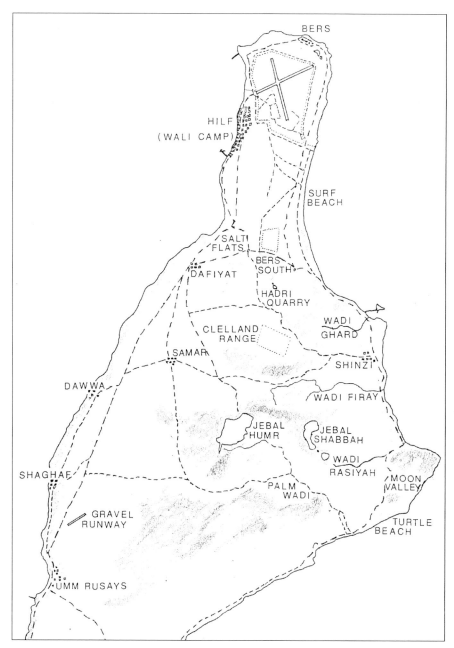

Map 29: North Masirah, 1982

not quite reached this critical height and speed and the pilots would have been justified in ejecting. However, the instructor decided to attempt a turn back and made a successful landing downwind on the runway. For saving the aircraft at some personal risk he was awarded the WKhM, the Sultan's Distinguished

Masirah Wildlife

Top: The RAF introduced chameleons from Southern Oman. They continue to thrive in the greenery of the domestic accommodation in spite of feral cats. (Photograph: Ann Richardson). *Middle:* The only known photo of the spiny-tailed lizard on Masirah (Photograph: Dennis Peet). *Bottom:* Flamingoes and donkeys at the sewage farm, 1994 (Photograph: Ann Richardson)

Service medal, which was well deserved. The Flight Commander noted that the medal is awarded for being extremely brave for a very short time, or for sterling service over many years. As he was a loan service officer he would not be there for many years, and he did not like the idea of being extremely brave for even a very short time. Yet he did want the medal, so he wondered whether it would be okay if he was fairly brave for a fairly long time. Thereafter he was known as Fairly Brave Dave.

Towards the end of the year the contractors had finished their work on the main runway and were switching to the sand runway. The ground sloped up towards its north-east end, and the general ground level had to be lowered in this area. Extremely large bulldozers dragged spurs of metal through the bedrock, ripping it up. Great rocks were left askew on the surface, and these had to be removed and dumped into a nearby wadi, but eventually the ground was levelled and smoothed and work began on the runway itself. It was paved and lengthened and a parallel taxiway was built on its southern side.

At the same time a sewage farm with several lagoons was built to the east of the airfield. The treated fresh water flowed down a gulley to the beach, and on each side a glade of Mesquite trees became well established. The semi-treated water was not pleasant but attracted many birds, including flamingos, and a small herd of wild donkeys which took up residence in the area. In the late 1990s the lagoons were taken out of use and the sewage is now treated in tanks above the ground. The birds and donkeys have left the area.

Christmas 1982 brought the usual generous hospitality by Global Chemical, the American company which built and operated the power station and desalination plant in the Wali Camp. The employees were Filipinos, and their Christmas invitations were to all other Christians on the island. Their mess hall was bedecked with Christmas decorations, and their tables groaned with the weight of gourmet food, and always a suckling pig roasting on a spit. When the alcohol and suckling pig had all been consumed the guests left and the men and children of the Wali Camp came flooding in through the gate.

The National Bank of Oman established itself on the island in a temporary cabin close to the sea and just to the north of the Global Chemical compound. The bank was set amid ruined water tanks and foundations dating from the early RAF tenure, close to corroding junk which had been dumped into the salt water stream which flowed constantly from the desalination plants on the air base. Since it was the only bank on the island it did attract customers, and after some years it moved from these unprepossessing surroundings to a proper building in the Wali Camp.

1983

In January No. 10 course were beginning their night-flying phase, the students were learning night take-offs and landings, and the circuit was full of aircraft. The runway controller was in his caravan at the beginning of the runway, and puzzled by what he could see. Individual runway lights were winking off and on again. He suddenly realised what was causing it – there was a camel on the runway, and the lights were winking off as its legs passed in front of the runway lights. He fired off a red Very light at an aircraft late on its final approach to land, and informed the tower why he had done this. All the aircraft were ordered to orbit the airfield until the camel was well clear of the runway. The aircraft were brought in for a final landing and the SOAF police were ordered to round up the camel and take it to the compound for stray animals. Once again the SOAF police combed the station for stray animals, and when they were satisfied the instructors and students walked out to their aircraft to start again. As they did so they saw a donkey walking towards the runway across the open doors of the lighted hangar. The Squadron Commander lost patience and said that he would not sanction any more night flying by 1 Squadron aircraft until the boundary fence was animal proof. Much of it was composed of coils of barbed wire which had rusted away since the departure of the RAF.

The following month there was a formal visit to the station by the Crown Prince of Bahrain, accompanied by Sayid Faher bin Taimur, the Sultan's uncle, and a number of other ministers. There was to be a static display of every type of SOAF aircraft, an Arabic presentation by the students, and a formal lunch with a forty-piece band. The contractors were not to be in evidence, no scruffy Airworkies, and the dog was to be shut up. There was a small fleet of Mercedes limousines which had arrived a few days earlier, which was just as well because the date was suddenly advanced by twenty-four hours. The VIPs arrived on the Sultan's VC10 airliner which did not have an auxiliary power unit so the ground starter unit was once again flown in from Thumrait, and as on a previous occasion it was unserviceable on arrival.

Later in February there was heavy rain which started at 4 o'clock in the morning and by that evening 8½ inches (216mm) had fallen. When there is that much rain there are bound to be difficulties. Torrents gushed through the officers' accommodation at about running speed, the rooms being flooded above the level of the electric wall sockets. The water level was even deeper in the Officers' Mess, and further downhill in the Sergeants' Mess it was 1½ feet deep which is nearly half a metre. The airfield was a lake, the runway and aircraft parking areas being deep under water. The airfield is in a slight depression yet a wadi to the east should have drained the area. The water level did not appear to be dropping. An expedition to the other side of the airfield revealed the reason – the contractors had dumped rubble and other waste into the wadi which had completely blocked it, so they sent an excavator round and removed the blockage. Once the water began to flow there was no need for further excavation and the water tumbled through, carrying all before it.

It was a spectacular cascade for over twenty-four hours. Then came the long task of sweeping the mud and sand off the paved areas of the airfield, which was mostly done by hand, everybody participating. Finally came the big clearing up operation in the rest of the station.

Airmail letters to the UK had always suffered serious delays, so outgoing mail was usually taken by people going on leave and posted at Heathrow. Incoming mail was more of a problem, and always had been. At one time it took up to seven weeks to reach the island. Enquiries from Masirah to the GPO in London revealed that there was never any delay in putting letters to Oman on the first available aircraft to Seeb Airport – the problem began in Oman. The Station Commander contacted HQ SOAF asking that the delays should be investigated, but was informed that there never had been any delays. That made everybody feel much better!

A great weight was lifted from the station in April when the Supply Officer was posted to Salalah. Vital supplies were released from the stores, and surreptitious visits to the Supply Squadron at Seeb were now no longer necessary.

Over the years the old RAF Clelland Weapons Range had received very little attention. It was used regularly by the Strikemasters, and sometimes by visiting fighters from Thumrait. The targets were old vehicles which by now had been shot to bits. The Squadron spent a day or two there assisted by MoD engineers who brought in a new air-to-ground target vehicle. That, and the dive-bombing target, were surrounded by rings of burmails. The rescue helicopter used its winch to drag old targets across to the wadi where they were dumped. The range was about ten kilometres south of the airfield, halfway between Dafiyat and Shinzi, an easy drive from the squadron crew room. The range safety officer used a handheld SARBE radio to control the aircraft and pass the weapons scores which were estimated by eye from a hillock close to the vehicle track. The syllabus for the students included dual air-to-ground firing early in the course, to emphasise that they were undergoing military training. Later, during the advanced fighter course, they were taught rocketing and dive-bombing, the bombs being small 25-lb practice bombs but the rockets were the real thing.

There were a couple of major air defence exercises during 1983. During the first, Masirah was attacked by Thumrait Jaguars and the defending Strikemasters were airborne merely to act as targets for them. The second exercise involved the Jaguars being detached to Masirah to defend it. The attackers were USAF F-111s which were based in the UK and detached to Thumrait. It was during August and the Americans were living in tents with no air conditioning. They had five generals at Thumrait, and no one was allowed to change into civilian clothes. The Strikemasters at Masirah acted as decoys to divert the attention of the attacking F-111s so that they could be more easily intercepted by the defending Jaguars.

Although the Strikemasters were totally outclassed 1 Squadron acquired a real operational role – the instructors were trained as forward air controllers. At first the training was at Masirah using the Strikemasters, then visiting Hunters were directed onto simulated targets on the island. The training next moved to the mainland where live weapons could be used by the fighters. Later the flying instructors were taught to use a laser target marker for the forward air control of Jaguars at night.

Towards the end of November a new squadron formed at Masirah. It was 20 Squadron with Jaguar fighter aircraft. Of the first six aircraft to arrive, three came from Thumrait and the other three were ferried in directly from the UK. 20 Squadron moved into the old RAF Hunter detachment building which had served as the village school for many years after the cyclone.

Land yachting had been a popular pastime for the pilots at Thumrait which is flat desert. Although Masirah could certainly be windy it did not have wide open spaces and was not so suitable for the 20 Squadron land yachts. Also for recreation 20 Squadron had a microlight aircraft made of metal tubing, wire and fabric. It was regularly crashed, and all sensible pilots viewed it from afar with considerable misgivings.

The Station Commander had to be a Jaguar-qualified pilot, so the CO at Thumrait was appointed as the new Station Commander at Masirah. The new CO at Thumrait was the 8 Squadron Jaguar Squadron Commander, so there were promotions there. At Masirah John Merry, a contract officer, had been

20 Squadron was formed at Masirah in 1983
(Photograph: Frank Milligan)

Station Commander for a number of years but had to step down and once again become OC 1 Squadron.

1984

At the beginning of February His Majesty Sultan Qaboos suddenly and unexpectedly arrived which had an electrifying effect on the station. The Jaguars were on their way to Abu Dhabi for an exercise, and were recalled. His Majesty was given a presentation in the Jaguar Squadron and was driven around the base on a tour of inspection which ended in the Officers' Mess with tea and biscuits. Here he chatted to his Omani and British officers. His Majesty was in good form and totally relaxed in this informal atmosphere and it seemed to be a very happy occasion for everybody. Before his departure he watched the Jaguars take-off on their delayed departure to Abu Dhabi.

1 Squadron was instructed to discontinue the advanced fighter course on Strikemasters and the transport training on Defenders, although these courses had drawn favourable comments from the CFS Examining Wing on its annual visits. The Examining Wing of the RAF Central Flying School is invited to visit many foreign and Commonwealth air forces to fly with the instructors and students, and assess the individual and general standard of their operations. The subsequent CFS report is an impartial outside review which is of value to the air force commanders.

Another unwelcome announcement was the abolition of Christmas festivities. There were to be no reciprocal visits between the Officers' and Sergeants' Messes, no Christmas dinner, no decorations and few, if any, family visits. All this was considered to be alien to the Moslem culture, but the Omani officers had always joined in all the festivities and enjoyed them. The Christmas and Easter school holidays provided an opportunity for the British personnel to see their children who were at boarding school, the weather in Oman being unsuitable during the school summer holidays. The British personnel were also told not to visit BERS where they could enjoy the company of another set of friends. The new restrictions were not greeted with much enthusiasm.

The officers had to move out of their accommodation while the contractor added showers and toilets to what were now two-room flats. Two large modern squares had been built further south, but the rooms were small and dark so almost everyone looked forward to moving back into the old RAF accommodation. Similarly the old RAF Officers' Mess was having the guts torn out of it in a complete rebuild, so the officers moved to a new mess which had been built immediately to the south. Eventually the two messes would be joined together. The Sultan had personally paid for high-quality furniture, fittings and carpets.

A new modern Sergeants' Mess was also being built a little further north than the old one. It would have its own fresh water swimming pool, but it would not have the mock Tudor decor in the bar. Many sergeants preferred their old mess.

1 Squadron had to abandon the Clelland Air Weapons Range which they had recently renovated, and instead were told to use the huge new Jaguar range which was being established at al Qarin in the southern part of the island. It took a long time to drive there so the Range Safety Officer had to start early and arrived back too late for lunch. Using the Clelland Range he could even come back to the Squadron for a cup of coffee in the middle of the morning.

For many years the golf course had been located behind the officers' accommodation, below the black hills at the back. Now this area was required for other developments including a splendid residence for the Station Commander. So the golf course moved to a larger and more suitable location on the north beach, between BERS and the threshold of runway 17.

On the mainland, there is a single tarmac road running down through the centre of Oman to the southern province of Dhofar. In July a Strikemaster passed over this road at low level during a dual navigation exercise. As it passed the road the instructor closed the throttle to simulate an engine failure to see what the student would do. The student correctly made a climbing turn to line up with the empty road for a simulated approach and landing. When it was evident that the forced landing would have been a success, the instructor opened the throttle again and turned away from the road, but the engine did not respond to the opening throttle. By the time this was realised the aircraft was below the minimum height for successful ejections and having turned away from the road the aircraft was now too low to line up with it again for a real forced landing, so the aircraft had to land alongside the road in the sand. There was no other choice. The first touchdown was smooth, but in front of the aircraft there was a large pile of sand dumped by the roadbuilders which was impossible to avoid, and the Strikemaster rammed into it. The aircraft was slammed back into the air and fell heavily to earth again, breaking off one wing. Luckily the ejection seats did not fire, but everything was so bent that the seat harnesses had tightened. One was so tight that it could not be released and the instructor had to cut through the straps with his survival knife. Eventually both pilots emerged from the wreck with cracked vertebrae, broken noses and sundry gashes and bruises.

By luck a passing vehicle containing Omani SOAF airmen picked up the two survivors and took them to Ghaba a few miles to the north. This was an oil company camp belonging to Petroleum Development Oman (PDO) where there was an airfield. A PDO aircraft took them to Seeb Airport, and from there they were flown to the RAF Hospital at Halton. Due to the cracked vertebrae the instructor and student were grounded for about six months, but did regain their flying categories. This was the only Strikemaster lost since the squadron's arrival at Masirah. A brand new Strikemaster was ordered in its place, and this arrived some years later. Eventually the Strikemasters were withdrawn from service in November 1999, one of them being from the first batch purchased over thirty years earlier. They were replaced by Swiss PC 9s.

During the closing months of 1984 the Jaguars intercepted a number of foreign aircraft which had entered Omani airspace without permission. Prominent among them were a total of seven IL–38 Mays which are anti-submarine and maritime patrol aircraft operated by the Soviet Navy from a base in South Yemen. Lockhead P-3 Orions are similar four-turboprop maritime aircraft and a number of these were intercepted, five of them Iranian and one belonging to the US Navy.

The Masirah airfield also provided a useful bolt hole for a number of US Navy carrier aircraft with emergencies such as the arrester hook failing to lower. Had it not been for Masirah these aircraft would have been lost – there was nowhere else they could land.

1985

The comprehensive upgrading of the station continued throughout 1985. Now that there was a paved parallel taxiway for runway 07/25, a new Air Movements terminal could be built next to it. The new terminal was built on the south side of the taxiway close to the threshold of runway 07. A road from the direction of the Wali Camp allowed people to come to the terminal without going through the boundary fence onto SOAF territory. Nearby a large SAF Shop was built with similar unrestricted access. There were SAF Shops at all the military garrisons in Oman, their purpose being to sell goods at subsidised prices to servicemen, their families and the locally employed civilians. BERS personnel were also allowed to shop here because there were no other similar shops on the island.

After some years the British personnel became suspicious about the SAF shop. A large number of local people were shopping there and buying up huge quantities of rice, sugar, and powdered milk, etc. At the check-out desks they seemed to be paying only a token amount, if that. Often they paid nothing. It appeared that fraud was rife and the SAF shop might have become the source of supply for the whole Wali Camp. After about ten years the shop was closed down, but the reason can only be guessed. The closure proved to be of great benefit to the Wali Camp where entrepreneurs found it profitable to open some good shops.

There was now a substantial chainlink boundary fence around the airfield and station buildings, and from it spurs went from coast to coast to delineate the now greatly extended SOAF territory. On the west the fence went down to the sea near the salt water stream from the desalination plants. The road to the jetty went through the fence with a cattle grid to stop goats and camels etc. passing through, but the animals soon learnt to negotiate the cattle grid to gain access to the grazing further north. In the east the fence went down to the sea at the first rocks to the north of Surf Beach. There was also a road through this fence to allow the BERS vehicles access to their satellite dish and HF site. Due to the inner boundary fence animals could not enter the airfield itself.

At the Wali Camp the low-cost housing had been completed and a large fish-processing and freezer plant had been built just to the south of the village. Opposite the plant a substantial stone mole was being built out towards deep water in the Masirah Channel. Ultimately this mole was over 500 metres long. At its end large dhows could moor up at any state of the tide, and an encircling arm to the north provided calm water in rough weather together with a landing stage.

Over the years there had been a considerable increase in the amount of fishing. The small heavy wooden canoes (houris) were losing favour because it was difficult to pull them up the beach to above the high-tide mark. Aluminium and fibreglass boats with outboard motors were much easier to handle, and there was an increase in the number of wooden launches with inboard motors. Sails had practically disappeared. Some years previously other Omani fishing vessels had appeared on the scene, large dhows from the Jaalan, mainly Sur, 130 miles up the coast to the north-east. The Masirah fisherfolk did not welcome outsiders coming into their waters and poaching their fish. There was some incident and apparently firearms were discharged. Three Buffalo aircraft of the Royal Oman Police landed on the mainland opposite the north of Masirah. They contained a posse of police to restore order. The whole area is very low lying and partially flooded even at low tide. The three aircraft landed on 'sabkha', a sunbaked crust covering a salt bog. When the aircraft stopped, their wheels broke through the crust and they were well and truly bogged in, so an overland convoy of recovery vehicles was sent, carrying pressed steel planking and jacks, etc. A number of police helicopters were detached to SOAF Masirah so that the recovery party could be brought in every night. The recovery operation took some days but eventually all three Buffalos were able to take off and return to Seeb.

1986

By this time 1 Squadron's building had been refurbished to a new design which was ideal for its task. Station Operations had moved out so this large room was brought into use in addition to the neighbouring room which had previously housed the central air-conditioning plant. Everything was very smart when the Sultan visited in February to award 'wings' to No. 14 Course. After the ceremony His Majesty unveiled a plaque marking the formation of the

Sultan Qaboos Air Academy. This consisted of two departments – one of them was 1 Squadron, and the other was the Department of Officer Training, housed in the adjacent buildings. The students were potential officers who had completed their recruit training as well as other stages of academic study and an English language course. They were from all branches, not just potential pilots. The course lasted for 16 weeks and was aimed at developing the cadets' leadership, self-reliance and self-confidence. There were adventure training exercises, map reading, team leading and camping down the island. Inevitably there were academic studies, mathematics, science, Islamic studies and more English; there was also drill and physical training.

In mid-July the Light Aircraft Flight was formed on 1 Squadron. The two aircraft were Swiss AS 202 Bravos from the disbanded Royal Flight Flying Club at Seeb, and were ferried from Seeb by the Squadron Commander and Flight Commander. Each cadet at the Department of Officer Training had up to four air experience flights in the Bravos, regardless of his branch. Another task of the Light Aircraft Flight, however, was grading potential pilots after they had passed the initial officer training course, it being cheaper to assess their pilot aptitude before embarking on the course of elementary flying training which was also on the Bravos. Two Bravos were not enough for this task so another two new ones were bought from the factory in Switzerland three years later. Hitherto the elementary flying training had been at flying schools in the UK, which was not always entirely satisfactory because it was difficult to monitor the students' progress and the quality of instruction. However, it did have the advantage of exposing the young Omanis to Western society, which widened their understanding of the non-Moslem world, hopefully without corrupting their culture. For some years the potential officers continued to go for further officer training at the RAF College Cranwell, after their initial course at the Department of Officer Training at Masirah. Cranwell provided an excellent environment in which the Omani cadets excelled. However, Oman's oil revenue was no more than modest and there were many other pressing calls on the national finances. After a few more years SOAF could no longer afford the Cranwell training for all the students and virtually stopped sending cadets. Both air forces were the poorer for this.

A squadron of surface-to-air missiles was formed at Masirah in May – 22 Squadron of Rapier missiles with two fire units. Deployment sites were prepared in the local area for airfield protection.

Around the time of his birthday in November Prince Charles and Princess Diana came to Masirah on a private visit. They stayed at BERS, a hideaway where they could be out of the spotlight and away from press photographers. It provided the seclusion that they needed.

Immediately after Prince Charles's birthday there was a very large exercise which received wide publicity in the British and Omani press as well as on television in both countries. Omani Jaguars of 8 Squadron and 20 Squadron

A Bravo of 1 Squadron's Light Aircraft Flight
(Photograph: Tam Syme)

participated, as did Tornado GR1s and F3s of the RAF and Royal Navy Sea Harriers. There was simulated close air support, ship attacks and dissimilar air combat. Part of the exercise was conducted at night and it lasted two full weeks.

1987

The build-up of the station continued throughout the year. Married quarters for Omani personnel were built on rising ground to the south-west of the single officers' accommodation. To the south of the station cinema a Mess for the Omani airmen was built together with three two-storey barrack blocks which were in the form of a hollow square. This is the classical form of an Omani fort, so they were named after Omani forts on the mainland. The officers' and sergeants' accommodation had always been in the pattern of a hollow square and were known as 'wadis', because the stone chippings in the square were reminiscent of the shingle in wadi beds. In the RAF days the wadis were named after RAF staff officers at headquarters, but SOAF renamed them after real wadis on the island. The wadis had barbecue emplacements, coloured lights in the trees, bars and large cable drums half buried to form round tables.

Due to the new pattern of roads the Giraffe House was demolished. This tall white building near the Medical Centre had been a prominent landmark for many years. Those who had known Masirah for a long time felt lost without this point of reference.

The RAF jetty had been built in 1964 and had survived the 1977 cyclone. However, it was now suffering from decay and its structure was no longer sound. From beneath it could be seen that the steel reinforcing beams had corroded and some had actually broken so that a heavy vehicle might well fall through the concrete deck into the sea. Another jetty was therefore built 100 yards to the north, closer to the Water Sports Club. The new jetty was longer, extending into water deep enough for small tankers to moor up alongside, making the discharge of fuel a much simpler process.

A flight of security police arrived towards the end of the year, their additional numbers bringing the total at SOAF Masirah to close on 1,000. When SOAF Masirah was formed in 1977 the total number of personnel was 182.

1988

In February and March 1988 two Motor Falke motor gliders arrived from Salalah where they had been used for recreation. Salalah was now a major civil airport with a long east-west runway to the north of the old airfield. It was still a SOAF base, and the number of air movements made it difficult to operate the motor gliders there. Often they would be taken away at weekends to unmanned landing grounds in the interior. At Masirah the Motor Falkes were to be used for air experience flying and with them from Salalah came Wakeel (Warrant Officer) Con Grieves who had been at SOAF Masirah in the early days. He had been the holder of several world gliding records. The Motor Falkes became part of the Light Aircraft Flight on 1 Squadron, but were only permitted to fly in the afternoons when there was no other air traffic. Omani ground branch officers and SNCOs were trained on the motor gliders so that they could give air experience flights when they became suitably qualified. The passengers were mostly cadets from the Department of Officer Training and the young Omani aircraft engineers. The motor gliders were put away into storage during the months of the south-west monsoon because it was not safe to fly them in strong winds.

1989

There was a large number of expatriate workers in Oman, including Masirah, who were a drain on the country's economy and created an underclass of unemployed Omanis. It was therefore decreed that the armed forces must employ Omanis with the intention of repatriating the workers from India, Pakistan, Sri Lanka and the Philippines. The employment of older, uneducated Omanis was not always successful, and Masirah was no exception. However, there was still a number of older islanders who had worked for the RAF and were invaluable. Perhaps the best was Abse who had worked in the Ration Supply Depot under both regimes, but who had been tragically killed some years previously trying to separate two fishing boats which had drifted into the shallows one foggy night. Abdul Malik was still the head laundryman. His father, Ali 'Dhobi', was Adenese and had been brought in by the RAF. Adam, a Somali, had arrived from Aden in 1957 and was still employed by the MoD engineers. Khalifa also served on after the departure of the RAF and was the excellent head waiter in the Officers' Mess. The RAF called some of the workers by British names, such as Bob in the Officers' Mess and Charlie in MT. The diminutive Tommy soldiered on, always happy to chat in English. These and others were faithful retainers. Their English, learnt from the RAF, was often quite colourful. On one occasion Hamed Humaid, a cleaner, discovered one of the contractor's workers in an officer's room and ordered him out with the words 'Out, you black bugger.'

The cleaners were not always welcome in the officers' rooms and could cause mayhem by, for instance, dusting the keys on a digital radio and thus reprogramming it in a random and bizarre fashion. An officer returned to his room one morning and found the cleaner sweeping it out. The broom head was upside down with the bristles pointing upwards. The officer removed the broomhead and replaced it with the bristles pointing downwards. The cleaner then removed the broom head and replaced it with the bristles pointing upwards again. Plainly there was a problem so the officer went to fetch the Pakistani Mess Manager, who was fluent in Arabic. He discussed the matter with the cleaner and the cleaner's dilemma was explained. 'He says,' explained the Mess Manager 'that if the bristles point downwards he gets left with a big pile of dust in the middle of the floor.'

A tribute must be paid to the Omani servicemen at Masirah who spent long periods away from home. They enjoyed a friendly and easy relationship with the British and their similar sense of humour was a great advantage. This was particularly so in pilot training which could sometimes be challenging. Most of the students surmounted these challenges and their progress was a source of pride to their instructors whose aim was to make the training a most enjoyable and stress-free experience. Many students were gifted pilots who progressed to more advanced aircraft. Those who failed the course joined other branches, and some of the ground crew were commissioned into the engineering branch. Such Omanis now fill top positions of responsibility for guiding the destiny of the air force which is in wise and safe hands.

CHAPTER XII

RAFO Masirah

1990

BY ROYAL DECREE SOAF became RAFO, the Royal Air Force of Oman. The British commander retired and was succeeded by the first Omani CRAFO His Excellency Liwa Rukn Tayyar Talib bin Meran al Raeesi. Later in June the last British Station Commander at Masirah departed after a tenure of seven years, handing over to Ameed Rukn Tayyar Mohammed bin Mahfoudh al Ardhi who was destined to become the next CRAFO.

In July Iraqi forces massed on the Kuwait border. Such threatening sabre rattling was frowned upon. Excited speculation in the media was passed off as hyperbole to enhance the circulation figures. Iraqi forces invaded Kuwait on 2 August 1990 which was unexpected, notably by British Airways which had a Boeing 747 Jumbo Jet on the ground at Kuwait Airport at the time. World leaders then realised that Kuwait was no more than the hors d'oeuvre and that Saudi Arabia was on the menu as the main course, with the Gulf States as the dessert course to round off a satisfying meal.

For a few days the invasion of Kuwait had little effect on Masirah. There were rumours of a possible Yemen involvement and that may be why RAF Jaguars were initially detached to Thumrait before moving to the Gulf.

After a few days RAFO Masirah went on to 24-hour manning. It was a period of uncertainty and no one really knew what to expect. The working hours were long and arduous but there was a great sense of cohesion and co-operation. The physical defence of the station was stepped up and a blackout was imposed with external lights switched off and windows covered in make-shift material; people kept tripping over kerbs and steps, and walking into things in the dark.

News broadcasts on the BBC World Service were keenly followed. The proximity of BERS was a particular advantage because, apart from the powerful broadcasts, there was a weak transmission on FM which lasted for twenty-four hours a day. The FM transmission was just for their own personnel, but it could also be received at RAFO Masirah. It is at times of crisis like this that the whole world listens to the BBC World Service, knowing that the news and comment is true and unbiased. From the news it was obvious that serious

The Gulf War 1990–91.
Here come the Yanks (Photograph: Bruce Watts)

Top left is Tent City to the south of the station. Top right are the Omani married quarters. Foreground – Medical Centre, and Officers' Mess opposite their quarters. (Photograph: Bruce Watts}

measures were beginning to be taken by some world powers. The Gulf States felt uneasy at the turn of events, their governments being aware that their countries were on Iraq's list of desirable acquisitions, so for self-protection they made facilities available to the United Nations allied forces. The local people, however, felt ambivalent about provoking a powerful neighbour by backing the pro-Israeli Americans. Many Omanis found little to admire in the Kuwaiti or Saudi regimes. Even in the UK itself British backing for the United Nations was condemned by the self-styled Moslem Parliament.

In the early hours of 12 August some USAF C-130 transport aircraft were crossing the Red Sea to Saudi Arabia, but were instructed by radio to change their destination and land at Masirah. Thus began Masirah's participation in the Gulf War. Up to this time the south-west monsoon had been particularly severe, but with the arrival of the first American aircraft the weather moderated and the rest of the monsoon period was comparatively mild.

These first Americans, from Pope Air Force Base in North Carolina, knew nothing of Arabia and did not know whether they had landed in Egypt, Saudi Arabia or even Kuwait itself. A whole new world awaited them. One aircrewman was heard to shout: 'Just show me to the hotel, man.' His face fell as part of a packaged tent was thrown to him. Over the next few days 'Tent City' took shape to the south of the RAFO officers' accommodation and grew to house over 1,200 personnel, more than RAFO Masirah itself. The tents were laid out in lines with the standard military austerity, but as time passed individual characteristics materialised – wooden doors appeared where once there had been flaps. The lines became named streets, avenues and boulevards which the occupants named after familiar places back home such as 10th Avenue South. Individual tents also had their own names. Initially they contained two rows of campbeds with lockers and canvas-backed chairs, but soon they became more homely with individual bed spaces partitioned off with reminders of home.

The huge American build-up continued. The new southern aircraft parking area had hydrant refuelling and was big enough for half a dozen Lockheed C-5 Galaxies as well as a handful of C-141 Starlifters. There were Boeing 707s and 747 Jumbo Jets as well as F-15 Eagles. There were visits by RAF Tornado GR1s and a detachment of air traffic controllers to share the load with the hard-pressed RAFO controllers. American controllers also assisted on occasions.

Down the island a natural surface runway had been prepared a little north of Umm Rusays, but not at the same place as the original RAF landing ground. It had been built for the Bravos' and motor gliders' circuit training, but at the beginning of the Gulf War it was lengthened and improved so that it could be used by the USAF C-130s. By Christmas fourteen KC-135 tankers were based at Masirah, from Wichita, Kansas and Great Falls, Montana. There was also a hospital and the facility for sending 40,000 dead back to the USA. In the sea off Masirah naval forces gathered, awaiting the order to move into the Gulf.

Christmas Day 1990 in Tent City
(Photograph: Bruce Watts)

Thanksgiving and Christmas were periods of great festivity with the atmosphere charged with excitement. Everyone was on a 'high' and keenly motivated. But with the New Year came the realisation that the allied preparations were nearly complete, and that soon Operation Desert Shield would become Operation Desert Storm. It concentrated the mind wonderfully. The gravity of the situation struck home when the KC-135 crews discovered that 15 per cent of them were expected to be killed in action. Some of the crew members were women with husbands and children back home, and the realisation of the real danger to come depressed their enthusiasm for the forthcoming operation. No one mentioned the old RAF adage: 'If you can't take a joke you shouldn't have joined'.

1991

The allied air attacks on Kuwait and Iraq began in the early hours of 17 January 1991. RAFO personnel were woken well before dawn by the shattering roar of the KC-135s taking-off. The tankers headed north to take up station in Saudi airspace north of Riyadh, remaining there for some hours to refuel fighters and strike aircraft returning from hostile territory. The tanker crews felt very vulnerable to Iraqi fighters sweeping in at low level and climbing up amongst them to fire their missiles, but surprisingly it never happened, and it soon

Air-to-air refuelling from a Masirah-based KC-135
(Photograph: Bruce Watts)

became apparent that the Iraqi Air Force had been paralysed by the onslaught. As the hours and days passed the tanker crews gained confidence.

There was massive resupply to Masirah, and from Masirah to the forward airfields in Saudi Arabia, largely carried out by two squadrons of C-130s, and much of the freight consisted of 2,000-lb bombs. The C-130 crews often had to spend the night at the forward bases in Saudi Arabia where sirens warned of the imminent arrival of Scud missiles which might well have had warheads containing lethal gas or biological agents. It was now the Masirah-based C-130 crews who felt vulnerable, but within a few days they were sent back to the safety of Masirah overnight. One of the Masirah-based KC-135 crews watched the first successful interception of a Scud by one of the Patriot anti-missile missiles. At the time the KC-135 was on station north of Riyadh which was the Scud target.

When hostilities began RAFO Masirah went onto the highest alert state, but RAFO aircraft did not participate in the war. Paradoxically the blackout measures at Masirah were rescinded because sabotage was seen to be more of a threat than attack from the air or sea.

After a week the weather in Iraq deteriorated to be the worst in many years. There was low cloud and heavy rain which hampered the precision visual bombing. High-level bombing would be unaffected by the bad weather lower down, so General Norman Schwarzkopf decided to use his heavy bombers a little earlier than planned. These were the B52s based at Diego Garcia 2,000 miles south of Masirah. The Masirah-based KC-135s were no longer required on the front line, and instead refuelled the B52s on their way into Iraq and on their return to Diego Garcia. The task of the B52s was round-the-clock carpet bombing of the Iraqi Army, particularly the Republican Guard which was being held in reserve behind the front-line troops. It was naturally desirable to destroy as much armour and supplies as possible, but also to demoralise and exhaust the Iraqi troops by denying them sleep for days on end. The B52 raids were irregular and unpredictable, concentrating on one location for several days and nights before suddenly switching elsewhere. The B52 bludgeon was an awesome weapon indeed.

As the allied ground advance started the doctors and nurses at Masirah stood by for a heavy influx of casualties, but it never happened. Casualties were light and Operation Desert Storm was soon over. Suddenly there seemed to be nothing to do with plenty of free time. In March the C-130s were given 48-hours notice to return home. The KC-135s stayed on for some time in support of American aircraft patrolling the 'No Fly Zone' in Southern Iraq. The crews told of the ecological horror of the burning oil wells that they had witnessed at Kuwait.

The final rundown began in May with the departure of the KC-135s; the hospital departed without having treated any battle casualties, and the morgue also left. The only death at Masirah had been a USAF servicewoman who had died of a heart attack. A chartered Boeing 747 collected almost all the remaining USAF personnel, and Masirah returned to normal. Tent city remained for some months but eventually it was packed away.

After all the excitement, RAFO Masirah had difficulty in settling back into a disciplined and controlled routine. Some motor glider pilots had adopted uninhibited practices which tempted fate, and the helicopter pilot touched his rotor blades on rising ground, resulting in a spectacular crash with the wreckage widely scattered; the crew and passengers were lucky not to be killed. 1 Squadron was in a rundown state and urgently needed good leadership to address its many shortcomings as a training organisation. There was a further deterioration with low morale until matters improved a year or two later. One of the Airwork employees had built himself an Evans VP2, a remarkably crude little aeroplane with a Volkswagen Beetle engine which produced only just enough power for flight. Its legal status was open to doubt both under British and Omani law. Its builder was allowed to fly the highly suspect 20 Squadron microlight, but one day its engine failed in flight as it often did and the Airwork employee was badly injured in the ensuing crash. When he was discharged from hospital he was posted to Salalah. Eventually his Evans VP2 was returned to the UK on one of the RAFO C-130s on its freight run to Bournemouth Airport.

20 Squadron also had an unfortunate time after the Gulf War when a young Omani Jaguar pilot flew into the ground shortly after a night take-off. The crash was near the BERS HF site and was heard by the duty engineer there.

1992

There was heavy rain in January, and small fish were seen in isolated rock pools in Palm Wadi. The mystery was how they got there. After more rain Palm Wadi became a flowing stream for some time. On the mainland five feet of snow was reported near the summit of the Jebel Shams which is the highest point in Oman.

Satellite television dishes appeared round the air base, and most people had television in their accommodation. Omani television was rebroadcast to the Wali Camp which was adopting its original name of Hilf. There were now shops in Hilf, and one or two restaurants, a post office and two banks. The post office seemed to be shut for most of the working day, and when open it had usually run out of airmail stamps, while the banks were often crowded with people shouting for attention and waving bits of paper in the air.

There were now a total of five flat-bottomed ferries sailing between Hilf and the mainland where there was a graded road to the north. The original small landing craft was still operating but by this time it was looking extremely battered. It nosed up to a ramp on a short mole just to the north of the village desalination plant, its arrival in rough weather being guaranteed to provide an entertaining spectacle. It seldom made an accurate approach to the landing ramp, and there were always contradictory orders shouted by everybody on the boat and everybody in the shore party who all pulled ropes in different

Hilf in 1998
Just north of the desalination plant, the hotel of Mohammed bin Khamis is near completion (Author's photograph)

Hilf in 1998
Approaching the shopping centre (Author's photograph)

directions. Often it took several attempts to make an accurate landing. The procedure was often complicated by kids jumping in and out of the sea, screaming and splashing each other and hanging onto the ropes, which only provoked more shouting from the shore party, the Arabic equivalent of 'Clear off, you little perishers!' Anyone in search of a free afternoon's entertainment could always go and watch, but should not leave before the nail-biting finale when the grossly overloaded vehicles engaged bottom gear and, tilting alarmingly, negotiated the boat's rolling ramp onto the upslope of the concrete ramp. It was a great relief when all were safely ashore.

Nonetheless, it was not as alarming as it was before the advent of flat-bottomed ferries. Civilian vehicles (mostly Land Rovers) were brought to the island on dhows. They were parked on planks laid across the gunwales of the dhow. The whole thing looked very top-heavy and unstable. On arrival at Masirah the dhow was brought in close, and sideways to the shore, then came the perilous unloading. A rope attached to the top of the mast was pulled by a shore party. That rolled the dhow a little towards the beach. Long planks were placed in front of the Land Rover's wheels, the other end of the planks being in shallow water near the shore. The Land Rover was then cautiously driven forward onto the planks, the displacement of the Land Rover's weight rolling the dhow even more towards the shore. Ideally the sloping deck would line up with the planks sloping down to the shore. The Land Rover could then be driven down the planks into the shallow water, and from there up onto the beach. Now relieved of its displaced load the dhow would roll back to its upright position. At the time this procedure provided the best spectator sport available on the island.

In October there was a hurricane warning. The 1 Squadron Strikemasters and Bravos were able to take cover with the 20 Squadron Jaguars. The eye of the storm was heading towards the southern tip of the island, but the weather was not as severe as had been feared. There was heavy rain on the base and the south end of the main runway was covered by floodwater. The lighter corrugated aluminium roofs flapped and tore away as was usual in any strong wind. Two very large wooden dhows were driven ashore on the east coast further down the island, but there was no loss of life, the wrecks providing plenty of firewood for the locals.

The Swiss University of Bern sent a geological expedition to the island during the winter of 1992/3. Their accommodation was in tents on the rocks to the north of Turtle Beach, but they had an office in Hilf where they could carry out their detailed work and telephone home, and in the evenings they usually dined at one of the restaurants before driving back to their camp.

With Omanis in command there were fewer inhibitions about Christmas. There was the Annual Draw in the Mess, and on Christmas Eve the officers were invited to the Sergeants' Mess for pre-lunch drinks. In the evening there was a Christmas Dinner in the Officers' Mess with crackers and paper hats. All nine Swiss geologists were invited as well as friends from BERS. Many officers and SNCOs were invited to the BERS New Year's Eve party. Omanis joined in these festivities, knowing that it was all good fun without any religious significance. Hitherto the wives of British officers had been allowed to come to Masirah for short family visits only, but now the Omani Station Commander allowed them to live permanently in their husband's accommodation, although none lived in the married quarters which were for Omanis only.

1993

Few Omani cadets were being sent to the RAF College Cranwell for their officer training, so RAFO took over the majority of this commitment at Ghalla in the capital area where for some years the Air Force had run the SAF boys' school. The Department of Officer Training at Masirah had been a preparation for Cranwell and was therefore no longer necessary and the staff moved to Ghalla. Occasionally the Ghalla cadets would visit Masirah en masse for a concentrated period of air experience flying in the motor gliders which would continue all day for several days over a long weekend.

In March 20 Squadron moved permanently from Masirah to Thumrait where it joined 8 Squadron, the other Jaguar squadron, and 6 Squadron which still had Hawker Hunters. For nearly a year 1 Squadron was once again the only flying unit on the station other than the rescue helicopter. Mirage 2000 fighters of the French Air Force arrived for an exercise early in the year, and USAF F-16s from South Carolina arrived in September for an exercise with 20 Squadron which returned to Masirah for a week or two. The F-16s flew non-stop from Germany to Masirah with in-flight refuelling from KC-135s. Lockheed C-5 Galaxies brought all their needs and the 120-man detachment operated out of another Tent City.

Over recent years the municipality had built a number of picnic shelters on Surf Beach. They had concrete floors with low surrounding walls and roofs to provide shade. They were built on sand and were therefore vulnerable to very high tides which sometimes washed them away. Towards the south of the island, on the channel side, is Rounders Bay. The whole bay became an encampment, except during the summer monsoon, with many large dhows anchored offshore This was the fishing fleet from the mainland town of Sur, perhaps joined by other fisherfolk from the Jaalan, who were taking advantage of the rich Masirah fishing grounds. Further south, just to the side of Ras abu Rasas, a small mole was built to enable people to come ashore. Apart from these small developments the island remained much as before except that the vehicle tracks were now graded. The villages down the island were larger but very much the same in character, although five years later, in the late 1990s, they were almost completely deserted except for Samar, Dawwa and Shaghaf. The expanding metropolis of Hilf had proved to be too great an attraction.

With the increase in fishing there were many more local fishing boats. These were beached just south of the RAFO jetty, and round the corner on the north beach halfway to BERS. Being in line with runway 17 they represented something of a hazard because flocks of sea birds were attracted to the area by the discarded fish. The birds would rise into the air and into the path of aircraft low on the approach to land. It was on RAFO territory and from time to time the RAFO Station Commander would have the fishing boats moved away, but in 1993 the boats would always move back again, the fishermen protesting that they had used that part of the beach for many years. This was not so, but no one in the Air Force had been there long enough to refute the claim and it was some years before the fishermen were permanently evicted. Camels roamed the area and this was also a hazard. On one occasion a camel walked into the headlight beam of a BERS Land Rover at night. The driver was unable to avoid it or stop, and the camel was killed. Its owner claimed 2,000 riyals from the driver, equivalent to about £3,000. The following few weeks were an anxious time for the driver, but fortunately for him the claim was thrown out by the court, probably because the camel should not have been there on RAFO territory.

The Omani go-kart grand prix was held at Masirah in September 1993 with participants coming from as far as the United Arab Emirates. The Masirah go-kart club had been thriving under the enthusiastic leadership of Daz Cosway, a young loan service fighter controller. The club members were both Omani

Recreation
Top: Go-Karts 1993 (Photograph: Martin Rigby). *Middle:* One of the motor gliders
1994. *Bottom:* Windsurfing 1992 (Photograph: Bruce Watts)

and British, including some from BERS, and a number of the go-karts were privately owned. Daz was accompanied by his wife Julie who produced the first baby born to a British couple on Masirah.

The ground training for the students on 1 Squadron was not all classroom work and included outdoor exercises. Occasionally the squadron ground instructor would take the students down the island after work and abandon them somewhere with a map and the contents of the survival pack in the ejection seat. They would have to make their way on foot to a pickup point where the helicopter would arrive at a prearranged time to take them back to base. It was an exercise in map reading and helicopter rescue techniques. The helicopter would not land, but hover and winch them up one by one if they reached the pickup point at the prearranged time. If they were not there for any reason they could use the SARBE radio and smoke flares to redirect the helicopter to wherever they happened to be. The Survival and Rescue Officer from HQ RAFO would sometimes arrive just before the weekend and take the students down the island for a two-day survival exercise. This unexpected interruption to their weekend arrangements was never welcomed by the students who knew that the next two days and nights were bound to be exhausting and uncomfortable. There was also 'wet winching' for instructors and students to practice rescue from the sea. Afterwards certificates were issued to the participants for record purposes. In October an instructor wrote the following report on the back of his certificate.

So there I was, one of four bobbing about in single seat dinghies in the sea near the jetty. Along comes the helicopter to winch us up. He turns and descends towards the first dinghy, and to my surprise he keeps turning and descending until he splashes down into the sea beside the dinghy. I couldn't believe what I was seeing. The pontoons on the skids do not inflate, and the pilot guns the engine to keep the helicopter afloat. There is obviously something wrong with the tail rotor because the helicopter is revolving in the water. Out pop various crew members and a large round multi-seat dinghy. As the helicopter revolves in the water the crew members and dinghy somehow avoid the tail rotor which is still under power and scything round and round in circles. After a few minutes the nose of the helicopter rears up, like an elephant trying to climb out of an African bog. The tail rotor hits the sea in a shower of spray, and stops.

The safety boat moves in and picks up the crew members, and closely attends the helicopter. It is still revolving in the water but the wind is slowly blowing it towards the beach. After 40 minutes it is beached on a falling tide and the pilot shuts down the engine.

The four of us in our dinghies are not the centre of attention. We drift off to the north-east in the general direction of Pakistan. Has everybody forgotten about us? Luckily we are spotted by a 'Charlie Boat', one of those

October 1993. After ditching in the sea the rescue helicopter is beached on a falling tide (Author's Photograph)

little flat-bottomed ships which the navy use to bring us supplies. We fire off our mini flares to indicate our distress, so the 'Charlie Boat' launches its Zodiac to pick us up. Thank God we've got a navy. The Zodiac takes us to where the helicopter is beached, and most Masirah personnel have arrived there to see what's happened. The four of us wade ashore with our dinghies in tow. We get a lot of 'What on earth are you doing here' looks from the curious on-lookers.

Later that evening the BERS heavy lift crane lifts the helicopter off the beach and lowers it onto a low loader which takes it back to base.

The Survival and Rescue Officer reckons all this counts as a wet winching and issues this certificate.

1994

At the beginning of 1993 sun shelters had been erected on the northern aircraft parking area. They had no doors, being simple half-cylinders made of corrugated metal. Some of them contained ground equipment but their real purpose was to shade the Strikemasters from the sun. The aircraft were taxied in and out, but were usually towed back to the hangar at the end of the working day. The shelters had been designed to withstand winds of 80 knots, but in January 1994 two of them collapsed in a wind of 48 knots, fortunately crushing only ground equipment. The reason for the collapse was the steel bars which

A Masirah-based Hawk of 6 Squadron
(Photograph: Pete Boothroyd)

October 1994. The author taxis a Strikemaster into a sun shelter at the end of his
last flight at Masirah

anchored the structures to the concrete beneath. The bars had completely rusted through in less than a year, so the sun shelters were only resting on the ground and not attached to it in any way. After another couple of years some more of the shelters buckled in a moderate wind, so all of them were removed.

6 Squadron was re-equipped with BAe Hawk aircraft and moved from Thumrait to Masirah. The role of the Hawks was much the same as the Hunters – for ground attack, reconnaissance, and interception of intruders (providing they were not too fast!). In addition they provided the next stage of training for students who had passed the Strikemaster course. 6 Squadron moved into the buildings next to 1 Squadron which had been used by the Department of Officer Training. The aircraft were hangared the other side of the runway, which was quite a long drive for the pilots. The Hawk aircraft used by the RAF enjoyed a fine reputation, but the 6 Squadron Hawks were the more modern 100 and 200 series two-seaters and single-seaters which had much enhanced capabilities. After a few years 6 Squadron moved to more suitable accommodation near SHQ, and a new hangar for the Hawks was built south of the armoury.

Towards the end of the year a Pakistan Air Force C-130 landed at Masirah, and inside were three Mushak aircraft and a team to assemble them. The Mushaks were Saab Safaris built under licence in Pakistan and used for elementary flying training at the Pakistan Air Force Academy; the wings were mounted shoulder high and were slightly swept forwards. The three aircraft were a gift from Pakistan. No doubt the Pakistanis hoped that the Light Aircraft Flight would sell their Swiss Bravos and re-equip the fleet with Mushaks, but actually the Bravos were much better aircraft. However, after another few years there was a reappraisal and a decision was made to sell the Bravos and have a fleet composed only of Mushaks.

1995

On 25 March a US Navy P3 Orion was carrying out an anti-submarine exercise 200 miles east of Oman. The Orion is a land-based maritime aircraft with four propeller turbine engines similar to the C-130 Hercules. During the anti-submarine exercise the Captain of the aircraft had stopped the two outboard engines to conserve fuel. After the exercise he attempted to restart them to climb up to 16,000 feet for his transit back to base. However, a warning light showed that there was a partial malfunction in the pitch change mechanism on the propeller of the outboard engine on the right-hand wing.

The warning light did not indicate that the aircraft was in any great danger, but it could lead to bigger problems. The Captain headed towards Masirah which was the closest airfield, and started reading the flight manual (commonly referred to as the 'Big Blue Sleeping Pill') to make sure he carried out the correct actions. According to some reports he did not follow the correct procedures but carried out his own experiments which reportedly made matters worse. The aircraft was still 80 miles from Masirah when a second warning light showed that there was a complete failure of the propeller pitch mechanism on that outboard engine, the propeller began to overspeed, and so did the heart rates of the crew. They were unable to prevent the overspeed and kept the aircraft at 16,000 feet until they reached Masirah, where they made a slow, cautious descent to reduce the strain on the propeller. At 5,600 feet there was an explosion. The co-pilot looked out at the right-hand engine and saw a huge cloud of black smoke. When the smoke cleared he could see that the propeller was missing and the reduction gearbox was on fire, so the engine was shut down and the fire extinguisher was operated. But the fire was not extinguished and kept burning fiercely, so the second fire extinguisher was operated – still the fire raged.

The inboard engine on that side then began to wind down having obviously been damaged by the explosion, so that engine too was shut down. The Captain opened the throttles to increase power on the two engines on the other wing, but glancing out at them he could see that the propellers on these two engines had almost stopped rotating, so they were also shut down. On the radio the aircraft Captain had been talking to his operating authority, but had failed to inform Masirah Air Traffic Control of his close proximity and serious emergency.

All four engines had been shut down, so there was no electrical power; everything went quiet. To regain electrical power the engineer attempted to start the auxiliary power unit, a small generator which is usually used only on the ground. Nothing happened. They were in a dead aircraft. Next the powered flying controls seized solid – it was like driving a car with a locked steering wheel. The Captain had lost control of the aircraft which rolled right into a turn of 45 to 50 degrees of bank and began to lose speed. It was not possible to parachute out of the problem because the aircraft was too low and the side cabin door was facing upwards.

All this happened in the 45 seconds since the explosion, it was plain for all to see that the aircraft was doomed, and so were they.

Then the control column suddenly unlocked. The pilots levelled the wings and looked towards the airfield but they were too low and too far away to make a glide landing, and they realised that they would have to ditch the aircraft in the sea, but there was no known procedure for a no-engine, no-flap, manual-control ditching. No one had ever done it, and no one ever thought that it might happen. The two pilots judged the roundout nicely and managed to correct a roll at the last moment. The aircraft hit the water, skipped several times and stopped. The Orion floated, and the crew were amazed to have survived. Escape hatches were jettisoned and soon the crew was outside the aircraft and into the sea. The Captain was covered in fuel from a ruptured

1995 – The US Navy P3 Orion Ditches
Top: The RAFO rescue helicopter arrives as the Orion sinks. *Bottom:* The Orion is lifted out onto a barge a month later (Both Photographs: Mike Crabtree)

fuel tank and his eyes stung, but otherwise the crew was completely uninjured. One of the life rafts would not inflate and three SARBE radios were tried before one would work. But the Masirah rescue helicopter arrived after only 10 minutes and needed only two journeys to rescue all eleven crew.

A month later a barge and crane arrived over the Orion which was in the Masirah Channel west of the airfield. When the aircraft was lifted out it could be seen that a propeller blade had detached from the right-hand outboard engine, and the sudden imbalance had caused the engine to explode. The detached propeller blade went clean through the fuselage, severing thirty-five of the forty-four engine and flight control cables and this shut down all four engines simultaneously. The fuel line to the auxiliary power unit was also cut. Of the nine intact cables two were the aileron cables, two were the elevator cables, two were the elevator trim tab cables and two were the rudder trim tab cables. So the crew were lucky that day. Or were they unlucky?

Epilogue

WHEN RESEARCHING for this book the author remembered that Sam Boyce, the last CO of RAF Masirah, had been searching for a crashed Vincent and the bodies of the crew, so the author contacted him and asked for details. Sam Boyce's reply is under the heading '1977'. Briefly, he found the crashed aircraft near Sur Masirah but not the bodies which were in a shallow cave.

The author knew that there were shallow caves along the southern edge of the old Sur Masirah landing ground and suspected that the bodies may have been buried there, so he wrote to his old friend Bruce Watts and asked him to have a look. Bruce Watts assembled a small search party and looked around the most obvious area and found human bones in a matter of minutes.

The single male body now had to be identified. The RAF Museum and the RAF Air Historical Branch were unable to find any reference to a fatal Vincent crash at Masirah. There had been three Vincent squadrons in the area, 8 Squadron at Aden, 84 Squadron at Shaibah and 55 Squadron at Habbaniyah. These squadrons' operations record books (Forms 540) are in the Public Record Office at Kew. The 8 Squadron F540s had been well kept and mentioned serious aircraft accidents, but there is no mention of a crash at Masirah. The F540s of 84 and 55 Squadrons had been kept extremely badly, with no entries for months on end. An 84 Squadron Vincent had crashed at Masirah in 1939, but although the aircraft had been written off the crew were uninjured. None of the surviving Vincent aircrew remember a fatal accident at Masirah. 244 Squadron at Shaibah were equipped with Vincents at the beginning of the Second World War, but Howard Alloway, the Squadron Commander at the time, states that none of his aircraft crashed at Masirah, so it is possible that the reported crash was not a Vincent. In order to leave no stone unturned, the author investigated the Vincents' predecessors, the Fairey IIIFs of 8 Squadron and the Wapitis of 55 and 84 Squadrons. The history of every aircraft is known and none of them was involved in a fatal crash at Masirah, nor were any of the flying boats of 203 Squadron or the transport aircraft of 70 Squadron. The Library of the Oriental and India Office in London contains the files of the British Political Agent in Muscat in the 1930s. The file index shows a file entitled 'RAF Graves', but the file is missing. The detective work was leading nowhere.

The author then contacted the RAF Personnel Management Agency at Innsworth, ancient files were unearthed, and yes, the file on the accident was there. There were even photographs of the temporary burial site. When the photographs reached the British Embassy in Oman they were taken to Masirah and it was soon realised that they were not of the burial site at Masirah. The photographs were of the burial site at Khor Gharim. The story of that accident in 1937 is related in this book.

Attention then switched to the bodies of the three aircrew buried at Khor Gharim. Commander Hugh Clark, the Naval and Air Attaché at the British Embassy in Oman, mounted an overland expedition to Khor Gharim and was there on 30 October 1997, the 60th anniversary of the fatal crash. From the photographs he located the site of the burial and found some fragments of bone which were removed for analysis. These proved positive and the Innsworth file showed where each individual had been buried. The remains were therefore carefully removed and taken to the British Embassy while the RAF Personnel Management Agency attempted to contact the next of kin. It proved impossible to find any relatives of Leslie O'Leary, the wireless operator (who had been only nineteen years old), or Robert McClatchey the Canadian pilot. However, relatives of Wing Commander Aubrey Rickards were traced.

But what of the fatal Vincent accident at Masirah? The author wrote to Malcolm Dennison, a close friend of the late Jasper Coates who served with him in the Sultan's army during the Jebal Akhdar war. Malcolm Dennison, who has since died, remembered Jasper telling him of the accident somewhere in South Arabia. He remembered only one such accident being mentioned and Jasper saying that the pilot was a Canadian.

John Clementson, the RAFO historian, found a photocopy of a letter from Jasper Coates dated 4 November 1976, which was therefore written during the last months of RAF Masirah. The letter was in an old 'put-away' file at SOAF Masirah, and is reproduced under the heading '1938'. Briefly, Jasper recounts how he flew in an 84 Squadron Vincent to inspect the bodies of Wing Commander Rickards and the pilot and W/T operator who had crashed at 'Sauqrah Bay'. Khor Gharim is in the wide Sawqirah Bay between Ras Madrakah and Ras Sharbatat. This was in 1938. The letter goes on to say that he spent the night at the Sur Masirah landing ground, but there is no mention of inspecting bodies there then, or on any subsequent visit.

The body in the shallow cave at Sur Masirah has been identified as that of a man, but it has not been possible to determine whether it is a European or an Omani. The crashed Vincent could be the one destroyed in 1939 when the crew survived. So has this research been nothing more than a wild goose chase? No. The remains of Aubrey Rickards, Leslie O'Leary and Robert McClatchey were laid to rest on 25 May 1998 at the PDO (Petroleum Development Oman) cemetery near Muscat. Relatives of Wing Commander Aubrey Rickards were flown to Oman for the funeral, and also present were Commander Hugh

25 May 1998. Immediately before the funeral of Wing Commander Aubrey Rickards, Pilot Officer Robert McClatchey and Aircraftman Leslie O'Leary

Clark, his sergeant and RAF officers on loan to RAFO. Unfortunately Charles Whitelock, the pilot of one of the other Vincents, was unable to be present. Owen Frame, the pilot of the third Vincent at Khor Gharim, died a few years ago. He never spoke of his ordeal at Khor Glarim, but after his death his surviving relatives found his report which is recorded in this book under '1937'.

If it was not for the author's research for this book, the three bodies would still lie forgotten at Khor Gharim and would probably have stayed there for ever.

Was there a fatal Vincent crash at Masirah? It seems unlikely, but why is the body of a man buried in such an un-Islamic grave? Possibly it is the body of a Masirah islander who was stoned to death at the place of execution near Sur Masirah. His remains may then have been interred in this unmarked grave without religious ceremony.

The Sur Masirah bones have been returned to their burial cave where they will remain.

Bibliography

Akehurst, John (1982), *We Won a War*, Michael Russell.

Allfree, P.S. (1967), *War Lords of Oman*, Robert Hale.

Ashworth, R.C.B. (1990), *The Shackleton*, Aston Publications Ltd.

Bailey, R.W. (1988, 1992), *Records of Oman* (12 volumes), Archive Editions.

Banks, Arthur (1996), *Wings of the Dawning*, Images Publishing (Malvern) Ltd.

Beckwith, Colonel Charlie A. and Knox, Donald (1984), *Delta Force*, Arms & Armour Press.

Burke, John (1970), *Winged Legend – The Story of Amelia Earhart*, Arthur Barker.

Corser, W.J.L. (1994), *The RAF Masirah Railway*, RAM Productions Ltd.

Deane-Drummond, A.J. (1992), *Arrows of Fortune*, Leo Cooper.

de la Billiere, General Sir Peter (1994), *Looking for Trouble*, HarperCollins.

Dudgeon, A.G. (2000), *Hidden Victory*, Tempus Publishing Ltd.

Geraghty, Tony, *Who Dares Wins* (1980), Fontana/Collins.

Halley, James J., MBE (1995), *The K File*, Air-Britain (Historians) Ltd.

Hitchcock, Fred (1993), *A Shillingsworth of Promise*, Milldam Press.

Jeapes, Colonel Tony (1980), *SAS Operation Oman*, William Kimber & Co. Ltd.

Kyle, James H. (1990), *The Guts to Try*, Crown Publishers Inc.

Lee, Air Chief Marshal Sir David, GBE CB (1980), *Flight from the Middle East*, HMSO.

Office of Air Force History (1949), *The Army Air Forces in World War II*, University of Chicago Press.

Overton, Bill (1990), *Blackburn Beverley*, Midland Counties Publications.

Shepherd, Anthony (1961), *Arabian Adventure*, Collins.

Skeet, Ian (1974), *Muscat & Oman – The End of an Era*, Faber & Faber.

Smiley, David (1975), *Arabian Assignment*, Leo Cooper.

Glossary

ADC	Aide-de-Camp, an assistant
AHQ	Air Headquarters
AOC	Air Officer Commanding
APL	Aden Protectorate Levies
AMDGW	Air Ministry Directorate General of Works
ASV radar	Air to Surface Vessel radar
ATC	Air Traffic Control
Bazaar	Market in an oriental country
Bedan	Old wooden Omani trading boat
BFAP	British Forces Arabian Peninsula
bin	Son of
BOAC	British Overseas Airways Corporation
Bughla	Old wooden Arab trading boat
Burmail	Metal 44-gallon drum
CFS	The Central Flying School of the RAF
CGI	Chief Ground Instructor
CO	Commanding Officer
CSOAF	Commander of the Sultan of Oman's Air Force
Desal plant	Desalination plant for producing fresh water from sea water
Dhow	Wooden Arab trading vessel
DO	Demi-Official
FAC	Forward Air Controller
FTS	Flying Training School
HBM	His (Her) Britannic Majesty
HE	High explosive
HH	His Highness
Houri	Dugout canoe

371

Jazirat	Island
Jebal	Mountain
Khor	Creek
LG	Landing Ground
Met	Meteorological
MO	Medical Officer
NCO	Non-Commissioned Officer
Negd	In Dhofar, the barren wilderness between the jebal and the sand sea
NFR	The Sultan's Northern Frontier Regiment
PA	Political Agent
PIA	Pakistan International Airways
PMO	Principal Medical Officer
PSI	President of the Service Institute
QFI	Qualified Flying Instructor
RAFO	Royal Air Force of Oman
Ras	Cape
RCL	Recoilless rifle. A rifle tube mounted on a tripod which fired a missile
RPG7	Rocket-propelled grenade
RSM	The Riyan-Salalah-Masirah air schedule from Aden
SAdO	Senior Administrative Officer
SAF	Sultan's Armed Forces
Sarbe	Search & Rescue Beacon
SAS	Special Air Service
Sayid	Prince
SEP	Surrendered Enemy Person
Sheikh	Arab tribal leader. A term of respect
SHQ	Station Headquarters
SMO	Senior Medical Officer
SNCO	Senior NCO
SNOPG	Senior Naval Officer Persian Gulf
SOAF	Sultan of Oman's Air Force
SOLF	Sultan of Oman's Land Forces
SON	Sultan of Oman's Navy

Suq	Market in an Arab country
TOL	Trucial Oman Levies
TOS	Trucial Oman Scouts
Very Light	A flare fired from a pistol for signalling or temporarily illuminating the surroundings.
Wadi	Water course – usually dry
Wali	District Governor appointed by the Sultan
WJR	The prefix of a distress message in Morse code

Index

1. Air Force and Navy Squadrons and Independent Flights – British and Omani
2. Land Forces – British, Omani, Adenese, Gulf, American, Iranian and Jordanian
3. People
4. Places
5. Ships

Squadrons and Flights

British

Omani

Land Forces

British

People

Places

Ships